Canadian Social Trends
Volume 3

Volume 1
ISBN 1-55077-010-1

Volume 2
ISBN 1-55077-062-4

Volume 3
ISBN 1-55077-105-1

Volumes 1 and 2: The contents of Volumes 1 and 2 are provided on pages vi-vii. Please check the website, call or e-mail for current availability and prices.

Thompson Educational Publishing, Inc.
Tel: (416) 766-2763 / Fax: (416) 766-0398
Website: www.thompsonbooks.com
E-mail: orderdesk@thompsonbooks.com

Canadian Social Trends

Volume 3

THOMPSON EDUCATIONAL PUBLISHING, INC.
TORONTO

Reproduced with the permission of the Minister of Supply and Services Canada.
These abstracts have been provided through the courtesy of Statistics Canada. If you would like to receive this or other related information on a continuing basis you may do so by subscribing to the appropriate Statistics Canada publication. For more information or to order call toll free in Canada 1-800-267-6677 or write to: Publications Sales, Statistics Canada, Ottawa, K1A 0T6, Ontario.

Canadian Social Trends, Statistics Canada's social statistical quarterly, is available by subscription with a discount for educational subscribers.

Thompson Educational Publishing, Inc. is an authorized user and distributor of selected Statistics Canada computer files under Licensing Agreement, 32400-6355.

E-mail: publisher@thompsonbooks.com
Website: www.thompsonbooks.com

Copies of this book may be ordered in the United States and Canada from our distributor:

CANADA:
General Distribution Services Limited
325 Humber College Boulevard
Toronto, Ontario M9W 7C3
1-800-387-0141 (ON/QC)
1-800-387-0172 (rest of Canada)
Fax: (416) 213-1917

USA:
General Distribution Services Limited
85 River Rock Drive, #202
Buffalo, New York 14207
Toll Free: 1-800-805-1083
Fax: (416) 213-1917

E-mail orders: customer.service@ccmailgw.genpub.com

Canadian Cataloguing in Publication Data

Main entry under title:

Canadian social trends, Volume 3.

Articles originally published in Canadian social trends issued by Statistics Canada.
ISBN 1-55077-105-1

1. Social Indicators - Canada. 2. Canada - Social conditions. I. Statistics Canada.

HN103.5.C32 1999   306'0971   C99-930768-1

Cover design: Elan Designs
Cover illustration: Design concept for First Ministers' Conference on Aboriginal Rights by Cecil Youngfox (1942-87). Cecil Youngfox was born in 1942 in Blind River, Ontario, of Ojibway and Métis parents. By the time of his death in 1987 at the early age of 45, Cecil Youngfox had established himself as one of Canada's leading native artists, renowned for his vivid, sensitive images of native cultural traditions. Among the many honours bestowed on him, Mr. Youngfox received the Aboriginal Order of Canada for his work in preserving his native heritage.

We acknowledge the financial support of the Government of Canada through the Book Publishing Industry Development Program (BPIDP) for our publishing activities.

Printed in Canada.
1 2 4 5   00 01 02 03 04 05

TABLE OF CONTENTS

COMPANION VOLUMES

For more information on Canada and Canadians, you may wish to obtain copies of Volume 1 and Volume 2, companion volumes to this volume. The tables of contents for Volumes 1 and 2 are given below.

Contents for Volume 1:

To order Volume 1 or 2, see the bottom of page viii.

Contents for Volume 2:

PREFACE

Canadian Social Trends is now available in three separate volumes. Each volume contains a vast amount of information about Canada and Canadians, past and present. We hope these three volumes will be useful to anyone who wants to understand what is happening in Canada today, why it is happening, and what is likely to happen in the future.

These three volumes are products of the information revolution. Together, they distil thousands of volumes of published and unpublished material about Canada. The material has been prepared to the highest standards of accuracy and is presented in an interesting and lively manner using photographs, charts, graphs and tables.

Like Volumes 1 and 2, Volume 3 has three major units:

- **Unit 1: Population, Human Geography and Health**
  Unit 1 contains material on the underlying population shifts in Canada, urbanization and changes in the health of Canadians.

- **Unit 2: Women, Marriage and the Family**
  The whole of Unit 2 is devoted to assessing the major and important changes that have occurred in the status of Canadian women, as well as in the institutions of marriage and the family.

- **Unit 3: Work, Life Style and Social Problems**
  Unit 3 examines changes in our working lives, our leisure, and concludes with a look at some major social problems in Canada today.

Our society has undergone enormous changes in recent years. What further changes will occur in our children's lifetime, not to mention our grandchildren's lifetime? It is, of course, impossible to know, or at least it is impossible to know very precisely. In part, where we go from here will depend on what each of us does to shape our society. These three volumes begin to look at some of the issues we will face. We hope it will encourage you to play a part in making Canada a better place for present and future generations.

Volumes 1 and 2: The contents of Volumes 1 and 2 are provided on the previous two pages of this book. Please check the website, call or e-mail for current availability and prices.

Thompson Educational Publishing, Inc.
Tel: (416) 766-2763 / Fax: (416) 766-0398
website: www.thompsonbooks.com
E-mail: orderdesk@thompsonbooks.com

POPULATION, HUMAN GEOGRAPHY AND HEALTH

Social Consequences of Demographic Change

by Yolande Lavoie and Jillian Oderkirk

Today's society bears little resemblance to that of the 18th and 19th centuries, a period when both fertility and mortality were high. In just over 100 years, life expectancy has doubled and the number of children per family has fallen by half. The social consequences of these changes have been particularly dramatic for women. Women no longer spend most of their lives in childbearing and childrearing, and as a result, have more opportunity to participate in paid labour, education and other public activities that were formerly the domain of men.

In the 18th century, the labour force was composed mainly of young adult males who could expect to work for about two decades. Today, in contrast, the labour force consists of an aging population of not only men but also of women, whose working lives are twice as long as those of their ancestors. Many new challenges accompany this increase in working life. For example, few workers can expect to work with the same skill set, perform the same job or even remain in the same field during their entire career. To cope with the likelihood of change, most are expected to participate in education and training programs throughout their lives.

From many early deaths to universal access to old age The lives of pioneers born in 1700 were very short, averaging only 30 to 35 years. Factors such as poor hygiene, infectious diseases, inadequate diet and limited means to control fertility lead to very high mortality rates. Four generations later, men born in 1831 lived an average of 40 years and women, 42 years. Although this was an improvement from the 1700s, infantile infectious diseases (scarlet fever, diphtheria, measles and others) and epidemics of cholera (1832), typhus (1846-1849), and smallpox (1885-1886), among others, were still taking the lives of many people.

During the next four generations, however, a spectacular increase in life expectancy occurred. From the 1831 cohort to the 1951 one, the average length of life almost doubled and the two-year survival advantage of women over men increased to eight years. For those born in 1951, life expectancy is 72 years for men and 80 years for women.

Increased opportunity to become a mother... The vast majority of women today have the opportunity to become a mother. In contrast, only about half of women born in the late 18th and 19th centuries had this chance. This is because many did not survive to reach puberty and many others died during their reproductive years. The period from age 15 to age 50 is considered by demographers to be the reproductive period of women's lives.

Just 667 of every 1,000 girls born in 1700 lived to reach age 15. By 1861, chances of survival had not increased very much, with only 691 of every 1,000

girls reaching that age. Improvements in the life expectancy of young women did not occur until the 20th century. For every 1,000 women, 874 of those born in 1921 survived to age 15, compared with 956 of those born in 1951. Less than one-half of all women born in the late 18th or early 19th centuries lived to age 50, whereas few Canadian women born around 1950 will die before reaching their 50th birthday.

...but lower fertility If every 1,000 women born in the early 18th century had survived to the end of their reproductive life, they would have given birth to 8,200 children, according to the reproductive behaviour prevalent at that time. This represents a lifetime fertility of slightly more than eight children per woman. However, since the majority of women

from that period did not survive to age 50, every 1,000 women born in 1700 bore only 4,300 children instead of 8,200.

By the 20th century, however, women's fertility had decreased substantially. Although the vast majority of women born in 1951 will live to age 50, they are expected to give birth to only 1,800 children for every 1,000 women, less than two per woman.

The population is replaced when each woman in the present generation is replaced by at least one daughter in the next. This daughter-to-mother ratio is called the net reproduction rate. In the 18th century, there were 2,100 daughters to replace 1,000 foremothers. With this reproduction rate the population doubled in 30 years. However, for every 1,000 women in the 1951 cohort, only 900 daughters are expected to be born, less

Female and male survivors at different ages, Canada, 1700 and 1831 to 1951						
Survivors per 1,000 females born in...						
Age	1700	1831	1861	1891	1921[1]	1951[1]
1 year	789	838	834	856	923	966
15 years	667	681	691	744	874	956
20 years	634	659	672	731	868	953
45 years	405	519	552	645	834	935
50 years	365	490	527	627	820	928
60 years	267	412	458	572	775	899
70 years	155	286	347	475	690	834
80 years	53	122	178	311	537	676
90 years	3	16	35	101	274	327
Survivors per 1,000 males born in...						
Age	1700	1831	1861	1891	1921[1]	1951[1]
1 year	789	814	811	835	907	958
15 years	667	666	674	724	856	944
20 years	634	646	656	710	847	937
45 years	405	502	531	624	798	901
50 years	365	466	500	603	775	889
60 years	267	371	414	527	695	833
70 years	155	237	295	389	549	704
80 years	53	89	137	198	329	462
90 years	3	10	22	43	108	147

[1] Survival projected for ages 40 and over.
Source: Statistics Canada, Catalogue 91-209E.

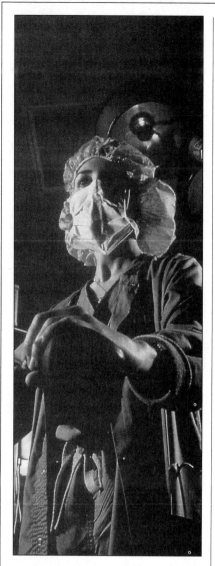

than the rate necessary to ensure replacement of the population.

Women's lives no longer devoted to childbearing In the late 18th and early 19th centuries, women's lives were devoted to motherhood. Canadian women born during this time, on average, married at age 22 and if they lived to age 50, bore about 10 children. Their first pregnancies usually occurred a few months after marriage and last pregnancies around age 40. At that age, these women had exhausted, on average, 70% of their expected years of life. For many, responsibilities associated with raising young children continued until their lives ended.

In sharp contrast to their foremothers, women in their early forties today are expected to have half of their lives still

ahead of them. In addition, the creation of couples is not as closely linked to reproduction as it was in the past, because the development and use of reliable contraceptive methods during the 20th century have enabled women and men to plan pregnancies. Couples may also choose to remain childless. As a result, women born in 1951 are expected to devote about two years of their lives to pregnancy and early infant care. Therefore, even after this period is subtracted from women's lives, because women generally live longer than men, they are expected to have the same number of years potentially available for public activities, such as paid work, as do men.

More women with paid work As the amount of time women had available for activities other than childbearing increased, so did their labour force participation. By 1961, the participation rate for women had grown to 30%, double the rate in 1901. During this period, however, it was mostly single women who were entering the labour force. Today, women's participation is much more pronounced and marital status does not have such a strong influence. In 1991, 77% of married women and 84% of single women aged 25-44 were participating.

The presence of children also does not restrict participation significantly. While mothers of very young children were less likely than mothers of older children to be in the labour market, the majority were still participating. In 1991, 62% of mothers with children under age 3, 68% of mothers with children aged 3-5 and 76% of mothers with children aged 6-15 were in the paid labour force.

Changing professional patterns The vast increase in the length of working life from the 18th to the 20th century combined with the increase in women's participation in public life have changed occupational patterns for both men and women. These changes present challenges which will likely lead to increased demands for training opportunities and flexibility in the workplace.

In the past, the labour force was not only primarily male but, because of its demography, was also young. During the second half of the 18th century, 7 out of 10 men aged 15-65 were aged 40 or less. Because of high mortality rates, those

born in the 18th century could expect to work for only 23 years on average, between ages 15 and 65.

Today, workers born in the 1950s can expect to work for 40 years before retirement. During such long careers, changes within the economy and industry may force many workers to upgrade their skills, switch jobs or even change vocations. Also, mature workers will dominate the labour force in Canada as early as the second decade of the next century. As a

result, there will be many workers competing for jobs at the top of organizational hierarchies.

In addition to the challenges associated with an aging labour force, women encounter gender-based biases in the workplace. In spite of some progress, such as an increasing acceptance of employment equity and a shift toward more equal sharing of parental responsibilities, many social mechanisms are not yet fully adapted to the reality that women have a permanent place in public life. For example, many women still encounter difficulty in obtaining parental leave, face job uncertainty after maternity leave and pay inequities between men and women.

Increasing uncertainty and competition in the workplace, for both men and women, are expected to result in greater demand for education and training programs. This may actually increase the relative importance of the educational system despite significant shrinking of the population of children and young adults.

Conclusion Increased longevity and controlled fertility are slowly changing traditional social hierarchies, within the family, workplace and community. In the 18th and 19th centuries, roles for both men and women, in the home and the public domain, were well defined. In addition, most of the population was young and those who were able to survive to older ages assumed positions of authority by virtue of their years of experience. The distribution of the population at that time, a pyramid with many young people at the bottom and fewer senior people at the top, corresponded to the hierarchical structure of most organizations.

Today, however, living to become a senior citizen is no longer limited to a select few. The population of older Canadians is growing relative to the size of younger age groups which are shrinking. This change in the age structure of the population expands the traditional pool for recruitment to the top levels of organizational hierarchies and substantially reduces the base. As a result, competition from both men and women for a limited number of positions of authority within social hierarchies, including those in the family, workplace and community, will likely increase.

Shifts in the demographic structure of society, however, cause social and economic change as much as they result from it. Totally unexpected situations often occur because as members of the population change over time, so do attitudes, beliefs and behaviours. Consequently, the future course of society can only be speculated upon by those who will be participants in roles they have not yet learned.

Yolande Lavoie is an independent consultant in demography and **Jillian Oderkirk** is an Editor of **Canadian Social Trends.**

- For more information consult Lavoie, Yolande, "Structure in Transition: Two Centuries of Demographic Change", in **Report on the Demographic Situation in Canada, 1992**, Statistics Canada, Catalogue 91-209E.

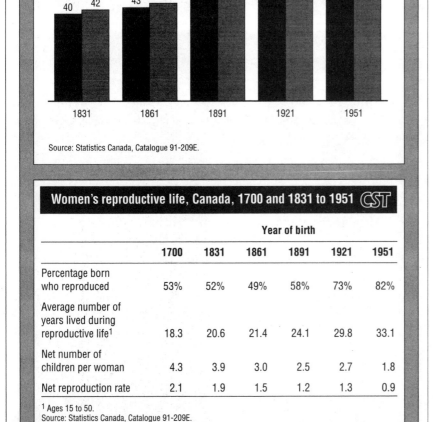

CANADIAN SOCIAL TRENDS BACKGROUNDER CST

Life expectancy at birth, 1831-1951 CST

Men ▪ Women ▪

Age

Year	Men	Women
1831	40	42
1861	43	45
1891	49	54
1921	63	70
1951	72	80

Source: Statistics Canada, Catalogue 91-209E.

Women's reproductive life, Canada, 1700 and 1831 to 1951 CST

	Year of birth					
	1700	1831	1861	1891	1921	1951
Percentage born who reproduced	53%	52%	49%	58%	73%	82%
Average number of years lived during reproductive life[1]	18.3	20.6	21.4	24.1	29.8	33.1
Net number of children per woman	4.3	3.9	3.0	2.5	2.7	1.8
Net reproduction rate	2.1	1.9	1.5	1.2	1.3	0.9

[1] Ages 15 to 50.
Source: Statistics Canada, Catalogue 91-209E.

CANADA'S
POPULATION
CHARTING INTO THE
21st CENTURY

by Tina Chui

CHANGES IN THE SIZE AND AGE STRUCTURE OF Canada's population result from shifts in fertility, mortality and migration patterns. These changes can have immediate and long-term consequences for society, affecting the demand for education, housing and health-care services, and the supply of workers to the labour force. Population projections play an important role in facilitating social and economic planning.

Canada's demographic future will likely be characterized by slow population growth and an aging population, largely due to low fertility and the aging of the baby boom generation. In 1995, Canada's population was estimated at 29.6 million, an increase of 9.6 million since 1966. Based on a medium-growth scenario, the population is projected to increase to 37 million by 2016.

Population growth: continuous, but slow in the coming decades

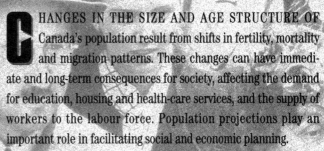

000,000s   Estimated | Projected

Source: Statistics Canada, Catalogue nos. 91-520-XPB and 93-310-XPB.

UNIT 1: POPULATION, HUMAN GEOGRAPHY AND HEALTH

The rate of population growth is expected to slow down. The annual growth rate will drop to 0.9% by 2016, from 1.4% in 1993. The decline of population growth is mainly due to the slowing down of natural increase (the difference between births and deaths). International migration will become increasingly important as the contribution of natural increase declines. By 2030, natural increase is expected to reach zero and from then on, immigration will be the sole source of population growth.

In addition to slow population growth, population aging will continue. The median age of the population (the point in the age distribution where half of the population is older and the other half is younger) is expected to increase to 40.4 years by 2016, from 33.9 years in 1993.

The baby boom Since the Second World War, the most important demographic development in Canada was the increase in fertility that took place roughly during the period 1946 to 1966.[1] This period has become known as the baby boom era. During the height of the baby boom in 1959, 473,700 babies were born, representing a 59% increase since the beginning of the boom in 1946.

The baby boom era, however, was only a temporary deviation in a long-term decline in fertility. In the late 1960s, Canada's fertility rate returned to its downward path. In 1966, women of childbearing age had an average of 2.8 births, compared with 3.9 births in 1959. Fertility continued to drop to below the replacement level of 2.1 births in 1972. Since then, fertility has remained fairly stable at around 1.7 births per woman.

Canadians are living longer As they have in other industrial countries, mortality rates in Canada have declined considerably due to improved quality of life and health care. In 1993, there were 7.1 deaths per 1,000 people, down from 9.9 in 1946. The declining mortality rate has resulted in increased life expectancy for Canadians. In 1993, a baby boy was expected to live to age 75 and a baby girl to age 81. This compared with 66.3 and 70.8 years for a baby boy and baby girl, respectively, in 1951.

Natural increase expected to fall to zero around 2030 Natural increase is a major determinant of population growth. In 1960, 88% of the population growth (339,300 people) was attributable to natural increase. With the onset of the "baby bust," however, natural increase dropped to 253,700 in 1966. The long-term trend of natural growth has been downward. If fertility remains at the current level of 1.7 births per woman, natural growth will decline to 147,100 in the year 2001. As boomers age, the number of deaths will increase. By 2030, natural increase is anticipated to fall to zero, and subsequently, deaths could exceed births.

Immigration and population growth International migration[2] is another potential source of population growth. Immigration is by far the most important component of international migration. The contribution of immigrants to Canada's population growth has fluctuated over the years, reflecting changes in the annual immigration levels set by government.

CANADIAN SOCIAL TRENDS BACKGROUNDER CST

Population projections

Population projections play an important role in the strategic decision-making process of business, professionals, planners, educators or anyone concerned about the size and characteristics of the population. Statistics Canada's population projections routinely provide possible scenarios of the population process. The most recent projections used as their base, the 1993 preliminary population estimates adjusted for net census undercoverage and included two new components: non-permanent residents and returning Canadians.

Three growth scenarios were used in the projections:

❏ *High-growth scenario* – assumes an increase in fertility to 1.9 children per woman by 2016; life expectancies at birth of 81.0 and 86.0 years in 2016 for men and women, respectively; and an annual immigration level of 330,000 by 2005.

❏ *Medium-growth scenario* (reported throughout this article) – generally reflects the continuation of current trends: a constant fertility of 1.7 births per woman; life expectancies at 78.5 and 84.0 years by 2016 for men and women, respectively; and an annual immigration level of 250,000.

❏ *Low-growth scenario* – fertility is assumed to decline to 1.5 births per woman; life expectancies are 77.0 and 83.0 years for men and women, respectively; and the annual immigration level is assumed to decline to 150,000 by 2005.

For all projections, emigration is assumed to increase from 46,800 in 1993 to between 49,600 and 58,300 by 2016. Non-permanent residents remain at 149,600 after 1994.[1] Returning Canadians are projected to increase from 21,800 in 1993 to 25,600 by 2016.

[1] Since the preparation of these projections, the estimates of non-permanent residents were revised. The estimate for 1995 was 258,500.

• For more information, see **Population Projections for Canada, Provinces and Territories, 1993-2016**, Statistics Canada, Catalogue no. 91-520-XPB. Also, for information on the projections of households, see **Projections of Households and Families for Canada, Provinces and Territories, 1994-2016**, Statistics Canada, Catalogue no. 91-522-XPB.

However, the role of immigration has become increasingly important in the face of declining natural increase.

In 1992, 216,000 people were added to Canada's population through net international migration; this number decreased slightly to 214,200 in 1993. In these two years, net migration actually surpassed natural increase (206,100 in 1992 and 190,600 in 1993). Although net international migration dropped to 184,800 in 1995, its contribution to overall population growth was about the same as that of natural increase (170,000).

As natural increase is expected to decline in the future, net migration will play an even more important role in population growth. If immigration targets remain at the recent annual level of 250,000 people, the contribution of net migration will continue to surpass that of natural increase. By 2030, when natural increase is projected to reach zero, immigration will be Canada's only source of population growth.

Low fertility and mortality result in an aging population[3] The age structure of a population is largely determined by its fertility and mortality levels. Over the years, the combined effects of low fertility and mortality levels in Canada have resulted in an age structure with a larger proportion of older and a smaller proportion of younger people.

In 1961, nearly four in ten people were under age 18, reflecting high fertility levels during the baby boom era. However, because of low fertility levels since the late 1960s, young people accounted for just one in four people (24%) in 1995. At the same time, seniors accounted for 12% of the population, compared with 8% in 1961.

This aging of the population is expected to continue because of improved longevity and the aging of the baby boom generation. By 2016, the number of seniors is expected to grow to nearly 6 million, accounting for 16% of the population. By 2041, the number of seniors will have tripled its present level to nearly 10 million. By then, almost one in four people (23%) will be aged 65 and over.

Because life expectancy for men is catching up with that for women, the imbalance in the sex ratio among seniors will decrease. In 1991, there were 81.6 men per 100 women aged 65 to 74, and 60.2 men per 100 women 75 years and over. These ratios will increase to 90.7 and 64.1 for the two age groups by 2016.

Population aging holds significant socio-economic implications for society. If people continue to retire in their mid-sixties, the ratio of pensioners to workers will continue to increase. The old-age dependency ratio between seniors and working-age people is expected to increase to 24.9 by 2016, from 18.6 in 1994. One effect of the increasing ratio of pensioners to workers will be the

[1] See "Canadian Fertility, 1951 to 1993: From Boom to Bust to Stability?" **Canadian Social Trends**, Winter 1995.

[2] Net international migration includes all landed immigrants and returning Canadians minus the number of people who leave Canada (emigrants). The number is also adjusted for non-permanent residents.

[3] See "Population Aging: Baby Boomers Into the 21st Century," **Canadian Social Trends**, Summer 1993.

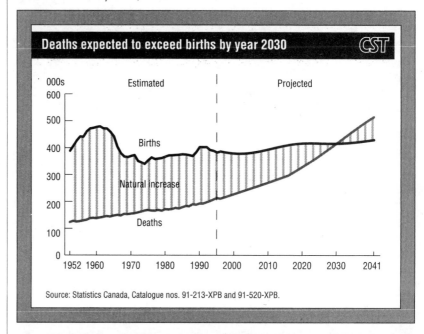

Deaths expected to exceed births by year 2030

Source: Statistics Canada, Catalogue nos. 91-213-XPB and 91-520-XPB.

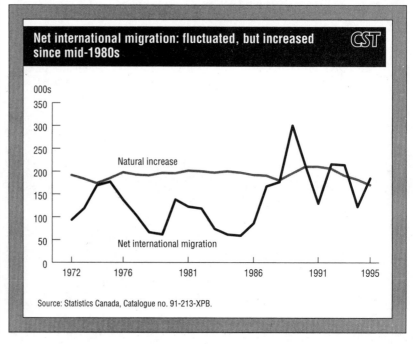

Net international migration: fluctuated, but increased since mid-1980s

Source: Statistics Canada, Catalogue no. 91-213-XPB.

UNIT 1: POPULATION, HUMAN GEOGRAPHY AND HEALTH

increased cost of maintaining public pension plans.[4]

An aging population will also result in an increase of medical-care needs and will raise the costs of providing that care. In particular, the costs of treating diseases common among older people, such as heart disease, stroke and cancer, will increase. With improved health care, people will live longer but will be more likely to suffer from chronic illnesses which require long-term care.

It is also true, however, that the coming generation of seniors will generally be healthier than previous generations. In addition, higher labour force participation among men and women will result in increased financial independence. Upon retirement, seniors' contribution to society will shift from paid to unpaid work.

More seniors today, particularly senior women, are living alone. A growing senior population raises issues such as housing affordability and design. Goods and services that will enable older people to maintain independent lifestyles will become increasingly important.

People under age 18: a growing number, but a declining proportion
Because of the large number of children born to the baby boom generation, the number of people under age 18 increased steadily to 7.2 million in 1995, from 6.7 million in 1986. If fertility remains at the current level, the size of this group is expected to grow to 7.5 million by 2016, and to 8.1 million by 2041.

However, this group will make up an increasingly smaller proportion of the total population. People under age 18 accounted for 24% of the total population in 1995. This proportion is expected to drop to 20% by 2016, and to 19% by 2041. Nevertheless, the steady increase of the school-age population will ensure a continued demand for primary and secondary education, and for child-care facilities.

Slow, but continuous growth of the young adult population The number of young adults aged 18 to 24 peaked at 3.5 million in 1982 when the majority of the baby boomers reached adulthood. This population, however, is expected to drop to 2.8 million by 1996, but will increase again to 3.3 million by 2016, and to 3.5 million by 2041.

Since it is at this age people pursue postsecondary studies, the demand for

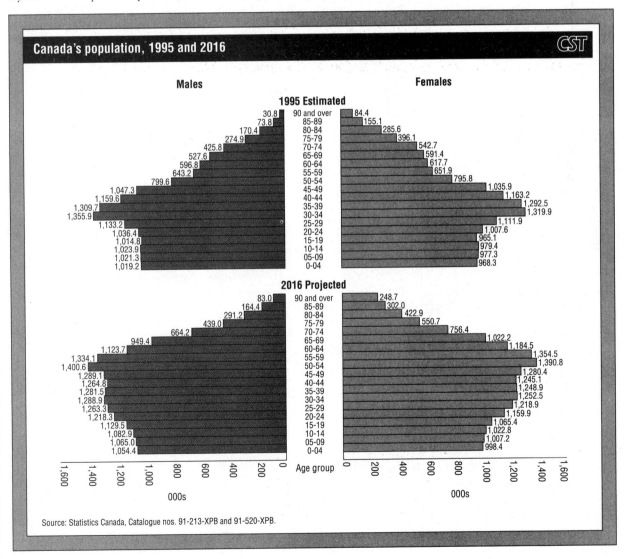

Canada's population, 1995 and 2016

Source: Statistics Canada, Catalogue nos. 91-213-XPB and 91-520-XPB.

this level of education will likely continue. Postsecondary education is currently undergoing funding and program review, and youth unemployment remains high. Therefore, improving access to higher education, and training an efficient and competitive work force for the next century are among the priorities facing policy makers.

Smaller proportion of the population will be of working age Generally, people start to enter the labour force at around age 18 and retire in their 60s. The size of the working-age population increased significantly in the late 1960s as the boomers reached working-age. In 1971, 12.5 million people were aged 18 to 64. This number increased to 15.6 million in 1981 and to 18.9 million in 1995. The working-age population is expected to continue to grow. By 2001, 20.4 million people will be of working-age, and the number will increase gradually to 23.7 million by 2016, and 25.1 million by 2041.

As a proportion of the total population, however, the working-age group will likely decrease as boomers start to reach retirement age around 2010. In 1971, 57% of the population were of working-age. The proportion increased to 64% in 1995. By 2011, 65% of the population will be of working-age. The proportion will then start to decline to 64% in 2016, and to 59% in 2041.

Older work force In the next twenty years, the baby boomers will be in their 40s and 50s, and thus, result in an aging work force. Almost one-third (32%) of working-age people were in the age range 45 to 64 in 1994. This proportion is expected to increase to 44% by 2016.

There are many issues related to an aging work force. Older workers are more experienced and less likely to change career, and therefore, are a more stable work force. However, the careers of many older workers may plateau as competition for more senior positions increases. This, in turn, may block the career advancement of younger workers.

Furthermore, an aging population will also result in more people with work disabilities. According to Statistics Canada's special projections of people with disabilities, 60% of people with work disabilities will be aged 45 to 64 by 2016, up from 46% in 1993.

Challenges for a greying work force are many. Older workers need to continue to update their skills in an economy increasingly based on technology, knowledge and information. Employers may need to become more innovative in managing their human resources. This could include offering part-time work to employees before retirement, and providing early retirement incentives which would create more opportunities for younger workers.

Population trends underlie many important policy concerns As the twenty-first century approaches, there are many issues facing policy makers and the public at large. For instance, what can be done to keep the economy viable with slow population growth and an aging population? How can we maintain a smaller but competitive and efficient labour force? How can we provide quality health care in response to increasing demands? And how can we minimize regional disparity and respond to the population changes faced by different regions in Canada? Population projections are useful tools that will assist decision-makers in both the public and private sectors in addressing these and other related issues.

[4] See "Government Sponsored Income Security Programs for Seniors: Canada and Quebec Pension Plans," **Canadian Social Trends**, Spring 1996.

• This article was adapted from **Population Projections for Canada, Provinces and Territories, 1993-2016**, Statistics Canada, Catalogue no. 91-520-XPB.

Tina Chui is an Editor with **Canadian Social Trends**.

CANADIAN SOCIAL TRENDS BACKGROUNDER

Non-family households to increase

Changing demographics also have implications for the household. The number of households is expected to reach 15.1 million by 2016, up from 10.3 million in 1991. Household growth results from a combination of factors, such as changes in the age at which people form a household, increasing divorce rates, fewer marriages, and the growing incidence of solo living. Non-family households[1] are projected to increase to 33% by 2016, from 29% of all households in 1991, while family households will drop to 67% from 71%.

Household size is also expected to drop to an average of 2.5 people by 2016, from 2.7 in 1991. This decline is mainly due to the growing number of non-family households, those headed by lone parents, and an on-going decline of multi-family households.

[1] Non-family households consist mainly of people living alone or unrelated people sharing a dwelling.

A History of Emigration from Canada

by Craig McKie

Since Confederation, emigration from Canada has been a significant and constant phenomenon. From 1851 to 1991, an estimated 7.9 million Canadian residents left Canada permanently to live in other countries. Immigration to Canada over that period, 12.5 million people, was not even double that total. Although most who emigrated to other countries were Canadian by birth, many had come to Canada as immigrants.

During the latter part of the 1800s and the early part of the 1900s, annual emigration flows were especially large and immigration flows were increased to replace those who had left. Emigration not only accelerated changes in the characteristics of Canada's population but also created large communities of ex-patriot Canadians in other countries.

The main destination of Canada's emigrants has always been the United States. Since the mid-1960s, however, this traditional route has been restricted by United States' immigration regulations.

Impact of emigration has lessened since the 1930s Emigrants represented 1% to 3% of Canada's total population each decade from 1931 to 1991. Before then, however, they represented between 5% and 17% of the total population each decade since the 1850s.

During the last half of the 1800s, emigration numbers were so large that the flow of people out of the country exceeded the flow of immigrants into the country. From 1851 to 1901, 2.2 million people emigrated from Canada, while only 1.9 million people immigrated to Canada.

Emigration totals remained very high until 1931. In fact, from 1911 to 1921, 1.1 million emigrants left Canada, the largest number ever recorded in a single decade. Overall, from 1901 to 1931, 2.8 million people emigrated from Canada, while 4.2 million people immigrated to Canada.

During the 1930s and 1940s, a period of economic depression and war, both

emigration and immigration totals dropped. From 1931 to 1941, numbers in both categories were the lowest ever recorded: 241,000 emigrants and 149,000 immigrants. Although totals were larger from 1941 to 1951 – 379,000 emigrants and 548,000 immigrants – they were much lower than those recorded before the 1930s.

After 1951, emigration increased, but, for the first time, not as quickly as immigration. Immigration totals returned to levels similar to those of the early 1900s, equalling or exceeding 1.4 million each decade since 1951. Emigration totals, on the other hand, increased from 462,000 in the 1950s to 707,000 in the 1960s, before falling to over a half million in the 1970s and 1980s.

Most Canadians living abroad are in the United States According to a Statistics Canada estimate based on United States' and United Nations' records, 1 million Canadian-born people were living outside of the country in 1980.[1] Most of these Canadians (84%) were living in the United States. The next largest concentrations of Canadians were in the United Kingdom (6%), Italy (2%), Australia (2%) and France (1%). Relatively few were in

[1] **Migration between the United States and Canada**, Statistics Canada Catalogue 91-530E. Data were based on 57 countries which collected information on Canadian born on their national censuses.

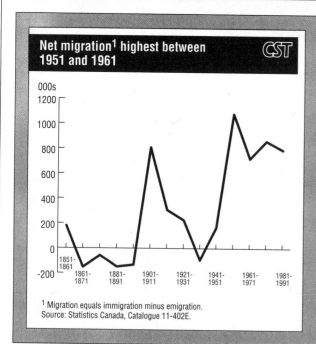

Net migration[1] highest between 1951 and 1961

CST

000s

[1] Migration equals immigration minus emigration.
Source: Statistics Canada, Catalogue 11-402E.

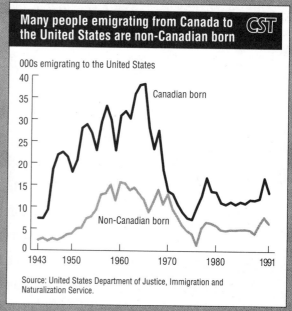

Many people emigrating from Canada to the United States are non-Canadian born

CST

000s emigrating to the United States

Canadian born

Non-Canadian born

Source: United States Department of Justice, Immigration and Naturalization Service.

the former West Germany, New Zealand, Yugoslavia, Mexico and Belgium (less than 1% each), with the remaining 2% in other countries.

According to the 1990 United States' Census, of all people living in the United States born in other countries, those born in Canada (745,000 people) were the third largest group, following those born in Mexico (4.3 million) and the Philippines (913,000). Over half of these Canadian-born people had become naturalized citizens of the United States.

Lower recent emigration linked to tighter American immigration laws In 1965, the United States, the predominant destination of Canadian emigrants, restricted immigration from Canada. Before 1965, migration flows between Canada and the United States proceeded with relatively little hindrance from national boundaries or immigration quotas. Amendments introduced to the United States' *Immigration and Nationality Act* in 1965, however, limited all Western hemisphere immigration for the first time to an annual quota of 120,000 people. Additional amendments in 1976 restricted the per-country limit for the Western hemisphere to 20,000 people and added a preference system for Western hemisphere natives. In 1978, Eastern and Western hemisphere quotas were combined, creating a world-wide ceiling on immigration to the United States.

According to the American Immigration and Naturalization Service (INS), the number of immigrants admitted to the United States who reported Canada as their last country of residence decreased by more than half from the 1960s to the 1970s, and then remained at that level. In both the 1950s and 1960s, there were about 400,000 immigrants admitted to the United States whose last country of residence was Canada. In contrast, the United States admitted only 169,900 Canadian immigrants between 1971 and 1980 and 156,900 in the following decade.

Canadian-born population in the United States has fallen The impact of restrictions on Canadian immigration to the United States is also reflected in United States' census counts. In 1990, there were 744,800 Canadian-born people living in the United States, down from 842,900 in 1980 and 812,400 in 1970.

These counts are much lower than those recorded earlier this century. From 1900 to 1950, for example, each United States' census recorded over 1 million Canadian-born residents. The lower figures in recent years reflect, in part, the high mortality among the large group of older Canadian-born residents in the United States.

Throughout Canada's history, fewer Americans have immigrated to Canada than Canadians to the United States and the population of Americans in Canada has always been small. According to the 1991 Census of Canada, 267,200 American-born residents were living in Canada.[2] This is down from 312,000 in 1981 and 309,600 in 1971. Although the 1971 count was higher than that in 1961 (283,900), the number of American born

---

CANADIAN SOCIAL TRENDS BACKGROUNDER

Canadian illegal aliens in the United States Every year, several hundred Canadians are apprehended by the United States' Immigration and Naturalization Service (INS) for violations of the United States' *Immigration and Nationality Act*. In 1991, the INS estimated that there were 7,300 Canadian illegal aliens living in the United States, that is, Canadians who could be deported. Of these, 64% had entered the United States without inspection and 32% had entered as visitors.

In 1991, 318 Canadians were expelled from the United States. Of these, 244 were deported and 74 left after having been informed that the INS had grounds to deport them (required departure under docket control). Almost half of those expelled were returned to Canada because of criminal or narcotics violations, 24% had failed to maintain or comply with conditions of non-immigrant status and 18% had entered the United States without inspection or had made false statements to gain entry.

Migrants to and from Canada, 1851-1991 — CST

Period of migration	Immigration	Emigration
	000s	
1851-1861	352	170
1861-1871	260	411
1871-1881	350	404
1881-1891	680	826
1891-1901	250	380
1901-1911	1,550	739
1911-1921	1,400	1,089
1921-1931	1,200	971
1931-1941	149	241
1941-1951	548	379
1951-1961	1,543	462
1961-1971	1,429	707
1971-1981	1,429	566
1981-1991	1,374	582

Source: Statistics Canada, Catalogue 11-402E.

in Canada declined between 1921 and 1961. During the first two decades of the 20th century, however, the number of American born in Canada increased to 374,000 in 1921 from 127,900 in 1901.

Many immigrants to Canada left to become residents of the United States Each decade from the 1950s to the 1980s and in both 1990 and 1991, 30% of immigrants to the United States whose last country of residence was Canada were not Canadian by birth, according to INS records. In contrast, during the 1940s, a decade of very low levels of Canadian immigration and emigration, less than 20% of immigrants to the United States from Canada were not Canadian born.

Although there is no earlier information, this phenomenon likely occurred in previous decades. It may have been even more prevalent during the early 1900s when both immigration and emigration levels were very high. From the mid-1800s until the 1960s, whenever immigration to Canada was high, emigration from Canada to the United States was also high. Similarly, when immigration to Canada was low, so was emigration to the United States. The movement of immigration flows to Canada in tandem with emigration flows from Canada to the United States suggests that at least some immigrants to Canada, particularly during the early 1900s, may have come to Canada with the intention of emigrating to the United States.

Many people hold multiple citizenships and residency rights As international travel and migration increase, the number of Canadians living outside the country and of those holding multiple citizenships or legal residency rights may also increase. According to the 1991 Census, 70,000 Canadian citizens by birth living in Canada were also citizens of at least one other country. In addition, 245,400 Canadians with citizenship through naturalization also reported being citizens of other countries. Many more

Canadian citizens are eligible for other citizenships or legal residency rights. For example, those who are Canadian by birth but who were born in another country may be entitled to citizenship in their country of birth. Other Canadian citizens may be entitled to citizenship in their parent's or grandparent's country of birth, depending on that country's laws.

The same principle also applies to the children of Canadian citizens who emigrated to other countries. In the United States, for example, over 2.2 million people reported on the 1970 Census that they had at least one parent born in Canada. Although this information was not collected in later United States' censuses, the 1970 results indicate that the number of people in the United States who might be eligible for Canadian citizenship is likely more than double the number of Canadian-born residents in that country. The same is also likely true for Canadian emigrants living in other countries.

EEC may attract future Canadian emigrants Migration is encouraged among European Economic Community (EEC) countries. According to EEC regulations, citizens of member countries have the right to seek employment and permanent residence in other member countries. As of 1991, the total number of people so relocated was 5.5 million (2% of the total

EEC population). As international labour mobility becomes more prominent and more advantageous to some individuals, Canadians entitled to citizenship in an EEC member country may choose to exercise that right to gain residency rights and employment in any EEC country.

Emigration opportunities are growing One effect of large scale emigration has been the creation of substantial ex-patriot populations of former Canadian residents in other countries, most notably the United States. For example, estimates calculated from Roman Catholic Church documentation indicate that approximately 5 million Roman Catholics of French-Canadian ancestry were living in the United States in 1970.

Compared to immigration flows, emigration has been much smaller in the past fifty years. This has resulted, in part, from tighter restrictions on emigration between Canada and the United States, the historical destination of most Canadian emigrants. Emigration from Canada may increase in the future, however, because Canadians now have more opportunities to live and work in other countries than they have had in the past few decades.

Canadians can move more freely within North America because the Free Trade Agreement between Canada and the United States has provisions which ease the flow of temporary labour from one country to another. Many Canadians may take advantage of opportunities to live and work outside of the country, particularly if employment and other life-style factors are perceived to be better in other countries than at home.

[2] Non-permanent residents were included in the census for the first time in 1991.

Dr. Craig McKie is an Associate Professor of Sociology, Carleton University and a Contributing Editor with *Canadian Social Trends*.

Recent immigrants in the workforce

by Jane Badets and Linda Howatson-Leo

During the first part of this decade, some 1.4 million people immigrated to Canada, contributing to one of the highest immigration flows since the 1940s. Nearly half of these new arrivals — 46% — were in the prime working ages of 25 to 44 years. As a result, recent immigrants have come to account for a growing proportion of new entrants to the labour force.

The ease with which these newcomers integrate into Canadian society depends, to a large extent, on their ability to find jobs. How have these recent immigrants fared in terms of employment (or unemployment) and the types of jobs they have found? And has their experience differed from that of others, including earlier groups of immigrants and people born in Canada? Using data from the Censuses of Population, this article explores the labour market experiences of recent immigrants in the 25 to 44 year age group from 1986 to 1996.[1]

Most recent immigrants speak English or French and are highly educated

Knowing the language of one's new country helps to understand that country's culture and allows one to take part in day-to-day life. Becoming part of the workforce also tends to

---

1. All populations discussed in this article refer to those aged 25 to 44 years, unless otherwise indicated.

CST   What you should know about this study

Recent immigrants: People who immigrated to Canada 5 years or less prior to the date of the Census. For example, in the case of the 1996 Census, recent immigrants refer to those who immigrated between 1991 and the first four months of 1996.

Canadian youth: People aged 15 to 24 who were not students (non-students) at the time of the Census, unless otherwise indicated.

Employment rate: The percentage of employed persons in the week prior to Census day in a particular population group (for example, women, immigrants, population aged 25 to 44). Also known as the employment-population ratio.

Unemployment rate: The percentage of unemployed people in the total labour force (which consists of the employed and the unemployed). The unemployed are those who, during the week prior to Census day, were without paid work but were available for work; they either had actively looked for work in the past four weeks or were on temporary lay-off or had definite arrangements to start a new job in four weeks or less.

Full-time or part-time employment: The total number of hours per week a person reported working in the Census reference year (the year preceding the Census). Full-time employment is considered to be 30 hours or more per week; part-time is less than 30 hours.

Full-year, full-time workers: Persons who said they worked 49 to 52 weeks in the Census reference year (1995), mostly full-time.

Part-year or part-time workers: Persons who said they worked less than 49 weeks in the Census reference year (1995), or who worked mostly part-time.

Occupation: The kind of work a person was doing during the week prior to the Census. If someone was not employed in the week prior to Census day, the information relates to the job of longest duration since January 1 of the previous year. The 1996 Census classified occupation information according to the 1991 Standard Occupational Classification (SOC).

be easier if one speaks and understands the language, particularly in professional occupations where communication is an essential part of the job. Among immigrants who spoke neither English nor French, people with lower levels of schooling had higher rates of employment than those who were highly educated. However, educated or not, in both the 1980s and the 1990s recent immigrants who could speak English or French were more likely to be employed than those who could not.

Canada's newcomers appear well equipped with language skills. In both the 1980s and the 1990s, the overwhelming majority of recent immigrants reported that they were able to conduct a conversation in one of the country's official languages.[2] In 1996, for example, 94% of men and 91% of women said that they spoke English or French. The figures in 1986 were similarly high: 93% of recent immigrant men and 89% of women claimed to speak at least one official language. One must, however, keep in mind that being able to converse informally does not necessarily indicate an ability to work in a language.

In general, education is also an important predictor of labour force performance. And newcomers who entered the country during the 1980s and the 1990s had, on average, higher levels of education than Canadian-born people in the same age group (25 to 44 years). In 1996, for example, the proportion of men with a university degree was twice as high among recent immigrants as among the Canadian-born: 36% versus 18%. Similarly, recent immigrant women were also more likely than Canadian-born women to have completed their university education: 31% compared with 20%. A similar pattern, although not as pronounced, appears at the other end of the educational spectrum: the proportion of men without high school graduation was

18% among recent immigrants and 23% among the Canadian-born aged 25 to 44. Among women, the proportion who had not completed high school was, at 19%, the same for both immigrants and those born in Canada.

Recent immigrants less likely to be employed in 1996
Despite their language abilities and high qualifications, recent immigrants are generally less likely to be employed than people born in Canada. In the short term this is not surprising, given that establishing oneself, making contacts and applying for jobs in a new environment tend to take time. However, compared with 1986, the employment situation of recent immigrants seems to have become more precarious both in absolute terms and relative to the Canadian-born; in 1996, immigrants found it substantially more difficult to secure jobs than did their predecessors in the 1980s. While this was also true for many Canadian-born, opportunities for immigrants have deteriorated more significantly.

For example, while in 1986 the employment rate of recent immigrant men aged 25 to 44 years was 81%, by 1996 it had declined to just 71%, indicating a substantial reduction in the likelihood of finding a job. Although during this period the employment rate of Canadian-born men also declined, it did so only slightly, from 87% to 84%. Immigrant men of the 1990s were notably worse off in the job market than their counterparts in the 1980s. And when

---

2. The census question on knowledge of official language asks respondents whether they are able to conduct a conversation in either or both of the official languages. The information collected, then, is based on respondents' self-assessment and may overstate (or understate) the actual abilities of these individuals in either or both languages.

CST **Education does not improve employment opportunity for recent immigrants as much as it does for the Canadian-born**

| Highest level of schooling completed | % employed age 25 to 44 | | | |
| | Men | | Women | |
	Canadian-born	Recent immigrants	Canadian-born	Recent immigrants
Total	84	71	73	51
Less than high school	71	65	52	38
Secondary school	85	69	71	44
Non-university	88	74	79	58
Some postsecondary	83	67	72	47
University	92	73	86	58

Source: Statistics Canada, 1996 Census of Population.

it came to finding a job, in 1996 they fell farther behind Canadian-born men than had immigrants a decade earlier.

Recent immigrant women were in an even more disadvantaged position. While their employment rate was already low at 58% in 1986, by 1996 it had fallen to an even lower 51%. Meanwhile, as a result of changing career aspirations, higher educational attainment and families' need for two incomes, Canadian-born women's employment rate continued its upward climb, from 65% in 1986 to 73% in 1996. It appears that immigrant women of the 1990s lost out in the job market. Their employment rates were lower than those of their counterparts in the 1980s, they lagged behind Canadian-born women with the gap rising over the years, and they were also substantially behind immigrant men when it came to finding employment.

Why employment was more problematic for immigrants of the 1990s is not clear, particularly since these newcomers had higher educational levels and better language skills than those who had arrived in the 1980s. Partly, it may be the result of the economy's difficulties in absorbing new entrants. But a host of other issues, such as the types of skills immigrants bring with them, their cultural background and their personal characteristics, are likely at work as well.

Education doesn't pay off for recent immigrants

For the Canadian-born, more often than not, education is the key to finding employment. The situation for recent immigrants, however, is very different.[3] Although their chances of finding employment did increase somewhat with higher levels of education, their employment rates continued to lag far behind those of the Canadian-born. Among men with less than high school, for example, some 71% of the Canadian-born and 65% of recent immigrants were employed in 1996. However, at the university level, 92% of those born in Canada had jobs, compared with only 73% of recent immigrants. The difference was even more pronounced for immigrant women. For Canadian-born women, employment rates climbed from 52% for those with less than high school to 86% for the university educated. In contrast, the employment rate of recent immigrant women with a university degree was just 58%.

Nearly one out of three recent immigrants work in sales and services

When looking for jobs, newcomers are often willing to make what they hope will be short-term sacrifices. To get established in a new country, some may initially take jobs that fall below their qualifications or expectations. Others may be able to find work in areas of their expertise.

---

3. The employment and unemployment rates for recent immigrants were adjusted to take account of the different educational profiles of the immigrant and Canadian-born populations. This adjustment (known as standardization) removes the effect of any differences due to education when comparing the two populations. As well, the unemployment rates were standardized by age to account for the fact that a higher proportion of recent immigrants are in the younger age group of 25 to 34 years.

CST Recent immigrants are most likely to work in sales and service occupations				
	Men		**Women**	
	Canadian-born	**Recent immigrants**	**Canadian-born**	**Recent immigrants**
All occupations	%		%	
Management	11	9	7	5
Business, finance and administrative	10	10	33	21
Natural and applied sciences and related	9	12	2	4
Health	2	2	10	6
Social science, education, government service and religion	5	5	10	5
Art, culture, recreation and sport	2	2	3	3
Sales and service	17	24	27	38
Trades, transport and equipment operators and related	27	18	2	2
Primary industry	6	2	2	1
Processing, manufacturing and utilities	10	17	4	15

Source: Statistics Canada, 1996 Census of Population.

Immigration to Canada in the past two decades has been characterized by several changes: source countries of immigrants, selection criteria, and higher numbers of immigrants entering Canada each year in the 1990s (over 200,000). The number and selection of immigrants entering Canada are determined to a large extent by government policies controlling admissions. Since the late 1970s, Canada's immigration policy has been guided by three broad objectives: to reunite families; to fulfill Canada's international legal obligations, and compassionate and humanitarian traditions with respect to refugees; and to foster a strong and viable economy in all regions of Canada.[1]

These objectives are reflected in the three categories under which people are admitted each year as permanent residents: family, humanitarian (refugees) and economic (skilled workers, business immigrants and their spouses and dependents). Only skilled workers and business immigrants (including investors, entrepreneurs and the self-employed) are selected on the basis of their labour market skills. Since 1967, skilled workers have been rated on a "point" system based on their age, education, training and occupation skills, demand for their occupation in Canada, existence of pre-arranged employment, and knowledge of one of Canada's official languages.

Between 1981 and 1985, the largest proportion (50%) of immigrants were admitted for reasons of family reunification, much higher than the 33% admitted in the economic category. In the following five year period (1986 to 1990) this pattern had changed, with the economic category accounting for the largest proportion (41%) of immigrants and a slightly smaller proportion (38%) in the family category. During the early 1990s, a higher proportion of immigrants was admitted in the family category than the economic category, a pattern similar to that of the early 1980s. In contrast to these shifting trends in the economic and family component of immigration, the proportion admitted to Canada as refugees has remained fairly constant throughout both the 1980s and 1990s at around 17% to 21% of total immigration.

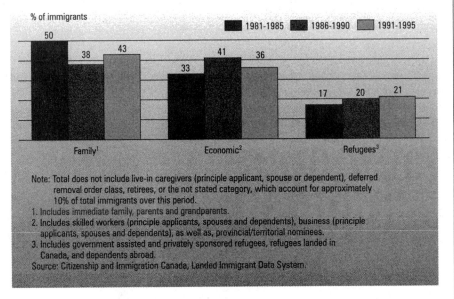

% of immigrants

■ 1981-1985   ■ 1986-1990   □ 1991-1995

Family[1]: 50, 38, 43
Economic[2]: 33, 41, 36
Refugees[3]: 17, 20, 21

Note: Total does not include live-in caregivers (principle applicant, spouse or dependent), deferred removal order class, retirees, or the not stated category, which account for approximately 10% of total immigrants over this period.
1. Includes immediate family, parents and grandparents.
2. Includes skilled workers (principle applicants, spouses and dependents), business (principle applicants, spouses and dependents), as well as, provincial/territorial nominees.
3. Includes government assisted and privately sponsored refugees, refugees landed in Canada, and dependents abroad.
Source: Citizenship and Immigration Canada, Landed Immigrant Data System.

A number of factors affect the extent to which recent arrivals integrate into Canada's labour market, as well as how quickly and easily this integration occurs. This article focuses on two important ones, level of education and knowledge of Canada's official languages. Other possible factors which may influence labour market outcomes are the selection of immigrants, their skills and attributes at the time of entry, their country of origin or visible minority status, as well as their intentions and aspirations for immigrating to Canada.

---

1. Citizenship and Immigration Canada. October 1994. Annual Report to Parliament. Ottawa. p.11.

For various reasons — such as the availability of jobs, proximity to others with the same origin, or educational opportunities for themselves or their children — most of Canada's recent immigrants have made their homes in the country's three largest cities. Toronto received the lion's share, with 42%, followed by Vancouver (18%) and Montreal (13%). The impact on the working-age population has been significant: in 1996, recent immigrants accounted for 14% of Toronto's population aged 25 to 44, some 13% of Vancouver's and 6% of Montreal's. It is in these cities that the majority of immigrants are working or looking for jobs. Immigrant unemployment, then, is mostly an urban phenomenon, belonging particularly to Canada's three largest cities.

Unemployment rate for men aged 25-44 ...

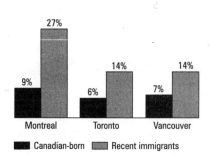

Canadian-born   Recent immigrants

- Recent immigrants – both men and women – had the highest unemployment rates in Montreal.

- In Toronto and Vancouver, recent immigrant men were about two times more likely to be unemployed than their Canadian-born counterparts.

- Recent immigrant women had higher jobless rates than either immigrant men or women born in Canada.

Unemployment rate for women aged 25-44 ...

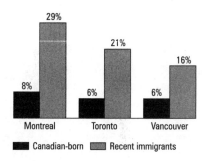

Canadian-born   Recent immigrants

... with a university degree

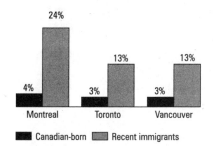

Canadian-born   Recent immigrants

- Unlike the Canadian-born, recent immigrants did not see their unemployment rate decline significantly with higher education.

- University educated recent immigrants — both men and women — were most likely to be unemployed in Montreal.

- In both Toronto and Vancouver, university-educated immigrant men's jobless rates were more than four times the rate of their Canadian-born counterparts.

... with a university degree

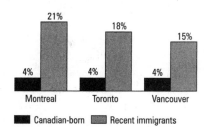

Canadian-born   Recent immigrants

... recent immigrants

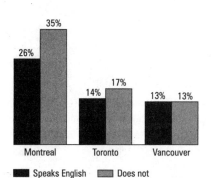

Speaks English or French   Does not speak either

- In all three CMAs, knowledge of an official language affected women's unemployment rate more than men's.

- In Vancouver, immigrant men's unemployment rate did not vary with official language knowledge.

... recent immigrants

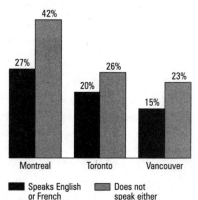

Speaks English or French   Does not speak either

Note: See footnote 3, page 18 about standardization of unemployment rates.
Source: Statistics Canada, 1996 Census of Population.

In 1996, recent immigrants were most likely to be employed in sales and service occupations. These jobs, which often require little or no previous experience and relatively few skills, tend to have easier entry requirements than other occupations. In addition, in today's increasingly service-oriented economy, sales and service jobs tend to be plentiful. It is not surprising, then, that some 31% of employed recent immigrants (38% of women and 24% of men) held these types of jobs compared with 23% of Canadian-born people aged 25 to 44 years. And although some in this sector were not highly educated (one-third of recent immigrants with less than high school worked in sales and services), others appear to have been considerably overqualified. For example, nearly one-quarter of recent immigrants with university degrees held jobs in sales and service occupations, making them about twice as likely to work at these jobs as their Canadian-born counterparts. It is possible that some highly educated immigrants whose qualifications are not recognized in Canada fell into this category.

On the other hand, substantial proportions of recent immigrants, particularly men, were employed as highly skilled professionals. Nearly one-quarter of immigrant men with university degrees were working in occupations in the natural and applied sciences as, for instance, computer

CST Youths and immigrants: new entrants facing a tough market

In some ways, the hurdles that recent immigrants face in the labour market resemble those faced by Canadian youths. While there are undoubtedly differences between these two groups – educational profile,[1] age, skills, social network, family responsibilities – youths and recent immigrants share some important characteristics. As new entrants to a competitive, and in some regions a tight, labour market, both groups are disadvantaged: they lack work experience (or Canadian work experience in the case of immigrants), tend not to have a well-established network of contacts, and are often under financial strain.

Indeed, even when they did succeed in finding employment, youths and immigrants were more likely than the rest of the population to work part-time or part-year and in entry-level service jobs. In 1995, the majority of employed people in both groups – 68% of youths and 58% of recent immigrants aged 25 to 44 years — were working part-time or part of the year compared with 42% of the Canadian-born between the ages of 25 and 44. While high levels of part-time employment are not a new development for either youths or immigrants (many in the 1980s were also in this situation), the incidence of this work arrangement has become more frequent since 1990. Industrial restructuring, rapid technological advances and a large baby-boomer workforce have all contributed to new entrants' increasing difficulties in securing full-time employment.

Both youths and recent immigrants were most likely to be employed in sales and service occupations. Among those in the labour force, 31% of recent immigrants and 43% of Canadian youth were employed in these jobs compared with 22% of the Canadian-born aged 25 to 44.

The parallel between these two groups does not, however, end with work arrangements or type of employment. The proportions of youths and recent immigrants who were not able to find jobs were also remarkably similar. Indeed, in 1996, the overall unemployment rate of recent immigrants was virtually identical to that of youths: 17% and 18%, respectively.[2] And as did immigrants, young people also had most difficulty trying to find jobs in Montreal, although their unemployment rate (18%) was not nearly as high as that of recent immigrants (27%). In Toronto and Vancouver, unemployment rates for both groups were the same.

While the unemployment scenario of Canadian youths and recent immigrants converged in 1996, the situation in the 1980s was quite different. For example, in 1986 the jobless rate was a relatively low 12% for recent immigrants compared with a much higher 17% for youths. So while finding jobs that year was already difficult for young people, immigrants had an easier time.

---

1. Immigrants aged 25 to 44 were more highly educated than Canadian youth. Immigrant men were seven times more likely than young Canadian men to have a university degree. Immigrant women were almost four times more likely than Canadian young women to do so. However, the education gap becomes smaller if the comparison is restricted to large urban areas, where most immigrants settle.

2. Because information on school attendance was not available in the 1986 Census, the unemployment rates for Canadian youths (in both 1986 and 1996) refer to the population aged 15 to 24, regardless of school attendance.

engineers, chemists and aerospace engineers. In contrast, 17% of Canadian-born men with university degrees worked in these types of jobs.

Summary

The labour market of the 1990s has undergone a number of changes. Significant shifts in the composition of the workforce, industrial restructuring, rapid technological advances and a prolonged recession altered employment opportunities. As new entrants to this labour market, immigrants who came to Canada during the 1990s experienced difficulties finding employment. These initial difficulties are often related to the fact that newcomers tend to go through a temporary adjustment period while they become established in their new country. In that they lack Canadian work experience, do not yet have a solid network of contacts, and have faced labour market difficulties in the 1990s, their situation is more difficult than that of their Canadian-born contemporaries.

Based on the experiences of earlier immigrants, however, one might expect that with time the 1990s wave of immigrants will find jobs and participate fully in the Canadian economy. Indeed, over a decade, the unemployment rate of immigrants who came in the early 1980s dropped to the point where the rate for men matched that of the Canadian-born. Women also experienced improvements, if to a somewhat lesser extent. It is true that the 1990s immigrants arrived during a different economic climate, and that factors not addressed in this article — such as cultural background, intentions and aspirations, types of skills and attributes — also affect the ease of labour market entry. However, it seems reasonable to assume that time will again improve the employment opportunities of Canada's newcomers.

Jane Badets is a senior analyst and **Linda Howatson-Leo** is an analyst with Housing, Family and Social Statistics Division, Statistics Canada.

Visible minorities in Toronto, Vancouver and Montréal

by Jennifer Chard and Viviane Renaud

In the past few decades, the visible minority population in Canada has grown considerably. In 1996, 3.2 million people identified themselves as members of a visible minority group. They represented 11.2% of Canada's population, up from 9.4% in 1991, with Chinese, South Asians and Blacks comprising the largest groups. Growth in the size of the visible minority population is due mainly to changes in immigration patterns: about seven in ten visible minorities are immigrants, with almost half having arrived in the country since 1981 and one quarter between 1991 and 1996.[1]

The increase in the number of visible minorities is particularly noticeable in larger metropolitan areas. Canada's major urban centres act as

---

1. Immigration has been the biggest contributor to the rapid growth of the visible minority population, but it is important to remember that some visible minority groups have long histories in this country. According to the 1996 Census, about two in three Japanese (65% or 44,000) and two in five Blacks (42% or 241,000) were born in Canada. As well, large numbers of Chinese (207,000) and South Asians (192,000) are Canadian-born.

CST

Visible minorities represented 11% of the total population in 1996, with Chinese, South Asians and Blacks the largest groups

| | Canada | Census Metropolitan Area | | |
		Toronto	Vancouver	Montréal
		%		
Total population ('000)	**28,528**	**4,233**	**1,814**	**3,288**
Visible minority population	11.2	31.6	31.1	12.2
Black	2.0	6.5	0.9	3.7
South Asian	2.4	7.8	6.6	1.4
Chinese	3.0	7.9	15.4	1.4
Korean	0.2	0.7	0.9	0.1
Japanese	0.2	0.4	1.2	0.1
Southeast Asian	0.6	1.1	1.1	1.1
Filipino	0.8	2.3	2.2	0.4
Arab and West Asian	0.9	1.7	1.0	2.2
Latin American	0.6	1.5	0.8	1.4
Visible minority, n.i.e.[1]	0.2	1.1	0.4	0.1
Multiple visible minority[2]	0.2	0.6	0.6	0.1

1. Not included elsewhere. Includes Pacific Islanders and other respondents likely to be in a visible minority group.

2. Includes respondents who reported more than one visible minority group.

Source: Statistics Canada, 1996 Census of Population.

important gateways for immigrants, who are drawn to these cities by family and community ties as well as by economic opportunities. In 1996, almost three-quarters of Canada's visible minority population lived in either Toronto (42%), Vancouver (18%) or Montréal (13%). These cities have been quickly transformed into increasingly vital components of Canada's cultural mosaic, each with its own distinctive composition: while Toronto has the greatest diversity of visible minority groups, Vancouver is known for its prominent Asian community and Montréal has attracted the largest number of French-speaking visible minorities.

One in three Toronto residents are visible minorities

Toronto has both the highest concentration of immigrants and the highest concentration of visible minorities in Canada, making it the nation's most diverse Census Metropolitan Area (CMA). Toronto was home to 1.3 million visible minorities in 1996. They represented 32% of the total population, with Chinese (335,200) and South Asians (329,800) the two biggest groups — each comprising 8% of the total population — followed by Blacks at 6% (274,900). In fact, the CMA of Toronto was home to the largest number of each of Canada's visible minority groups, except for Arabs and West Asians, and Japanese.

Recent immigrants in particular have shaped the cultural landscape in Toronto, since almost 80% are members of a visible minority group. Of the 441,000 immigrants living in the CMA who arrived between 1991 and 1996, three in five were born in Asia or the Middle East. The top five places of birth were Hong Kong, Sri Lanka, the People's Republic of China, the Philippines and India.

Among Toronto's visible minorities, there are considerable differences in immigrant status and age. Nearly seven in ten Japanese and four in ten Blacks were born in Canada, compared with less than 25% of all other visible minority groups. More than four in ten Blacks, Southeast Asians, Latin Americans and South Asians were under the age of 25, while about three in ten Chinese and Japanese were in this age group — similar to the total population of Toronto (33%).

Scarborough has highest proportion of visible minorities in the nation

Within the Toronto CMA, some municipalities stand out as having particularly large visible minority populations.[2] Scarborough had the highest concentration in Canada, with over half (52%) of the population belonging

---

2. Since most census subdivisions follow the boundaries of municipalities or townships, this article uses "municipalities" as a synonym.

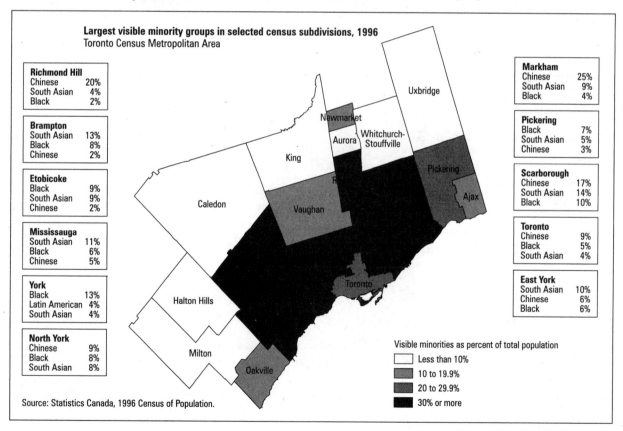

Largest visible minority groups in selected census subdivisions, 1996
Toronto Census Metropolitan Area

Richmond Hill
Chinese	20%
South Asian	4%
Black	2%

Brampton
South Asian	13%
Black	8%
Chinese	2%

Etobicoke
Black	9%
South Asian	9%
Chinese	2%

Mississauga
South Asian	11%
Black	6%
Chinese	5%

York
Black	13%
Latin American	4%
South Asian	4%

North York
Chinese	9%
Black	8%
South Asian	8%

Markham
Chinese	25%
South Asian	9%
Black	4%

Pickering
Black	7%
South Asian	5%
Chinese	3%

Scarborough
Chinese	17%
South Asian	14%
Black	10%

Toronto
Chinese	9%
Black	5%
South Asian	4%

East York
South Asian	10%
Chinese	6%
Black	6%

Visible minorities as percent of total population
- Less than 10%
- 10 to 19.9%
- 20 to 29.9%
- 30% or more

Source: Statistics Canada, 1996 Census of Population.

	Total population	Visible minority population %
Visible minorities accounted for at least one-third of residents in 10 municipalities, 9 in the Toronto or Vancouver CMAs (CST)		
Scarborough, On.	554,525	52
Richmond, B.C.	148,150	49
Markham, On.	172,735	46
City of Vancouver, B.C.	507,930	45
North York, On.	584,675	40
Burnaby, B.C.	176,825	39
Saint-Laurent, Qc.	73,760	36
York, On.	145,785	34
Mississauga, On.	542,450	34
Richmond Hill, On.	101,480	33

Note: Excludes the University Endowment Area, British Columbia, which is also a census subdivision. The total population was 6,680, and it had a visible minority population of 35%.

Source: Statistics Canada, 1996 Census of Population.

to a visible minority group, followed by Markham (46%), North York (40%), York (34%), Mississauga (34%) and Richmond Hill (33%). As well, about three in ten residents in East York (31%), Brampton (30%), Etobicoke (30%) and the city of Toronto (28%) were members of a visible minority group. Still, in some areas of Toronto, visible minorities comprised a very small proportion of the population, accounting for less than 5% of residents in several municipalities, including Caledon, Halton Hills and Georgina.

Chinese, South Asians and Blacks are the largest visible minority groups in almost all Toronto municipalities, though some areas have more diverse visible minority populations than others. In 1996, Scarborough and North York were among the most varied, with large proportions of Chinese, South Asian and Black residents. In comparison, Chinese were the predominant visible minority group in Markham and

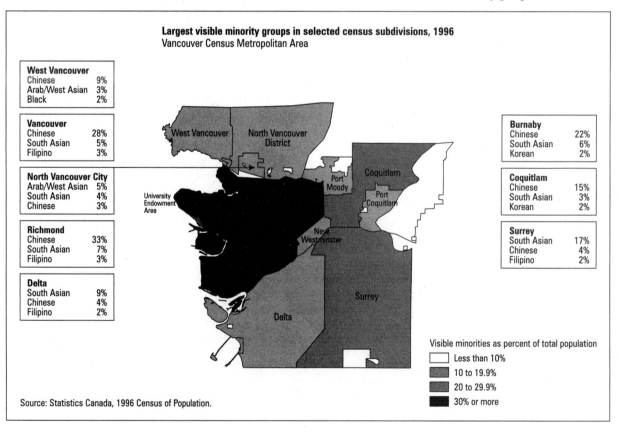

Largest visible minority groups in selected census subdivisions, 1996
Vancouver Census Metropolitan Area

West Vancouver
Chinese 9%
Arab/West Asian 3%
Black 2%

Vancouver
Chinese 28%
South Asian 5%
Filipino 3%

North Vancouver City
Arab/West Asian 5%
South Asian 4%
Chinese 3%

Richmond
Chinese 33%
South Asian 7%
Filipino 3%

Delta
South Asian 9%
Chinese 4%
Filipino 2%

Burnaby
Chinese 22%
South Asian 6%
Korean 2%

Coquitlam
Chinese 15%
South Asian 3%
Korean 2%

Surrey
South Asian 17%
Chinese 4%
Filipino 2%

Visible minorities as percent of total population
☐ Less than 10%
◻ 10 to 19.9%
▨ 20 to 29.9%
■ 30% or more

Source: Statistics Canada, 1996 Census of Population.

Richmond Hill, Blacks were the most numerous group in York and South Asians the largest in Mississauga.

The CMA of Vancouver is Canada's most Asian metropolitan area

Vancouver is home to several large Asian communities. A total of 565,000 residents, or 31% of the total population of the CMA, belonged to a visible minority group in 1996, with the Chinese accounting for about half. Vancouver's 279,000 Chinese represented 15% of all residents, while its 120,100 South Asians comprised the second largest group at 7%. Notably, Vancouver was home to the largest number of Japanese in Canada, as well as to the second largest numbers of Chinese, South Asians, Filipinos and Koreans.

The high level of Asian representation in Vancouver is not surprising, given patterns of immigration to the CMA. Four in five of Vancouver's 190,000 recent immigrants were from Asia, with Hong Kong, China, Taiwan, India, the Philippines, South Korea, and Viet Nam among the top ten birthplaces. About three-quarters of Chinese, Southeast Asians, Koreans and Filipinos living in Vancouver in 1996 were immigrants. In contrast, over half of Japanese (54%) and one-third of South Asians (34%) had been born in Canada.

Although visible minorities tended to be slightly older in Vancouver than in Toronto or Montréal, they were still young relative to the total population. About 30% of the CMA's population was under age 25 in 1996, compared with over 40% of South Asians, Southeast Asians, Koreans, Blacks and Latin Americans.

Richmond, City of Vancouver and Burnaby home to largest visible minority populations

Most municipalities in the Vancouver CMA have substantial visible minority populations. In particular, almost half the residents of Richmond (49%) belonged to a visible minority group, as did 45% in the City of Vancouver, 39% in Burnaby, 29% in Surrey and 28% in Coquitlam. Unlike Montréal and Toronto, very few municipalities in Vancouver had visible minority populations of less than 5%.

In most municipalities, Chinese and South Asians were the largest visible minority group, followed by Filipinos or Koreans. The Chinese accounted for a very significant proportion of the population in Richmond, the City of Vancouver and Burnaby, while South Asians were the largest group in Surrey, Delta and New Westminster. Interestingly though, Arabs and West Asians were the most numerous visible minority population in the City of North Vancouver.

Blacks are Montréal's largest visible minority group

Montréal's visible minority population has its own distinctive composition. In 1996, 401,000 people, or 12% of the total CMA population, were visible minorities. Blacks were the largest group, numbering 122,300 and representing 4% of all residents, while Arabs and West Asians, with nearly 74,000 people, made up 2%. Montréal is home

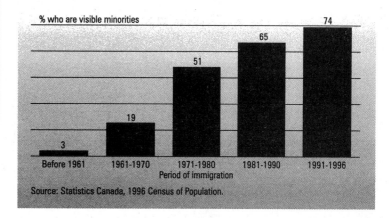

CST Growth in visible minority population fuelled by immigration

Since the 1970s, the sources of immigration to Canada have changed, with fewer immigrants entering from Europe. In addition, amendments to the *Immigration Act* in 1967 introduced a new universal points system for evaluating all applicants on an equal basis, regardless of their ethnic origin or place of birth. While earlier immigrants to Canada were mainly of European descent, newer arrivals are more likely to have been born in countries outside of Europe.

Today, Canada's newest residents tend to be Asian-born. Almost six in ten immigrants who arrived between 1991 and 1996 were from Asia, with Eastern Asia (for example, Hong Kong and the People's Republic of China) accounting for 24% and Southern Asia (for example, India and Sri Lanka) for 13%. Recent non-Asian immigrants were most likely to be from Europe (19%), Africa (7%), Central and South America (7%) or the Caribbean and Bermuda (6%). As a result, the proportion of visible minorities among immigrants has been increasing in the past two decades.

% who are visible minorities

Before 1961	1961-1970	1971-1980	1981-1990	1991-1996
3	19	51	65	74

Period of immigration

Source: Statistics Canada, 1996 Census of Population.

to the largest Arab and West Asian population in the country and the second largest Black, Latin American and Southeast Asian communities.

CST — What you should know about this study

This article uses data from the Census of Population, last conducted in May 1996.

Visible minority population: the *Employment Equity Act* defines visible minorities as "persons, other than Aboriginal peoples, who are non-Caucasian in race or non-white in colour." In Canada, the visible minority population includes the following groups: Blacks, South Asians, Chinese, Koreans, Japanese, Southeast Asians, Filipinos, Arabs and West Asians, Latin Americans and Pacific Islanders.

Immigrants: people who are, or have been at one time, landed immigrants in Canada. A landed immigrant is a person who has been granted the right to live in Canada permanently by immigration authorities. Some are recent arrivals, while others have resided in Canada for a number of years.

Recent immigrants: people who immigrated to Canada between 1991 and 1996.

As in the other large metropolitan areas, immigrants have contributed to the growth of the visible minority population in Montréal; seven in ten recent immigrants in the CMA were members of a visible minority group. Montréal has attracted a relatively large number of immigrants from countries where French is spoken. Between 1991 and 1996, almost 135,000 people immigrated to Montréal, with the most common places of birth being Haiti and Lebanon. Compared with Canada as a whole, Montréal has almost doubled its share of recent immigrants from West Central Asia and the Middle East, Africa and the Caribbean.

Among Montréal's largest visible minority groups, Blacks were most likely to be Canadian-born: nearly four in ten compared with fewer than two in ten Arabs and West Asians or Latin Americans. In fact, about 30% of Arabs and West Asians and Latin Americans arrived in Canada between 1991 and 1996.

Visible minorities in Montréal are younger than those in other CMAs, and are also younger than Montréal's

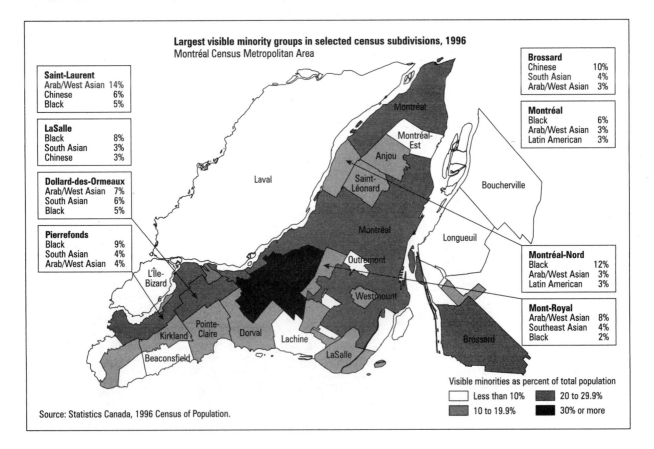

Largest visible minority groups in selected census subdivisions, 1996
Montréal Census Metropolitan Area

Saint-Laurent
Arab/West Asian	14%
Chinese	6%
Black	5%

LaSalle
Black	8%
South Asian	3%
Chinese	3%

Dollard-des-Ormeaux
Arab/West Asian	7%
South Asian	6%
Black	5%

Pierrefonds
Black	9%
South Asian	4%
Arab/West Asian	4%

Brossard
Chinese	10%
South Asian	4%
Arab/West Asian	3%

Montréal
Black	6%
Arab/West Asian	3%
Latin American	3%

Montréal-Nord
Black	12%
Arab/West Asian	3%
Latin American	3%

Mont-Royal
Arab/West Asian	8%
Southeast Asian	4%
Black	2%

Visible minorities as percent of total population
- Less than 10%
- 10 to 19.9%
- 20 to 29.9%
- 30% or more

Source: Statistics Canada, 1996 Census of Population.

total population. While 32% of all Montréal residents were under age 25 in 1996, 42% of visible minorities were in this age group. Blacks and Latin Americans were the youngest — nearly half the members of each group were not yet 25 years old.

Visible minorities centered in municipalities on the island of Montréal

In Montréal, the visible minority population is more geographically centralized than in Toronto or Vancouver. For the most part, visible minorities are concentrated on the island of Montréal where they comprised 36% of residents in Saint-Laurent, 26% in Dollard-des-Ormeaux, 22% in Pierrefonds and 20% in the City of Montréal. In only one other municipality, the south shore community of Brossard, did visible minorities account for more than one-fifth of the population (26%).

Blacks and Arabs and West Asians were prominent in most municipalities. Both were among the largest visible minority populations in the city of Montréal, Saint-Laurent, Dollard-des-Ormeaux, Pierrefonds, Montréal Nord, Mont-Royal, Saint-Léonard and Roxboro. The Chinese, South Asian, Latin American and Southeast Asian groups were also a significant presence in many parts of the CMA, with the Chinese the largest group in Brossard.

The future

The visible minority population is expected to grow rapidly over the next few decades, the result of continuing high levels of immigration from non-European countries and a relatively youthful visible minority population. It is projected that by the year 2016, visible minorities will account for one-fifth of the Canadian population.[3]

The majority of this visible minority population is expected to continue to live in Ontario in 2016 (56%), with most of the remainder in British Columbia (18%) and Quebec (14%). Thus, Toronto, Vancouver and Montréal will likely become increasingly differentiated from other regions of Canada in terms of cultural diversity and the presence of visible minorities.

3. Statistics Canada. 1995. *Projections of Visible Minority Population Groups, Canada, Provinces and Regions, 1991-2016*. Product No. 91-541-XPE.

Jennifer Chard and **Viviane Renaud** are senior analysts with Housing, Family and Social Statistics Division, Statistics Canada.

Mapping the conditions of First Nations communities

by Robin Armstrong

The majority of Registered Indians in Canada reside in approximately 900 small First Nations communities, which form a 5,000 kilometre archipelago across the Canadian landscape. Although many of these communities have much in common, they are by no means a homogeneous group. Separated by distance and differentiated by history, language and culture, individual communities often developed unique ways of life. Nearly all, however, have a substantially lower standard of living than the average Canadian community.

Comparing First Nations communities with each other reveals that living conditions in these communities vary considerably according to several factors. One of these factors is location. Regional differences in patterns of well-being — if indeed there are such patterns — may highlight some of the characteristics that are associated with these diverse living conditions. Using levels of schooling, employment rate, income and housing as indicators of well-being, this article examines the location of First Nations communities whose well-being is above average, average and below average. It then compares the living conditions of these First Nations communities with those of other Canadian communities.

Nearly one in four Registered Indians live in above average communities

In 1996, approximately 23% of the Registered Indian population lived in above average First Nations communities. They reported better incomes, higher employment rates, lower levels of crowding and generally higher levels of education than

Although it seems important, location is neither an assured nor an only path to socioeconomic well-being

did residents in average and below average communities. Most above average communities were clustered in Quebec, mid- and southern Ontario, and British Columbia's southern and coastal regions. However, smaller pockets were present in every province, at times adjacent to First Nations communities with substantially lower standards of living.

Approximately 47% of the Registered Indian population lived in communities with average socioeconomic conditions. Compared with above average communities, low educational attainment and crowding were marginally higher while employment rates and income were considerably lower. Average communities were most prevalent in the Maritimes, southern Manitoba and southern Saskatchewan.

The third group of communities, where nearly 32% of the Registered Indian population lived, exhibited below average conditions. In these communities, high rates of crowding combined with low levels of education, employment and income. The largest concentrations of below average communities were found in mid-Quebec, northwestern Ontario, northern Manitoba and Saskatchewan, and throughout Alberta.

Communities near urban centres better off than others

Geographic patterns suggest that being near urban or resource-rich areas aids development. Communities in these locations are able to pursue socioeconomic well-being by accessing resources and integrating with urban labour markets. Location, however, is neither an assured nor an only

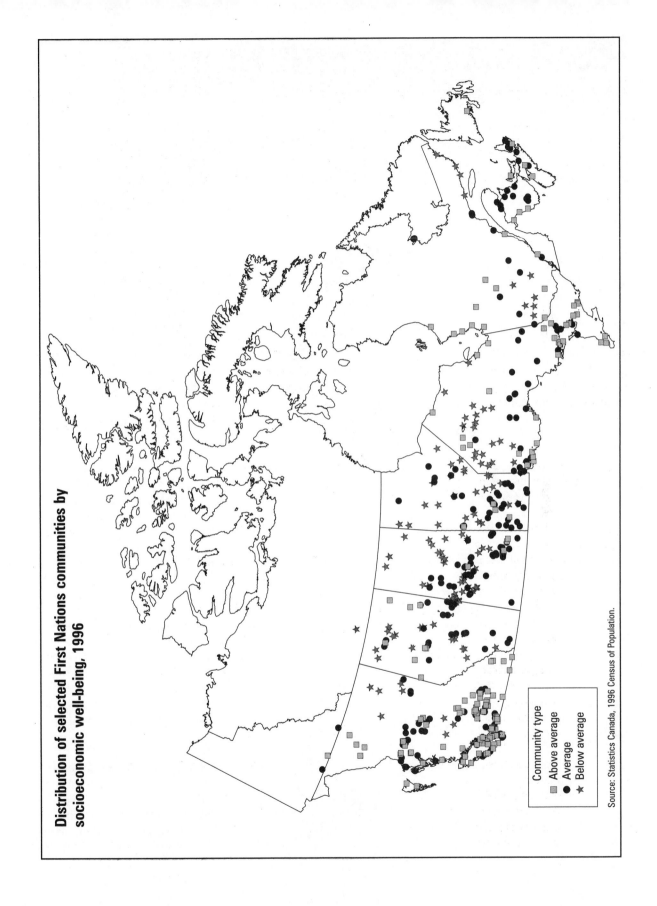

Distribution of selected First Nations communities by socioeconomic well-being, 1996

Community type
- ■ Above average
- ● Average
- ★ Below average

Source: Statistics Canada, 1996 Census of Population.

Data for this study have been drawn from the 1996 Census of Population. First Nations communities are defined as census sub-divisions (CSDs) classified as reserves, settlements, Indian government districts, terres reservées or villages cris. In 1996, Statistics Canada collected data from 751 First Nations CSDs. Of these, communities with populations less than 65 were eliminated, accounting for 2.5% of the Registered Indian population of enumerated First Nations communities. This left almost 500 First Nations communities in the study population. Cluster analysis was used to identify and group communities with similar characteristics: 154 were classified as above average, 218 as average, and 124 as below average.

The following four variables are used to measure socioeconomic well-being:

Education: the percent of population aged 20 to 64 with less than grade 9 education as their highest level of schooling. High percentages indicate the extent to which a population is inadequately educated for the modern economy.

Employment: the percent of population aged 20 to 64 employed during the week prior to the census. This variable is a measure of the general health of the local wage economy as well as the paid labour force success of a population.

Income: average annual income from all sources, in 1995, for individuals with income. Income serves as a proxy for the general material well-being of a population.

Housing: mean number of persons per room. Higher values indicate more crowded housing conditions. Not counted as rooms are bathrooms, halls, vestibules and rooms used solely for business purposes.

The remaining two indicators provide further aid in interpreting well-being:

Language: indicates the percent of population that speaks an Aboriginal language at home. It is a proxy for how successfully traditional culture has been preserved. However, a low percentage does not necessarily indicate a loss of uniquely Aboriginal culture.

Youth: indicates percent of population that is under 18 years old. This, in turn, points to the fertility of the population and may, where low, indicate out-migration of population from these areas.

path to success. Some First Nations communities near major cities have below average characteristics, while others in more isolated locations show above average attributes.

Other variables also help explain why some communities are better off than others. First it appears that, in general, First Nations communities that have adopted more "mainstream" ways of doing things are more likely to have better socioeconomic conditions. Indeed, in above average communities, a substantially lower proportion of people spoke an Aboriginal language at home than in below average communities (10% versus 52%), implying that more people conversed in English or French. Above average communities were also more like mainstream society in that they had older populations and were more highly educated.

There are, however, exceptions to mainstream-adaptation models of success. In a small group of eight above average communities (seven of which are James Bay Cree), nearly 90% of the population spoke an Aboriginal language at home. High proportions of Aboriginal home language use (35% to 75%) also occurred in another six above average communities. And some of these well-off groups have very young populations (45% to 55% under 18 years), which further differentiates them from mainstream society. These examples suggest that there are several models for socioeconomic success. Perhaps characteristics that above average First Nations communities share with other Canadians are more superficial than would appear at first glance.

First Nations communities still lag behind non-Aboriginal Canada

Substantial socioeconomic disparities continue to exist between residents in First Nations communities and other Canadians. Compared with the overall Canadian population, in 1996,

CST	More than 4 in 10 people in a typical below average First Nations community had less than a Grade 9 education		

| | **First Nations communities** | | |
	Above average	Average	Below average
% of Registered Indian population	23	47	32
% with less than Grade 9[1]	15	20	44
% employed[1]	60	42	35
Number of persons per room	0.8	0.9	1.3
Average annual income	$16,000	$11,000	$10,000
% speaking Aboriginal language at home	10	15	52
% under 18 years	38	43	48

1. As percentage of population aged 20 to 64.

Source: Statistics Canada, 1996 Census of Population.

on-reserve Registered Indians were more than twice as likely to have less than grade 9 schooling. In addition, their employment rates were 60% lower, and their average income was only half as much ($25,000 versus $12,000). Data on family and housing conditions reveal a similar pattern: First Nations families were twice as likely to be lone-parent families (26% versus 13%) and dwellings were over six times more likely to be crowded (31% versus 5%).

But averages often mask individual differences. To see how specific First Nations communities compared with the rest of the country, non-Aboriginal Canada was divided into five regions of well-being, and a new group of "best-off" Aboriginal communities was created. This best-off group, whose socioeconomic well-being was the highest among First Nations, comprised a set of 45 communities located primarily in southern Ontario and in southern and coastal British Columbia. When levels of education, employment, housing and income were compared between best-off Aboriginal communities and the five non-Aboriginal regions, the results spoke for themselves: First Nations

communities with the best socio-economic circumstances met the standards of only the poorest regions of non-Aboriginal Canada.

Then and now

While several factors preclude making an exact comparison between 1986 and 1996, sufficient similarities in methodology exist to allow a general contrasting of the two periods. Results indicate that the distribution of First

Nations by relative levels of socioeconomic well-being has not changed significantly during the 10 years.

Geographical patterns in 1996 also resembled those 10 years before. Conditions remained mostly poor in northwestern Ontario, northern Manitoba and northern Saskatchewan; they continued to be relatively good in southern and northern Ontario, along the U.S. border, and in southern British Columbia. Meanwhile, conditions eroded somewhat in the northern and central coastal regions of British Columbia and central Alberta, while they improved in Atlantic Canada and in isolated pockets in the northern parts of provinces from British Columbia to Quebec.

Summary

The vast majority of First Nations communities have considerably lower standards of living than non-Aboriginal regions. In fact, the best-off First Nations communities compare only with the worst-off areas of non-Aboriginal Canada. But substantial variations also exist between Aboriginal communities depending on several geographic and socioeconomic factors. For example, First Nations communities appear to do better

CST	Conditions in even the poorest non-Aboriginal regions were better than those in the best-off First Nations communities	

	Best-off First Nations communities	Worst-off non-Aboriginal regions
% with less than Grade 9[1]	12	20
% employed[1]	58	57
Number of persons per room	0.7	0.6
Average annual income	$18,200	$18,900
% speaking Aboriginal language at home	2	n.a.
% under 18 years	36	25

1. As percentage of population aged 20 to 64.

Source: Statistics Canada, 1996 Census of Population.

socioeconomically when near an urban centre or resource-rich area. Their situation becomes better yet when certain factors — language, age structure of population, education — reflect those of the non-Aboriginal majority. At first glance, this may suggest that adopting mainstream ways may be the model for socioeconomic success. However, the numerous exceptions to this observation imply that there are alternative paths to development, making the situation more complex than may appear at first sight.

• This article is adapted from "Geographical patterns of socioeconomic well-being of First Nations Communities," *Rural and Small Town Canada Analysis Bulletin,* Volume 1, No. 8, Statistics Canada, Catalogue 21-006-XIE. June 1999. http://www.statcan.ca/english/freepub/21-006-XIE/ 199900821-006-XIE.pdf

Robin Armstrong is Assistant Director of Census Operations Division, Statistics Canada.

LANGUAGE & CULTURE OF THE MÉTIS PEOPLE

by Josée Normand

The 1982 Constitution recognizes three Aboriginal peoples in Canada – the Indian, the Inuit and the Métis. While general knowledge of North American Indians and Inuit has grown in recent years, the non-Aboriginal public knows comparatively little about the Métis. Perhaps this is because defining the Métis people can be difficult. In previous centuries, the term "Métis" was commonly used to describe people of mixed Indian and French or Indian and British ancestry; for some Métis people, however, it has a more specific historical and geographical meaning. Considering themselves neither Indian nor White, the Métis' dual heritage is evident in their present-day lifestyle, including language, dress, music, dance and spirituality. This article draws on Statistics Canada's 1991 Aboriginal Peoples Survey to provide a brief linguistic portrait of the Métis and outline their participation in traditional Aboriginal activities.

Métis presence strongest in the Prairies In 1991, over 135,000 Canadians – more than one in five Aboriginal people – identified themselves as Métis, as measured by the Aboriginal Peoples Survey. In common with the other Aboriginal peoples, they are a very young population: well over one-third (38%) of the Métis people were under the age of 15 in 1991, compared with only 21% of the general Canadian population.

Many historians consider the Métis to be linked to the Red River Métis of Manitoba. Indeed, most Métis consider the Prairies their historic homeland and their ties to the West are very strong. In 1991, almost three-quarters of self-identified Métis lived in the Prairie provinces – 29% in Alberta, 25% in Manitoba and 20% in Saskatchewan. Outside the Prairies, the Métis people were most numerous in Ontario (9%).

The Métis are the most heavily urbanized of the Aboriginal peoples. In 1991, about 65% of the self-identified Métis population lived in urban areas, compared with 48% of North American Indians.[1] Many lived in large urban centres; in fact, more than one in five Métis lived in either the Winnipeg (15,000) or Edmonton (13,500) census metropolitan areas (CMAs). Many Métis were also residents of Saskatoon (5,500), Calgary (4,300) and Regina (3,700).

In 1991, only 1% of self-identified Métis lived on lands designated for Aboriginal peoples, compared with 36% of North American Indians. The Métis people tend to live in urban areas more so than other Aboriginal peoples mainly because they have no legally recognized land base. Land is being allocated in some provinces, however, and land claims negotiations are underway in the Northwest Territories. For example, eight Métis settlements in Alberta and several parcels of land in Saskatchewan have been designated as Métis land, while Ontario has allocated reserve land and recognized, as Registered Indians, some members of the Métis population of Rainy River.[2]

English and French the mother tongue of many Métis For many Métis, the language of their community is English or French, an inheritance from their European ancestors. Not only did all Métis aged 15 and over speak at least one official language in 1991, both English and French were spoken by 14%, a rate much higher than that reported by North American Indians (6%). The ability to speak both official languages was much more common among older Métis: those

aged 65 and over were almost three times more likely to speak both official languages than those aged 15 to 24.

Given their European heritage, perhaps it is not surprising that only 18% of Métis aged 15 and over, compared with 39% of North American Indians, could converse in an Aboriginal language. Most spoke either Cree (70%) or

Métis and North American Indian populations, by size of area of residence, 1991   CST

	Métis		North American Indian	
	000s	%	000s	%
Canada	135	100	461	100
On-reserve	2	1	166	36
Urban	88	65	219	48
Rural	45	34	76	16

Source: Statistics Canada, **A Profile of the Métis**, Catalogue no. 89-547-XPE.

CANADIAN SOCIAL TRENDS BACKGROUNDER   CST

The Aboriginal Peoples Survey

The 1991 Aboriginal Peoples Survey (APS) was developed in consultation with Aboriginal organizations and federal, provincial, territorial and municipal government departments. It collected detailed information about people who identified themselves as North American Indian, Métis or Inuit, and/or were Registered Indians according to the *Indian Act of Canada*. The sample for the APS was chosen using the 1991 Census of Population question on ethnic origin. Individuals who reported on the census questionnaire that they had Aboriginal ancestry, and/or were registered according to the *Indian Act*, were contacted; however, only those individuals who *self-identified* with an Aboriginal group were interviewed for the survey. In other words, while the census measured everyone's ethnic background, the APS measured only those individuals who explicitly described themselves as belonging to an Aboriginal group. Although there is much debate about the definition of the Métis people, and the APS was criticized in some quarters, it still offers a valuable source of information, illuminating the distinct character of the Métis people.

• For more information, see the "User's Guide to 1991 Aboriginal Data," or contact the Aboriginal Data Unit of the Housing, Family and Social Statistics Division, Statistics Canada, 7th Floor Jean Talon Building, Ottawa K1A 0T6.

---

[1] For the sake of brevity, this article does not compare the Métis with the Inuit, who account for only 6% of the total Aboriginal population.

[2] Royal Commission on Aboriginal Peoples, **Sharing the Harvest: The Road to Self-Reliance**, Ottawa, 1993.

Ojibwa (16%). However, about 6% spoke Michif, an exclusively oral *lingua franca* developed by the Métis from many languages – among them Chippewa, English, Gaelic and Assiniboine – but dominated by French and Cree.[3]

The fact that young Métis adults were least likely to speak an Aboriginal language in 1991 – 8% of 15- to 24-year-olds, compared with 54% of seniors – suggests that these languages are being passed to fewer Métis with each successive generation. In fact, 6% of Métis aged 15 and over could no longer converse in an Aboriginal language they had once spoken. The most common reasons reported for this loss were lack of contact with others who spoke the same language (46% of former speakers) and simply forgetting it (31%). However, about 9% of former speakers cited the fact that they had been forbidden to use their language.[4]

The urban Métis population, particularly in CMAs, was somewhat less likely to speak an Aboriginal language – 12% of those aged 15 and over, compared with 29% of Métis living in rural areas in 1991. It seems probable that a rural area better preserves the close community contact necessary to maintain verbal fluency in an endangered language. This suggestion is supported by data showing that 20% of urban and 17% of rural Métis understood an Aboriginal language, even though they did not speak it.

Many Métis tune in to Aboriginal-language media The fact that more people understand than speak an Aboriginal language may help to explain the use of Aboriginal-language media in the Métis community. In 1991, over 80% of Métis aged 15 and over reported that some type of Aboriginal-language media – television, radio, recordings or videos – was available where they lived. Métis with access to native media were less likely to use it than North American Indians; for instance, 36% of Métis watched Aboriginal-language television programs, compared with 41% of Indians, and 20% versus 31% respectively, listened to radio. Interestingly, native broadcast media are less readily available in areas where Aboriginal languages are more commonly spoken in the community. For example, 83% of Métis living in urban centres had access to Aboriginal-language television, compared with 70% in rural areas. To a smaller extent, the same was true of Aboriginal-language radio,

Official languages spoken by Métis and North American Indian populations aged 15 and over, 1991

Age group	Métis			North American Indian		
	English only	French only	Both English and French	English only	French only	Both English and French
	%			%		
15 and over	82	4	14	86	4	6
15 – 24	88	3	9	90	4	5
25 – 44	82	3	14	88	4	7
45 – 64	77	5	17	82	5	7
65 and over	64	3	26	70	5	6

Figures may not add due to rounding.
Source: Statistics Canada, **A Profile of the Métis**, Catalogue no. 89-547-XPE.

Métis in rural areas were most likely to speak an Aboriginal language

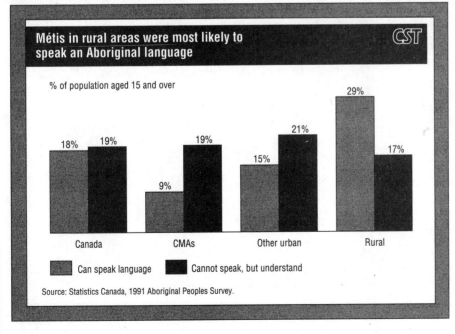

% of population aged 15 and over

- Canada: Can speak language 18%, Cannot speak, but understand 19%
- CMAs: Can speak language 9%, Cannot speak, but understand 19%
- Other urban: Can speak language 15%, Cannot speak, but understand 21%
- Rural: Can speak language 29%, Cannot speak, but understand 17%

■ Can speak language   ■ Cannot speak, but understand

Source: Statistics Canada, 1991 Aboriginal Peoples Survey.

[3] Michif possesses "a pattern of combination which is most unusual, and in its way, very rigorous." John C. Crawford (ed.), **Michif Dictionary: Turtle Mountain Chippewa Cree**, Pemmican Publications, Winnipeg, 1983.

[4] Missionaries, teachers and the non-native community actively discouraged the Métis, especially children, from using the Michif language. The Métis National Council, **The Métis Nation**, Vol. 2, no. 2, November 1993.

which was received by 85% of Métis in towns and cities and 82% of those living in rural areas.

A considerable proportion of Métis who did not actually speak an Aboriginal language were among those using native media. For example, 60% of Métis who could speak an Aboriginal language watched native TV, but so did 32% of those who could not. The figures are even more startling in terms of the actual television audience: 72% of the 26,000 Métis tuning in to native TV could not converse in the language of the programs they were watching. As one would expect, the older the viewing audience, the more likely that they could speak an Aboriginal language – 48% of those aged 45 and over compared with only 19% of those aged 15 to 44.

Aboriginal languages used more often in the classroom Education is an important medium by which a community's language and traditions are passed from one generation to another. Much of this teaching may be done informally within the family, but formal education can also play a role. However, in 1991, only 10% of Métis children aged 5 to 14 had been taught in an Aboriginal language in elementary school, compared with 26% of North American Indian children. Métis children were also considerably less likely to have had Aboriginal teachers, at only 22% compared with 41% of North American Indian children. These differences most probably reflect the more urban character of the Métis population – Métis children are simply less likely to attend native schools than other Aboriginal children.

At the same time, the APS data suggest that efforts are being made to introduce a stronger Aboriginal presence in the schools. Though only a small minority of Métis children under age 15 had encountered an Aboriginal language or teacher in the classroom, an even smaller percentage of older Métis aged 15 to 49 had done so when they had attended elementary school. A total of only 4% had been taught in an Aboriginal language and only 16% had had an Aboriginal teacher.

Participation in traditional activities Traditional activities are another expression of the Métis culture. In 1991, many self-identified Métis aged 15 and over – almost 41% – participated in activities traditional to the Aboriginal community. These included economic activities – hunting, fishing and trapping – and cultural ones – storytelling, traditional dancing, fiddle playing,

jigging and doing arts and crafts. Interestingly, younger people were more involved than older Métis: 42% of Métis aged 15 to 44 took an active part in traditional activities, while only 37% of those aged 45 and over did so. In contrast, over half of North American Indians in the two age groups (54% in each) participated in traditional activities. In this case, the differences do not appear to stem from the urban concentration of the Métis, since even Métis in rural areas were much less likely to take part in traditional Aboriginal activities, at 47% compared with 62% of North American Indians.

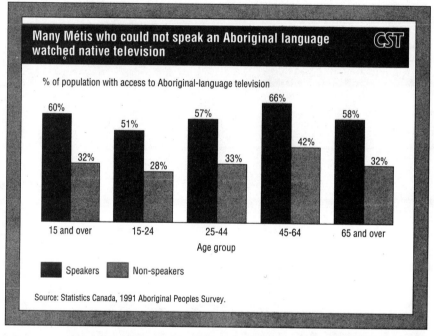

Many Métis who could not speak an Aboriginal language watched native television CST

% of population with access to Aboriginal-language television

	Speakers	Non-speakers
15 and over	60%	32%
15-24	51%	28%
25-44	57%	33%
45-64	66%	42%
65 and over	58%	32%

Age group

Source: Statistics Canada, 1991 Aboriginal Peoples Survey.

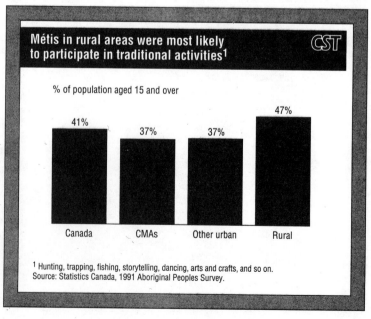

Métis in rural areas were most likely to participate in traditional activities[1] CST

% of population aged 15 and over

Canada	CMAs	Other urban	Rural
41%	37%	37%	47%

[1] Hunting, trapping, fishing, storytelling, dancing, arts and crafts, and so on.
Source: Statistics Canada, 1991 Aboriginal Peoples Survey.

for Aboriginal-language television, even though only one-quarter of the viewers can conduct a conversation in the language of the broadcast. Two-thirds of Métis live in urban areas – many in cities of 100,000 or more – yet over half eat fish and game obtained through hunting and fishing. The most active participants in traditional Aboriginal activities are not the older members of the community, but those under the age of 45. The Métis people's ties to Aboriginal culture may not be as strong as those of North American Indians, but there is no doubt that they are a unique community with a clear desire to sustain and strengthen their culture and traditions.

• For more information, see **A Profile of the Métis**, Statistics Canada, Catalogue no. 89-547-XPE.

Josée Normand is an analyst with the Target Groups Project, Housing, Family and Social Statistics Division, Statistics Canada.

Hunting, trapping and fishing are important traditional Aboriginal activities, and with no legally recognized land base, the Métis people are currently subject to the same restrictions on these activities as non-Aboriginal people. Nevertheless, in 1991, about 13% of the Métis population (17% rural and 9% urban) lived away from home for at least a week to hunt, trap, fish or otherwise participate in traditional activities. Most were away for a relatively short time, but one-third (34%) were absent for more than four weeks. Hunting and fishing, even if only for a few weeks, are notable because fish and game supplement the diet of more than half of the Métis community. For 13% of Métis aged 15 and over, hunting and fishing supplied over half of their meat and fish, and for an additional 40% of the community, at least some of their meat and fish.

Out of their dual ancestry, the Métis people have created a distinct cultural life. English or French is the mother tongue of many Métis, and only about one in five can speak an Aboriginal language, but another one in five can understand a native language. Thus, outsiders observe apparent contradictions, such as a large Métis audience

Temporary Residents of Canada

by Craig McKie

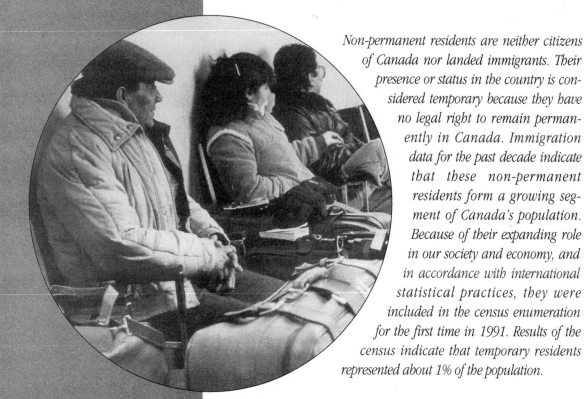

Non-permanent residents are neither citizens of Canada nor landed immigrants. Their presence or status in the country is considered temporary because they have no legal right to remain permanently in Canada. Immigration data for the past decade indicate that these non-permanent residents form a growing segment of Canada's population. Because of their expanding role in our society and economy, and in accordance with international statistical practices, they were included in the census enumeration for the first time in 1991. Results of the census indicate that temporary residents represented about 1% of the population.

Many non-permanent residents are working in Canada at the request of an employer and possess an employment authorization that allows them to reside legally in this country. Some temporary residents have student visas allowing them to stay in Canada to attend school or university. Others have been admitted into the country on humanitarian, compassionate or national interest grounds, such as applicants for refugee status and those holding Minister's permits authorizing residence in Canada. Some are visiting Canada with documented visitor's visas, while others are living in the country without legal permission.

Non-permanent residents concentrated in Toronto, Montreal and Vancouver Of non-permanent residents enumerated by the 1991 Census, almost three-quarters were living in Toronto, Montreal and Vancouver. In 1991, 44% of non-permanent residents were living in the Toronto census metropolitan area (CMA), while 18% were in the Montreal CMA and 10% in the Vancouver CMA.

Non-permanent residents represented 2.5% of the Toronto CMA's total population. The next highest concentration was in the Vancouver CMA (1.4% of the population), followed by the Montreal CMA (1.3% of the population). Non-permanent residents formed less than 1% of the populations of all other CMAs.

Numbers more than double in 10 years According to administrative data from the Citizenship and Immigration Canada Visitors Immigration Data System (VIDS),[1] the number of non-permanent residents more than doubled during the 1980s, rising to 369,100 in 1990 from 143,000 in 1981. By 1990, the annual number of non-permanent residents was 73% greater than the annual intake of permanent residents, that is, landed immigrants. In contrast, in 1981, the number of non-permanent residents was only 11% greater than the annual intake of permanent residents.

In addition to a growth in the population of non-permanent residents during the 1980s, the length of their residency in Canada has also increased. Among non-permanent residents who arrived in Canada in 1989, 50% stayed for a year or more. In contrast, only 25% of non-permanent residents admitted in 1981 stayed for a year or more.[2]

Non-permanent residents are more likely than landed immigrants to be of working age. In 1990, 88% of non-permanent residents were aged 20-49, while only 60% of landed immigrants admitted that year were that age.[2] Therefore, if non-permanent residents had been included in counts of new immigrants admitted in 1990, the dependency ratio of this population, the proportion who were seniors and children, would have been much lower.[2]

According to VIDS, most (80%) non-permanent residents in 1990 lived in either Ontario or Quebec, with 43% in the Toronto CMA alone.[1] Males outnumbered females, with 135 male non-permanent residents of Canada for every 100 females. Among landed immigrants admitted in 1990, the ratio also favoured males but less so, with 102 males for every 100 females.[2]

Temporary workers form largest group
Growth in the population of non-permanent residents during the 1980s was largely concentrated among those in Canada as paid workers. According to VIDS, the number of non-permanent residents with employment authorizations staying in Canada for one year or more increased six times to 162,900 in 1990 from 26,300 in 1981. Some of this large increase occurred because, in 1989, employment authorizations were granted to almost 100,000 people already living temporarily in this country as refugee applicants.[2] By

[1] Michalowski, M., "Temporary Immigrants to Canada: Numbers and Characteristics in the 1980s." Paper presented at the 1990 North American Conference on Applied Demography, Bowling Green, Ohio, October 18-21, 1990.

[2] Michalowski, M., "Redefining the Concept of Immigration in Canada," **Canadian Studies in Population**, Vol. 20(1), 1993.

CANADIAN SOCIAL TRENDS BACKGROUNDER

Administrative data and census counts

The 1990 VIDS total (369,100) exceeds that obtained from the 1991 Census (223,400), indicating that a large number of non-permanent residents did not respond to the census. Many may have been reluctant to complete a government census form because of a language barrier, a fear of undermining their residency or a lack of awareness of the need to participate.

VIDS provides a record of documents issued to non-permanent residents and, as a result, individuals may be represented more than once on the VIDS data base. To convert VIDS to a register of non-permanent residents, estimation procedures were developed to eliminate multiple counting of the same person.[1]

VIDS includes non-permanent residents with employment authorizations, student visas, Minister's permits and those with documented visitor's visas. The census counted those with employment authorizations, student visas, Minister's permits and those who were refugee applicants as non-permanent residents.

[1] Michalowski, M. and C. Forier, "Two Neglected Categories of Immigrants to Canada: Temporary Immigrants and Returning Canadians," **Statistical Journal of the United Nations**, ECE 7: 175-204, 1990.

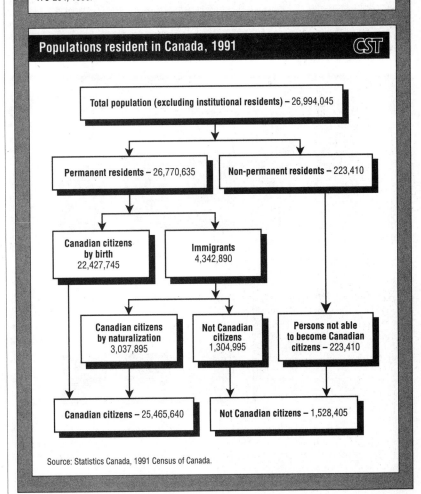

Populations resident in Canada, 1991

Source: Statistics Canada, 1991 Census of Canada.

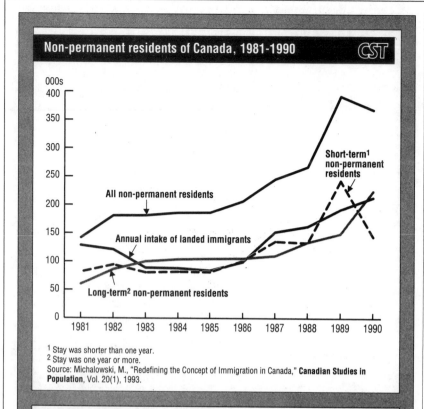

Non-permanent residents of Canada, 1981-1990

000s

- All non-permanent residents
- Short-term[1] non-permanent residents
- Annual intake of landed immigrants
- Long-term[2] non-permanent residents

[1] Stay was shorter than one year.
[2] Stay was one year or more.
Source: Michalowski, M., "Redefining the Concept of Immigration in Canada," **Canadian Studies in Population**, Vol. 20(1), 1993.

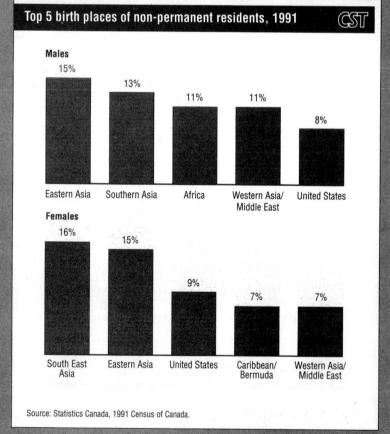

Top 5 birth places of non-permanent residents, 1991

Males

Eastern Asia	Southern Asia	Africa	Western Asia/ Middle East	United States
15%	13%	11%	11%	8%

Females

South East Asia	Eastern Asia	United States	Caribbean/ Bermuda	Western Asia/ Middle East
16%	15%	9%	7%	7%

Source: Statistics Canada, 1991 Census of Canada.

1990, the number of non-permanent residents with employment authorizations staying in Canada for one year or more was four times greater than the number holding student visas, eight times greater than the number with Minister's permits, and eleven times greater than the number of documented visitors.[2]

Historically, the non-permanent labour force consisted of foreign agricultural workers admitted to Canada during harvest times to augment the domestic labour force when it was seen to be inadequate for short-term surges in demand for particular types of labour.[3] Although seasonal labour still attracts non-permanent residents, work requiring longer stays has become more the norm.

Much is unknown about the occupations of those with employment authorizations who stay in Canada for one year or more. This is because 79% of non-permanent residents who worked in Canada for one year or more in 1990 held exempted employment authorizations, from which occupation information was not available. Exempted employment authorizations were created, not to fulfil unmet demands for labour, but so that people already living in Canada, such as refugee applicants, could obtain jobs and thus not be as dependent on Canada's social safety net.[2]

Among non-permanent workers who stayed in Canada for one year or more, for whom occupation information was known, service occupations dominated. In 1990, 35% held these types of occupations. Service occupations were the most common jobs held by females (63%), many of whom were live-in care givers. Other predominant occupational groups included teaching (16%), managerial and administrative (13%), entrepreneurs and investors (8%), and natural sciences, engineering and mathematics (7%).[2]

There has always been a flow of foreign nationals in and out of Canada for business purposes. Under the Free Trade Agreement between Canada and the United States, special provisions for the temporary entry of Canadian and American citizens into one another's territory for business purposes were adopted. These terms facilitate the flow between the two countries of consultants, professionals, sales representatives and maintenance personnel.

UNIT 1: POPULATION, HUMAN GEOGRAPHY AND HEALTH

Many are applicants for refugee status Applicants for refugee status are those who arrive at Canada's borders on their own initiative and seek asylum by making a special application for permission to stay in Canada as a refugee. These applicants are entitled to remain in the country temporarily until their claim is heard to completion by the Canadian Immigration and Refugee Board (IRB). Those receiving a positive decision by the board become permanent residents of Canada. Refugee applications are governed by Bill C-86 which came into force January 1, 1989, superseding Bill C-55. That year, there was a backlog of 95,000 refugee applications.

To provide an opportunity for refugee applicants to financially support themselves, many are granted exempted employment authorizations. Refugee applicants with exempted employment authorizations are included in VIDS totals, while those without are excluded. The IRB, however, has data on all refugee applicants. IRB data indicate that the number of claims for refugee status climbed to almost 3,150 per month during 1992, representing a steady influx of non-permanent residents.

According to the IRB, refugee status and thus permanent residence was granted to 17,437 refugee applicants living temporarily in Canada in 1992. This intake was down from 19,425 in 1991.[4] Similarly, the overall percentage of applicants obtaining refugee status was down to 57% in 1992 from 64% in 1991. In 1992, about 7,000 applicants whose claims were held over from previous years were granted status, but were not included in the 1992 totals.[5] That year, applicants from Somalia (91%) were more likely than applicants from any other country to be granted refugee status.

In the first quarter of 1993, 14,068 refugee claims were made, according to the IRB. Of these claims, 6,798 cases were completed. Of the completed cases, 51% were granted refugee status. As in previous years, most claimants in 1993 came from Sri Lanka, followed by the former Soviet Union and Somalia.[6]

Student visas, Minister's permits and documented visitors Many foreign students are attending Canadian schools and universities. According to VIDS, the number of non-permanent residents with student visas increased to 40,200 in 1990 from 23,900 in 1981.

According to VIDS, the number of non-permanent residents who held Minister's permits authorizing their residence in Canada because of humanitarian, compassionate or national interest grounds remained about the same each year during the 1980s. In 1990, there were 22,100 non-permanent residents with Minister's permits, up slightly from 20,300 in 1981.

Documented visitors form a small but growing group of non-permanent residents. In 1990, there were 14,500 documented visitors, up from 8,300 in 1981.

Non-permanent residents contribute to social change Non-permanent residents are a heterogeneous element in the Canadian population. The group includes workers, students, applicants for refugee status, those who possess Minister's permits, visitors and an unknown number of people without any legal status in Canada.

Although non-permanent residents may not stay in Canada for substantial amounts of time, as a group, they are a growing component of the overall population. By the last half of the past decade, the number of non-permanent residents each year was about double the annual intake of landed immigrants.

Non-permanent residents are concentrated in Toronto, Montreal and Vancouver. These metropolitan areas, which all have large landed immigrant populations, likely attract temporary residents because they offer communities of people of the same nationality, areas in which people's mother tongues can be used in daily life, and arrays of services for those of their national origin.

Inflows of non-permanent residents and landed immigrants to these few urban centres are resulting in social change, including a significant shift in the ethnic origins of these populations. New residents affect the demand for local services, such as health care, education, social assistance and employment programs. In addition, as workers, consumers and taxpayers, non-permanent residents have become important contributors to these urban economies.

[3] The legal basis for short-term admission of workers to Canada as paid workers was laid with the Employment Authorization Program begun in 1973.

[4] **Annual Report for the Year Ending December 31, 1992**. Ottawa: Immigration and Refugee Board Catalogue MQ1-1992.

[5] In addition to refugee claimants whose applications were approved, 16,000 refugees were sponsored to come to Canada in 1992. These individuals have landed immigrant status when they arrive in Canada.

[6] "Refugee claims totalled 14,068, board reports," **Globe and Mail**, May 29, 1993, p.A-3.

Dr. Craig McKie is an Associate Professor of Sociology, Carleton University and a Contributing Editor with *Canadian Social Trends*.

Non parlo né inglese, né francese

"I Can't Speak English or French"

by Brian Harrison

A ccording to the most recent Canadian census, more people unable to speak English or French were living in Canada in 1991 than at any other time this century. In total, 308,500 people over age 5, 62% of whom were women, had this language barrier. Accessing services or finding employment may be very difficult for these people. In addition, their educational opportunities may be limited by the inability to speak one of Canada's official languages.

UNIT 1: POPULATION, HUMAN GEOGRAPHY AND HEALTH

Heavy immigration during the 1980s, particularly during the last half of the decade, contributed to a large increase in the number of people unable to speak either official language. This has put a strain on services, such as language training and translation, required to help those unable to speak an official language cope within Canadian society.

51% of immigrants unable to speak English or French have been in Canada for more than ten years Most people who could not speak English or French in 1991 (86%) were immigrants to Canada while the remainder were non-permanent residents[1] and Canadian-born individuals. Notwithstanding the impact of recent high immigration levels, more than half (51%) of immigrants who could not speak one of the official languages had been living in Canada for more than ten years.

Although these individuals settled in Canada before 1981, they may not yet have learned English or French because their daily responsibilities isolate them from other Canadians. Immigrant women working in the home, for example, often live in communities where daily activities are conducted in their mother tongues. Others who arrived in Canada more recently have not yet had an opportunity to learn an official language. Of immigrants who could not speak English or French in 1991, 36% arrived after 1985 and 13% arrived between 1981 and 1985.

Knowledge of official languages varies Of all immigrants with a mother tongue other than English or French, 10% were unable to speak either official language well enough to conduct a conversation. Knowledge of English or French, however, varied widely by language group. Similar proportions of those with a Chinese (21%) or Portuguese (20%) mother tongue were unable to speak English or French. In contrast, just 1% of those with a German mother tongue and less than 1% of the Dutch mother tongue group were unable to speak an official language.

Broad differences in language knowledge exist, at least in part, because the proportion of people who could speak

---

1 People who hold student or employment authorizations, Minister's permits or who are refugee claimants.

English or French prior to coming to Canada varies by language group. Recent immigration from countries where neither English nor French is widely spoken has led to an increase in the proportion unable to speak an official language.

More women than men Among adults 20 years or older who could not speak English or French, women outnumbered men in all age groups. The proportion of women rose with age, from 53% of those aged 20-24 to 67% of those aged 65 and over. Women's domestic responsibilities and more limited labour force participation likely restrict both their interaction

---

with other Canadians outside of the home and their access to language training programs.

Most live in large households... People who could not speak English or French lived in larger households in 1991 than Canadians overall. Most people who were unable to speak an official language, 62%, lived with four or more people. In contrast, just 47% of all Canadians lived in a household that size. About 27% of those with this language barrier lived with six or more people.

Some people unable to speak English or French (6%), however, lived alone. Of

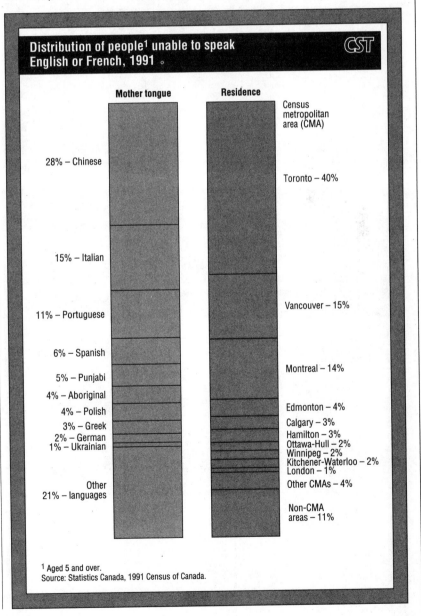

Distribution of people[1] unable to speak English or French, 1991

Mother tongue
- 28% – Chinese
- 15% – Italian
- 11% – Portuguese
- 6% – Spanish
- 5% – Punjabi
- 4% – Aboriginal
- 4% – Polish
- 3% – Greek
- 2% – German
- 1% – Ukrainian
- Other 21% – languages

Residence — Census metropolitan area (CMA)
- Toronto – 40%
- Vancouver – 15%
- Montreal – 14%
- Edmonton – 4%
- Calgary – 3%
- Hamilton – 3%
- Ottawa-Hull – 2%
- Winnipeg – 2%
- Kitchener-Waterloo – 2%
- London – 1%
- Other CMAs – 4%
- Non-CMA areas – 11%

1 Aged 5 and over.
Source: Statistics Canada, 1991 Census of Canada.

those living alone, mostly women, 43% had a Chinese or Italian mother tongue.

...and urban areas Concentrations of people unable to speak English or French are especially high in large urban areas where sizeable ethnic communities exist. More than 300 of every 10,000 people living in Toronto and Vancouver census metropolitan areas (CMAs) had this language barrier in 1991, while in the CMAs of Montreal, Calgary, Edmonton and Kitchener-Waterloo the ratio was about 150 for every 10,000 people. In contrast, rates in Hamilton (140), Windsor (133), Winnipeg (114) and London

(103) were much closer to the national average of 124 for every 10,000 people. Those who could not speak either official language represented less than 100 of every 10,000 people living in Canada's other large urban areas.

More than two-thirds of those unable to speak English or French in 1991 lived in Toronto (40%), Vancouver (15%) and Montreal (14%). Many people with this language barrier also lived in Edmonton (4%), Calgary (3%) and Hamilton (3%). As a result, four provinces were home to almost all people who could not speak one of Canada's official languages: Ontario (53%),

British Columbia (17%), Quebec (16%) and Alberta (8%). Other provinces and territories had far fewer people with this language difficulty, ranging from 3% (9,785 people) in Manitoba to an almost negligible percentage in Prince Edward Island (75 people) and the Yukon (30 people).

Rapid growth since 1981 The number of people unable to speak English or French grew by 32% from 1981 to 1991. The four largest provinces, as well as urban areas that already had large populations with this language barrier, experienced high growth rates. The number of those who could not speak English or French increased by 67% in British Columbia, 45% in Alberta, 31% in Ontario and 27% in Quebec. Among the largest urban areas, the number increased by 88% in Vancouver, while rising 38% in both Toronto and Montreal. Large increases have an impact on social services, such as language training and translation, required to integrate this population into Canadian society.

Many Chinese, Italian and Portuguese People whose mother tongue was Chinese, Italian or Portuguese accounted for more than half of those unable to speak English or French in 1991. Chinese, the fastest growing language group in Canada since 1986, was the mother tongue of 28% of those who could not speak English or French, while Italian was the mother tongue of 15% and Portuguese of 11%.

Most of those with a Chinese mother tongue who could not speak English or French lived in Toronto (37%) or Vancouver (32%), while most Italians with this language barrier lived in Toronto (56%) or Montreal (24%). The majority of those who spoke Portuguese and could not speak either official language lived in Toronto (63%).

Brian Harrison is a senior analyst with the Demolinguistics Division, Statistics Canada.

• Adapted from the **1991 Census Short Article** of the same title.

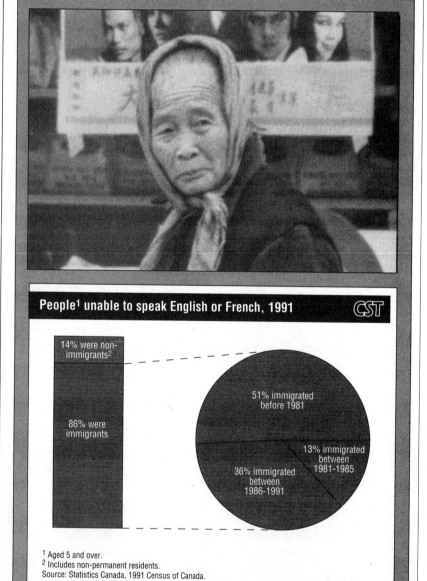

People[1] unable to speak English or French, 1991   CST

14% were non-immigrants[2]

86% were immigrants

51% immigrated before 1981

13% immigrated between 1981-1985

36% immigrated between 1986-1991

[1] Aged 5 and over.
[2] Includes non-permanent residents.
Source: Statistics Canada, 1991 Census of Canada.

In sickness and in health: The well-being of married seniors

by Susan Crompton and Anna Kemeny

With the aging of the population, Canadians have become increasingly concerned about the well-being of senior citizens. In recent years, many sectors of society have discussed how best to help seniors maintain their independence as well as what seniors themselves can do to minimize the problems that can develop with aging. Researchers agree that "successful aging," like successful living, is generally best achieved by some combination of physical, mental and emotional health; close relationships with friends and family; financial stability; and ongoing involvement with life.[1]

However, it seems that good physical health is simultaneously a condition for, and a contributor to, aging well: more opportunities are available to a healthy person, and a wider variety of activities, both mental and physical, seems in turn to improve a person's health.[2] This would suggest that seniors whose everyday activities are restricted by illness or disability are in greatest jeopardy of isolation and perhaps loss of independence.

Using some selected indicators, this article compares the psychological and social well-being of married seniors in poor health with those of seniors in good health. It also examines whether a person's well-being is affected by their spouse's health. To control for the well-known effects of socioeconomic status on health, the study population are middle-income homeowners living in two-person households in which at least one spouse is age 65 or over.

Healthy or not, most married seniors were doing well psychologically

The majority of married seniors described themselves as happy — but those in good health were more likely to do so. Over 90% of healthy senior men and women reported that they were happy, regardless of their partner's health. In comparison, no more than about three-quarters of men and fewer than two-thirds of women in poor health claimed to be happy. But while it appears that seniors in ill health are more likely to report feeling happy if their partner is healthy rather than ill, there is no statistically significant difference between the two groups, suggesting that a spouse's physical health has a minimal impact on happiness.

Although the majority of married seniors scored very low on the scale for mental distress, a very real degree of emotional discomfort seems to attend the lives of people whose day-to-day activities are compromised by illness. Many seniors in poor health are likely living with chronic pain, which is often associated with increased levels of mental distress. According to the distress scale — which measures feelings of restlessness, hopelessness, worthlessness or sadness — married seniors who were ill reported

---

1. Rowe, John W. and Robert L. Kahn. 1998. *Successful Aging*. New York: Dell Publishing. pp. 35-52.

2. Ibid. pp. 35-52.

This article uses data from the cross–sectional component of the 1996-97 National Population Health Survey (NPHS), designed to collect information about the health of Canadians. Almost 82,000 respondents answered in-depth health questions, covering items such as health status, use of medication, risk-taking behaviour and mental and psychological well-being.

For this article, persons living in middle-income two-person homeowning households in which at least one person was age 65 or over — more than 2,050 respondents representing almost 600,000 persons — were identified; of these, persons in either poor or good health living with a spouse in either poor or good health — almost 800 respondents representing over 220,000 men and women — were selected for inclusion in the study population. In the great majority of these households, both the respondent and the spouse were 65 or older; in some cases, the respondent was younger. For the sake of brevity, however, all respondents will be referred to as "seniors."

Poor health: having an activity limitation and at least two long-term health problems. Also referred to as "ill."

Good health: not having an activity limitation and having no or only one long-term health problem. Also referred to as "healthy."

Middle-income: annual household income of $20,000 to $40,000 in 1996-97.

Activity limitation: refers to any long-term physical or mental condition or disability that limits a person's activities at home, at school, at work or in other settings. Physical limitations common among seniors include mobility (ability to get around), non-correctable hearing and vision problems.

Long-term health problem/chronic health problem: a diagnosed health condition lasting, or expected to last, at least six months. Common long-term conditions among seniors include arthritis or rheumatism, non-arthritic back problems, heart disease, high blood pressure and diabetes.

Distress: based on a set of questions designed to assess mental and emotional well-being. Respondents were asked how frequently (from none of the time to all the time) they felt very sad, nervous, restless or fidgety, hopeless, worthless, and that everything was an effort. Higher scores indicate more distress.

Depression: measures the symptoms associated with a major depressive episode using a subset of questions from the Composite International Diagnostic Interview.

Emotional support: based on four questions that ask (yes or no) if the respondents has someone they can confide in, someone they can count on, someone who can give them advice, and someone who makes them feel loved. A higher score indicates greater perceived social support.

Frequency of social contact: measures the frequency (every day, at least once a week, two or three times a month, once a month, a few times a year, once a year, never) with which the respondent had contact in the past 12 months with friends, neighbours and family members who are not part of the household. A higher score indicates more contacts.

Frequency of social involvement: measures the frequency (at least once a week, at least once a month, at least three or four times a year, at least once a year, never) of the respondent's participation in associations, voluntary organizations and religious services. A higher score indicates greater social involvement.

Cognitive function: measure of memory and thinking capacity, based on the respondent's usual ability to remember things and usual ability to think and solve day-to-day problems.

Physical activity index: measure of intensity of leisure-time physical activity based on energy expenditure. An *active* person expends a minimum of 3.0 calories per kilogram of body weight per day in activity during their leisure time; a person at a *moderate* level expends a minimum of 1.5 calories. A person will achieve cardiovascular benefits from active physical activity and health benefits from moderate activity. Persons who are *inactive* expend less than 1.5 calories per kilogram of body weight per day and are deriving no health benefits from physical activity.

higher levels of distress than their healthy counterparts. Nevertheless, having a healthy spouse seemed to help men in poor health, since almost all 94% of them reported a low level of distress (less than 7 out of 24), compared with only 63%[3] of those whose spouse was also ill. Women in poor health did not seem to benefit in the same way, since there was no statistically significant difference in distress levels recorded by those with a healthy compared to an ill partner.

Average scores are another way of looking at levels of distress and they tell the same story: the average scores of seniors in poor health (except for men with healthy wives) were almost four to six times higher than those of seniors in good health.

The depression index probes the likelihood that a period of feeling blue or sad may have escalated into an episode of clinical depression. Depression is actually quite uncommon among people who are married, and even more uncommon among the elderly.[4] Even when burdened with ill health, over 96% of married seniors had exhibited no symptoms of depression during the previous year.

Medical studies have consistently shown that emotional support, especially from a partner, has direct positive effects on health. Researchers believe this is because some of the health-related effects of aging are buffered when people have someone they can confide in and can count on, and who can give them advice and make them feel loved. Conversely, lack of such support is a powerful risk factor for poor health, perhaps because people have no one to help shield them from the effects of various stressors.[5]

According to the NPHS, married seniors had a high rate of emotional support, with the overwhelming majority of both men and women scoring at least 3 out of 4 on the emotional support scale, regardless of their own or their spouse's health. (Although only 78% of men in poor health married to part-

ners in poor health scored high, the difference between them and other men was not statistically significant.)

The love and companionship received at home is reinforced by keeping in touch with friends, relatives and neighbours. The great majority of seniors reported that they visited with and talked to people in their social network at least several times a month. Women in both good and poor health, and with both healthy and ill partners, scored consistently high on the frequency of contact scale (over 94% scored at least 3 out of 6 and had average scores of over 4). Men, healthy or not, also had high scores (over 96% scoring 3 out of 6 with average scores of 4 and over) as long as their partner was healthy. However, if married to someone in ill health, men's scores dropped visibly, implying in the case of social contact that the health of their wives made a greater difference than their own.

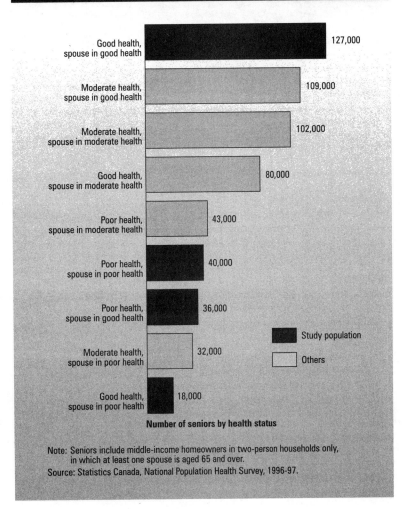

Over one in five married seniors is in good health and lives with a spouse in good health

Good health, spouse in good health — 127,000

Moderate health, spouse in good health — 109,000

Moderate health, spouse in moderate health — 102,000

Good health, spouse in moderate health — 80,000

Poor health, spouse in moderate health — 43,000

Poor health, spouse in poor health — 40,000

Poor health, spouse in good health — 36,000

Moderate health, spouse in poor health — 32,000

Good health, spouse in poor health — 18,000

■ Study population
□ Others

Number of seniors by health status

Note: Seniors include middle-income homeowners in two-person households only, in which at least one spouse is aged 65 and over.
Source: Statistics Canada, National Population Health Survey, 1996-97.

---

3. Subject to high sampling variability.

4. In 1994-95, 6% of married persons and 3% of seniors were classified as having had a major depressive episode in the previous year. Beaudet, M.P. 1996. "Depression," *Health Reports* 7, 4. (Statistics Canada catalogue 82-003-XPB)

5. Rowe, J. W. and R. L. Kahn. 1998. *Successful Aging*. New York: Dell Publishing. pp. 152-166.

Some gerontologists believe that continuing engagement with life, sometimes reflected as involvement at the community level, also contributes to successful aging, and is associated with better health, self-worth and connection with others.[6] However, according to their scores, few seniors ranked above the mid-point on the social involvement scale (at least 4 out of 8); the exception, not surprisingly, was healthy seniors with healthy partners — some 68% of men and 61% of women in healthy couples. Average scores indicated gender differences in involvement in community activities: women (both healthy and ill) living with a partner in poor health had average scores higher than men in the same situation, perhaps indicating their greater desire to "get out and about."

The fact that seniors in poor health were less likely to participate in volunteer organizations and associations, or to attend religious services, may reflect the limits imposed by their physical restrictions: attending meetings when one's mobility is restricted, or participating in group activities with a hearing problem, may be difficult to undertake.

There is another benefit to social interaction that seniors may enjoy. Regular use of the powers of thinking, reasoning and solving problems is central to supporting day-to-day health and independence. Some medical studies show that seniors who are involved in a variety of activities appear to have strong cognitive capacity, while those with very little social involvement report having trouble concentrating, solving problems and remembering events. Over eight in 10 seniors in healthy couples reported having no difficulty with cognitive function. In contrast, over half of seniors living in couples in poor health had at least some cognitive difficulty (for example, being forgetful, having trouble thinking clearly). This could be due to a variety of factors related to their physical condition, such as chronic pain and discomfort or the effects of medication.

Interestingly, regardless of their own health, seniors with healthy spouses were more likely to report good cognitive function than those with ill spouses.

Seniors not likely to be physically active, even if they are healthy

According to many researchers, physical fitness is also crucial to aging well: fitness boosts muscular strength, reduces the impact of other health risks, maintains bone mass and improves psychological well-being.[7] Health benefits can be derived from walking for as little as 30 minutes a day, and cardiovascular benefits from one hour's walking.[8]

While leisure-time exercise in its various forms — walking, gardening, swimming — provides its own rewards, one of its benefits lies in keeping seniors in shape so they can perform the regular, mundane tasks of daily life — walking upstairs, doing laundry, preparing meals or doing yardwork. In the long-term, physical fitness can

CST — Senior men in good health living with a partner in good health were most likely to report feeling happy

		Distress index	
	% who are happy	% under 7 of 24	Average score
Senior men			
In good health			
Spouse in good health	96	98	1.0
Spouse in poor health	88	98	0.8
In poor health			
Spouse in good health	77	94	2.1
Spouse in poor health	64[1]	63[1]	6.1
Senior women			
In good health			
Spouse in good health	90	96	1.5
Spouse in poor health	94	93	1.8
In poor health			
Spouse in good health	64	72	4.0
Spouse in poor health	60[1]	60[1]	5.6

Note: Seniors include middle-income homeowners in two-person households only, in which at least one spouse is aged 65 and over.

1. Subject to high sampling variability.

Source: Statistics Canada, National Population Health Survey, 1996-97.

6. Ibid. pp. 167-180.

7. Ibid. p. 98.

8. Example calculated for a 70-kilogram (154-pound) adult, using the NPHS definitions of energy expenditure at the moderate and active levels.

reduce a couple's dependence on outside help with their everyday activities.

One would not expect people with multiple chronic illnesses and an activity limitation to engage often in recreational physical activities. Indeed, about two-thirds of ill seniors with partners in poor health were physically inactive, compared with only half of healthy seniors living in healthy couples. What is somewhat surprising are the results for healthy seniors living with a spouse who is ill: two-thirds are inactive during their leisure time. This may suggest that the time available for their own activities is curtailed by the need to provide care for their partners.

Regardless of their own or their spouse's health status, women were more likely than men to be physically inactive during their leisure time: over eight in 10 women in poor health, and over half of those in good health, did not meet the basic minimum level of physical activity for maintaining their health. Some of this inactivity may be due to their inability to participate in traditional recreational activities,

but the special fitness classes now offered in many communities — aquafit, "chair aerobics" and seniors' yoga and weight training classes — may provide an opportunity for these seniors to enjoy the benefits of physical activity.

Summary

Results of the NPHS show that homeowning middle-income married seniors in poor health do not score as well on some indicators for psychological well-being (happiness, distress) as their healthy counterparts. They also report having more trouble in their day-to-day cognitive function. However, much of the malaise reported by seniors in poor health, as well as some of their difficulty with remembering things or thinking clearly, could be due to medication or chronic pain and discomfort related to their illnesses and physical limitations. On the other hand, married seniors in poor health enjoy a high level of emotional support and are just as socially engaged as those in good health.

CST — The vast majority of seniors reported receiving high levels of emotional support

	Emotional support		Frequency of contact		Social involvement	
	% at least 3 of 4	Average score	% at least 3 of 6	Average score	% at least 4 of 8	Average score
Senior men						
In good health						
Spouse in good health	96	3.8	96	4.4	68	4.4
Spouse in poor health	98	3.8	--	3.5	--	2.9
In poor health						
Spouse in good health	100	4.0	98	4.0	50[1]	3.0
Spouse in poor health	78[1]	3.3	82[1]	3.6	24[1]	1.7
Senior women						
In good health						
Spouse in good health	93	3.6	94	4.2	61	4.3
Spouse in poor health	96	3.9	97	4.4	48[1]	3.4
In poor health						
Spouse in good health	96	3.8	100	4.2	42[1]	2.7
Spouse in poor health	98	3.9	99	4.3	36[1]	2.7

Note: Seniors include middle-income homeowners in two-person households only, in which at least one spouse is aged 65 and over.

-- Sample too small to provide reliable estimate.

1. Subject to high sampling variability.

Source: Statistics Canada, National Population Health Survey, 1996-97.

For reasons which are not clear, higher socioeconomic status is strongly associated with good health. People in the upper-middle and upper income brackets are more likely to enjoy very good to excellent health than those in lower income groups. Researchers have proposed that this may be because high-income persons most often have a high education and are employed in less hazardous jobs; earning higher incomes also allows them greater control over their lives. Other researchers suggest that higher education helps people to better understand health risks, since well-educated people generally maintain healthier lifestyles, including more exercise, good nutrition, more medical check-ups and less risky behaviour (for example, not smoking and using seat belts).

The link between socioeconomic profile and health is less pronounced among older than younger people, but the association nonetheless persists. Among seniors, the link to socioeconomic status may not be simply the "heritage" of good or poor health from their youth, but the level of involvement in maintaining their health into old age. Some studies suggest that seniors with higher socioeconomic status are better able to understand health education material provided by their doctors and to participate actively in making decisions about their health care. Also, the International Adult Literacy Survey showed that Canadian seniors with good literacy skills (which are strongly associated with higher income and education) are exposed regularly to a wider range of information — newspapers and magazines, books and radio — than seniors with poor skills. With many media sources now carrying health news, researchers suggest that seniors with access to more information in their daily lives may be alerted sooner to potential health problems, leading to earlier diagnosis and treatment.

• For more information, see Paul Roberts and Gail Fawcett. 1998. *At Risk: a Socio-economic Analysis of Health and Literacy Among Seniors* (Statistics Canada, Catalogue 89-552-MPE, no. 5)

The impact of a spouse's health on successful aging cannot be overlooked, since the well-being of someone close generally influences one's own state of mind. For most indicators of well-being examined, healthy seniors married to healthy people are better off than seniors in poor health married to people who are ill. The situation of "mixed health" couples is not as clear. Having a spouse who is ill does not seem to adversely affect the general well-being of healthy seniors; meanwhile, having a healthy spouse appears to be quite beneficial to seniors who are ill, especially men, suggesting that the healthy partner offers help and support that makes life more comfortable and enjoyable. Further research into this issue would be rewarding.

Susan Crompton is Editor-in-Chief and **Anna Kemeny** is an editor with *Canadian Social Trends*.

WWNo Needs Short-Term Help?

by Kelly Cranswick

Who Needs Short-Term Help?

Who Needs Short-Term Help?

C aregiving often brings to mind visions of frail seniors being cared for by their families. However, people who are experiencing a temporarily difficult period in their lives — they may have lost a loved one, broken a leg or just given birth — also need help to look after the children, cook dinner or shop for groceries.

People who need assistance just for a short time often find themselves having to rely on the help of family and friends. But many people live far from their support networks, particularly parents and siblings, who are especially important sources of help. Divorce or separation, and step or blended families, can also complicate the situation since a person may feel unsure about who they can turn to when they need help.

According to the 1996 General Social Survey, 900,000 Canadians accepted help while they were going through a temporarily difficult time. Despite its importance, however, little recognition is given to short-term caregiving. Perhaps this is because it is largely unstructured and makes few, if any, demands on public sector resources. Whatever the reason, most caregiving studies focus on long-term care, especially to seniors.

This article addresses the gap in the research by providing a first glimpse of Canadians who receive help because of a temporarily difficult time. It also identifies the people whose needs are likely to be neglected during a period of short-term difficulty.

Who receives help due to a temporarily difficult time?
Women were more likely than men to receive help during a difficult time. Five percent of women 15 years and over (about 600,000) compared with 3% of men (about 290,000) received help at some point during 1996 because of a short-term problem. Women most likely to require assistance were those aged 25 to 44 (6%), who are of prime child-bearing age, and women 65 years and over (6%[1]), whose health tends to be failing. Among men, seniors were most likely to receive help to get through a tough time (4%[1]).

Living alone or with one's family made little difference as to whether a person received help. Five percent of people living alone were assisted during a temporarily difficult time. This compared with 4% of people living with their spouse and 4% living with their spouse and children. Three percent of people living in "other" situations, including single parents and people 15 years and over living with their parents, also accepted short-term help.

While living arrangements did not reveal much about who received help during a temporary difficulty, the presence of young children living in the household was somewhat more telling. People with children under 5 years of age were most likely to be recipients (6%); those with older children were less likely (4%). The somewhat higher demand of people with preschool children reflects the fact that people often need assistance after the birth of a child, and helps to explain why women were more likely to require short-term caregiving.

What tasks do people need help with? To learn about the assistance Canadians received during a short-term crisis, the 1996 General Social Survey (GSS) asked people to identify the help they obtained for four specific sets of activities: personal care, tasks around the house, running errands, and childcare.

Personal care The greatest number of care-receivers — almost 400,000 — got help with their personal care,[2] with fewer men receiving assistance than women. People are not likely to seek assistance with their personal care unless absolutely necessary, therefore, it was not surprising that short-term illness[3] or serious injury was cited by 8 out of every 10 people as the reason they needed help with these intimate tasks.

As might be expected, a large proportion of caregivers providing personal care during a short-term crisis were spouses. Daughters, sisters and mothers also offered assistance. And, although some people received care from their friends, the numbers were somewhat small, probably because it is often

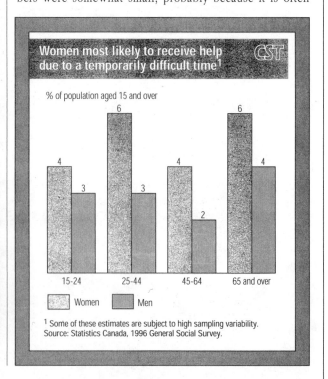

Women most likely to receive help due to a temporarily difficult time[1] · CST

% of population aged 15 and over

	15-24	25-44	45-64	65 and over
Women	4	6	4	6
Men	3	3	2	4

☐ Women   ■ Men

[1] Some of these estimates are subject to high sampling variability.
Source: Statistics Canada, 1996 General Social Survey.

uncomfortable to accept assistance for tasks such as bathing from someone who is not a close family member.[4] However, people must feel differently about formal caregivers as the largest proportion of care-receivers chose to entrust their personal care to professionals.

Tasks around the house Over 385,000 Canadians received help with the tasks around their house because they were in the midst of a temporarily difficult time. Most got help with house cleaning, laundry and sewing. Many other care-receivers needed someone to lend a hand with preparing meals and cleaning up afterwards, while some got help with house maintenance and outside work. For each type of task, more women than men received assistance.

In the majority of cases (58%), help with household chores was provided because the care-receiver had a short-term illness. The birth of a child (pregnancy or adoption) and/or problems with children (19%) were also relatively common reasons. Spouses and mothers most often provided support with household chores.

Running errands Often times, people have responsibilities that take them out of the house. In 1996, more than 219,000 Canadians with a temporary problem received assistance running their errands. A slightly larger number got help with transportation than with shopping, while a smaller proportion received help with their banking and bill-paying. Gender differences were pronounced, with more women then men receiving assistance with each task. Short-term illness (66%) was again the main reason why people were unable to leave their homes to run errands.

The caregivers who ran errands were different than those who provided help with the other tasks. Daughters and sisters were called on most frequently to take on these responsibilities. While many people still turned to spouses during a difficult time, even more turned to other family members, and some went to friends. Possibly it is easier to ask for help from someone who is already running an errand, especially if they are not a member of the household; for example, asking friends to do one's shopping when they do their own.

Childcare In 1996 more than 137,000 Canadians with children under age 15 received help with childcare when they were going through a difficult spell. One-third[1] received childcare because of the birth of a child (pregnancy or adoption) and/or problems

with their children; one-fifth[1] cited "other" reasons, such as school responsibilities. Not unexpectedly, Canadians receiving help with childcare were most likely to turn to their mothers.

Most help for temporarily difficult times was given by immediate family[1]　CST

| Relationship | % of people receiving help from a specific caregiver | | | |
	Personal care	Tasks at home	Running errands	Childcare
Spouse	34	28	25	--
Mother (in-law)	16	29	17	37
Daughter (in-law) & sister (in-law)	18	21	34	--
Other relatives	--	25	30	--
Formal caregiver	36	21	--	31
Friends[2]	9	18	21	--

-- Data too small to be released.
[1] Many of these estimates are subject to high sampling variability.
[2] Included friends, neighbours, co-workers and ex-partners.
Note: Columns do not add to 100 as a person could have been receiving help from more than one person.
Source: Statistics Canada, 1996 General Social Survey.

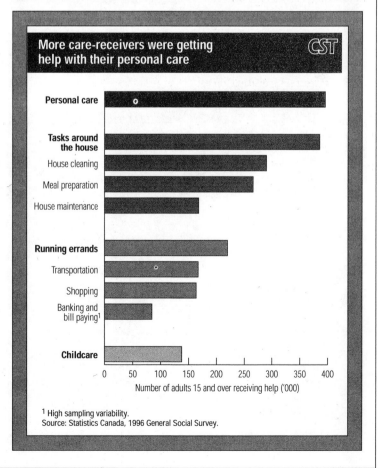

More care-receivers were getting help with their personal care　CST

Number of adults 15 and over receiving help ('000)

[1] High sampling variability.
Source: Statistics Canada, 1996 General Social Survey.

---

[1] This estimate has high sampling variability.

[2] Help with personal care includes assistance with bathing, brushing teeth or dressing, etc.

[3] Short-term illness also includes minor injuries.

[4] Leroy O. Stone, 1993. "Social consequences of population ageing: The human support systems dimension." Proceedings of International Population Conference. Montreal: International Union for the Scientific Study of Population. Vol. 3, pp. 25-34.

Age, employment status biggest predictors of having unmet needs

CST

Social network		Odds ratio of needing additional assistance
Parent(s) still living	Yes	1.0
	No	1.9
Sibling(s) still living	Yes	1.0
	No	0.6*
Child(ren) still living	Yes	1.0
	No	0.3
Feel close to friends and relatives	Yes	1.0
	No	1.4*
Attend religious services weekly or monthly	Yes	1.0
	No	1.4*
Main activity		
Employment Status	Working	1.0
	Not working	2.7
Personal characteristics		
Age	65 and over	1.0
	45-64	2.0*
	25-44	6.0
	15-24	3.7
Sex	Men	1.0
	Women	1.2*
Marital status	Married	1.0
	Separated/divorced	2.0
	Widowed	2.1*
	Single	0.8*

* Difference not statistically significant.
Source: Statistics Canada, 1996 General Social Survey.

The significant number of people getting formal help also suggests that many parents hire childcare workers to help out on a short-term basis.

The need for additional assistance While 900,000 people who went through a temporarily difficult time in 1996 received assistance, there were more than 200,000 people who did not get enough, if any, help. This total included approximately 120,000[1] people who had received help but needed more, and over 90,000[1] people who had wanted assistance but did not receive any. What were the odds that someone would not get sufficient help during a temporarily difficult time?

Since parents, especially mothers, often provide help during a temporarily difficult time, it seems reasonable to assume that a person without family would be more likely to lack the help they need. Data from the 1996 GSS support this belief. After controlling for other factors, the odds of having unmet needs were twice as great for people with deceased parents than for people who had at least one living parent.

On the other hand, people without children were less likely to have unmet needs, compared to people with children. This could be because children make demands that can be inconsistent with a parent's own needs, especially during a tough time, a conflict that childless people do not have to cope with.

People not working more likely to need added help The odds of needing additional assistance were almost three times greater for people not employed in the work force as for those who were employed. People who were "not employed" included individuals with long-term illnesses, retirees or seniors, women on maternity leave, and people looking for work, which can be a stressful time. In other words, people undergoing a temporarily difficult time may be over-represented among those outside the workforce. However, it should be noted that employed people often develop social networks at work, and may call on their colleagues to provide assistance.

The likelihood of having unmet needs generally declined with age. When all other factors were accounted for, the probability of needing additional short-term assistance was about 6 times greater for people aged 25 to 44 than for those 65 and over. This may seem surprising, but is probably explained by the fact that many seniors receiving assistance are getting long-term help, so are less likely to have unmet needs because of a temporary problem.

Divorced or separated people were twice as likely as married people to report they had unmet needs during a difficult time. One obvious reason is that married people are often able to rely on their spouse for support. Another possibility is that the temporarily difficult time may itself be the process of separation or divorce. This is suggested by the finding that the odds of other unmarried people — widows or widowers and single people — having unmet needs were not significantly different than the odds of married couples. These unmarried people may have found sources of support outside marriage, something divorced people had not yet developed.

Some unexpected findings Several other characteristics, especially social network factors, that might be expected to be associated with unmet needs were not. When other factors were controlled for, women faced no higher odds than men in finding help during a difficult spell. This result is interesting, since more women than men reported having received help for a short-term difficulty in 1996, and accounted for two-thirds of people with unmet needs. Also, even though sisters were often cited as caregivers, the odds of people without siblings having unmet needs were no different than the odds of people with brothers and sisters.

Similarly, having close friends and relatives was not a significant factor in having unmet needs, probably because people most often rely on immediate family members, such as spouses and parents, for assistance. And, while one would suspect that a strong social network is developed through participation in religious activities, it would seem that fellow members are not called upon for help in a crisis. The odds of having unmet needs during a temporarily difficult time were not different for people who did not attend religious services regularly, than for those who did.

So, who typically needs additional assistance during a temporarily difficult time? People with unmet needs were likely to be divorced, 25 to 44 years of age with children, suggesting that these people may be single parents. Generally they were not employed in the paid labour force and their parents were deceased.

Summary According to the General Social Survey, 900,000 Canadians who went through a temporarily difficult time in 1996 received assistance. While the findings suggest that most people who required short-term help were getting it, there still remained more than 200,000 people who needed temporary assistance, and who were not getting enough, if any, help.

Receiving help because of a temporarily difficult time can be viewed as part of a dynamic exchange: for every person who no longer needs help, there is another who is going through a short-term crisis and requires assistance. And the demand for such help is likely to increase. The growing practice among hospitals of discharging patients early, and the expansion of out-patient treatment, may increase the number of people needing help as they recover at home. Meanwhile, with the number of divorces each year remaining steady at approximately 78,000, people undergoing the trauma of marital breakdown are likely to need short-term help with childcare and other tasks.

Kelly Cranswick is an analyst with Housing, Family and Social Statistics Division, Statistics Canada.

Dementia among seniors

by Mary Anne Burke, Joan Lindsay, Ian McDowell and Gerry Hill

The aging of the Canadian population has focused a spotlight on people suffering from Alzheimer's disease and other forms of dementia. Dementia, a clinical syndrome characterized by severe losses of cognitive and emotional abilities, interferes with daily functioning and the quality of life. According to the recent Canadian Study of Health and Aging, the number of Canadian seniors with dementia is likely to more than triple by the year 2031.

The public and private costs to society as the numbers of elderly Canadians with dementia increase will be high, given the nature of care they will require.[1] Since dementia is a disease of aging, the impact will be disproportionately high for women, as there are more elderly women than men. Also, women shoulder a much larger load than men in caring for those suffering from dementia. Canadians will be increasingly challenged to find equitable, cost-effective and viable solutions for the care of those suffering from dementia.

UNIT 1: POPULATION, HUMAN GEOGRAPHY AND HEALTH

Prevalence of dementia The prevalence of dementia increases sharply with age. According to the 1991 Canadian Study of Health and Aging (CSHA), 8% of Canadians over age 64 suffered from various forms of dementia — including 2.4% of seniors aged 65 to 74, 11% of those aged 75 to 84 and 35% of those over 84. There are more women than men with dementia: in 1991, 68% of those over age 64 with dementia were women. While women's greater longevity may explain some of this difference, it does not account for it all. Age-specific rates also indicated women are more likely than men to be diagnosed with dementia.

Alzheimer's disease is the most prevalent form of dementia, accounting for 64% of all cases in 1991. Vascular dementia accounted for another 19% of cases, and other forms of dementia for the remaining 17%. While women were more likely than men to suffer from Alzheimer's, the opposite was true for vascular dementia. In 1991, among women over age 64 suffering from dementia, 69% were reported to be suffering from Alzheimer's disease and 14% from vascular dementia; among men the same age with dementia, 53% were reported to have Alzheimer's and 30% to have vascular dementia.

Current care practices People suffering from dementia are fairly evenly divided between those in institutions and those living in the community under the care of informal, usually unpaid, caregivers. In 1991, 51% of the 252,600 Canadian seniors with dementia lived in institutions — a relatively costly form of care. Community care is dependent on an informal caregiver. Although daughters and, to a lesser extent, sons may be available to care for parents with dementia, they tend

[1] Ostbye, T., and E. Crosse. "Net economic costs of dementia in Canada," *Canadian Medical Association Journal.* 1994; 151:1457-1464.

Dementia increases with age and is more prevalent among women   CST

Age group	Age-specific rate		
	Living in the community	Living in institutions	Total
	(per 1,000)		
65-74			
Male	10	437	19
Female	20	406	28
Both sexes	16	419	24
75-84			
Male	71	536	104
Female	68	532	116
Both sexes	69	533	111
85 and over			
Male	173	618	287
Female	180	673	371
Both sexes	178	660	345
All			
Male	39	555	69
Female	45	572	86
Both sexes	42	569	80

Source: "Canadian Study of Health and Aging: Study methods and prevalence of dementia" – Reprinted from, by permission of the publisher, *CMAJ*, 1994; 150(6), pp. 906.

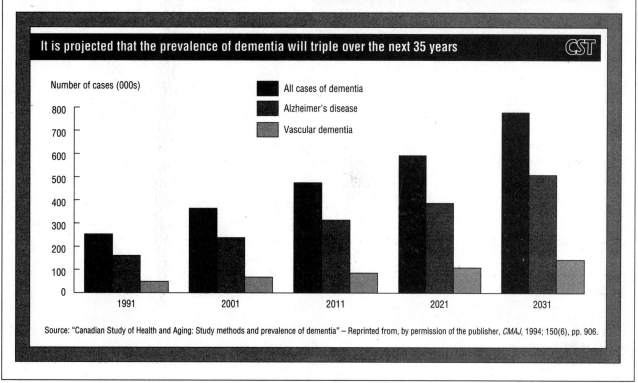

It is projected that the prevalence of dementia will triple over the next 35 years   CST

Source: "Canadian Study of Health and Aging: Study methods and prevalence of dementia" – Reprinted from, by permission of the publisher, *CMAJ*, 1994; 150(6), pp. 906.

Data source and definitions

The Canadian Study of Health and Aging (CSHA) is a joint effort of the Department of Epidemiology and Community Medicine at the University of Ottawa and the federal government's Laboratory Centre for Disease Control. The CSHA working group conducted a study of the elderly in 18 centres across Canada, excluding the Yukon, Northwest Territories, Indian reserves and military bases. The first phase of the study was conducted from February 1991 to May 1992. A representative sample of people aged 65 and over was chosen randomly: 9,008 living in the community and 1,255 in institutions. Participation rates were 72% for residents of the community and 82% for those in institutions.

One of the initial objectives of the study was to determine the prevalence of dementia in these two populations. Respondents in the community were interviewed at home and screened for the likely presence of dementia using a simple psychometric test. Those who failed the test, and all residents of the institutions, were offered a standardized examination which resulted in a clinical classification into one of four categories: cognitively normal, Alzheimer's disease, vascular dementia, or other types of dementia.

Dementia is a clinical syndrome characterized by progressive loss of cognitive function, in particular memory, leading to inability to function physically and socially. The syndrome is associated with many diseases of the brain. In late life the most common are Alzheimer's disease and vascular dementia. Other less common causes of dementia include genetic diseases (e.g. Huntington's disease), infectious (e.g. Creutzfeldt-Jacob disease) and degenerative diseases such as Parkinson's disease.

Alzheimer's disease (AD) — a primary degenerative disease of the brain — is characterized by progressive memory impairment, beginning with loss of short-term memory. The decline in cognitive functioning is progressive. In severe cases there is extreme disability, which frequently requires 24-hour care. Alzheimer's disease does occur before age 65 but the prevalence at younger ages is too low to measure. The prevalence of Alzheimer's disease increases exponentially with age.

Findings from the 1991 CSHA confirmed a number of previously reported risk factors for Alzheimer's: family history of dementia; a history of head injury; age; and low educational status — possibly as an indicator of other socio-economic factors affecting the risk of AD, such as poor diet. A weak link to aluminum exposure was also established, but evidence was not clear, underscoring the need for further research. The CSHA also identified, for the first time, a link between AD and occupational exposure to glues, pesticides and fertilizers. This relationship also requires further study. The use of non-steroidal anti-inflammatory drugs (NSAIDs) was identified as a preventive factor that should be explored in further research.[1]

Vascular dementia is an irreversible, progressive disease usually caused by arteriosclerosis of the cerebral arteries. It progresses by steps, with sudden decrements as more brain tissue is damaged by the underlying diseases, followed by periods of stability.

[1] The Canadian Study of Health and Aging (CSHA) Working Group, 1994. "The Canadian Study of Health and Aging: Risk Factors for Alzheimer's disease in Canada." *Neurology*, November 1994.

to have conflicting roles in terms of caring for their own families. Typically, then, elderly women care for their ailing spouses either until their husband dies or until their own declining health makes it impossible. As wives tend to outlive their husbands, women, more often than men, do not have full-time community caregivers and thus require institutional care. In 1991, for example, 54% of women with dementia were living in institutions, compared with 44% of men. Once institutionalized, women with dementia are also there longer: in 1991, women with dementia could expect to live on average 1.4 years in an institution compared with just 0.6 years for men.[2]

Women have shouldered a disproportionate share of the informal care burden, either caring for their husbands or their ailing parents. The economic and human costs to women as care providers have not been quantified but are potentially enormous.

Mounting pressures for new models of care There are three issues that will necessitate careful planning for new models of care. First, the increase in the number of seniors with dementia will add to the institutional care required — and to the attendant costs. In 1993-94, Canadian seniors accounted for 75% of beds and 64% of spending by residential care facilities in Canada. Costs have continued to increase in these facilities, reaching $94 per resident day in 1993-94, with the cost of direct care (nursing services, therapeutic services and medications, but not meals and administrative expenses) rising to $46 per resident day.[3]

Second, the devolution of health care already necessitates new models of health care. For example, for the past decade, the workload of hospitals has continually shifted from inpatient to outpatient treatment, with outpatient visits increasing by 13% between 1986-87 and 1992-93, and the number of hospital beds dropping steadily by 14% over the same period.[4] As such, ongoing patient care for all but the

[2] Hill, G., W. Forbes, J-M Bethelot, J. Lindsay and I. McDowell. "Dementia among seniors," *Health Reports*, Catalogue no. 82-003-XPB, Autumn 1996.

[3] Statistics Canada, 1996. *Residential Care Facilities*, 1993-94, Catalogue no. 83-237.

[4] Statistics Canada, 1996. *Hospital Annual Statistics*, 1992-93, Catalogue no. 83-242, and *Hospital Indicators*, Catalogue no. 83-246.

acutely ill has been increasingly shifted to informal caregivers. A similar move towards devolution of long-term institutional care may also be likely. The provincial government in Ontario, for example, already plans to shift responsibility for long-term health-care from the province to municipalities.

Third, recent time-use surveys show that women already face a considerable "time crunch" in coping with their current paid and unpaid responsibilities. A drop in the number of women able and willing to provide the intensive informal care required for a growing number of people suffering from dementia will add to the increased demand for high-cost institutional care; at the very same time, pressures to reduce institutionalization may grow.

No matter what scenario unfolds, communities will be challenged to find ways of sharing the heavy burden of caring for those suffering from dementia.

Conclusions Current projections estimate that by 2031, the number of Canadian seniors with dementia — many of whom will be women — will triple. The social and fiscal costs to society of having such a large group of ill people are not yet calculable. New studies suggesting that hormone replacement therapy can delay the onset of dementia and improve memory and concentration for those already affected offer some hope,[5] as do other research efforts currently under way.[6] Strategies that focus on a clear understanding of the risk factors and the development of preventative strategies may improve quality of life and reduce the number of Canadians with dementia. Both the challenge and the solution may lie in moving dementia from a private to a community health issue.

[5] Veterans Affairs Puget Sound Health Care System, Tacoma, Washington. Lead researcher, Dr. Sanjay Asthana.

[6] Canadian Study on Health and Aging Working Group, 1994.

Mary Anne Burke was an analyst with **Canadian Social Trends**, **Gerry Hill** is an analyst with the Social and Economic Studies Division, Statistics Canada; **Ian McDowell** is an analyst with the Department of Epidemiology and Community Medicine, University of Ottawa; and **Joan Lindsay** is an analyst with the Cancer Bureau of the Laboratory Centre for Disease Control.

15 Years of AIDS
in Canada

by Jeffrey Frank

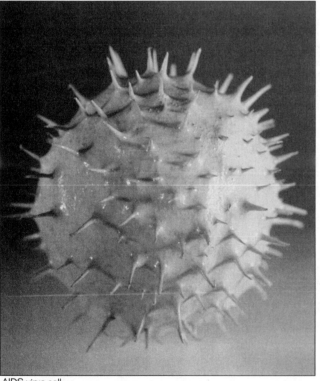

AIDS virus cell

Fifteen years ago, few Canadians had even heard of Human Immunodeficiency Virus (HIV) or Acquired Immunodeficiency Syndrome (AIDS). Indeed, the first documented AIDS case in Canada was not reported until 1982. HIV/AIDS today represent one of the most pressing health and social issues facing society. An estimated 16,000 people had been diagnosed with AIDS in Canada by the end of 1994, and over half of these people had already died from AIDS-related causes. It is further estimated that up to 45,000 people have been infected with HIV, the virus that causes AIDS. There is no vaccine or cure and the full impact of the disease has yet to be realized.

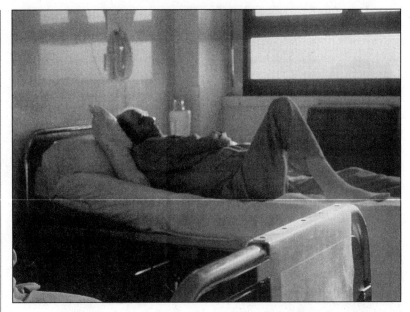

The XI International Conference on AIDS will take place in Vancouver, British Columbia from July 7 to 12, 1996. As many as 15,000 people from all over the world will meet to help find solutions for AIDS. The information shared will contribute to the development of effective prevention techniques and to progress towards finding a cure. With Canada hosting this year's international conference, it seemed an appropriate time to provide our readers with an update on the AIDS situation in Canada.

HIV is a blood-borne virus that is most often transmitted sexually, through needle sharing, or through blood products and transfusions. A person infected with HIV can carry the virus for a long time before developing any AIDS-related illnesses or symptoms. Studies suggest that about one-half of HIV carriers develop AIDS within ten to eleven years of infection. Thus, HIV disease is a preventable, chronic and progressive condition of which AIDS is the final stage. With the onset of AIDS, the body's capacity for combatting disease is diminished. People with AIDS become susceptible to various life-threatening infections and illnesses.

HIV and AIDS exact immense social and economic costs. Like other disabling conditions, HIV/AIDS threaten the independence and social well-being of people infected, as well as their families, friends and caregivers. In addition, a diagnosis of HIV is often accompanied by stigma and discrimination. Economically, the growing number of HIV-infected people will continue to bring increased pressure on Canada's health and social welfare systems. The annual cost to the health-care system of treating people living with AIDS has been estimated at over $200 million. Other costs, including those related to lost productivity, insurance settlements and social services, could be as high as $800,000 per person living with HIV.[1]

The annual number of AIDS diagnoses among adults continues to grow in all regions of the country and among all risk groups, with the exception of blood product recipients. In the overall population, the rates of AIDS cases and deaths due to the disease are still relatively small. For young adult males, however, rates are high, and the disease is among the leading causes of death. Evidence suggests that the incidence of HIV in recent years has occurred among people who tend to be younger than those previously infected, and among people in a variety of risk groups. This has important implications for efforts directed at prevention.

Incidence of AIDS on the rise An estimated 16,000 AIDS cases had been diagnosed in Canada by the end of 1994.[2] One-third of these cases were diagnosed over a period of eleven years. Another third developed over the next three years, and the final third occurred during the last two years. Thus, the frequency of diagnosed AIDS cases has increased.

Canada recorded its first case of AIDS in 1982, but an examination of medical records indicated that the first case had actually been diagnosed in 1979. By the

[1] **National AIDS Strategy, Phase II – Building on Progress**, Health and Welfare Canada, 1993.

[2] Determining the actual incidence of AIDS is complicated by delays in the reporting of confirmed diagnoses, and by the fact that some cases go unreported. Nonetheless, the Laboratory Centre for Disease Control, the agency responsible for monitoring AIDS in Canada, has developed methods of adjusting for reporting delay and under-reporting.

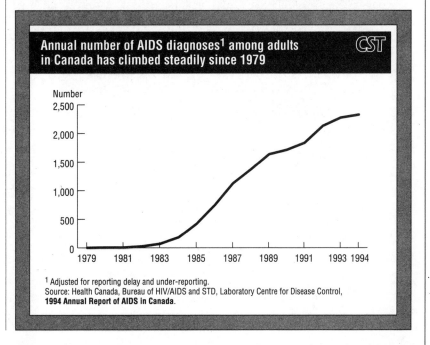

Annual number of AIDS diagnoses[1] among adults in Canada has climbed steadily since 1979

CST

[1] Adjusted for reporting delay and under-reporting.
Source: Health Canada, Bureau of HIV/AIDS and STD, Laboratory Centre for Disease Control, **1994 Annual Report of AIDS in Canada**.

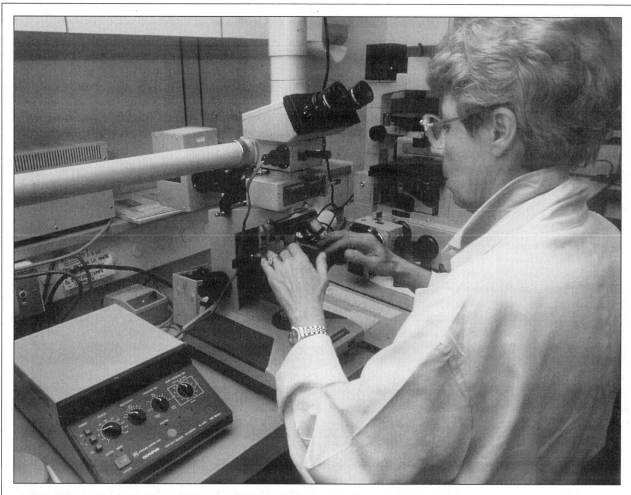

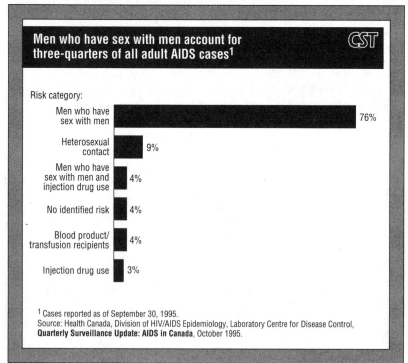

Men who have sex with men account for three-quarters of all adult AIDS cases[1]

Risk category:

Men who have
sex with men — 76%

Heterosexual
contact — 9%

Men who have
sex with men and
injection drug use — 4%

No identified risk — 4%

Blood product/
transfusion recipients — 4%

Injection drug use — 3%

[1] Cases reported as of September 30, 1995.
Source: Health Canada, Division of HIV/AIDS Epidemiology, Laboratory Centre for Disease Control,
Quarterly Surveillance Update: AIDS in Canada, October 1995.

end of 1984, 257 adult cases had been diagnosed. After adjusting for reporting delay, the annual incidence rate of diagnosed AIDS cases increased steadily from 1.8 cases for every 100,000 adults in 1985, to 9 cases per 100,000 in 1994.

In all years, the incidence of AIDS cases was much higher among men than it was among women. In 1994, the incidence rate among men was 18.4 cases per 100,000, compared with 1.2 cases for every 100,000 women. Among children under age 15, the rate was 0.4 cases for every 100,000 children in that age group in 1994, up from 0.2 cases in 1985.

Men who have sex with men still most at risk Risk factors for contracting AIDS include men having sex with men, heterosexual contact with a person at risk or with a person from a country where AIDS is endemic, injection drug use, receiving blood products or transfusions, and perinatal transmission. For men in Canada, having sex with other men is the most significant risk factor. As of the fall of 1995, sex with other men accounted for four out of five AIDS cases (81%) ever diagnosed among adult males. Heterosexual contact with a person at risk is also an important factor, accounting for 38% of AIDS cases among women and 3% of those among men. Heterosexual activity with a person from a country where AIDS is endemic accounted for 26% of cases among women and 3% among men.

Fifteen percent of AIDS cases among women and 3% of those among men were contracted through injection drug use. Blood products or transfusions accounted for 14% of cases among women and 3% among men. Finally, expectant parents with HIV can transmit the virus to their unborn child. In fact, perinatal transmission accounted for about three-quarters (76%) of AIDS cases among children – the remainder having been infected through blood products or transfusions.

Importance of risk factors shifting
The proportion of annual AIDS cases accounted for by exposure to various risk factors has shifted in recent years. Men who have sex with men still comprise the largest risk group, although the proportion of annual AIDS cases attributable to this risk factor has been decreasing since 1987. That year, eight out of ten AIDS cases (79%) involved men who had sex with men. By 1994, this group accounted for just under seven out of ten cases (69%). Similarly, the proportion of AIDS cases involving blood-product recipients was 2% in 1994, down from nearly 6% in 1988. Improvements in blood screening have substantially reduced the likelihood of infection through blood products or transfusions.

Injection drug use is a risk factor of increasing significance. In 1987, injection drug users made up only 1% of AIDS cases; by 1994, this proportion had increased to 6%. Women who contract the disease through heterosexual contact also make up a small but increasing proportion of AIDS cases. Between 1986 and 1990, the proportion of annual AIDS cases accounted for by women was 4.6%. This proportion averaged 5.6% from 1991 to 1994.

Men in their 30s most likely to be diagnosed with AIDS By the end of 1994, men who were aged 30 to 39 at the time

CANADIAN SOCIAL TRENDS BACKGROUNDER

National AIDS Strategy

Launched by Health and Welfare Canada in June 1990, the National AIDS Strategy is Canada's blueprint for preventing the spread of HIV/AIDS. After widespread consultation, the initial phase of the strategy established the following goals: to stop the transmission of the Human Immunodeficiency Virus; to search for effective vaccines, drugs and therapies; and to treat, care for and support people inflicted with HIV/AIDS, their caregivers, families and friends. The National AIDS Strategy established the federal government's framework for action involving research; support to non-governmental organizations; education and prevention; care, treatment and support; and coordination and collaboration.

In March 1993, the federal government outlined the financial details of the second phase of the National AIDS Strategy. In total, $40.7 million annually or $203.5 million over five years was targeted. The annual resource allocation involves $17.8 million for research and epidemiological monitoring; $9.8 million for community development and support to national non-government organizations; $6.2 million for education and prevention initiatives, $5.4 million for care, treatment and support; and $1.5 million for coordination and collaboration.

HIV/AIDS prevention and community action programs Health Canada's HIV/AIDS Prevention and Community Action Programs (PCAP) exist to help stop the transmission of HIV. In consultation and collaboration with various partners, the Prevention Program provides leadership for the development of national prevention policies, strategies and initiatives for groups most vulnerable to HIV/AIDS. The Program addresses a number of areas including: collaborative prevention program strategies; prevention and behavioral research; information synthesis and knowledge development; experimental development programming; intergovernmental initiatives; and support of non-governmental partners, through core funding and project funding. For more information on the Prevention Program, see **National AIDS Strategy, Phase II, Projects Funded by the AIDS Education and Prevention Unit, Status Report as of September 15, 1995**, Health Canada, Population Health Directorate.

The AIDS Community Action Program (ACAP) provides operational and project-specific funding for community-based, non-governmental organizations. The Program is delivered through the national and regional offices of Health Canada. For more information on ACAP, see **AIDS Community Action Program Funding Guidelines**, which are available from the National AIDS Clearinghouse.

General requests for information should be directed to:

The National AIDS Clearinghouse
Canadian Public Health Association
400-1565 Carling Avenue,
Ottawa, Ontario, K1Z 8R1
Telephone (613) 725-3434; Fax (613) 725-9826

of diagnosis[3] accounted for 42% of all reported AIDS cases, and 45% of cases among men. Another 27% of male AIDS cases were among men aged 40 to 49, and 17% were among those aged 20 to 29 at the time of diagnosis. Females accounted for 6% of all reported cases. Among females, 38% involved women aged 30 to 39, 30% were 20 to 29, and 14% were aged 40 to 49 at the time they were diagnosed as having AIDS. Children under age 15 accounted for only 0.01% of all reported cases. These 115 cases were nearly evenly distributed between boys (54%) and girls (46%).

Younger people becoming HIV-positive

The Laboratory Centre for Disease Control (LCDC) estimates HIV incidence using AIDS surveillance data, taking into account the delay between HIV infection and the onset of AIDS. Although the number of HIV infections has increased annually, LCDC calculations indicate that the incidence of HIV infection probably peaked in the early 1980s, mainly among men who had sex with men.

There also appears to have been a recent acceleration of HIV infections that started in 1990. What is different about this new resurgence in HIV infections is that it seems to have occurred not only among men who had sex with men, but also among injection drug users, heterosexuals, as well as some people with no identified risk. The annual incidence of HIV infection is growing more rapidly among these other risk groups and has yet to peak.

Prior to 1982, the estimated median age of people infected with HIV was 32 years. This declined to 27 years of age during the peak years of the early epidemic (1983 and 1984). During the period 1985 to 1990, however, the median age at HIV infection was 23 years. Thus, those who become HIV-infected today can be in any of several risk categories and tend to be considerably younger than those who were infected previously. This has obvious but important implications for the targeting of information and education programs, and for AIDS prevention measures generally.

Number of AIDS-related deaths approaching 10,000 By the end of 1995, 9,133 AIDS-related deaths had been

[3] A diagnosis of AIDS can follow many years after HIV infection. Therefore, these people were much younger when they became infected with HIV.

CANADIAN SOCIAL TRENDS BACKGROUNDER

International context of HIV/AIDS

Allowing for under-diagnosis, incomplete reporting and reporting delay, and based on available data on HIV infections around the world, it is estimated that over 4.5 million AIDS cases have occurred worldwide since the late 1970s.[1] The vast majority of these cases occurred in Africa, South Asia and the Americas. As of late 1994, an estimated 18 million adults and 1.5 million children, had been infected with HIV since the beginning of the pandemic. Countries in southern and central Africa, and South Asia accounted for over three-quarters of these infections.

In the United States, AIDS is a much more common disease than it is in Canada. In 1994, there were 1,542 AIDS cases for every million people, compared with 380 cases per million in Canada. Moreover, the distribution of cases by risk factor is different in the United States, with a much larger proportion of cases in that country contracted through injection drug use. Rates in some other developed countries included 578 cases per million people in France; 426 cases per million in Italy; 302 cases in Australia; 173 in the United Kingdom; and 7 cases for every million people in Japan.

[1] **Weekly Epidemiological Record**, 13 January 1995, vol. 70, no. 2, World Health Organization.

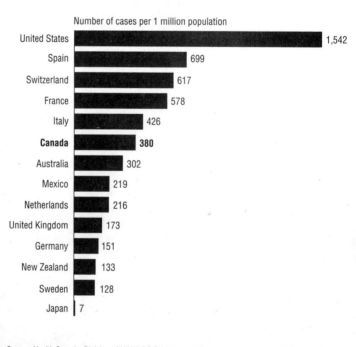

Rates of AIDS cases for selected countries, 1994

Source: Health Canada, Division of HIV/AIDS Epidemiology, Laboratory Centre for Disease Control, **Quarterly Surveillance Update: AIDS in Canada**, January 1995.

Estimated distribution of total adult HIV infections from late 1970s/early 1980s until late 1994

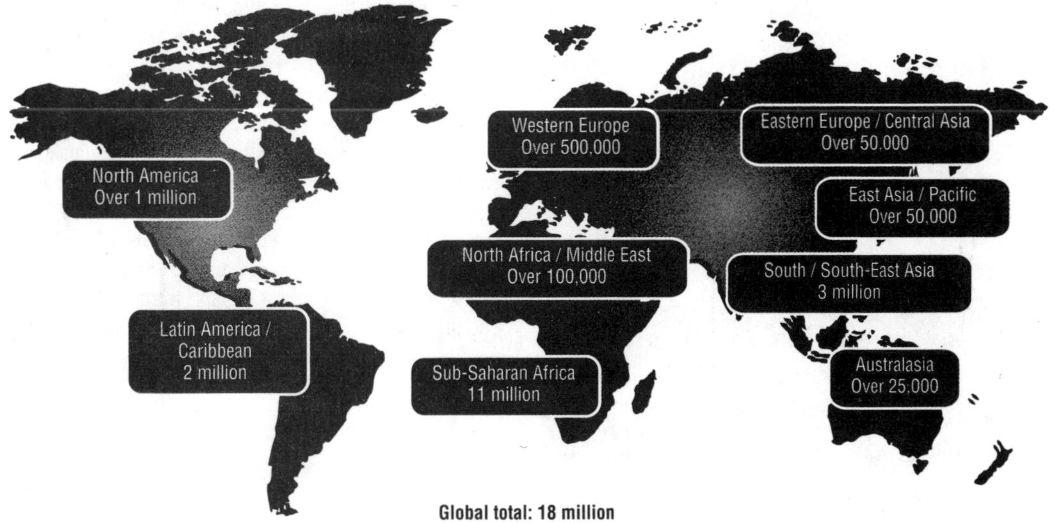

North America
Over 1 million

Western Europe
Over 500,000

Eastern Europe / Central Asia
Over 50,000

East Asia / Pacific
Over 50,000

North Africa / Middle East
Over 100,000

South / South-East Asia
3 million

Latin America /
Caribbean
2 million

Sub-Saharan Africa
11 million

Australasia
Over 25,000

Global total: 18 million

Estimated distribution of HIV-infected adults alive as of late 1994

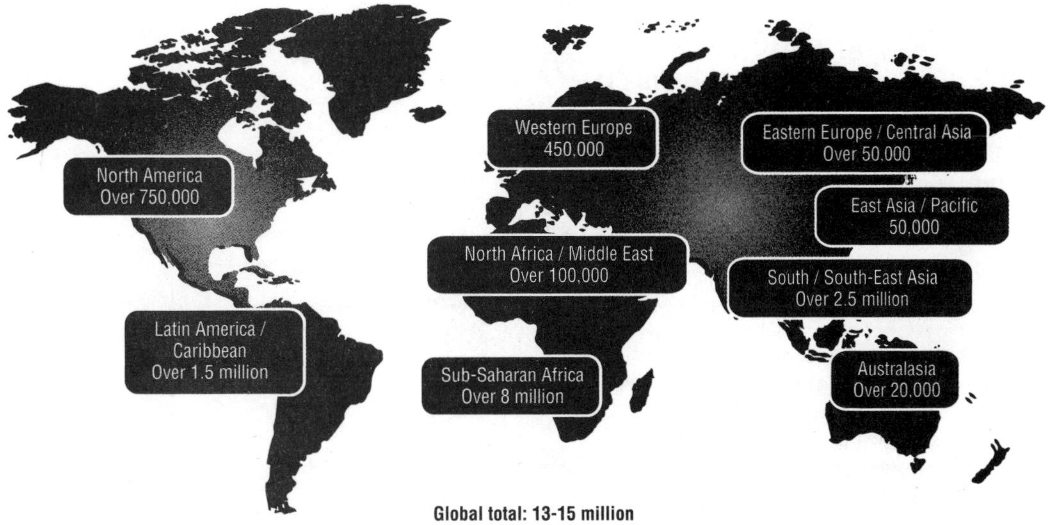

North America
Over 750,000

Western Europe
450,000

Eastern Europe / Central Asia
Over 50,000

East Asia / Pacific
50,000

North Africa / Middle East
Over 100,000

South / South-East Asia
Over 2.5 million

Latin America /
Caribbean
Over 1.5 million

Sub-Saharan Africa
Over 8 million

Australasia
Over 20,000

Global total: 13-15 million

Source: World Health Organization, **Weekly Epidemiological Record**, vol.70, no.2, 13 January 1995.

reported. The annual number of deaths due to diseases brought on by AIDS increased in each successive year since the early 1980s until 1993. For that year, 1,293 deaths due to AIDS had been reported by the end of 1995. The numbers for 1994 and 1995 were 1,248 and 901, respectively.

Delays in the reporting of AIDS-related deaths, however, mask what is likely a continuing increase. For example, 126 deaths that occurred in 1994, and 36 deaths that occurred in 1993 were reported only during the second half of 1995. Thus, the numbers for recent years will continue to be adjusted upwards as reports of more deaths due to AIDS are received.

The pattern of AIDS-related deaths closely follows the age-sex profile of AIDS cases, with men in their 30s and 40s, and to a lesser extent those in their 20s, being the most likely to succumb as a result of the disease. In fact, for men aged 20 to 44 in 1993, HIV/AIDS was the third leading cause of death, representing 18 deaths for every 100,000 men that age. Only suicide (28 deaths per 100,000) and motor vehicle crashes (21 per 100,000) caused more deaths among men in this age group. The AIDS death rate

for men this age was slightly higher than the rate of deaths caused by cancer (17.5 per 100,000). In 1993, AIDS caused 1,077 deaths among men aged 20 to 44, compared with only 68 among women that age (1 death per 100,000).

Rates highest in British Columbia, Ontario and Quebec Of all adult AIDS cases reported by the end of 1994, 42% were in Ontario, 29% in Quebec and 18% were in British Columbia. At 75 cases for every 100,000 adults, however, the incidence rate was highest in British Columbia. This was followed by Ontario with 73 cases per 100,000, and Quebec with 69 cases for every 100,000 adults.

Nearly one-half (49%) of all AIDS cases among women in Canada were in Quebec. The higher rate for Quebec women is partly a result of immigration patterns. Immigrants in Quebec are more likely to come from countries where AIDS is as common among females as it is among males. Haiti, for example, is one of these countries and accounted for nearly one in ten immigrants who arrived in Quebec between 1981 and 1991. In that province, heterosexual activity with a person from a country where AIDS is endemic was identified as the risk factor in 11% of all cases, compared with less than 1% in the rest of Canada.

Jeffrey Frank is an Editor with **Canadian Social Trends**.

CANADIAN SOCIAL TRENDS BACKGROUNDER CST

Laboratory Centre for Disease Control

Data used in this article were produced by the Laboratory Centre for Disease Control, Health Canada. The Centre collects data on AIDS cases and deaths on a quarterly basis. For more information, see **1994 Annual Report of AIDS in Canada**, Health Canada, Bureau of HIV/AIDS and STD, Laboratory Centre for Disease Control. Also available is the **Quarterly Surveillance Update: AIDS in Canada**. Copies of these and other publications are available in either official language, free of charge:

By Mail:
Health Canada, Division of HIV/AIDS Surveillance, Bureau of HIV/AIDS and STD, Laboratory Centre for Disease Control, Ottawa, Ontario Canada, K1A 0L2, Postal locator: 0202A.

By Internet:
The **Quarterly Surveillance Update: AIDS in Canada** can be accessed electronically using a Web browser at http://hpb1.hwc.ca:8300 or via Gopher at hpb1.hwc.ca port 7300 (select Laboratory Centre for Disease Control, HIV/AIDS, HIV/AIDS statistics).

By Fax:
Documents can also be accessed via FAXLINK. Dial (613) 941-3900 using the handset on your fax machine and, when asked, indicate number 111.

UNIT 2

WOMEN, MARRIAGE
AND THE FAMILY

Attitudes Toward Women, Work and Family

by Nancy Zukewich Ghalam

Men and women in Canada have long performed very different kinds of work. For much of the 20th century, men earned an income working in the labour force, while women were responsible for the unpaid work of caring for home and family. The mass entry of women into the labour market over the past few decades, however, has challenged this conventional division of labour according to sex and has led to changing work and family roles for both men and women. Today, nearly half the Canadian workforce is made up of women and the majority of husband-wife families are supported by the employment earnings of both spouses.

Using data from the 1995 General Social Survey (GSS), this article asks: Are people's ideas still shaped by the traditional division of labour by sex or does their thinking reflect the new reality of women in the workforce? Attitudes are important for many reasons. For instance, they collectively shape public opinion and public policy. Attitudes also influence the behaviour of people and the choices available to them as employers, workers, family members and, more generally, participants in Canadian society.

Women's roles have changed dramatically Although men's roles have evolved in the past few decades, the changes for women have been much more dramatic. Men may be more involved with domestic work and child raising today than they were in the past, but being both a husband/father and a wage earner are still viewed as compatible roles. In the not so distant past, however, being both a wife/mother and a wage earner were not considered compatible by most people. As recently as 1982, only four out of ten Canadians agreed that women should participate in the labour force when they have young children, while nine out of ten agreed if the women had no young children.[1] In the past, a woman was expected to leave the formal workforce when she married to fulfil her role as

[1] Boyd, Monica, *Canadian Attitudes Towards Women: Thirty Years of Change*, Ottawa: Supply and Services Canada, 1984, p.12.

Measuring attitudes

In the 1995 General Social Survey, the following questions were asked of a representative sample of the Canadian population.

(1) In order for you to be happy in life, is it very important, important, not very important or not at all important to be able to take a paying job either outside or inside the home?

(2) Can you tell me if you strongly agree, agree, disagree or strongly disagree with each of the following statements?

❑ An employed mother can establish just as warm and secure a relationship with her children as a mother who does not work for pay.

❑ Having a job is the best way for a woman to be an independent person.

❑ Both the man and the woman should contribute to the household income.

❑ A pre-school child is likely to suffer if both parents are employed.

❑ A job is all right, but what most women really want is a home and children.

Measuring attitudes accurately can be a tricky process. Careful thought goes into planning survey questionnaires, especially regarding the language and wording of the questions. The meaning of words and questions can vary, for example, across regions and from one age or socio-economic group to another. Also, the way a question is worded can lead a respondent to agree with the question as it is presented, instead of responding objectively. As well, questions may have a social desirability or politeness bias. For instance, respondents may choose answers that correspond with societal norms, or they may respond the way they think the interviewers expect them to, out of a desire to be polite and co-operative.

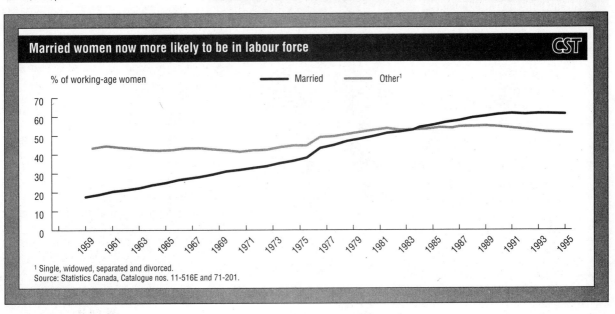

Married women now more likely to be in labour force

% of working-age women — Married — Other[1]

[1] Single, widowed, separated and divorced.
Source: Statistics Canada, Catalogue nos. 11-516E and 71-201.

wife, mother and care giver — duties which centred on unpaid work in the domestic sphere. For instance, in 1960, less than 20% of married women were labour force participants, compared with 45% of women who were single, divorced, separated or widowed. Since 1984, however, married women have been more likely than their unmarried counterparts to be in the labour force.

Some changes in attitudes seen...
Today, we live in a society in which half of employed people are women and dual-earner families are the norm. In many respects, the attitudes of Canadians reflect this reality. According to the 1995 General Social Survey, 86% of men and 64% of women responded that it is important or very important to their personal happiness to be able to take a paying job. In fact, research has suggested that "[w]ork in the formal economy is an important source of feelings of usefulness and worth for many women."[2]

Analysis of Gallup poll data from the 1950s to the 1980s indicates that younger people and those with higher levels of education were most likely to hold views supportive of less traditional roles for women. This was also true of people's attitudes in 1995. For example, among those aged 15 to 24, the vast majority of both men (91%) and women (83%) stated that being able to work for pay is important or very important to their personal happiness. Among those aged 65 and over, this view was held by 75% of men and only 37% of women.

The attitudes of women appear to be more closely related to age than to educational attainment. According to the 1995 GSS, young women were more likely than their older counterparts to respond that being able to work for pay is important or very important to personal happiness, regardless of their educational background. For example, among women who had attended university, 80% of those aged 15 to 24 held this view, compared with 35% of women aged 65 and over. On the other hand, men's views on this subject tended to be similar at all ages and levels of educational attainment.

Independence important to women
Overall, women were somewhat more likely than men to express attitudes that support women's participation in the labour force and acknowledge the expansion of women's roles beyond the domestic sphere. For example, 73% of women, compared with 68% of men, agreed or strongly agreed that both spouses should contribute to household income. The support for shared responsibility for family income, especially among women, may stem from the fact that working for pay also provides a certain

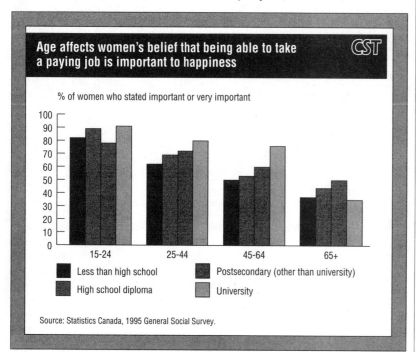

Age affects women's belief that being able to take a paying job is important to happiness

% of women who stated important or very important

Less than high school
High school diploma
Postsecondary (other than university)
University

Source: Statistics Canada, 1995 General Social Survey.

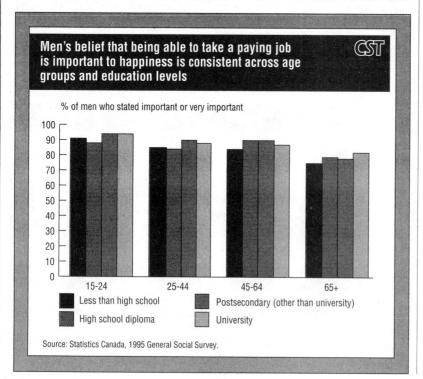

Men's belief that being able to take a paying job is important to happiness is consistent across age groups and education levels

% of men who stated important or very important

Less than high school
High school diploma
Postsecondary (other than university)
University

Source: Statistics Canada, 1995 General Social Survey.

[2] Armstrong, Pat and Hugh Armstrong, *The Double Ghetto: Canadian Women and Their Segregated Work*, Third Edition, Toronto: McClelland and Stewart, 1994, p.211.

degree of economic security and independence. Employment earnings are the main source of personal income for the vast majority of people in Canada. Therefore, the inability to earn an income has a significant bearing on the risk of living in a low-income situation. In fact, many husband-wife families rely on the earnings of both spouses to stay above the low income cut-offs.[3]

Surprisingly, contrary to the general trend, men and women with higher levels of schooling were somewhat *less likely* to agree or strongly agree that both the man and woman should contribute to household income. The decline was most noticeable among men: agreement levels ranged from 73% of men with less than a high school diploma to 65% of men with a university degree.

Working for pay the best way for a woman to be independent On the issue of independence, women and men were equally likely to agree that having a job is the best way for a woman to be an independent person (45% and 44%, respectively), but women were twice as likely as men (10% versus 5%) to strongly agree with this statement. Furthermore, about 50% of men at all levels of educational attainment agreed or strongly agreed that a job is the best way for a woman to be an independent person. Among women, levels of agreement varied slightly, from 53% of women with a high school diploma to 59% of women who had attended university.

...yet traditional views persist The persistence of traditional views in a modern society has resulted in conflicting attitudes. People see value in women being in the workforce but feel that the family, especially young children, may suffer as a result. For example, 59% of men and 67% of women agreed or strongly agreed that an employed mother can establish just as warm and secure a relationship with her children as a mother who does not work for pay. At the same time, over half of those surveyed (59% of men and 51% of women) agreed or strongly agreed that a pre-school child is likely to suffer if both parents are employed. The latter question, however, referred specifically to children of pre-school age, whereas the former referred to children of all ages. This suggests that respondents may believe that younger children have a greater need for maternal attention than older children.

Overall, people's attitudes tended to correspond with their own work and family arrangements. For example, 78% of women who were employed or looking for a job in 1995[4] agreed or strongly agreed that an employed mother can establish just as warm and secure a relationship with her children as a mother

---

Attitudes of people aged 15 and over, by sex, 1995   CST

	Very important	Important	Not important	Not at all important	Don't know[1]	Total[2]
Importance of being able to take a paying job						
			%			
Men	37	49	9	1	3	100
Women	18	46	26	4	4	100
Total	27	48	18	3	4	100

	Strongly agree	Agree	Disagree	Strongly disagree	Don't know[1]	Total[2]
Employed mother can have warm relationship with children						
			%			
Men	8	51	27	3	10	100
Women	14	53	20	2	9	100
Total	11	52	24	3	10	100
Having a job is best way for a woman to be independent						
			%			
Men	5	44	35	3	12	100
Women	10	45	33	3	8	100
Total	7	45	34	3	10	100
Man and woman should contribute to household income						
			%			
Men	12	56	19	0	11	100
Women	15	58	15	1	9	100
Total	13	57	17	1	10	100
Pre-school child will suffer if both parents are employed						
			%			
Men	11	48	28	2	9	100
Women	11	40	34	3	10	100
Total	11	44	31	3	9	100
A job is all right, but what most women really want is a home and children						
			%			
Men	4	42	32	2	18	100
Women	6	40	37	4	11	100
Total	5	41	35	3	15	100

1 Includes "No opinion"
2 Includes "Not stated". Also, rows may not add to 100% because of rounding.
Source: Statistics Canada, 1995 General Social Survey.

---

3 See Statistics Canada, *Characteristics of Dual-Earner Families in 1994*, Catalogue no. 13-215-XPB.

4 Main activity during the 12 months prior to the survey.

who does not work for pay. In contrast, 64% of women whose main activity was keeping house agreed or strongly agreed that a preschool child is likely to suffer if both parents are employed.

Women remain primary care givers

Despite high levels of female labour force participation, many Canadians believe that home and children take precedence over working for pay in women's lives. In 1995, 46% of both men and women agreed or strongly agreed that "while a job is all right, what most women really want is a home and family." However, a considerable share of people (34% of men and 41% of women) disagreed or strongly disagreed with this statement, while the remainder (18% of men and 11% of women) responded that they did not know or had no opinion.

These data suggest that the expectation remains for women, even when employed, to maintain primary responsibility for home and family. In 1992, men and women aged 25 to 44 who worked full-time and had children under age 19 each spent, on average, about ten hours per day on total paid and unpaid work activities. However, these women devoted 1.6 hours more per day to unpaid work than their male counterparts.[5]

Conclusion Attitudes are dynamic and constantly changing. Our ideas and experiences shape the world around us and, in turn, the world shapes our ideas and experiences. As this analysis has shown, attitudes can vary by sex, age and level of education. However, characteristics such as age and education may be interrelated (i.e., people aged 25 to 44 are more likely than people over age 65 to have attended university). Thus, it is difficult to determine from this preliminary analysis which factors have the greatest impact on people's views.

Do Canadians still hold traditional ideas about appropriate roles for women and men? The findings of this analysis confirm previous research that suggests "traditional sex roles for women and men fade slowly."[6] It is perhaps not surprising that people's attitudes toward women, work and family are somewhat contradictory and characterized by both traditional and contemporary views of the division of labour by sex.

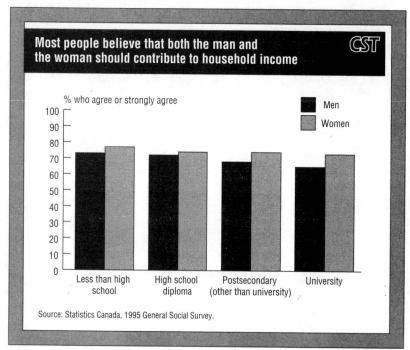

Most people believe that both the man and the woman should contribute to household income

% who agree or strongly agree

Legend: Men, Women

Categories: Less than high school, High school diploma, Postsecondary (other than university), University

Source: Statistics Canada, 1995 General Social Survey.

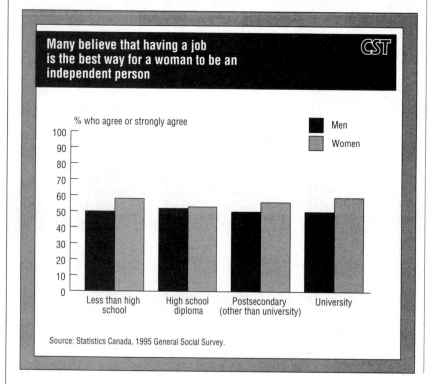

Many believe that having a job is the best way for a woman to be an independent person

% who agree or strongly agree

Legend: Men, Women

Categories: Less than high school, High school diploma, Postsecondary (other than university), University

Source: Statistics Canada, 1995 General Social Survey.

[5] Frederick, Judith A., *As Time Goes By... Time Use of Canadians*, Statistics Canada, Catalogue no. 89-544E.

[6] Boyd (1984), p.23.

Nancy Zukewich Ghalam is an analyst with Housing, Family and Social Statistics Division, Statistics Canada.

CST

education of women in canada

by Josée Normand

*In the last half of the twentieth century,
higher education has become a prerequisite for a
growing share of occupations, and a requirement of most jobs paying
above average wages. Moreover, the department of Human Resources Development estimated that just under
one-half of jobs created during the 1990s will require more than sixteen years of education or training. Thus,
for both women and men, the attainment of a postsecondary education has become increasingly important.*

Men's enrolment in universities and colleges grew rapidly immediately following the Second World War. Among women, on the other hand, most of the increase in enrolment in higher education occurred during the past twenty-five years. Also over this time, women's labour force participation rose sharply, and women increasingly entered higher-paying occupations.

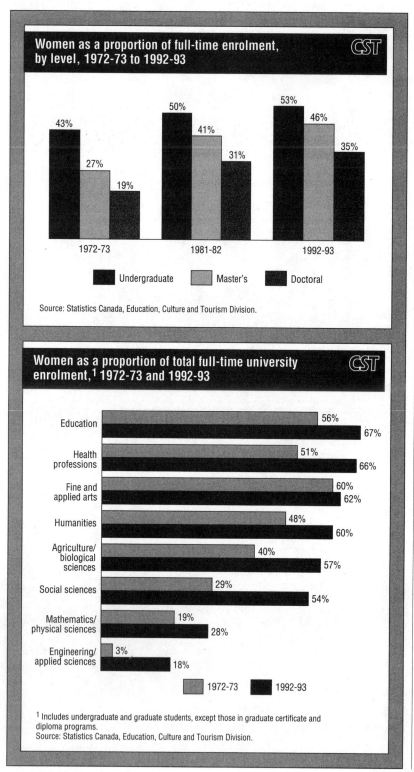

Women as a proportion of full-time enrolment, by level, 1972-73 to 1992-93

CST

- 1972-73: Undergraduate 43%, Master's 27%, Doctoral 19%
- 1981-82: Undergraduate 50%, Master's 41%, Doctoral 31%
- 1992-93: Undergraduate 53%, Master's 46%, Doctoral 35%

■ Undergraduate ■ Master's ■ Doctoral

Source: Statistics Canada, Education, Culture and Tourism Division.

Women as a proportion of total full-time university enrolment,[1] 1972-73 and 1992-93

CST

	1972-73	1992-93
Education	56%	67%
Health professions	51%	66%
Fine and applied arts	60%	62%
Humanities	48%	60%
Agriculture/biological sciences	40%	57%
Social sciences	29%	54%
Mathematics/physical sciences	19%	28%
Engineering/applied sciences	3%	18%

■ 1972-73 ■ 1992-93

[1] Includes undergraduate and graduate students, except those in graduate certificate and diploma programs.
Source: Statistics Canada, Education, Culture and Tourism Division.

Despite improvements in educational attainment, however, women are still concentrated in female-dominated fields of study at both the university and community college level. At the same time, they continue to be underrepresented in many of the engineering, mathematics and applied science programs. In addition, although women now account for the majority of students at the undergraduate level, they remain the minority at the graduate level.

Proportion of women with a university education increasing rapidly
Over the past two decades, the proportion of women with a university degree increased faster than the proportion of men with this level of education. By 1991, 10% of women aged 15 and over had a university degree, up from only 3% in 1971. Over the same period, the proportion of men with a university degree increased to 13% from 7%. Nonetheless, the proportion of women with this level of education remained lower than that of men.

Both women and men were almost twice as likely in 1991 as in the early 1970s to have other postsecondary education, such as a diploma or some university or college courses. The proportion of women with this level of education rose to 32% in 1991 from 18% in 1971. Similarly, the proportion among men rose to 31% from 17%.

Given these increases in educational attainment, it is not surprising that relatively few women and men have less than a Grade 9 education. In 1991, 14% of both women and men had this level of education, less than half the proportions in 1971 (31% of women and 33% of men).

Young women more likely to be highly educated than young men In 1991, 10% of women aged 20 to 24 had a university degree, compared with 8% of men that age. Young women were also more likely (21%) than young men (14%) to have a postsecondary certificate or diploma.

Women aged 25 to 44, on the other hand, were less likely than men that age to have a university degree (16% compared with 18%), but were more likely to have a postsecondary certificate or diploma (22% compared with 17%). Both senior women and men tended to have less formal education than did younger people. Among seniors, 3% of women and 8% of men were university graduates, and 9% of women and 6% of men had a postsecondary certificate or diploma.

Women majority at undergraduate level, but not in graduate schools The difference in the proportions of all women and men with a university degree will likely close even further in the future, because women's share of university enrolment is higher now than it was during the 1970s. At the undergraduate level, women accounted for 53% of full-time enrolment in 1992-93, up from 43% in 1972-73. The proportion of women at the graduate level increased even more rapidly over the two decades. In 1992-93, 46% of full-time Master's students and 35% of full-time doctoral students were women, up from 27% and 19%, respectively, in 1972-73. As a result of these increases, most full-time university students were women in 1992-93 (52%).

Few women enrolled in mathematics or engineering At the undergraduate level, women accounted for the majority of full-time enrolment in 1992-93 in six out of eight major fields of study: health professions (68%), education (67%), fine and applied arts (62%), humanities (61%), agriculture and biological sciences (59%) and social sciences (54%). Women remain underrepresented, however, in mathematics and the physical sciences (30%), and in engineering and applied sciences (19%).

At the Master's level, women accounted for the majority of full-time enrolment in four major fields of study: education (66%), health (62%), fine and applied arts (59%), and humanities (56%). At the doctoral level, however, education was the only major program in which women accounted for the majority of full-time students (60%).

Similar to the situation at the undergraduate level, relatively few women were enrolled in graduate studies in mathematics or engineering. Of all full-time students at the Master's level, women accounted for 27% of those in mathematics and the physical sciences, and 18% of those in engineering and applied sciences, proportions similar to those at the undergraduate level. At the doctoral level, however, the proportions

were lower: 19% in mathematics and the physical sciences, and only 11% in engineering and applied sciences.

At the undergraduate level, part-time studies more common among women Almost 200,000 women were attending university part-time in 1992-93. Part-time enrolment accounted for 40% of total enrolment of women, compared with about 30% of that of men.

At the undergraduate level, the number of women studying part-time in 1992-93 (175,800) was much higher than that of men (102,400). As a result, women accounted for 63% of part-time undergraduate students. At the graduate level, however, the number of women enrolled part-time (22,100) was only slightly above that of men (20,600), and women accounted for just over one-half (52%) of part-time graduate students.

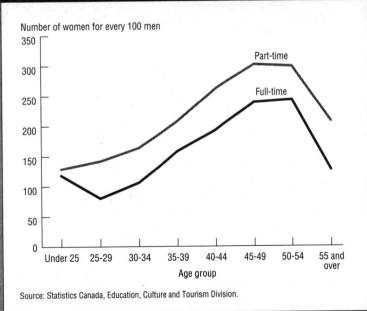

Women as a proportion of full-time enrolment, by level, 1992-93 CST

Field of study	Undergraduate	Master's	Doctoral
		%	
Health professions	68	62	43
Education	67	66	60
Fine and applied arts	62	59	46
Humanities	61	56	46
Agriculture/biological sciences	59	50	33
Social sciences	54	47	45
Mathematics/physical sciences	30	27	19
Engineering/applied sciences	19	18	11

Source: Statistics Canada, Education, Culture and Tourism Division.

Ratio of female to male undergraduates, 1992-93 CST

Number of women for every 100 men

Part-time

Full-time

Age group: Under 25, 25-29, 30-34, 35-39, 40-44, 45-49, 50-54, 55 and over

Source: Statistics Canada, Education, Culture and Tourism Division.

When education was less valued, men left school earlier than did women

In the early part of this century, the proportion of women aged 15 to 19 who were attending school exceeded that of men.[1] This was perhaps because, at that time, there were fewer employment opportunities for young women than for young men. By 1951, however, the situation had reversed and proportionately more young men aged 15 to 19 were attending school. In the following decade, young men remained more likely to be in school, although school attendance became much more common among both women and men. During that period, the educational requirements of many occupations were rising and enrolment of young men in university programs began to grow. At the same time, increased urbanization resulted in greater employment opportunities for young women. This was perhaps why school attendance did not increase as much among young women as it did among young men.

Since the 1960s, the proportion of women and men aged 15 to 19 who were attending school has continued to rise. It was not until 1981, however, that the proportion of women attending school equalled that of men.

In contrast, from 1921 to 1981, men aged 20 to 24 were proportionately more likely than women that age to be attending school. By 1981, however, the gap between the proportions for men and women narrowed considerably. In 1991, the proportion of women aged 20 to 24 attending school full-time[2] equalled that of men.

[1] Discussion of trends from 1921 to 1961 is from Statistics Canada, 1961 Census of Canada, Vol. 7, Part 1, General Summary and Review, p. 10-5. Data exclude Newfoundland, and the Yukon and Northwest Territories.

[2] From 1971 to 1991, full-time attendance was used to best approximate the concepts used in earlier years.

Proportion of young men and women attending school, 1921-1991[1]

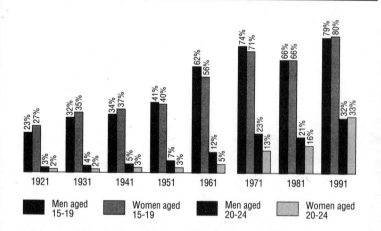

| | Men aged 15-19 | Women aged 15-19 | Men aged 20-24 | Women aged 20-24 |

[1] From 1971 to 1991, full-time attendance was used to best approximate the concepts used in earlier years. Data from 1921 to 1961 exclude Newfoundland, and the Yukon and Northwest Territories.
Source: Statistics Canada, 1961 Census of Canada, Vol.7, Part 1 and Catalogues 92-742, 92-743, 92-914 and 93-328.

Part-time university attendance was most common among women aged 25 and over. In 1992-93, only 7% of female undergraduates under age 20 and 19% of those aged 20 to 24 were enrolled part-time. In contrast, 60% of female undergraduates aged 25 to 29 and 87% of those aged 40 to 44 were part-time students. The proportion of male undergraduates who were enrolled part-time also rose at a similar rate with increased age.

More women undergraduates in most age groups Since students under age 25 studying full-time made up about one-half (54%) of all undergraduates in 1991, it was the growing number of women under age 25 that was mainly responsible for the female majority on campus. Nonetheless, among students in undergraduate programs, women outnumbered men in most age groups.

Of full-time students under age 25 in 1991, there were 119 women for every 100 men. This ratio declined to a low of 81 women for every 100 men among those aged 25 to 29. In each subsequent age group, the ratio increased, reaching 244 women for every 100 men among those aged 50 to 54. At ages 55 and over, however, the ratio fell to 128 women for every 100 men.

Women accounted for an even larger proportion of all part-time undergraduate students. Among those under age 25, there were 129 women for every 100 men. The ratio of women to men widened consistently with each age group. By age 45 to 54, there were about 300 women for every 100 men in part-time undergraduate programs. The ratio of women to men was lower among part-time students aged 55 and over, but women still outnumbered men (208 women for every 100 men).

Many women over age 25 may be pursuing a university education, either part-time or full-time, because they did not have the opportunity to do so when they were younger. Some may have been divorced or widowed, and are increasing their educational attainment to improve their job opportunities. Others, perhaps in the empty-nest family stage, have more time for studies in their older years than they did when they were younger. By age 55, however, many men are retiring and also have increased time available to pursue their education. This perhaps explains why the ratio of women to men is closer among people in this age group, even though in the population that age women outnumber men.

Women account for over half of full-time community college enrolment In 1991-92, 53% of all full-time community college students were women, a figure virtually unchanged since the mid-1970s. As in universities, women accounted for the majority of students enrolled full-time in most fields of study, with the exception of applied science and technology programs. For example, almost all students enrolled full-time in secretarial sciences were women (96%), as were those in educational and counselling services (90%) and nursing (89%). In contrast, women accounted for only 32% of those in natural science and primary industry programs, 30% of those in mathematics and computer science, and only 12% of those in both engineering and other technologies.

Many employed women upgrading their job qualifications In 1991, 25% of employed women were taking non-academic courses to improve their employment skills, while 8% were taking academic courses with the same objective. Some of these women were upgrading their qualifications by taking both types of job-related training. The proportions of employed men taking non-academic (24%) and academic (7%) courses designed to improve their skills were similar to those of women.

Few women in trade apprenticeship programs Women accounted for only about 1% of people enrolled in the fifteen largest trade apprenticeship programs in 1992, the same proportion as in 1988. The number of women participating in such programs, however, doubled to 1,580 from 760 over the same period.[1] The largest proportions of women apprentices were in machinist, and painting and decorating programs in 1992 (about 4% of each). Women made up between 1% and 2% of apprentices in carpenter, construction

electrician, and motor vehicle body repair and mechanic programs, and less than 1% of those in bricklayer, industrial electrician, heavy-duty equipment mechanic, millwright, plumber, refrigeration, sheet metal, pipe fitter and welder programs. These major trades, each with at least 3,000 registrants in 1992, accounted for 73% of all apprentices in the 170 recognized programs.

Only two trades with over 3,000 registered apprentices in 1992 were not almost completely dominated by men: hairdresser (hairstylist) and cook. Between 1988 and 1992, about 86% of apprenticing hairdressers (hairstylists) and 26% of apprenticing cooks were women.

Most Canadians do not have a postsecondary education Despite rapid increases in higher education, almost 60% of both women and men in 1991 did not have any formal education beyond high school. Even among people aged 25 to 44, this was the case for about 40% of women and men. With nearly half of new jobs requiring at least sixteen years of education, people with lower levels of educational attainment will likely become increasingly disadvantaged in the job market.

In addition, with the progression of the information age, many jobs created in the future will require advanced technical and science-related skills. Women may have difficulty obtaining this type of employment because they lack the necessary qualifications. Even in recent years, women have accounted for a very small proportion of students enrolled in engineering, mathematics, computer science and other applied science programs. Similarly, partly as a result of historically low enrolment in such programs, women account for only about one in five professionals employed in natural science, engineering and mathematics-related occupations.

[1] Karl Skof, "Women in Registered Apprenticeship Training Programs," **Education Quarterly Review**, Statistics Canada Catalogue 81-003: Vol. 1, No. 4.

• For additional information, see **Women in Canada: A Statistical Report**, Third Edition, Statistics Canada Catalogue 89-503E.

Josée Normand is an analyst with the Target Groups Project, Housing, Family and Social Statistics Division, Statistics Canada.

Changes in women's work continuity

BY JANET FAST AND MORENO DA PONT

Long-term employment inter-ruptions play a significant role in shaping the career paths of individuals who experience them. Employment discontinuity has been shown to affect future employability, advancement opportunities, earnings, and the attitudes of employers and co-workers. Since work and income are considered important to our sense of identity, employment discontinuity can affect our psychological and emotional well-being as well.

Because women are more likely to interrupt their employment for a long period of time, their attachment to the labour force has traditionally been viewed as weaker than men's. But over the last 30 years, women's participation in the paid workforce has increased dramatically. By 1995, the vast majority (91%) of women aged 20 and over had worked for pay at some time during their lives. Contemporary women have also shown increased commitment to life-long careers, reporting fewer and shorter periods of employment discontinuity than earlier generations of women. However, women continue to experience more career discontinuity than men, and they experience longer interruptions than men. This article describes how women's employment continuity has changed.

Work interruptions occur early in women's careers Almost two-thirds (62%) of all women who had ever worked experienced an interruption in paid work of six months or more. In contrast, just over one-quarter of men (27%) experienced work discontinuity. Regardless of the historical era in which an interruption in paid work occurred, most occurred when women were in their early 20s. Between 1990 and 1994, 43% of women in their early 20s who had ever worked experienced their first interruption. In contrast, 9% of those aged 35 to 44 experienced their first interruption. Interruptions were even less common among those aged 45 and over. The high rate of interruptions in paid work among younger women may be related to their limited work experience and also to higher fertility rates compared with older women.

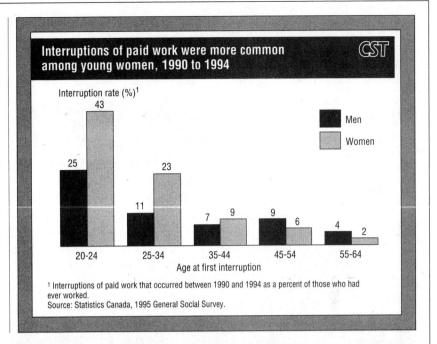

Interruptions of paid work were more common among young women, 1990 to 1994

Interruption rate (%)[1]

Men / Women

Age at first interruption	20-24	25-34	35-44	45-54	55-64
Men	25	11	7	9	4
Women	43	23	9	6	2

[1] Interruptions of paid work that occurred between 1990 and 1994 as a percent of those who had ever worked.
Source: Statistics Canada, 1995 General Social Survey.

CANADIAN SOCIAL TRENDS BACKGROUNDER

Defining an interruption in paid work

"Work interruptions" was one of the topics covered by the 1995 General Social Survey (GSS). Respondents who had worked steadily for pay for at least six months were asked if they had ever stopped working for pay for a period of six months or more. Respondents who had done so are said to have experienced a long-term interruption in paid work, whether they returned to work or not after the stoppage. Respondents were asked when each interruption of six months or longer started and why it started. If they had returned to paid work, they also were asked how long the interruption had lasted, whether they had returned to the same job, whether the job had similar duties and whether they had returned to a full- or part-time job.[1] Detailed information was collected for as many as four long-term work interruptions. These retrospective questions allow the work interruption patterns of several generations of women to be examined.

The GSS relied on the ability of respondents to recall work interruptions over a lifetime of work. Consequently, this study is subject to recall error because some people may have forgotten interruptions that occurred many years before. This recall task may have proven more difficult for people with longer work histories.

People under age 20 and full-time students who had worked part-time were excluded from the study because of short-term labour market experience. Many older workers indicated that their first interruption occurred at retirement. While retirement has become less permanent than it once was, the nature and consequences of this type of interruption are likely to be quite different from those due to other causes. Consequently, interruptions at retirement were not considered to be interruptions in this study.[2]

Work interruptions were first investigated in a supplement to the Labour Force Survey in 1972. Statistics Canada's Family History Survey in 1984 also examined work interruptions and found that 50% of women and 18% of men who had ever worked experienced a work interruption lasting one year or more.[3] This earlier survey underestimated the differences between men and women because it excluded any interruptions that lasted less than one year, many of which could have been for childbirth. The 1995 GSS addressed this problem by inquiring about work interruptions of six months or more.

[1] Respondents were not asked if they returned to the same employer. A return to the same employer has implications for seniority rights, pension credits and maintenance of rates of pay.

[2] For more information on retirement see "Retirement in the 90s," *Canadian Social Trends*, Autumn 1996.

[3] Thomas K. Burch, *Family History Survey - Preliminary Findings*, Statistics Canada, Catalogue no. 99-955-XPB, 1985.

Most women return to work Most women (71%) return to paid work after an interruption. Many of them (31%) settled back into the same job and duties. About one-quarter returned to a job with similar duties, while slightly less than half found new jobs.

However, less than half (47%) of women who had full-time jobs returned to a full-time job; a quarter returned to part-time work. The remainder had not yet returned to paid work at the time of the survey. Many women who worked part-time before they interrupted their paid work returned as part-time employees (42%), while 37% had not re-entered the paid labour force as of 1995. The Canadian National Child Care Survey shows that 31% of part-time workers with children under age 13 worked part-time because of family responsibilities. Since most lengthy interruptions of paid work for women are a result of family responsibilities, a woman's return to paid work may be greatly influenced by the availability of supports such as daycare facilities and home support for children and, in some cases, help for elderly parents.

Women's work interruptions are getting shorter Women's first completed interruptions are now much shorter than they were — an average of 1.4 years for women 25 to 34 compared with 8.1 for women 55 to 64. Shorter interruptions (for women) may have occurred because attitudes toward the role of women in the family and toward paid work have changed. Examining the interruption patterns of older women may give a glimpse of the work attitudes and conditions they experienced when they first started paid work and when their families were first formed. For example, most women aged 55 to 64 in 1995 had started their first job in the 1950s and experienced interruptions during the 1950s and 1960s. In contrast, most women aged 25 to 34 in 1995 had started their first paid jobs in the 1980s and most of their long-term interruptions occurred in the late 1980s and early 1990s.

In the 1950s and 1960s, women often left the labour force for extended periods to care for their children. This is reflected in the lengthy career interruptions of older women. Today, young women interrupt their careers for much shorter periods. In the 1950s, only one out of eight women who interrupted their paid work returned to paid work within two years. In the 1990s, over half (55%) returned to work within two years.

Women interrupt their careers for family-related reasons Women's role as caregiver within their families is evident from the work interruption data.

CANADIAN SOCIAL TRENDS BACKGROUNDER

Measuring the duration of interruptions in paid work

The duration of work interruptions reported in this article refers to those who have returned to paid work (i.e., completed interruptions). On average, women's completed interruptions lasted 4.6 years. However, 29% of women who experienced interruptions had not returned to paid work by the time they were interviewed in 1995 (i.e., incomplete interruptions). If incomplete interruptions were also included in the calculation, the average duration would be 8.0 years. Some women who had incomplete interruptions at the time of the survey may eventually return to paid work, thereby increasing the duration further, while others may never return.

The completed interruptions for young women are brief in part because those who had the shortest interruptions would have returned to paid work in 1995. As more young women return to paid work, the average duration of their completed interruptions will increase. However, it is unlikely that it will ever approach that of older women.

Another way of looking at how quickly women return to paid work is to examine the percentage of women who return to paid work within a certain period of time, say two years. The value of this approach is that it covers both complete and incomplete interruptions.

Work interruptions of younger women were much shorter than those of older women

Age in 1995	Ever worked for pay[1]	Interrupted paid work[2]	Returned to paid work within two years of the start of the first interruption[3]	Average duration of first completed interruption
	%			years
Total	91	62	35	4.6
20 to 24	76	33	52	1.0
25 to 34	95	52	62	1.4
35 to 44	96	65	46	3.4
45 to 54	97	70	28	5.6
55 to 64	92	72	18	8.1
65 and over	78	64	7	11.1

[1] As a percent of all women.
[2] As a percent of women who ever worked for pay.
[3] As a percent of women who interrupted their paid work.
Source: Statistics Canada, 1995 General Social Survey.

Marriage, maternity leave and care of children or elderly relatives (family-related reasons) were the reasons for 62% of women's interruptions of paid work. Although these reasons are still dominant, they are less prevalent than they once were. In the 1950s, family-related reasons accounted for 88% of all women's interruptions, while economic reasons[1] accounted for less than 1%. In contrast, in the early 1990s, less than half (47%) were family-related while economic reasons had grown to represent 22% of all women's interruptions of paid work. Factors that may have influenced this change include lower fertility rates, delayed childbearing and changes in the workplace that enable women to resume work after childbirth.

Contemporary women have fewer children[2], more frequently delay childbearing until they have established their careers, are less likely to interrupt their careers for six months or more for childbirth or child care, and return to paid work after childbirth much more quickly than new mothers of earlier generations.

Looking back at mothers who gave birth to their first child in the 1950s, 63% had steady paid work at some time prior to giving birth, of whom 39% took at least six months leave of absence from paid work at childbirth. Sixty-five percent of women who interrupted their paid

[1] Includes layoff or end of contract, lack of work, business or company closure and seasonal work.

[2] David Ford and François Nault, "Changing Fertility Patterns, 1974 to 1994," *Health Reports*, Statistics Canada, Catalogue no. 82-003-XPB, Vol. 8, no. 3, Winter 1996.

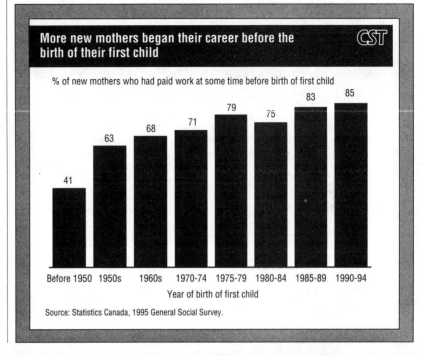

More new mothers began their career before the birth of their first child

% of new mothers who had paid work at some time before birth of first child

Before 1950: 41
1950s: 63
1960s: 68
1970-74: 71
1975-79: 79
1980-84: 75
1985-89: 83
1990-94: 85

Year of birth of first child

Source: Statistics Canada, 1995 General Social Survey.

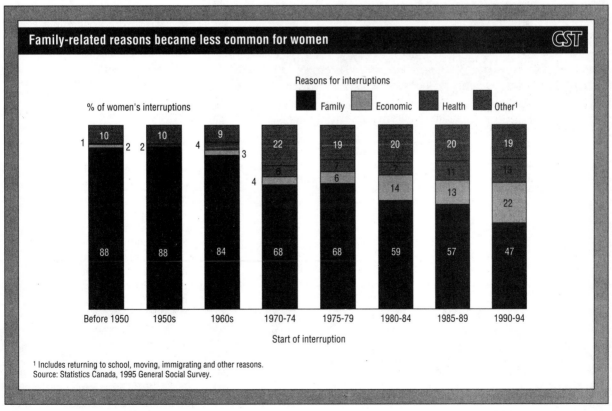

Family-related reasons became less common for women

% of women's interruptions

Reasons for interruptions: Family, Economic, Health, Other[1]

Start of interruption	Family	Economic	Health	Other
Before 1950	88	1	2	10
1950s	88	2	2	10
1960s	84	3	4	9
1970-74	68	6	4	22
1975-79	68	6	7	19
1980-84	59	14	7	20
1985-89	57	13	11	20
1990-94	47	22	13	19

Start of interruption

[1] Includes returning to school, moving, immigrating and other reasons.
Source: Statistics Canada, 1995 General Social Survey.

work for the birth of their first child returned to paid work afterwards, but only 1% did so within two years of the start of the interruption. Although many employed mothers of the 1950s interrupted their work because of childbirth, 20% interrupted their paid work more than three years before the birth of their first child, usually for reasons of marriage or personal or family responsibilities.

By the early 1990s, 85% of new mothers worked for pay at some time prior to the birth of their first child. Fifty-seven percent of employed new mothers interrupted their paid work at childbirth. Unlike mothers of the 1950s, 78% of new mothers who interrupted their paid work returned to work after the birth of their child, 56% within two years of the start of the interruption.

Education: a factor in work interruptions In general, women with more education experience fewer work interruptions.[3] These findings are expected, as those with more education usually have the most marketable skills and are therefore able to obtain the highest paying and most stable jobs. As well, perhaps those with higher levels of education have the greatest incentive to return quickly to paid work after an interruption because they have the most to lose in foregone earnings. University graduates were least likely to experience interruptions and also had by far the shortest interruptions.

Implications of work interruptions Work interruptions have more serious implications for women than men in terms of earnings, employability and long-term economic well-being because women experience more frequent and longer work interruptions. Many women report not returning to paid work at all and nearly one quarter of those employed full-time before an interruption returned to part-time work. Childbirth and child care remain the predominant reasons for a hiatus in a career, often resulting in interruptions lasting longer than a year.

When a woman does return to paid work, the role of caregiver does not end. Part-time jobs may be viewed as a way of improving the balance between family and job responsibilities. Part-time employment may also be the only available option after a lengthy interruption. Skills may have deteriorated or job requirements may have increased, making it difficult to find a full-time job. Regardless of the reason why women work in part-time jobs, current earnings are affected.

Recent new mothers were more likely to interrupt their paid work at child birth — CST

Mothers who worked at some time prior to the birth of their first child

Year of birth of first child	Interrupted three or more years before birth of first child	Interrupted paid work for six months or more at birth of first child	Did not interrupt paid work for six months or more at birth of first child
	%		
All new mothers	10	47	43
Before 1950	29	25	46
1950s	20	39	41
1960s	13	49	38
1970-74	10	53	37
1975-79	7	47	46
1980-84	4	50	46
1985-89	6	50	44
1990-94	5	57	38

Source: Statistics Canada, 1995 General Social Survey.

Recent new mothers returned to paid work more quickly — CST

Mothers who interrupted paid work for six months or more at birth of their first child

Year of birth of first child	Completed interruptions	Returned to work within two years after birth of first child	Average duration of completed interruption at birth of first child
	%		years
All new mothers	81	34	5.1
Before 1950	64	1	10.6
1950s	65	8	11.6
1960s	82	19	7.1
1970-74	84	15	6.6
1975-79	91	25	6.1
1980-84	88	42	3.4
1985-89	84	45	2.0
1990-94	78	56	1.0

Source: Statistics Canada, 1995 General Social Survey.

[3] On average, older women have less education than younger women. Age and education interact to influence both the likelihood and duration of interruptions in paid work. Education has a significant effect on interruptions after accounting for differences in age.

Future income can also be affected. Canada Pension Plan, Quebec Pension Plan and private pension plan benefits are based on both length of time over which contributions were made to the pension plan and the amount of earnings upon which contributions were made. Therefore, interruptions can reduce retirement benefits and the long-term well-being of women. Both the Canada and Quebec Pension Plans have provisions to drop low-earning years for periods of reduced labour force attachment while caring for a child under the age of seven. However, private pension plans rarely have these provisions. Because interruptions also often coincide with a reduction in women's earnings, women's ability to invest in Registered Retirement Savings Plans is also hindered.

The rapid pace of technological change may make re-entering the paid work force after an interruption in paid work more difficult as skills and qualifications become obsolete more quickly. This reality may induce people to accelerate their return to paid work. Certainly in today's world, the employability of those who remain out of the paid work force for extended periods is at risk because their once-valued skills may become obsolete and new skills may not have been acquired.

Conclusion Women are less likely today than they were in past decades to interrupt their paid work. In addition, those who do interrupt return to work, and they return more quickly than ever before. Increasing opportunities for post-secondary education have improved the employability of women. The introduction of legislation protecting the jobs of women on maternity leave has provided more recent cohorts of women with greater assurances of re-employment should they interrupt their paid work. Women's earnings are also increasing relative to men's and their earnings increasingly represent a larger portion of family income than in the past.

There will always be work interruptions. But the likelihood, frequency and duration of them is changing, and will probably continue to do so. With the adoption of more family-friendly work arrangements and employment policies, women are better able to remain in the work force and still care for children and other family members. Many other factors also influence work interruptions. Economic conditions, the life cycle, foregone income, decisions on how to care for children or elderly parents, attitudes toward the role of men and women within the family and availability of affordable daycare may all have an effect.

Janet Fast is an associate professor with the Department of Human Ecology at the University of Alberta and **Moreno Da Pont** is an analyst with the Service Division of Statistics Canada.

University graphs are least likely to experience paid work interruptions

Educational attainment in 1995	Interrupted paid work[1]	Returned to paid work within two years of first interruption[2]	Average duration of first completed interruption
		%	years
University graduates	51	50	3.1
College graduates	61	46	4.1
Trade/technical school graduates	56	34	5.5
High school graduates	67	32	5.1
Never completed high school	65	18	6.7

[1] As a percent of women who ever worked for pay.
[2] As a percent of women who interrupted their paid work.
Note: Respondents' highest level of education in 1995; interruptions may have occurred much earlier when respondents had less education. To reduce the impact of education upgrading, first interruptions due to a return to school are excluded from this table.
Source: Statistics Canada, 1995 General Social Survey.

CANADA'S REFUGEE FLOWS
Gender Inequality

by Monica Boyd

"ONE IMPRESSION STANDS OUT ABOVE ALL OTHERS: THE FACES OF THE REFUGEES ARE OVERWHELMINGLY THE FACES OF WOMEN AND CHILDREN."

Susan Forbes Martin, then a member of the United States Commission on Refugees, wrote this statement in her journal while on a 1986 site visit to a refugee camp in Thailand.[1]

People in flight from their home countries, because of persecution and fear, face many challenges. Relations between women and men, and children and parents, are altered. The maintenance of culture is often difficult. Many refugees, particularly those living in camps, have problems obtaining basic necessities, like food and water, as well as accessing supplies, health care and education. Many struggle daily for their family's survival.

Of all world refugees, estimated to total 16.7 million in 1990, only a small minority will have their needs met through asylum in Canada.[1] Between 1981 and 1991, Canada admitted 279,000 people as permanent residents on humanitarian grounds. Of these, 30% were UN convention refugees and 70% were members of designated groups.

People admitted to Canada as UN convention refugees or as members of designated groups may be sponsored to come to Canada or they may arrive at Canada's borders and apply for refugee status. Those who are sponsored by the government or by organizations such as churches are given permanent residence upon their arrival in Canada. Those who arrive at Canada's borders on their own must apply for refugee status. If their application is accepted, they may stay in Canada until their claim is heard by the Immigration and Refugee Board (IRB). Only those who receive a positive decision by the board may apply to remain in Canada as a permanent resident.

Most world refugees are women and children
Comprehensive and detailed data on the world refugee population are not available. However, the distribution of world refugees by gender and age is expected to approximate that of the total populations of areas where most refugees live – Africa, South Asia and the Middle East.[2] This is because the conditions which produce refugee flows, including abrupt changes in regimes and the formation of new nation

[1] Martin, Susan Forbes, **Refugee Women**, Atlantic Highlands, New Jersey: ZED Books Ltd., 1992.

[2] Keely, Charles B., "The Resettlement of Women and Children Refugees," **Migration World**, Vol. 20, No. 4(Fall): 14-18, 1992.

states, usually affect the whole population in areas where they occur.

The populations of Africa, South Asia and the Middle East are characterized by relatively high fertility rates. As a result, in many countries in these areas, about half of the population is under age 15. Assuming that the numbers of adult men and women in these countries are similar, then about 75% of the populations of these areas consist of children (50%) and women (25%).

Estimates of the percentage of world refugees who are women and children range between 75% and 85%. Estimates that exceed 75% reflect upward adjustments to account for the higher percentage of women and children that have been observed in some United Nations' High Commission on Refugees (UNHCR) camps. It also includes the expectation that men are less likely to be present in refugee camps or among groups in flight because of death or imprisonment or because of continued insurgency or military involvement in their area of origin.

Men predominate among refugees admitted to Canada as permanent residents Among those admitted to Canada as permanent residents on humanitarian grounds during the past decade (UN convention refugees and members of designated groups), there were over one and a half times as many men as women. Men are estimated to represent one-quarter of the world refugee population. According to Citizenship and Immigration Canada records, however, men accounted for 48% of UN convention refugees and 47% of designated groups admitted to Canada from 1981 to 1991. In contrast, 27% of UN convention refugees and 30% of designated groups admitted to Canada during that period were women.

Children under age 15 were greatly under-represented among refugees admitted to Canada as permanent residents. Although it is estimated that half of populations in flight are usually children, they accounted for 24% of both UN convention refugees and designated groups admitted to Canada from 1981 to 1991.

Only in classes of immigrants where admission was not based on humanitarian grounds did women predominate. From 1981 to 1991, women represented 43% of those accepted under classes where admission was not based on humanitarian grounds, while men represented 37% and children 19%. The higher representation of women in these other classes largely results from a concentration of women in the family class, where they outnumber men by 50%. From 1981 to 1991, 304,282 women were admitted in this class, compared with 219,418 men. Many women admitted in the family class were entering Canada to rejoin family members already in the country.

Men more likely than women never to have been married According to Citizenship and Immigration data, between 1981 and 1991, 59% of men admitted as UN convention refugees and 45% admitted as members of designated groups were never married. Among women admitted, the corresponding percentages were 37% and 33%, respectively. Of those admitted to Canada as permanent residents under other classes where admission was not based on humanitarian grounds, 38% of men and 32% of women never had been married. A high proportion of never-married men in the UN convention refugee and designated group categories may result in a limited number of refugee women and children immigrating to Canada on the basis of family ties.

Those admitted to Canada on humanitarian grounds and who have permanent resident status can sponsor the migration of close relatives to Canada, many of whom are also victims of flight or persecution.[3] By definition, never-married people admitted on humanitarian grounds will have no spouses and likely no

CANADIAN SOCIAL TRENDS BACKGROUNDER

What is a refugee?[1] According to Article 1 of the 1951 United Nations Convention Relating to the Status of Refugees, a refugee is a person who "...owing to well founded fear of being persecuted for reasons of race, religion, nationality, membership of a particular social group or political opinion, is outside the country of his nationality and is unable, or owing to such fear, is unwilling to avail himself of the protection of that country...."

Canada is a signatory to this convention and thus uses the UN definition of a refugee in assessing who is eligible to enter Canada as a refugee. The Canadian *Immigration Act*, 1976 and amendments introduced in Bill C-86 (December, 1992) also provide for the admission of other groups on humanitarian grounds.[2] "Designated classes" is a term used to capture a variety of "refugee like" situations including mass outflows (such as those from Indochina), disproportionate punishment for violation of strict exit controls (self-exiles) and, for specific countries, the internally displaced (political prisoners and oppressed people).

[1] Citizenship and Immigration Canada, Refugee Affairs Immigration Policy Group, 1993.

[2] See subsection 6(3) of the *Immigration Act*.

children to sponsor. In contrast, married people admitted to Canada on these grounds may sponsor the eventual migration of spouses and children. Unfortunately, there is no way to determine from the Canadian landed immigrant data base which migrants admitted to Canada on the basis of family ties are actually a continuation of an earlier refugee movement.

Process for selecting refugees eliminates many women Compared to worldwide estimates of the composition of refugee populations, women are underrepresented in humanitarian-based admissions to Canada for a number of reasons. Men are more likely than women to travel to Canada's borders and become refugee applicants. Among the 57,455 claims finalized in 1991 and 1992 by the Immigration and Refugee Board (IRB), 66% were claims from men. Men are also more likely than women to be politically active participants when repression, insurgency and civil war occur and thus meet the criteria of a UN convention refugee.

The UN convention definition of a refugee considers race, religion, nationality and membership in a particular social group or political opinion as reasons why an individual may fear being persecuted in their home country. In many countries, however, women undergo persecution as a consequence of the actions of other family members. Such experiences, which can involve rape, torture and beatings, may not be considered "persecution" by IRB adjudicators.

Recognizing that many refugee claimants fear gender-related persecution, on March 9, 1993, the IRB released guidelines assisting members in assessing claims based on gender persecution. These guidelines are directed to members of the IRB who review refugee claimant cases and are not part of Canada's immigration legislation.

The process used to select refugees from outside Canada also results in men being more likely than women to be admitted. To be admitted into Canada as a permanent resident, those seeking asylum must first meet the United Nations' criteria of a UN convention refugee or be a member of a designated group. In addition, people from outside Canada, such as those in refugee camps, must be considered admissible, which generally means that they should exhibit the potential for eventual successful resettlement in Canada.

Men are more likely than women to meet admissibility standards that major settlement countries, like Canada, impose. This is because socio-economic characteristics, such as exposure to Western lifestyles, education, knowledge of English or French, and job skills, are used to assess claimants' potential for successful settlement. As women in many countries where refugees originate receive fewer educational, employment and social opportunities than men, they are less likely to meet admissibility standards on their own merits. In addition, because refugee service agencies and national governments emphasize eventual repatriation rather than permanent resettlement, they do not usually select women and children who are temporarily separated from husbands and fathers.

When women are admitted to Canada on humanitarian criteria, they are much more likely than men to enter as part of a larger family unit in which another individual has satisfied admission standards. According to Citizenship and Immigration data for 1981 to 1991, less than half of women admitted to Canada as UN convention refugees or as members of designated groups were principal applicants, compared with 91% of men

[3] Refugees with permanent resident status are no longer required to sponsor the migration of their spouses and children. Instead, when the applicants receive permanent resident status so do their spouses and children.

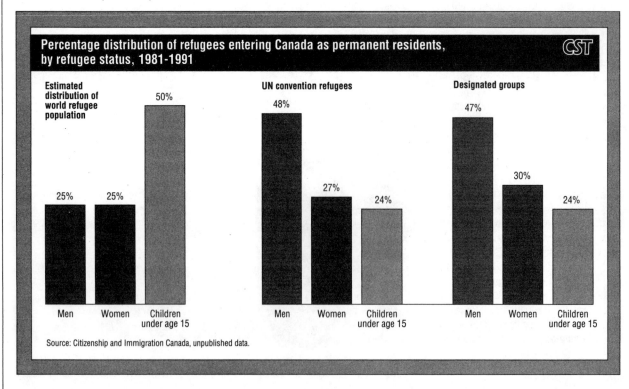

Percentage distribution of refugees entering Canada as permanent residents, by refugee status, 1981-1991   CST

Estimated distribution of world refugee population

Men	25%
Women	25%
Children under age 15	50%

UN convention refugees

Men	48%
Women	27%
Children under age 15	24%

Designated groups

Men	47%
Women	30%
Children under age 15	24%

Source: Citizenship and Immigration Canada, unpublished data.

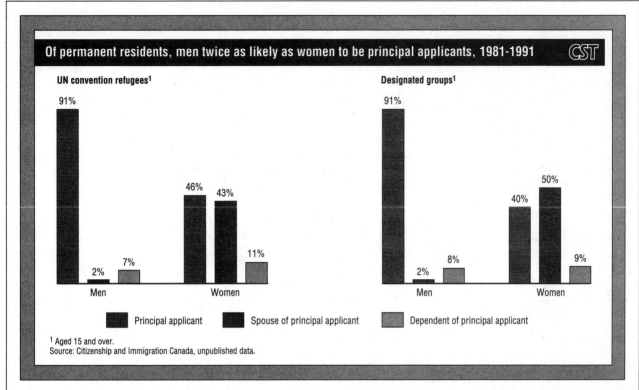

Of permanent residents, men twice as likely as women to be principal applicants, 1981-1991

UN convention refugees[1]

- Men: Principal applicant 91%, Spouse of principal applicant 2%, Dependent of principal applicant 7%
- Women: Principal applicant 46%, Spouse of principal applicant 43%, Dependent of principal applicant 11%

Designated groups[1]

- Men: Principal applicant 91%, Spouse of principal applicant 2%, Dependent of principal applicant 8%
- Women: Principal applicant 40%, Spouse of principal applicant 50%, Dependent of principal applicant 9%

■ Principal applicant   ■ Spouse of principal applicant   ■ Dependent of principal applicant

[1] Aged 15 and over.
Source: Citizenship and Immigration Canada, unpublished data.

admitted. Whereas 43% of women who were convention refugees and 50% of women who were members of designated groups entered as spouses of principal applicants, less than 2% of men in each of these groups were admitted as spouses.

"Women at risk" program initiated to address problems
The difficulties that refugee women face in meeting settlement criteria resulted in the UNHCR taking an initiative in the mid-1980s to target "women at risk." Canada started a women at risk program in 1987, and women have been admitted through this program since 1988. From 1988 to 1991, however, the total number of people admitted under this program, including women as well as their family members, was very small (391), representing only 0.3% of all UN convention refugees and members of designated groups admitted during that period.[4]

The women at risk program is designed to allow women who meet the eligibility criteria of a UN convention refugee or a member of a designated group to be admitted into Canada, even if they do not meet admissibility standards due to low educational attainment, limited labour-market skills or heavy child-care responsibilities. In general, this program admits women in precarious situations where local authorities can not ensure their safety and protection, such as those experiencing harassment by local authorities or members of their own communities. This situation most likely occurs when adult males are absent from the household.

Many women left behind Women and children are less likely than men to be accepted for settlement in Canada and other Western countries on humanitarian grounds. Given that women and children form a large proportion of populations in flight, this implies that they disproportionately remain in their initial country of refuge.

In addition to problems faced by all refugees, such as separation from family members, poor living conditions, inadequate health care and difficulty maintaining culture,[5,6,7] refugee women are often the targets of violence. For many refugee women, however, the persecution they face goes unrecognized and the barriers to acceptance for resettlement they encounter are unbreakable.

[4] **Immigration Statistics**, annual reports, 1988-1991. By September 1993, 620 people had been admitted under this program.

[5] Martin, Susan Forbes, **The Economic Activities of Refugee Women**. Washington, D.C.: Refugee Policy Group, The Center for Policy Analysis and Research on Refugee Issues, 1988.

[6] Ptolemy, Kathleen, "First International Consultation on Refugee Women: Geneva (November, 1988)," **Canadian Woman Studies** 10 (Spring): 21-24, 1989.

[7] Taft, Julia Vadala, **Issues and Options for Refugee Women in Developing Countries**. Washington, D.C.: Refugee Policy Group, 1987.

Dr. Monica Boyd, past president of the Canadian Population Society, is currently the Pepper Distinguished Professor, Department of Sociology and Research Associate, Center for the Study of Population, Florida State University, Tallahassee, Florida.

- For additional information on this topic, see **Conference Proceedings: Gender Issues and Refugees: Development Implications**. Centre for Refugee Studies, York University, North York, Canada (forthcoming).

MEASURING AND VALUING

Households' Unpaid Work

In Canada and elsewhere, people spend roughly as much time on unpaid work as they do on paid work. No matter how unpaid work is valued, it represents a major use of resources with substantial costs and benefits to individuals, households and society. This article summarizes the activities included as unpaid work, Statistics Canada's most recent estimate of its value, and how demographic, economic and social trends have influenced unpaid work over the past thirty years.

by Chris Jackson

Issues related to unpaid work have drawn increasing interest in recent years. These include: child care, care of the growing number of seniors, the disproportionate share of unpaid work done by women, the pressures of balancing family and job responsibilities, and the inclusion of unpaid work in national statistics such as the System of National Accounts. Attention has also focused on the adjustment of taxation, pension and income support policies and programs to recognize the contribution of unpaid work to the economic and social well-being of Canadians. Courts are also engaged in assessing the value of unpaid work. For example, lawyers and judges need to know its value in cases of negligence causing injury or death, and in divorce settlements.

Unpaid work covers a wide range of activities International guidelines recommend limiting the scope of unpaid work to those unpaid activities that produce goods and services which could be exchanged in the market. Unpaid work includes: domestic chores, looking after children, shopping and management of the household, volunteer work, helping friends, relatives and others, and transportation to and from these activities.

Women still do most of the unpaid work In 1992, adult Canadians spent 25 billion hours on unpaid work. This represented 1,164 hours per adult, down from 1,223 hours in 1961.

Women, on average, spent 78% more time in 1992 on unpaid work than men did (1,482 hours per year, compared with

CANADIAN SOCIAL TRENDS BACKGROUNDER CST

Measuring unpaid work

Time use surveys are essential for estimating the value of unpaid work. These surveys provide information on the amount and types of unpaid work done, and who does this form of work. Statistics Canada's initial efforts in the mid-1970s to estimate the value of household work relied upon data from time use surveys in Halifax and Toronto in 1971-72.

Subsequent studies used the 1981 Canadian Time Use Pilot Study, and the 1986 and 1992 General Social Surveys (GSS) on time use. Each survey asked respondents to keep a 24-hour diary of their daily activities, including paid work, unpaid work, education, personal care and leisure.

The 1986 and 1992 surveys covered a representative sample of the household population aged 15 and over in the ten provinces. The 1981 pilot survey included people at fourteen locations across Canada. Although everyone's unpaid work contributes to family and social well-being, that of children under age 15, people living in institutions and temporary residents of Canada was not measured.

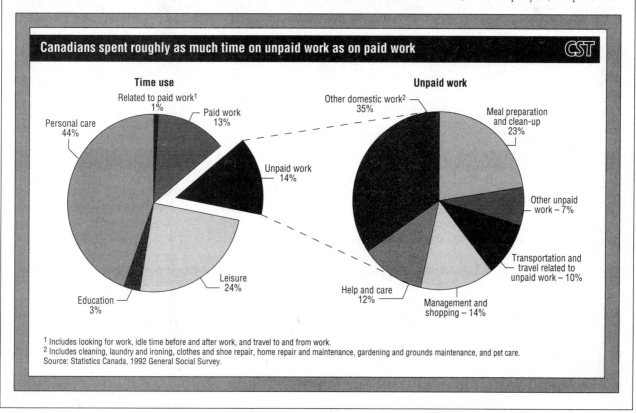

Canadians spent roughly as much time on unpaid work as on paid work CST

Time use
- Related to paid work[1] 1%
- Paid work 13%
- Personal care 44%
- Unpaid work 14%
- Leisure 24%
- Education 3%

Unpaid work
- Other domestic work[2] 35%
- Meal preparation and clean-up 23%
- Other unpaid work – 7%
- Transportation and travel related to unpaid work – 10%
- Management and shopping – 14%
- Help and care 12%

[1] Includes looking for work, idle time before and after work, and travel to and from work.
[2] Includes cleaning, laundry and ironing, clothes and shoe repair, home repair and maintenance, gardening and grounds maintenance, and pet care.
Source: Statistics Canada, 1992 General Social Survey.

831 hours). They also spent 11% less time on unpaid work in 1992 than in 1961, though their participation in the labour force had nearly doubled over the same period. In contrast, men spent 6% more time on unpaid work. Nonetheless, women still did about two-thirds of the unpaid work in 1992. If paid and unpaid work were combined, women spent the same amount of time working as men did.

Meal preparation and clean up the biggest chore Meal preparation and clean up is by far the single most time-consuming activity, taking close to one-quarter of the time spent on unpaid work. Household work represents about 95% of unpaid work, with the balance devoted to volunteer work and helping others outside the household. Although volunteer work and helping others represented only 5% of unpaid work, it was still equivalent to more than 730,000 full-time jobs in 1992.

A changing composition of tasks and division of labour Canadians spent less time on meal preparation and care of household members in 1992 than in 1961. But, they spent more time on cleaning, clothing care, repairs and maintenance, household management and shopping.

The division of these tasks between the sexes has also changed since 1961. By 1992, women were spending relatively more time on cleaning, management and shopping, transportation, volunteer work and helping others outside the household. Meanwhile, men were spending more time on repairs and maintenance, and on the traditionally female tasks of meal preparation and clothing care.

Valuing unpaid work The value of unpaid work is estimated on the basis of hourly wage rates from census data on employment earnings. The two most common wage-based methods are derived from the notions of "opportunity cost" and "replacement cost." Opportunity cost methods assign a value to unpaid work based on the wage rate of the person doing the unpaid work.[1] The value of

---

[1] Household members doing unpaid work could have worked for pay instead. The value of unpaid work is equivalent to its opportunity cost, the foregone wage.

What is unpaid work? | CST

A: Household work

Domestic work	Examples
✓ Meal preparation	making a pot of tea, setting the table, cooking, baking, cleaning up after meals or baking, washing/drying dishes
✓ Cleaning	mopping floors, dusting, vacuuming, making beds, taking out the garbage
✓ Clothing care	washing laundry, hanging it out to dry, folding clothes and linen, mending clothes, sewing on buttons, shining shoes, hemming
✓ Repairs and maintenance	painting, plastering a wall, plumbing, fixing or washing the car, renovations, mowing and watering grass, weeding, composting, raking leaves, watering house plants
✓ Other domestic work	packing for a move or vacation, rearranging furniture, putting groceries away, feeding and grooming pets

Help and care	
✓ Child care	feeding, changing and bathing babies and other children, putting them to bed, teaching them to learn, helping with school work, reprimanding, reading and talking to children, administering first aid, medicines or shots, taking temperature, playing games with children, walking or biking with them, unpaid baby-sitting by household members (not parents or guardians), visiting children in hospital
✓ Adult care	washing and cutting hair, running a bath, providing help to disabled and elderly members of the household, administering first aid, preparing and administering medicines, taking temperature
Management and shopping	paying bills, balancing chequebooks, making shopping lists, preparing tax returns, shopping for groceries, clothing, hardware, gasoline, looking for a house or apartment, getting appliances repaired
Transportation and travel	travel related to management and shopping for goods and services, taking family members to day care, work, school, hospital and other places, other travel related to domestic work

B: Other unpaid work

✓ Volunteer work	fund raising, answering a crisis line, delivering meals
✓ Other help and care	helping friends, neighbours, relatives and others with housework, cooking, transportation, repairs and maintenance
✓ Transport: other unpaid work	travel related to volunteer work and other help and care

Source: Statistics Canada, Catalogue no. 13-603-XPE, no. 3.

Dramatic influx of women into the labour force
Women's participation in the labour force almost doubled over the past thirty years, reaching 58% in 1992. Labour force participation of women with children under age 3 also nearly doubled to 61% in 1992 from 32% in 1976. This significantly reduced the time spent on unpaid child care and increased the demand for paid child-care services.

Fewer children and more seniors At the height of the postwar baby boom, children under age 5 comprised more than 12% of the population. This proportion declined to about 7% in 1992. As a result, Canadians needed less time for child care and related activities with fewer and older children. This has repercussions on the market economy as well, as women with young children often withdraw from the labour market temporarily, work part time or seek child-care services.

In 1992, seniors made up 12% of the population, up from 8% in 1961. Although seniors are healthier than in the past, many need help and care, especially the most elderly. On the other hand, they do not have the pressing commitments related to having a paid job or to having children at home. Consequently, seniors have more time to engage in volunteer work and other informal helping and caring activities.

Households are getting smaller Average household size declined to 2.6 in 1992 from 3.9 people in 1961. Smaller households do less household work than larger ones. However, they also have fewer opportunities to take advantage of "economies of scale." The time taken to prepare dinner for three, for example, is often not much different from that required to prepare a comparable dinner for two.

More rooms to clean and more amenities Canadians are living in dwellings with more rooms and amenities than in 1961. The average number of rooms per dwelling increased to 5.9 in 1992 from 5.4 in 1961. Indoor cleaning tends to increase with the number of rooms. Nearly all dwellings today have hot water supply, a bath, shower and flush toilet. Roughly 15% to 20% of dwellings were without such facilities in the early 1960s. These amenities ease many unpaid activities such as cooking, child care and washing dishes, although they also require time for their upkeep.

In 1992, 57% of households lived in single-detached dwellings, compared with 65% in 1961. This also affects the amount and type of unpaid work that Canadians do. Apartment dwellers generally spend less time on home repair and maintenance, outdoor cleaning, gardening and grounds maintenance.

More appliances than ever before In 1992, most households had an electric stove, a refrigerator and a vacuum cleaner. Roughly three out of four households had a microwave oven, a freezer, an automatic washer and dryer. Forty-four percent had a dishwasher in 1992, compared with less than 2% in 1961. The use of household appliances potentially saves time and makes some tasks easier to do. On the other hand, it may also lead to more time being spent on appliance repairs and maintenance or on seeking repair services.

Paradoxically, time spent on household work has remained almost constant over time. Part of the explanation lies in rising standards of quality and cleanliness. For example, automatic washers have made doing laundry easier compared with old-style wringer washers. Nowadays, however, Canadians are cleaning their clothing and linen more often. In addition, the availability of cheaper and more efficient appliances leads households to do some things themselves rather than purchase similar goods or services in the market.

More income to manage and spend The increase in women's employment since 1961 has coincided with a rise in family income. Average family income increased to $53,700 in 1992 from $28,500 in 1961 (1992 dollars). With more money to manage, expenditures to make and investments to consider, shopping and managing household finances have become more time consuming.

Spending patterns have changed In some cases, households relied more on market services in 1992 than they did in 1961. For example, Canadians spent more of their food budgets on meals outside the home in 1992 (32%) than they did in 1961 (17%). Similarly, spending on child care outside the home, one of the fastest growing components of personal spending, increased to $2.8 billion in 1992 from $37 million in 1961.

In other instances, household self-reliance may have increased. In 1992, 83% of households owned at least one vehicle, up from 68% in 1961. This, combined with increased multiple vehicle ownership, has slowed the growth in personal spending on public transit and taxi services. Similarly, laundry and dry-cleaning services account for a smaller proportion of household budgets, as households have replaced these services with their own washer and dryer. This has occurred despite an increase of more than 190% in spending on clothing between 1961 and 1992.

unpaid work at opportunity cost is calculated both before and after taxes.

The replacement cost method puts a value on unpaid work based on the wage rate paid to people who do similar types of work.[2] This can be calculated in two ways. The generalist approach values each unpaid activity using the wage rate of domestic employees (housekeepers). The specialist approach uses the wage rates of specialized occupations. For example, the value of meal preparation is based upon the wages of cooks or chefs.

Both the opportunity and replacement cost methods have the weakness of being only indirectly related to the value of goods and services produced by households. With the opportunity cost method, for example, the value of washing dishes could be $100 per hour for a lawyer or $10 per hour for a sales clerk, although both may do the job equally well.

Replacement cost methods assume that household members are as efficient as the businesses or domestic staff who, in theory, could do their unpaid work. For example, a household member may take one hour to mow the lawn. The replacement cost of that unpaid work equals the price of one hour of a groundskeeper's or domestic worker's time. This value is used although it might take these workers less time to do perhaps an even better job. Replacement cost methods

also assume that tasks such as household management and volunteer work can be delegated to domestic employees which may not be possible.

Many researchers favour the generalist replacement cost method. Domestic employees work in a similar setting and under similar conditions as household members. Moreover, the method is easier to apply.

Value of unpaid work equalled almost $11,000 per adult in 1992 Using the generalist replacement cost method, the value of unpaid work was $136 billion in 1961 (in 1992 dollars) and $235 billion in 1992. For both years, this represented about one-third of Gross Domestic Product (GDP), the total value of market-produced goods and services.

The value of unpaid work averaged $10,900 per adult in 1992, down from $11,300 in 1961. The averages hide some significant variations among demographic groups. For instance, the unpaid work of married women who were not employed and had children was worth $24,400 in 1992. That year, the average paid worker earned $24,900.

Much work to be done Despite advances in the measurement of unpaid work, debate continues on what counts as unpaid work and how to place a value on it.

The distinction between unpaid work and leisure or personal activities (nonwork) is not always clear. Should unpaid work include activities such as exercising, learning, producing domestic crafts and commuting to work? Are other activities often included as unpaid work, such as gardening, window shopping or playing with children, too much like leisure?

Resolving the difficult issue of valuation of unpaid work is also important. Should the value of unpaid work be estimated based on the time spent doing unpaid work or should it be based on the value of goods and services produced as a result? Is a market-based value even appropriate for valuing households' unpaid work?

The evolution of the debate on the measurement and valuation of unpaid work undoubtedly will shape Statistics Canada's future efforts in the field. Meanwhile, Statistics Canada is undertaking research toward creating a system of unpaid work statistics. The 1996 Census was the first Canadian census to measure the time spent on housework, child and elder care. The resulting data will form an integral part of this system.

Better information on unpaid work can lead to a more thorough understanding of the use of human resources. It can foster a greater understanding of the economy and the links between its market and non-market sectors. Measuring unpaid work provides information on what types of work are undertaken, what goods and services result, what costs are incurred, who provides and who benefits. Perhaps even more importantly, it recognizes the unpaid but beneficial tasks that Canadians do for themselves, their families and friends, and for the community at large.

[2] Instead of doing work themselves, household members could have purchased goods or services. The value of unpaid work is equivalent to the cost of paying someone else to do it (its replacement cost).

• This article was adapted from **Households' Unpaid Work: Measurement and Valuation**, Statistics Canada, Catalogue no. 13-603-XPE, no. 3.

Chris Jackson is a research economist with the National Accounts and Environment Division, Statistics Canada.

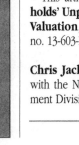

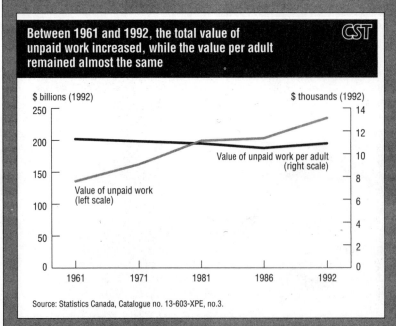

Between 1961 and 1992, the total value of unpaid work increased, while the value per adult remained almost the same

$ billions (1992) — left scale

$ thousands (1992) — right scale

Value of unpaid work per adult (right scale)

Value of unpaid work (left scale)

Source: Statistics Canada, Catalogue no. 13-603-XPE, no.3.

Marriage in Canada

Changing Beliefs and Behaviours 1600-1990

Adapted by Jillian Oderkirk

*From Jean Dumas, **Report on the Demographic Situation in Canada, 1992.** Statistics Canada Catalogue 91-209E and Jean Dumas and Yves Péron. **Marriage and Conjugal Life in Canada**, Statistics Canada Catalogue 91-534E.*

From the beginning of Canada's colonial period until the 1960s, most Canadians viewed marriage as a lifetime commitment, and the only circumstances under which a couple could live together and raise a family. In the past twenty-five years, however, attitudes toward marriage have changed profoundly. Marriage is no longer necessarily a lifetime commitment, as a large minority of couples now divorce. Many Canadians of all ages do not consider marriage a necessary prerequisite to living with a partner and have chosen common-law arrangements – sometimes temporary, sometimes permanent. Mainly for this reason, births outside of marriage are not as unusual and the legal distinction between legitimate and illegitimate births has been abolished.

Although these changes have affected the stability and exclusivity of marriage, they have not caused the institution to disappear. Indeed, the majority of Canadians are still expected to marry, at least once, before their 50th birthday. Compared with twenty-five years ago, however, marriage is now less prevalent, occurs later in life and often does not last long enough for couples to raise their families.

Marriage beliefs and practices From its remote origins, the traditional marital institution was a means of passing assets, real or symbolic, from one generation to another. Satisfaction of spouses was not considered very important and dissatisfaction with a marriage was not grounds for breaking a union. This rationale for traditional marriage made divorce virtually impossible and marriage annulments were almost the only way to terminate a union. Divorce only became possible when marriage began to be based on spousal affection and fulfilment. When such fulfilment lapsed, spouses could seek a break of the union. Despite this, few divorces occurred. At that time, large families were common, and the resultant childrearing responsibilities limited women's access to the labour market. The institution of marriage was also reinforced by churches that considered the union sacred.

Social changes in the last few decades, however, have eroded these century-old beliefs and practices. The change with perhaps the greatest impact was the emergence of widely available, reliable birth-control methods. This facilitated a huge decrease in fertility and family size and, in turn, gave women greater opportunity to achieve financial independence. Following these changes, it became more difficult for religious institutions to keep couples together who wanted to break their marriage bonds. Increased societal demand for legal dissolution of marriages led to the emergence of laws liberalizing divorce.

Colonization: men married late, women married early During Canada's colonization in the 17th century, Europeans emigrating to Canada predominantly were men. The imbalance between the genders resulted in women marrying at young ages and in men, many of whom had difficulty finding a partner, marrying at older ages or not at all. Data from this period are limited to the colony of New France.

In New France, Roman Catholic marriage and the civil laws of France were adopted and records of marriages were maintained by the church. Divorce was illegal because the Roman Catholic religion considered marriage a sacrament that could not be dissolved, even after the physical separation of spouses.

Most early Quebec settlers were unmarried men who came to the colony as soldiers or indentured workers. Because there were few women to accommodate the resultant demand for wives, Louis XIV of France recruited 800 young women of marriageable age to travel to the colony between 1663 and 1673. Nonetheless, before 1700 there were still two men for every woman among the colonists. This imbalance resulted in a high proportion of early marriages among women born between 1640 and 1679. The average age at first marriage of women was 20, while the average age of men was 28. The imbalance lessened for those born from 1700 to 1739. Women's age at first marriage increased to 23, while that of men fell slightly to 27.

During 19th century, many married late or not at all Cultural beliefs among people in Canada in the 1800s, most of whom were immigrants from Northern and Western Europe, reflected those prevalent in their countries of origin. In Northern and Western Europe, children who were not heirs to the family estate usually left the family home when they married. In contrast, in Southern and Eastern Europe, it was common for married children to remain in one of their parent's households.

Throughout this period, households were the unit for the production of goods and services, and setting up an independent home required a large investment. To afford a marriage, young people in Northern and Western Europe often had to spend several years doing paid work. As a result, it was common for people to be either older when they married or to remain single.

Estimated from census records, the average age at marriage for both Canadian men and women in the 1800s was high. For example, among those born from 1821 to 1830,[1] the average age at first marriage was 26 for men and 23 for women. Among those born four decades later, 1861 to 1870, the average age at marriage rose to 29 for men and to 26 for women.

Fewer men and women born during the second half of the 19th century married than did their predecessors. The proportion of men still single at age 50 increased from 10% of those born from 1826 to 1845 to a high of 15% of those born from 1861 to 1865. Of men born during the remaining decades of the 19th century, the proportion who never married fluctuated between 13% and 14%. The pattern was similar among women, with the proportion who were still single at age 50 rising from just under 11% of those born before 1846 to 12% of those born from 1851 to 1870. Among women born during the remaining decades of the century, the proportion was about 11%.

Divorce unobtainable in 19th century Ontario and Quebec Before Confederation, English civil law, which recognized religious marriages and civil marriages conducted by public officials, was established in the provinces, with the exception of Quebec. Under English civil law, cohabitation between unmarried people was considered a common-law marriage if the relationship was stable or resulted in children. Such unions were

[1] The average age at first marriage of birth cohorts includes only those married before age 50.

UNIT 2: WOMEN, MARRIAGE AND THE FAMILY

unusual, however, as most couples married. The various colonies were free to adopt English divorce laws, although only New Brunswick and Nova Scotia did so before Confederation. In Quebec, which maintained its own Civil Code under provisions of the *Quebec Act* of 1774, divorce was not legal.

The *British North America Act* of 1867, the terms of Confederation, respected regional diversity in marriage laws. Provincial legislatures were granted authority over marriage and the definition of its legal effects, marriage annulment and legal separation. Jurisdiction over divorce was shared between the federal parliament that enacted the law and the provincial legislatures that gave their courts authority to grant divorces. Quebec and Ontario did not endow their courts with this authority and thus, divorce was unobtainable in Canada's two most populated provinces.

Conscription during World War II led to earlier marriages As was the case for Canadians in the 19th century, those born during the early 20th century tended to marry late, and many did not marry at all – more than one-in-ten remained single at age 50. The economic problems of the early 1930s contributed to the postponement of many marriages. Among those born from 1906 to 1914, the average age at first marriage was 28 for men and 25 for women.

World War II caused an upswing in marriages culminating in 1940, 1941 and 1942. Canada entered the war in 1939, but was geographically far from the battlefield, and thus initially sent only career soldiers and volunteers. Conscription was extensively debated and was not decided upon until a 1942 referendum. During these years of uncertainty, the prospect of being drafted into the armed forces was a potent stimulant to marriage for young single men, since they would be called first to go to war. Among those born during the last half of the 1910s and early 1920s, the average age at first marriage dropped to 27 for men and to 24 for women.

Marriage earlier and more universal from mid-1940s to 1970 The generations who married following World War II, from the mid-1940s to the 1960s, were not only more likely to marry than their elders, but to do so at increasingly younger ages. The average age at first marriage among men dropped from 26 among those born from 1924 to 1929 to 25 among those born from 1930 to 1938. For women, the average age at first marriage fell from 23 among those born from 1924 to 1932 to 22 among those born from 1933 to 1938. In addition, the proportion remaining single at age 50 also dropped to under 5% of those born during the 1930s.

Those born in the 1940s also showed a strong tendency to marry. As of 1988, only 5% of those born from 1939 to 1943 had not married by age 45 and only 8% of those born from 1944 to 1948 had not married by age 40.

Since 1973, marriage is less common and occurs later in life It was not until 1973 that marriage rates among single people began dropping significantly and uninterruptedly, reaching levels in the 1980s and 1990s comparable with those at the height of the Great Depression. This decline led to a corresponding increase in

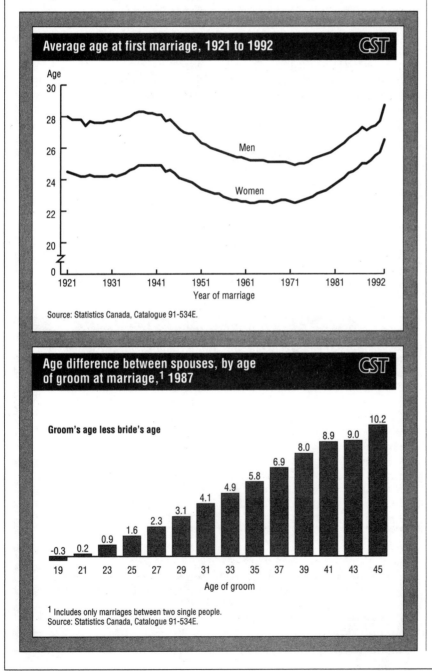

Average age at first marriage, 1921 to 1992

Age

Men

Women

Year of marriage

Source: Statistics Canada, Catalogue 91-534E.

Age difference between spouses, by age of groom at marriage,[1] 1987

Groom's age less bride's age

Age of groom	Groom's age less bride's age
19	-0.3
21	0.2
23	0.9
25	1.6
27	2.3
29	3.1
31	4.1
33	4.9
35	5.8
37	6.9
39	8.0
41	8.9
43	9.0
45	10.2

[1] Includes only marriages between two single people.
Source: Statistics Canada, Catalogue 91-534E.

the proportion of young singles, which also reached or surpassed 1930s' levels.

Today, first marriages are not only less prevalent, they are also taking place later. By 1992, the average age at first marriage was 29 for men and 27 for women. This is an increase, for both genders, of three years since 1989 and four years since 1980. In contrast, during the 1960s and most of the 1970s, the average age at first marriage remained stable at 25 for men and 23 for women.

Following the propensity to marry observed in 1990, only 631 of every 1,000 men and 674 of every 1,000 women in Canada are expected to marry at least once before age 50. In contrast, from 1939 to 1972, total first marriage rates remained above 900 of every 1,000 men and women. Since the early 1970s, however, total marriage rates declined below 900 per 1,000, falling steadily to under 700 per 1,000 by 1980. This was the first time since the Great Depression that marriage rates were this low.

The total marriage rate in 1990 varied across Canada, particularly between Ontario and Quebec. Ontario appears to be a more traditional society with the highest total marriage rates of all provinces and territories. In 1990, 725 of every 1,000 men and 769 of every 1,000 women in Ontario were expected to marry at least once before age 50. In contrast, total marriage rates in Quebec, 438 per 1,000 men and 481 per 1,000 women, were the lowest in Canada with the exception of the Northwest Territories. In the Northwest Territories, where there is a large Aboriginal population among whom legal unions have always been less common, only 363 per 1,000 men and 372 per 1,000 women in 1990 were expected to marry at least once before age 50.

Divorce laws liberalized in 1968 Legal separation and annulment are integrated into Canadian civil laws and for centuries have been accepted by Christian churches, including the Roman Catholic Church. Until the 20th century, these were the only two recourses available to married couples in most provinces. Provincial courts have been empowered to grant divorce only since 1930 in Ontario, since 1945 in Prince Edward Island and since 1968 in Quebec and Newfoundland. Before then, it was possible to submit requests for divorce to

the federal parliament, but such requests were few. Existing laws were very restrictive and, generally, divorce was only granted with proof of adultery.

It was only after the 1968 *Divorce Act* that divorce became truly accessible in all provinces. This Act was innovative because it recognized lasting separation as sufficient grounds for divorce. The Act required that when a divorce was requested, an abandoned spouse must have been separated for three years and a departing spouse, for five years.

Couples already separated at the time of the Act were the first to benefit from this provision. Thus, these couples accounted for a more than doubling of divorces between 1968 (11,300) and 1970 (29,800). The first divorces under these new grounds were not granted until July 1971. After that, the number of divorces rose from 32,400 in 1972 to 54,200 in 1976.

A new *Divorce Act* that came into effect in the spring of 1986 resulted in an increase in divorces in 1986 and 1987. This Act reduced the minimum separation time to one year until a divorce could be granted. A decrease in divorces in 1984 and 1985 suggests that some couples, anticipating new legislation, postponed their divorce requests until after the Act came into effect. The number of divorces in the late 1980s peaked at 90,900 in 1987 before falling to 78,200 in 1990.

Marriages can be legally dissolved by either the death of a spouse, a divorce or an annulment. Since 1980, the proportion of legal marriages dissolved by divorce has risen dramatically and, as a result, divorce is rapidly becoming nearly as important a factor in marital dissolutions as the death of a spouse. While divorce accounted for only 2% of marriage dissolutions between the two world wars, it represented 9% to 12% of dissolutions during the 1950s and 1960s. Its share climbed to 28% in the early 1970s and reached 42% in 1990.

Rising divorce rates lead to an increase in remarriage Since the late 1960s, divorce has become more common and divorce rates have risen substantially. According to the 1990 total divorce rate, 3,800 of every 10,000 marriages would end in divorce before 25 years, an increase of almost three times since 1969 (1,400 per 10,000). Consequently, the annual number of people becoming eligible for remarriage has grown considerably, since each divorce adds two new people to the marriage pool, whereas the death of a spouse adds only one.

Unlike most widowed people, many re-entering the marriage pool after divorce are still at an age when the likelihood of finding a new partner is high. This continuous influx of many young marriageable

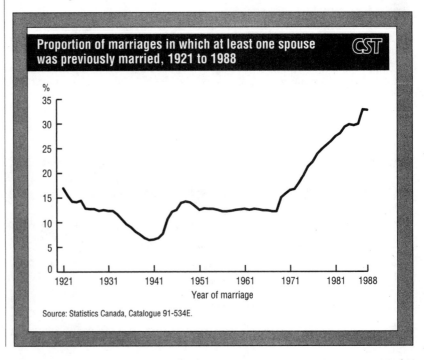

Proportion of marriages in which at least one spouse was previously married, 1921 to 1988 CST

Year of marriage

Source: Statistics Canada, Catalogue 91-534E.

UNIT 2: WOMEN, MARRIAGE AND THE FAMILY

people has triggered a steep annual increase in remarriages since the 1960s. Over the same period, first marriages between single people have fallen sharply. This is partly because of an increase in the number of single people marrying divorced people and also because many single people are living common law.

Up to 1968, over 90% of both men and women who married were single before their marriage and the proportion who were divorced was less than 5%. Since then, the proportion of newly-married people who were single before their marriage has continued to decline for both genders. By 1988, about 75% of men and women were single before their marriage, while about 20% were divorced. Combining people who had been widowed as well as those who were divorced, one-third of all marriages in 1988 included at least one spouse who was remarrying.

Early marriages most unstable

Marriages among teenagers are the most likely to result in divorce. From 1976 to 1987, the annual divorce rate for every 10,000 first marriages of men who were aged 15-19 at the time of their marriage was more than 5,000 every year except 1985 when it was 4,700.[2] Similarly, over that period, the divorce rate for every 10,000 women who married when they were aged 15-19 was more than 4,000 each year. In contrast, divorce rates among those aged 25 and older at the time of their first marriage were much lower. From 1976 to 1987, the annual number of divorces for 10,000 first marriages of people aged 25 and over at the time of their marriage was fewer than 4,000 among men and fewer than 3,500 among women each year.

Marriages of divorced women tend to be more unstable than those of single people or divorced men. This may be because divorced women often have custody of children from their previous marriages. In 1985, there were 1,600 divorces for every 10,000 marriages between a divorced woman and a single man, and 1,500 divorces for every 10,000 marriages between a divorced woman and a divorced man. In contrast, there were 1,300 divorces for every 10,000 marriages between a divorced man and a single woman, the same rate as that for marriages between two single people.

Cohabitation before marriage For three centuries, Canadians considered marriage necessary for establishing a conjugal relationship and, accordingly, people's first marriage coincided with the beginning of their first union. However, with each new generation born since World War II, marriage has become a less and less common part of early conjugal life.

According to the 1990 General Social Survey (GSS), people born just before or during World War II were the last to almost exclusively marry before living together as a couple. Among people aged 45-54 in 1990, only 5% of men and 2% of women had lived common law before marriage or before age 30. Following them, those born from 1946 to 1955, the first members of the baby boom, reached marriageable age at the same time that modern contraceptive methods became widely available. Among this group, 19% of men and 16% of women had lived common law before marriage or before age 30. Subsequent generations have been involved in common-law unions in greater numbers. Among those born from 1956 to 1960, 40% of men and 36% of women had lived common law before marriage or before age 30. Even higher proportions are expected for those born

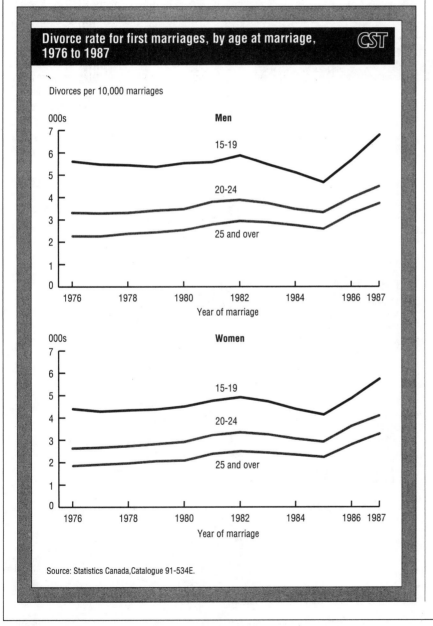

Divorce rate for first marriages, by age at marriage, 1976 to 1987 CST

Divorces per 10,000 marriages

000s — Men

15-19
20-24
25 and over

1976 1978 1980 1982 1984 1986 1987
Year of marriage

000s — Women

15-19
20-24
25 and over

1976 1978 1980 1982 1984 1986 1987
Year of marriage

Source: Statistics Canada, Catalogue 91-534E.

during the 1960s, many of whom are choosing common-law unions over marriage in early conjugal life.

According to the 1990 GSS, common-law unions were often a prelude to marriage. Slightly more than half of common-law unions formed during the 1970s resulted in marriages between the same partners. Of unions formed during the first half of the 1980s, more than 40% had been legalized at the time of the survey (42% among men and 46% among women). Presumably, for many couples, marriage is often already planned or expected when the union begins.

Most who reported that their first union was by common law were no longer living common law in 1990, but had married either their common-law partner or another person. This was true for 75% of those who began a common-law union during the 1970s. For those who entered a common-law union during the first half of the 1980s, the proportion who were married by the time of the survey was lower (51% of men and 59% of women), but could increase with time.

In addition, most first common-law unions had led quite rapidly to either marriage or separation. Among those who entered their first union between 1980 and 1984, only 16% of men and 12% of women were still living common law with their first partner in 1990. The corresponding proportions were even lower among first unions formed before 1980.

Future trends uncertain Following three centuries of relative stability, the institution of marriage has been in turmoil since the 1970s and the future of the institution is unclear. Marriage has become less of a prerequisite for a couple to live together and has tended to vanish from early conjugal life. Marriage also seems increasingly fragile, as marriage breakdown occurs more frequently and with increasing ease. Nevertheless, it appears that most singles who live common law eventually marry and many divorced people remarry.

Increasing marital instability combined with decreasing fertility affects society in several ways. More and more adults alternate between conjugal and solo-living periods, and there are fewer children. Private pacts between partners – common-law unions – whose terms can be questioned at any time by either partner without any social sanction, increasingly are being favoured over marriages. In addition, more and more children are being born into common-law families and as a result, divorce indices increasingly underestimate union breakdown and the formation of lone-parent families.

[2] The annual divorce rate includes all divorces from marriages lasting up to 25 years (90% of all divorces).

Jillian Oderkirk is an Editor with *Canadian Social Trends*.

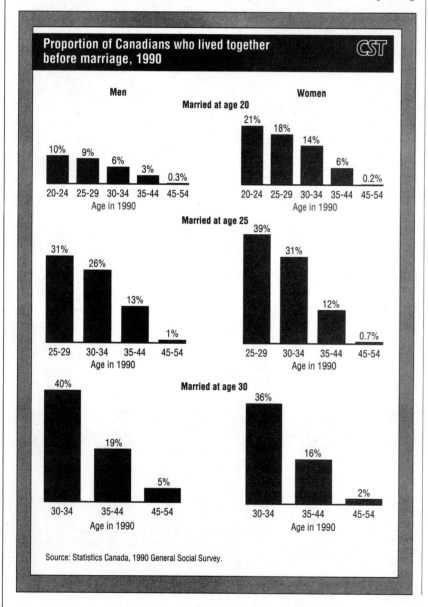

Proportion of Canadians who lived together before marriage, 1990

Source: Statistics Canada, 1990 General Social Survey.

1994 International Year of the Family
Année internationale de la famille

Canadian Attitudes to Divorce

by Judith A. Frederick and Jason Hamel

"Oh, life is a glorious cycle of song, A medley of extemporanea; And love is a thing that can never go wrong; And I am Marie of Roumania."[1]

Over the past thirty years, Canada has undergone major demographic and socio-economic changes that have radically altered family life. In the past, if a man and woman wanted to live together, they got married and expected the marriage to blossom with the arrival of children. But the advent of reproductive freedom has changed women's lives dramatically and conjugal life has become more complicated. With the ability to control their fertility, women became better-educated, entered the labour force in droves and began to earn their own income. Women's increased independence has allowed marital partners greater freedom to dissolve an unhappy relationship. Responding to changing social realities, divorce laws eased and the divorce rate doubled in 25 years. In the 1990s, the social stigma surrounding divorce has virtually disappeared.[2]

Despite the prevalence of divorce, little is known about why some marriages succeed and others fail. But research has found that attitudes are among the strongest predictors of divorce.[3] Exploring the factors that influence attitudes may help us better understand our increasingly complex conjugal lives. This article examines a number of socio-demographic characteristics that affect Canadians' beliefs about the conditions that justify breaking up a marriage.

[1] Dorothy Parker, *The Quotable Woman*, Running Press Book Publishers, 1991, p.41.
[2] In this article, divorce includes the dissolution of both cohabiting and legally married couples.
[3] Don Swenson, "A Logit Model of the Probability of Divorce," *Journal of Divorce and Remarriage*, Vol. 25 (1/2), 1996, p.173.

Most Canadians agree abusive behaviour, infidelity and disrespect justify divorce There was nearly unanimous agreement among Canadians aged 15 and over (95%) that abusive behaviour from a partner is sufficient reason to leave a marriage. Almost nine in ten also believed that an unfaithful partner or lack of love and respect are sufficient reasons to break up. All three generations — Elders, Boomers and Gen-Xers — expressed similarly strong opinions on these issues. Less solid support was apparent about a partner who drinks too much, but nearly three-quarters believed it is sufficient grounds for divorce. These four reasons constitute the fundamental beliefs that Canadians of each generation share

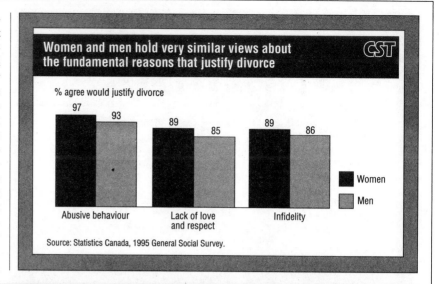

Women and men hold very similar views about the fundamental reasons that justify divorce

% agree would justify divorce

Source: Statistics Canada, 1995 General Social Survey.

CANADIAN SOCIAL TRENDS BACKGROUNDER

Data source and limitations

The 1995 General Social Survey (GSS) on family and social support collected data from nearly 11,000 Canadians aged 15 and over living in the ten provinces, excluding full-time residents of institutions. In addition to gathering a wide array of information about the respondent's family and marital history, the survey explored attitudes towards several family-oriented issues. One of the issues was marital dissolution; specifically, respondents were asked "... if you think the following reasons are sufficient for splitting up a marriage or common-law relationship."

The ten reasons presented fell into three general categories: fundamental issues such as abusive or disrespectful behaviour of a partner; experiential issues such as conflict over money, households chores and raising the children; and fertility issues such as inability to have children or to agree on the number of children to have. In a more personal vein, respondents were also asked if they themselves would stay in a union for the sake of their children.[1] The responses offer insight into the issues Canadians agree are justifiable grounds for divorce and those that are more contentious.

Methodology Certain variables can interact together and influence the results of the analysis. For example, since 57% of Canadians in their first common-law union are Gen-Xers, the attitudes they express may stem from their age rather than their marital history; the same could be said of people in their first marriage, almost 91% of whom are Boomers and Elders. To control for some of these interaction effects, a statistical technique called multiple classification analysis (MCA) has been applied to the data, so that the results presented in

this article show the effect of only the one variable, while holding other factors such as religiosity, province of residence and country of birth constant. For example, the first table in this article shows the effect of generation on opinions about divorce, holding constant marital history and other factors, while the second table shows the effect of marital history, holding constant generation and other factors. (Several other variables that did not significantly affect the results — e.g. number of children, education and labour force status — were excluded from the model.)

The generation gap This article adopts Michael Adams's definition of "generations" or age groups.[2] Adams divides the Canadian population into three categories: Elders (born before 1946), Boomers (born between 1946 and 1965) and Gen-Xers (born after 1965). Adams suggests that three factors largely determined the values of the Elders — gender, age and income — and notes that their society was fairly static and supportive of well-established institutions like marriage. The Boomers — more affluent, educated, traveled and informed — used their position in society to challenge these institutions and the values they represented. Meanwhile, the Gen-Xers — less affluent than their parents but with broader and more multidimensional horizons — consider these institutions and values less relevant than the two earlier generations.

[1] The 1995 GSS also asked respondents whether their own relationship was very happy, fairly happy or not too happy. Fewer than 2% reported that they were "not too happy." While social pressure may inhibit some respondents from reporting an unhappy union, it could be that many unhappy unions have already been dissolved.

[2] Adams, Michael, *Sex in the Snow: Canadian Social Values at the End of the Millennium*, Penguin Canada, 1997.

Elders more likely than younger Canadians to agree with more reasons to divorce

	Gen-Xers 15 - 29	Boomers 30 - 49	Elders 50 and over	Total
	% of population aged 15 and over			
Fundamental issues				
Abusive behaviour from the partner	95	95	94	95
Unfaithful behaviour from the partner	89	85	89	88
Lack of love and respect from the partner	86	87	87	88
Partner drinks too much	68	73	80	74
Experiential issues				
Constant disagreement about how the family finances should be handled	28	40	49	40
Unsatisfactory sexual relationship with the partner	21	37	45	35
Unsatisfactory division of household tasks with the partner	12	16	21	17
Conflict about how the children are raised	14	17	21	17
Fertility issues				
Inability to have children with the partner	8	12	17	13
Disagreement about the number of children to have	3	6	11	7
Would stay for the children	44	39	52	43

Source: Statistics Canada, 1995 General Social Survey.

Men are less likely to tolerate an unsatisfactory sexual relationship

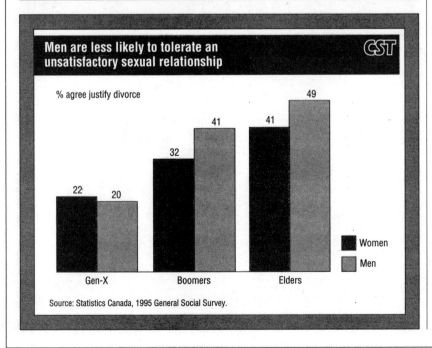

% agree justify divorce

Source: Statistics Canada, 1995 General Social Survey.

about grounds for divorce, and a strong positive correlation exists among them.

Younger adults less likely to agree experiential issues are valid reasons to split The real differences among the generations emerge with respect to experiential issues — that is, dealing with finances, sexual relationships, household chores and raising children. It appears that the more experience Canadians have dealing with these aspects of marital life, the less tolerant they become. Experiential issues were more often seen as grounds for divorce by Elders (61%) than either Boomers (55%) or Gen-Xers (49%).

About 40% of all Canadians aged 15 and over believed that constant disagreement about handling the family's finances is sufficient grounds for divorce, but very different results were observed among the generations. About one-third of Gen-Xers held that continual squabbling over money justifies divorce, while nearly half of Elders did. Perhaps with their greater likelihood of being a one-income family, Elders have stronger views about allocating the family's money. Women's and men's attitudes toward disagreements about money were quite similar.

Gen-Xers were also only half as likely as Elders to consider an unsatisfactory sex life sufficient reason to split up. This may reflect younger Canadians' relative lack of experience with the kind of problems that can develop in a sexual relationship over time. Men were more likely to agree that this issue justified leaving a marriage, especially in the older generations. Interestingly, responses to this question are highly correlated with the question about conflict over division of household labour.[4]

Few adults (17%) considered an unsatisfactory division of household tasks a valid reason for marital dissolution, but the level of agreement rose with each generation and Elders were almost twice as likely as Gen-Xers to concur. It was men rather than women (19% versus 14%) who most frequently agreed that this type of conflict justifies divorce; one might expect sharing housework to be a bigger issue among women, since they still retain primary responsibility for the household even when they are employed outside the home.[5]

Only a small minority of Canadians (17%) considered conflict over raising children valid grounds for leaving a partner. But as with the other experiential issues, Elders were most likely to agree that arguing about the children was sufficient reason for divorce.

Fertility issues not likely to justify marriage break-up... Fewer people think that divorce is justified by infertility or the number of children to have than by conflict over the way the children are being raised. Only 13% of adults believed that inability to have children was a valid reason to end a marriage, while conflict

[4] Arlie Hochschild has noted that unresolved conflict over the sharing of household chores can lead to resentment in the bedroom; the 1995 GSS findings tend to support her theory. *The Second Shift*. New York: Viking (1989)

[5] Judith A. Frederick, *As Time Goes By: Time Use of Canadians*, Statistics Canada, Catalogue no. 89-544-XPE.

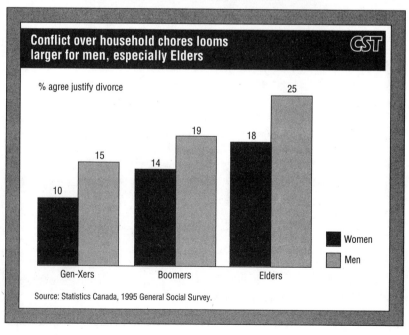

Conflict over household chores looms larger for men, especially Elders

CST

% agree justify divorce

	Gen-Xers	Boomers	Elders
Women	10	14	18
Men	15	19	25

Source: Statistics Canada, 1995 General Social Survey.

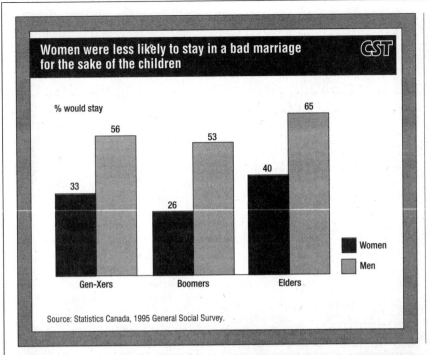

Women were less likely to stay in a bad marriage for the sake of the children

CST

% would stay

	Women	Men
Gen-Xers	33	56
Boomers	26	53
Elders	40	65

Source: Statistics Canada, 1995 General Social Survey.

about the number of children to have won even less support (7%). There was no significant difference between women's and men's opinions. Nonetheless, a substantial difference is evident between generations: Elders were more than twice as likely as Gen-Xers to concur that conflict over fertility issues is grounds for divorce.

... but majority would not stay married for the kids' sake The majority of Canadians would not stay in a bad marriage for the sake of their children. About 40% of adults said they would remain; Boomers, who are currently most likely to be faced with this issue, would be least likely to stay. Also, women were less inclined than men to want to hold the family together simply for the children's sake, with fewer than one-third of women reporting they would stay, compared with nearly 60% of the men.

Percent of population aged 15 and over who agree ... is sufficient reason to split up a marriage or common-law relationship, by marital history

CST

	Total	Common-law		Married		Previously married		Single
		First	Second or subsequent	First	Second or subsequent	Wid-owed	Divorced/ separated	
Fundamental issues				% of population aged 15 and over				
Abusive behaviour from the partner	95	95	94	94	99	92	95	96
Unfaithful behaviour from the partner	88	91	86	86	89	83	87	90
Lack of love and respect from the partner	88	87	86	86	88	83	88	91
Partner drinks too much	74	76	79	71	81	72	77	77
Experiential issues								
Constant disagreement about how the family finances are handled	40	44	43	37	41	36	45	43
Unsatisfactory sexual relationship with the partner	35	44	36	33	32	32	38	39
Unsatisfactory division of household tasks with the partner	17	25	18	14	15	12	18	21
Conflict about how the children are raised	17	23	21	14	18	14	25	20
Fertility issues								
Inability to have children with the partner	13	17	13	11	11	16	14	14
Disagreement about the number of children to have	7	11	7	6	8	6	7	9
Would stay for the children	43	36	33	49	30	57	33	42

Note: A second or subsequent common-law union refers to individuals who had a previous relationship, either cohabitation or a legal marriage. A second or subsequent marriage refers to individuals who have been married before. If individuals living in a common-law union then married, they are included in the first marriage category.
Source: Statistics Canada, 1995 General Social Survey.

Marital history colours attitudes to divorce Of course, marital history also plays an important role in Canadians' views about divorce. People who have remained in their first marriage take a less liberal view than those who have not. Thus, Canadians in their first marriage (49% of adults in 1995) as well as widows and widowers (6%) were least likely to agree that any of the issues described justify breaking up a marriage. In contrast, individuals who are currently divorced or separated (7% of all adults), in a common-law union or a second marriage (14%) generally found divorce more acceptable.

Most probably reflecting their own experiences, separated or divorced people agreed more frequently than any other marital group that most issues are valid grounds for divorce. On the other hand, individuals in their first marriage, as well as the widowed, held much less liberal views about divorce. But although the married and the widowed expressed similar opinions about fundamental and experiential issues, widows and widowers were more likely than married Canadians to believe that infertility is grounds for divorce. The importance that the widowed placed on children is reflected in the fact that they believed most strongly that partners should stay in an unhappy marriage for the sake of the children.

A relatively high proportion of individuals in their first common-law union also considered infertility a valid reason to separate, but they were also sympathetic to conflict over sharing chores and an unsatisfactory sexual relationship. The attitudes of cohabitants were tangibly less traditional than those of married couples.

Singles held some of the most liberal views of divorce for fundamental reasons, but were more likely than other marital groups to view experiential issues or infertility as valid grounds for divorce. They appear to have a more idealized view of a relationship than others with more experience in living together.

Summary Almost all Canadians say they believe one should not tolerate an abusive or disrespectful partner; over one-third think constant arguments about money or an unsatisfactory sex life are grounds for divorce; less than one-fifth think conflict over raising the children, sharing household tasks or disagreements over fertility issues justify leaving a marriage. However, less than half of Canadians would stay in an unhappy relationship because of their children.

Without longitudinal studies, it is not possible to speak with authority about the extent to which values and attitudes toward divorce have been changing in recent years.

But the findings from the 1995 GSS may help to explain why the risk of divorce has increased while the characteristics of those most at risk have not changed significantly. Both age and experience appear to shape attitudes to divorce: people over 50 are much less tolerant of problems with a partner than Canadians under 30, and people in their second marriage accept a wider variety of reasons to dissolve a relationship than people in their first.

Judith A. Frederick is a senior analyst and **Jason Hamel** was a co-op student with Housing, Family and Social Statistics Division, Statistics Canada.

CANADIAN SOCIAL TRENDS BACKGROUNDER

Divorce in the 1990s

Between 1971 and 1982, the annual divorce rate in Canada more than doubled, from 135 to 280 divorces per 100,000 population. For the next three years, divorce rates declined; then, following passage of the Divorce Act of 1985, divorce rates increased dramatically, peaking in 1987 at 362 divorces per 100,000 population. By about 1990, rates had leveled off, and rates have fluctuated relatively little since then.

However, a more precise way to examine the trend is to restrict the calculation to people who are eligible to divorce, that is, legally married couples. Viewed in this way, it can be seen that the marital divorce rate in 1995 (1,222 divorced per 100,000 legally married couples) was not much higher than in the early 1980s (1,180 in 1981). But while this 1.2% risk of divorcing in a given year is not very high, the risk of divorcing during the life of the marriage is much greater. For example, almost one in three couples (31%) who married in 1991 will eventually split up, if the 1991 divorce rates prevail.

The chance of divorcing increases rapidly during the first few years of marriage, peaking after five years and then declining gradually as the marriage continues. In light of this, it is not surprising that the divorce rate is highest for men and women in their twenties and early thirties, at about 2,000 divorced per 100,000 legally married couples per year. The divorce rate decreases with age after the mid-thirties, declining by age 75 to less than 85 divorced per 100,000 legally married couples. Men who divorce between the ages of 65 and 87 have been married an average of 27 years; women, 29 years. These averages, however, mask the fact that these seniors are most likely to have divorced either after a very long first marriage (of more than 40 years duration) or after a short second or subsequent marriage.

• For more information, see Jane F. Gentleman and Evelyn Park, "Divorce in the 1990s," *Health Reports*, Statistics Canada Catalogue 82-003-XPB, Vol. 9, no. 2.

Moving in *together:*

by Pierre Turcotte and Alain Bélanger

The formation of first common-law unions

The first conjugal union has a special meaning in one's life. The circumstances attending its creation are generally quite different from those leading to subsequent relationships, as it often coincides with the end of formal schooling, the start of one's working life or leaving the home where one grew up. But in Canada, as in a number of industrialized countries, domestic and family relationships have become much more diverse in the past 30 years. One aspect of this diversification is that new forms of families have appeared; among the main trends is a marked increase in the prevalence of common-law unions.

This study analyzes the influence of selected demographic and socioeconomic characteristics on the likelihood of establishing a common-law union as the first union. The results of the analysis do not differ greatly between men and women, so to avoid repetition, most of the discussion centres on the dynamics of union formation for women.

Majority of first unions are now common-law Nowadays, it appears that Canadian women prefer to live common-law in their first conjugal relationship. Over half (57%) of first conjugal unions formed between 1990 and 1995 were common-law. The proportion is much higher in Quebec, where 80% of all first unions formed during this period were common-law. This form of first union has more than tripled over the past two decades: only 17% of first unions formed in 1970-74 (21% in Quebec) were common-law. This remarkable growth leads us to examine the variety of factors that influence the formation of such unions.

Women in recent birth cohorts choose common-law for first union The probability of living in a first union outside marriage is significantly higher for women in more recent birth cohorts. For women born between 1971 and 1980 (i.e. aged 15 to 24 at the time of the survey), the likelihood of cohabiting was approximately 30% higher than for those born between 1961 and 1970 (aged 25 to 34 at the time of the survey). The probability declines for women born before 1961. Women in these older cohorts generally began their conjugal life before the mid-1970s, well before common-law unions became a widely accepted alternative to marriage.

Choosing a common-law union as the first union is more popular among francophones, regardless of their province of residence. The risk ratio for forming such a union is greater for women whose mother tongue is French, even if they live outside Quebec, than it is for women whose mother tongue is English or a language other than French.

Women who attend religious services every week are half as likely to experience a first common-law union as women who attend only occasionally, and native-born Canadian women are nearly twice as likely as immigrants to opt for a common-law relationship as their first form of conjugal union. The parents' marital history also exerts a major influence on the type of first union that women choose; if their parents' marriage had collapsed before they were 15 years old, women were 75% more likely to opt for a common-law union.

Women with children more likely to enter a first common-law union Women who have a child before entering their first conjugal union have a higher risk of forming a common-law relationship. This result differs from that obtained

CANADIAN SOCIAL TRENDS BACKGROUNDER

Analyzing the formation of first common-law unions

Most of the data that appear in this article are drawn from the 1995 General Social Survey (GSS). The 1995 GSS collected data from nearly 11,000 respondents aged 15 years and over living in private households in the ten provinces; almost 2,500 of these respondents (just under 1,000 in Quebec and about 1,500 elsewhere in Canada) reported that their very first conjugal union was a cohabitation outside marriage. Other data are drawn from the censuses of 1981, 1986 and 1991, which have collected information on the total number of persons who describe themselves as living in common-law unions.

Determining the risk factors The technique called "event history analysis" was used to analyze the 1995 GSS data. This technique combines two tools — life tables and regression analysis — and is ideal for analyzing data gathered by a retrospective survey such as the 1995 GSS, which collects information about life history from respondents. Using life tables in conjunction with regression analysis allows the researcher to measure the net effect of different factors on an individual's probability (or "risk") of experiencing an event. In this article, event history analysis is used to measure the likelihood that, given certain characteristics, Canadians will choose a common-law relationship as their first conjugal union.

The results of the event history analysis are presented in a table showing the risk ratios for a number of variables. Each variable used in the model includes a reference category (shown in parentheses); by definition, the risk ratio for this reference group is equal to 1. The ratios calculated for the other categories of a variable are interpreted in relation to the reference category. If the ratio for the non-reference group is more than 1, the risks of forming a first common-law union (compared with forming no union at all) are greater than for the reference group. Conversely, a ratio less than 1 indicates that the risks are lower for the non-reference group than for the reference group.

An increasing proportion of first unions are common-law unions

Period of formation	% of all first unions		
	Canada	Quebec	Other provinces
1970-74	17	21	15
1975-79	37	47	33
1980-84	41	64	33
1985-89	51	70	44
1990-95	57	80	50

Source : Statistics Canada, 1995 General Social Survey.

Age and employment status are important risk factors for women forming a first common-law union

	Characteristic (Reference variable in parentheses)	Relative risk (Reference ratio = 1)
Birth cohort	1971-1980	1.319
	(1961-1970)	1
	1951-1960	0.697
	Before 1951	0.130
Mother tongue and region of residence	(French, Quebec)	1
	French, other provinces	0.814
	Other languages, Quebec	0.590
	Other languages, other provinces	0.599
Religious practice	Never	1.423
	(A few times per month or year)	1
	At least once a week	0.523
Place of birth	(Canada)	1
	Abroad	0.512
Dissolution of parent's marriage	Yes	1.740
	(No)	1
Employment status	Employed	1.958
	(Not employed)	1
Educational level	Less than secondary diploma	0.932*
	(Secondary diploma/college)	1
	University	1.082*
Birth of first child	Before union	1.462
	(Not before union)	1

Note: Significant at the 0.05 threshold unless marked with an asterisk (*).
Source : Statistics Canada, 1995 General Social Survey.

Common-law unions: a growing phenomenon

Since the early 1980s, the number of persons living common-law has nearly tripled. By 1995, 2 million people (nearly 1 in 7 Canadian couples) were living common-law, compared with 700,000 (less than 1 in 16 couples) in 1981. Not only has the prevalence of common-law unions increased rapidly, but their rate of increase has also accelerated.

	% of couples living common-law		
	Canada	**Quebec**	**Other provinces**
1981	6	8	6
1986	8	13	7
1991	11	19	9
1995	14	25	11

Sources: Statistics Canada, 1981, 1986 and 1991 Censuses; 1995 General Social Survey.

in a study based on the 1984 Family History Survey, which found that out-of-wedlock births tended to lower the risk of entering a common-law union.[1] Other studies have also shown that the majority of single mothers ultimately marry, often within a few years of the child's birth. The 1995 GSS results seem to support recent research in the United States, which found that the probability of a first marriage declines if a child is born before the first union, but that the likelihood of a first common-law union increases.[2]

Being employed[3] increases the probability that a woman's first union will be common-law; in fact, women who had held a job were twice as likely as those not working outside the home to opt for a common-law union. This finding appears to indicate that women's participation in the labour market gives them a degree of financial autonomy that allows them greater flexibility in choosing their conjugal arrangement.

The likelihood of entering a common-law union does not vary significantly among women with different levels of educational attainment. Women with less than a secondary school diploma and those with university education showed approximately the same probability as those who had a secondary school diploma.[4] On the other hand, women who were presently enrolled in an educational program were 30% less likely to form first common-law unions than those who were not going to school. Similar findings have been obtained in the United States and Europe.[5]

Men's behaviour is similar to women's, with one exception In general, the demographic and socioeconomic factors that influence the formation of first common-law unions are no different for men than for women. That is, if a characteristic such as mother tongue increases the likelihood that women will experience a first common-law union, it also increases the likelihood for men. The magnitude of the effect is not always the same, but it is usually within the same range. However, while women's probability of living common-law increases from one birth cohort to the next, the same is not always true of men. For example, men born between 1971 and 1980 (aged 15 to 24 at the time of the survey) are not significantly more likely to opt for a common-law union than those born between 1961 and 1970 (aged 25 to 34).

[1] Desrosiers, Hélène and Céline Le Bourdais, "Les unions libres chez les femmes canadiennes: étude des processus de formation et de dissolution", *Population, reproduction, sociétés. Perspectives et enjeux de démographie sociale*, Montréal, Les Presses de l'Université de Montréal, 1993, pp. 197-214.

[2] Bennett, Neil G., David E. Bloom and Cynthia K. Miller, "The influence of Nonmarital Childbearing on the Formation of First Marriages", *Demography*, Vol. 32, No 1, 1995, pp. 47-62.

[3] "Employed" is defined as holding a job for more than six months.

[4] The approach used to estimate transition periods for education does not take account of the fact that some people temporarily interrupt their education.

[5] Blossfeld, Hans-Peter (editor). *The New Role of Women - Family Formation in Modern Societies*, Westview Press, Social Inequality Series, Boulder, 1995.

A few words about marriage The same techniques used to assess the risk factors associated with forming a first common-law union were also applied to first marriages. The analysis identified two major groups of characteristics: those that affect the likelihood of forming a conjugal union of either type, and those that influence the choice between marriage and a common-law union. For example, two factors that appear to have a strong influence on union formation are being employed and/or having a child. However, a woman's age and cultural characteristics seem to influence which type of union she chooses. Interestingly, the dissolution of her parents' marriage has no significant effect on the likelihood that a woman will marry, but it does have a significant impact on the probability that she will live in a common-law relationship.

Summary The proliferation of common-law unions is thought to be associated with many recent social changes that have influenced trends in family behaviours and attitudes. Several factors appear to underlie these changes, including the massive entry of women into the labour market (with the resulting increase in women's autonomy); the dissociation between sexuality and marriage and between fertility and marriage; the decline in religious practice; and the redefinition of the roles and expectations of spouses. The 1995 GSS does not address these issues directly, but it has identified several characteristics that have a significant effect on the probability that people will live common-law in their first conjugal relationship.

This article is an excerpt from "Dynamics of Common-law Unions in Canada," a Statistics Canada Research Paper, available on the Internet. The URL is http://www.statcan.ca/english/Vlib/other9.htm

Pierre Turcotte is a senior analyst with Housing, Family and Social Statistics Division and **Alain Bélanger** is a senior analyst with Demography Division, Statistics Canada.

Religious Observance

Marriage and Family

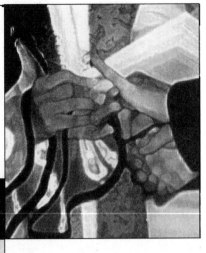

A person's behaviour may be greatly influenced by his or her religious convictions. Religious convictions may be displayed in different ways, such as attendance at religious services, prayer, meditation or reading of religious scriptures, all of which may be indicators of the importance of religion in a person's life. For many, regular attendance at religious services may be a reflection of a deep religious commitment and belief. Religious devotion, or the lack of it, has been associated with marital stability, family size, and premarital sex.

by Warren Clark

Religion can be viewed as a system of thought, feeling, and action shared by a group that gives members an object of devotion; a code of ethics governing personal and social conduct; and a frame of reference relating individuals to their group and the universe.[1] Most major religions teach compassion and helpfulness, and research has shown that religious attendance is associated with positive social behaviour.[2] Also, those who attend religious services more frequently are more likely to state that they have spiritual needs.[3] This may indicate that frequent attenders at religious services attach more importance to finding purpose and meaning in life than those who do not.

Using attendance at religious services as a proxy for religious conviction, this article examines the influence of religiosity on the attitudes of Canadians toward children, marriage and family relationships, and upon overall well-being, health and marital behaviour.

Religion plays an important role in the formation of attitudes to marriage and subsequent marital behaviour. For example, acceptance of biblical teachings about the sanctity of marriage and prohibitions against adultery may act as a barrier against divorce by reducing the likelihood of infidelity.[4] The 1995 General Social Survey (GSS) found that the most common reasons why someone might decide to pursue a divorce were abusive behaviour, unfaithfulness, lack of love and respect, and a partner who drinks too much.[5] While religious people were just as unwilling as those who never attended religious services to forgive a spouse's abusive or unfaithful behaviour, they were less likely to view lack of love and respect, and a partner's drinking too much as grounds for divorce. Religious couples were also more likely to state that they would stay married for the sake of their children.

Weekly attenders place more importance on home life The 1995 GSS asked Canadians to rate several areas of life in terms of their importance to the

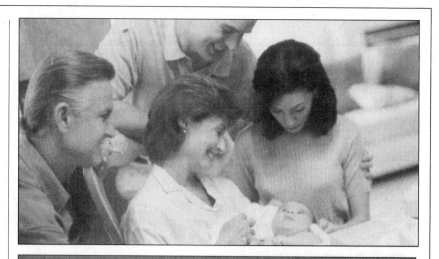

CANADIAN SOCIAL TRENDS BACKGROUNDER

What you should know about this study

Statistics Canada's General Social Survey (GSS) collects data from a sample of approximately 10,000 Canadians aged 15 and over living in private households in the ten provinces. Since 1985, two religion questions have been asked on each survey: one concerning religious affiliation, and the other, attendance at religious services or meetings. Religiosity (religious commitment), as measured by attendance at religious services, may vary substantially from time to time. This article relates attendance at religious services at the time respondents were interviewed; religious commitment at the time of an event (e.g., marriage breakdown) may have been quite different than it was at the time the respondent was interviewed.

Throughout this article, the terms "religious people" and "weekly attenders" are used to indicate adults who attend religious services every week.

Religious people more likely to want to keep the family together

Valid reasons for divorce	Attends religious services weekly	Never attends religious services
	%	
Abusive behaviour	92	96
Unfaithful behaviour	86*	88*
Lack of love and respect	76	92
Partner drinks too much	68	75
Would remain married for the sake of the children	57	36

* Difference not statistically significant.
Source: Statistics Canada, 1995 General Social Survey.

[1] The Concise Columbia Encyclopedia 1995.

[2] Beutel 1995, pp. 438-439.

[3] Bibby 1995, p.135.

[4] Call 1997, p. 383.

[5] Frederick 1998, pp. 7-8.

Religious people tend to place greater importance on marriage, family and children

	Average score	
	Attends religious services weekly	**Never attends religious services**
Importance to happiness of...	(0=not at all important, 3=very important)	
• a lasting relationship	2.60*	2.45*
• being married	2.35	1.80
• having at least one child	2.27	1.95
• being able to have a paying job	1.89	2.10
Agreement with following statement	(0=strongly disagree, 4=strongly agree)	
• Employed mothers can establish just as warm a relationship with their children as mothers who do not work for pay	2.26	2.54
• Keeping house is just as fulfilling as working for pay	2.60	2.28
• A job is alright but what women really want is a home and children	2.32	1.94
• A pre-school child is likely to suffer if both parents are employed	2.54	2.22
• Having a job is the best way for a woman to be an independent person	2.03	2.28
• If a man brings enough money home so his wife and children have a comfortable life, he has fulfilled his role as a husband and a parent	1.62	1.36
• A man should refuse a promotion at work if it means spending too little time with his family	2.24	2.01
• A woman should refuse a promotion at work if it means spending too little time with her family	2.30	2.05
• Both the man and woman should contribute to the household income	2.56*	2.73*
• Having a family is alright, but what most men really want is to be successful in their job	2.13*	2.09*
• A man does not have to be very involved in sharing the everyday tasks of raising children; this is not primarily a man's responsibility	0.91*	0.81*

* Difference not statistically significant.

Note: Some of the differences between weekly attenders and those who never attended during 1995 is accounted for by age differences between the two groups. Young people have different values than older people; also young people are less likely to attend religious services on a weekly basis. Even after accounting for age differences between the two groups, all differences remained statistically significant except for those marked.

Source: Statistics Canada, 1995 General Social Survey.

respondent's happiness. On a scale from 0 to 3, 0 indicated the issue was not at all important, while 3 meant it was very important to their happiness.

Weekly attenders of religious services — both men and women — placed greater importance on lasting relationships, being married, and having at least one child than those who did not attend. Regardless of how often men attended religious services, they placed almost equal importance on being able to have a paying job. In contrast, women who attended weekly services believed a paying job was less important (1.59) than women who never attended (1.93). These views were common to all weekly attenders, regardless of their age.

Individuals were also asked to rate their agreement with certain statements relating to attitudes toward work and family. The scale ranged from 0 (strongly disagree) to 4 (strongly agree).

Weekly attenders of both sexes agreed more strongly with statements supporting family and the nurturing role of women than those who never attended. "Keeping house is just as fulfilling as working for pay" was the statement with which weekly attenders agreed most strongly.

Although they showed less agreement with the statement that "a job is alright but what women really want is a home and children", their opinion on this statement contrasted more starkly with non-attenders than on any other issue.

On other issues, weekly attenders' and non-attenders' attitudes were very similar. In fact, there was no real difference in their belief that men and women should contribute to the household income and the statement that men should share in the raising of children.

Religious people feel better Studies have found links between religion and mental health suggesting that people who regularly attend religious services have a more optimistic view of life than those who never attend. According to these studies, religious people are less likely than others to become delinquent, to abuse drugs and alcohol, to divorce or be unhappily married, and to commit suicide. Religiously active people may even tend to be physically healthier and to live longer, in part because of their healthier smoking, eating, and drinking habits.[6]

The 1996 GSS echoes some of these earlier findings. After taking account of income, family structure, education, age, sex and employment status (all of which may contribute to a person's sense of well-being), the odds of feeling very satisfied with their lives were 1.7 times higher for weekly attenders than those who had not attended religious services during the last 12 months.

People attending religious services every week also felt they had less stress in their lives. According to the 1996 GSS, weekly attenders had about half the odds (0.6) of having a very stressful life as non-attenders after accounting for other socio-demographic factors. Young weekly attenders under age 35 also were more likely to feel they had very good or excellent health than non-attenders. Young adults' feelings of better health may be related to less smoking. In 1996, only 18% of weekly young attenders were cigarette smokers compared with 38% of those age 15 to 34 who never attended. Older adults felt the same about their health, regardless of how often they attended religious services.

Weekly attenders have happier, longer marriages Many things contribute to happy marital or common-law relationships. While religion may sometimes be a source of conflict in some relationships where partners differ strongly in their religious views, it seems that regular

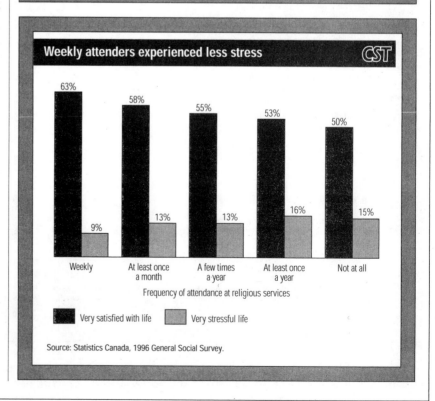

Decade when marriage began and attendance at religious services	Duration of first marriage		
	At least 5 years	At least 10 years	At least 15 years
	%		
Married in 1950s			
Weekly	99	98	96
Not at all	98	94	91
Married in 1960s			
Weekly	97	93	89
Not at all	92	83	73
Married in 1970s			
Weekly	95	89	84
Not at all	88	74	66
Married in 1980s			
Weekly	94	89	80
Not at all	85	69	57

Marriages of weekly attenders last longer

Source: Statistics Canada, 1995 General Social Survey.

Weekly attenders experienced less stress

Frequency of attendance at religious services

■ Very satisfied with life   ▪ Very stressful life

Weekly: 63% / 9%
At least once a month: 58% / 13%
A few times a year: 55% / 13%
At least once a year: 53% / 16%
Not at all: 50% / 15%

Source: Statistics Canada, 1996 General Social Survey.

[6] Myers 1995, p.16; Bradley 1995, pp. 259-267; Larson, 1994; National Institute for Healthcare Research, 1998.

attendance at religious services is related to stronger marriages. The odds of having a very happy marital relationship were 1.5 times greater for those attending religious services weekly than for those who didn't attend at all (after accounting for differences in age, education, income, religion, province, employment status and the decade when the marriage began). Interestingly, income appeared to have no influence on marital happiness, after the other factors were controlled for.

An earlier study based on the 1984 Canadian Fertility Survey found that women who attended church weekly were less likely to want to dissolve their marriage.[7] The 1995 GSS supported these findings, showing that compared with those who never attended religious services, the odds that a weekly attender's marriage would break down were less than half.[8] Marriage longevity of weekly attenders was greater than that of non-attenders regardless of which decade they were married. For example, 89% of the marriages of weekly attenders who were married in the 1970s lasted at least 10 years, compared with 74% of non-attenders' marriages.

Those who attended religious services each week were also less likely to have lived common-law prior to marriage (6%) than non-attenders (21%).

Summary Canada appears to be becoming increasingly secular as organized religion plays a less important role in Canadians' lives. The number of Canadians reporting no religious affiliation is increasing and attendance at religious services is declining. The long-term effect of these trends on the fabric of society is difficult to foresee.

CANADIAN SOCIAL TRENDS BACKGROUNDER

"No religion" continues to grow

At the time of the 1961 Census, less than 1% of Canadians claimed to have no religion. By 1991, this proportion had increased to almost 13%.[1] Between 1981 and 1991, the number of Canadians reporting no religious affiliation increased from 1.8 million to 3.4 million. While the 1996 Census did not have a question on religion, the 1996 General Social Survey revealed that 14% of Canadians aged 15 and over had no religious affiliation.

Historically, Canada has been predominantly Christian, with most of the population divided between Protestants and Catholics. In the last 10 years (1986 to 1996), Roman Catholics remained at about 45% of the Canadian adult population, but the share of mainline Protestant denominations (United, Anglican, Presbyterian, Lutheran) has dropped from 28% of the adult population to 20%. At the same time, the conservative Protestant denominations[2] have remained at 6% of the adult population, while Eastern non-Christian Religions (Islam, Hinduism and Buddhism and other smaller groups) have grown to represent almost 3%, reflecting the increased cultural diversity of Canada.

Attendance at religious services declines Since the mid-1940s, people have been attending religious services less and less. In 1946, the Gallup Poll reported that 67% of Canadian adults had attended religious services during the previous week. By 1996, the GSS reported that only 20% of adult Canadians had attended religious services every week.[3]

The greatest decline in weekly attendance has been among Roman Catholics, falling from 37% in 1986 to 24% in 1996. Corresponding to the decline in weekly attendance has been an increase in the number of people who did not attend religious services during the year. While in 1986 only one in seven Roman Catholics did not attend church, by 1996 nearly one in three did not. Over the same time period, weekly attendance of mainline Protestants has declined from 17% to 14% of adults,

while conservative Protestants have maintained weekly attendance figures in the 50% to 60% range.

Religious service attendance has declined across all age groups, indicating a broad disenchantment with institutionalized religion. Not surprisingly, seniors showed the most enthusiasm for religious services. In 1996, 34% of those aged 65 and over attended weekly, compared with only 12% of 15- to 24-year-olds.

In 1996, many adults (32%) who said they were affiliated with a religion did not attend religious services at all. Another significant minority (10%) said they only attended once or twice a year. This suggests either that people are less committed to their religion or that religion has become more a personal commitment than communal worship. In the United States, attendance made a comeback in the early 1970s and 1980s as the baby boomers began to form families. Weekly attendance rates remained almost constant at 30% from 1986 to 1993.

Although attendance at religious services has declined substantially in Canada over the last 20 years, in 1995, Reginald Bibby's Project Canada survey indicated that the vast majority (81%) of Canadians still believed in God. This compares with 89% in 1975, implying that although attendance has declined sharply, most people have retained their belief in God.[4]

[1] The 1961 Census asked "What is your religion?" but had no check-off category to indicate "no religion". Respondents wishing to indicate this had to write in "no religion" in the space provided. Since 1971, each decennial Census has had a mark-in response category for "no religion".

[2] Includes Baptist, Pentecostal, Nazarene, Evangelical Free, Mennonite, Salvation Army, Reformed, Christian and Missionary Alliance and other smaller groups. Mainline Protestant and Conservative Protestant are defined based on definitions used by Nock 1993, p.47,48,54 and Bibby 1987, p.28.

[3] The Gallup poll asked whether respondents had attended church services in the last 7 days; the GSS asks how frequently respondents have attended religious services in the last year. Since some people who attend infrequently may have actually attended last week, the Gallup Poll results may be somewhat inflated compared with the stricter GSS definition of religious observance.

[4] Bibby 1995, pp.130-131.

Attendance at religious services can influence attitudes, which in turn have an impact on behaviour. Weekly attenders tend to be more forgiving of marital problems and less likely to cite these problems as a valid reason for ending a relationship. Religious people also hold more traditional family values, placing greater importance on children and the family and on the nurturing role of women within the family. In addition, religious people tend to report having happier, less stressful lives and happier relationships with their partners.

[7] Balakrishnan, 1987, p. 396.

[8] After accounting for the effect of a variety of socio-demographic factors including decade when the marriage began, education, religion, pre-marital births, teenage pregnancy, province, age difference between spouses and whether a common-law union preceded marriage.

Warren Clark is an analyst with *Canadian Social Trends*.

References

Balakrishnan, T.R. and K Vaninadha Rao, Evel Lapierre-Adamcyk, Karol J. Krotki, "A hazard model a ysis of the covariates of marriage dissolution in Canac Demography, Vol. 24, No. 3, August 1987, pp. 395-40(

Beutel, Ann M. and Margaret Mooney Marini, "Gender values," American Sociological Review, Vol. 60, J 1995, pp. 436-448.

Bibby, Reginald W., "The Bibby Report-Social Tre Canadian Style," Toronto: Stoddart Books, 1995.

Bibby, Reginald W., "Fragmented Gods, The Poverty Potential of Religion in Canada," Toronto: Stodc Publishing Co. Ltd., 1987.

Bradley, Don E., "Religious involvement and so resources: Evidence from the data set America Changing Lives," Journal for the Scientific Study Religion, Vol. 34, No. 2, 1995, pp. 259-267.

Call, Vaughn R.A. and Tim B. Heaton, "Religious influe on marital stability," Journal for the Scientific Study Religion, Vol. 36, No. 3, 1997, pp. 382-392.

The Concise Columbia Encyclopedia, New York: Colum University Press, 1995.

Frederick, Judith A. and Jason Hamel, "Canadian attitu to divorce," Canadian Social Trends, Ottawa: Statis Canada, Spring 1998.

Larson, David B. and Susan Larson, "The Forgot Factor in Physical and Mental Health: What does research show," Washington, D.C., Rockville, N National Institute for Healthcare Research, 1994.

Myers, David G. and Ed Diener, "Who is Happ Psychological Science, Vol. 6, No. 1, January 19 pp.10-19.

National Institute for Healthcare Research, "Scient Research on Spirituality and Health: A consensus repc Rockville, MD: 1998.

Nock, David A., "The organization of religious life Canada," in The Sociology of religion — A Canac Focus, edited by W.E. Hewitt, Toronto: Butterwort 1993.

Eastern non-Christian religions and those reporting no religion have grown fastest

Religion	1986	1991	1996
	millions		
Roman Catholic	9.0	9.3	10.4
Mainline Protestant	5.6	5.0	4.8
Conservative Protestant	1.2	1.1	1.4
Other Protestant	0.7	0.7	1.2
Jewish	0.2	0.2	0.2
Eastern Orthodox	0.3	0.2	0.2
Eastern non-Christian religions	0.3	0.5	0.7
No religion	2.0	3.5	3.4
Not reported, don't know	0.4	0.5	1.2

Source: Statistics Canada, General Social Survey.

Attendance at religious services continues to decline

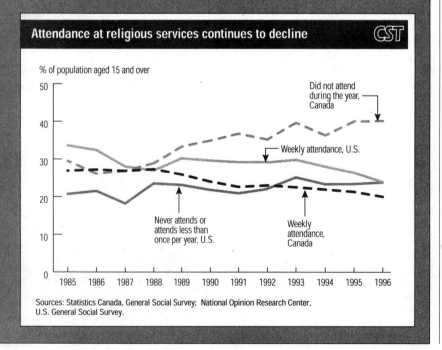

% of population aged 15 and over

Did not attend during the year, Canada

Weekly attendance, U.S.

Never attends or attends less than once per year, U.S.

Weekly attendance, Canada

Sources: Statistics Canada, General Social Survey; National Opinion Research Center, U.S. General Social Survey.

Births

Over the last thirty years, and particularly during the past decade, the proportion of births to unmarried mothers has increased dramatically. In addition, the circumstances surrounding these births has changed. Until recently, unmarried mothers tended to be young and unattached. Today, however, women having children outside of marriage are older and many are in common-law relationships.

outside marriage

A Growing Alternative

by Marilyn Belle and Kevin McQuillan

Growth in the proportion of births to unmarried women has varied across the country, resulting in large provincial differences. In Quebec, where the proportion of couples living common law is double that of other provinces, the proportion of births outside of marriage is the highest. On the other hand, in Ontario, where the proportion of common-law couples is relatively low, the proportion of births outside of marriage is the lowest. These large provincial variations result from emerging and long-standing differences in beliefs regarding the role of legal marriage in family formation.

Proportion of non-marital births now 6 times higher than in 1961 The proportion of births to unmarried mothers has been increasing almost continuously since 1921, when only 2% of all Canadian births were outside of marriage.[1] The rate increased slowly in the decades that followed, reaching almost 5% by the end of World War II. This upward trend was briefly reversed during the 1950s' baby boom when the percentage of non-marital births fell to 4% before returning to just under 5% in 1961.

Since 1961, however, there has been a much stronger upward trend in non-marital births. The proportion of births to unmarried women doubled between 1961 and 1971 to 9%, and then grew to 14% in 1981. Since then, rapid increases continued and by 1991, 27% of births occurred outside of marriage.

Such a large growth in the proportion of births to unmarried women during the

1980s is related to the emergence of common law as an alternative living arrangement for couples. According to the census, 11% of all Canadian couples were living common law in 1991, up from 6% in 1981. In addition, common-law couples account for an increasing proportion of all couples with children. By 1991, 8% of all couples with children were living common law, up from only 3% in 1981.

Non-marital fertility up since mid-1970s Although the proportion of births outside of marriage increased over the last three decades, factors influencing this trend changed. During the 1960s and early 1970s, decreases in the fertility rate of married women (births per 1,000 married women) and increases in the proportion of unmarried women of childbearing age were the major causes of this growth. It was not until the mid-1970s that a sharp rise in the fertility rate of unmarried women began to drive the increase in the proportion of births outside marriage. By 1991, the number of births for every 1,000 unmarried women had increased to 32 from 21 in 1981 and 18 in 1961.[2]

Age of unmarried mothers rising Both the circumstances surrounding a birth and the consequences for a mother and child are quite different for a teenaged mother living at home than for a woman in her early thirties in a cohabiting relationship. Three decades ago, giving birth outside of marriage was very much a young woman's experience. In 1961, 72% of non-marital births occurred to women under age 25. Today, however, almost half of births outside of marriage occur to mothers aged 25 and over. This reflects, in part, the declining proportion of married women aged 25-34 and the increasing likelihood that unmarried women this age – many of whom are in common-law unions – will bear a child.

Non-marital fertility rates for women aged 25 and over increased sharply in the 1980s, after having declined during the late 1960s and early 1970s. Among

[1] National data exclude Newfoundland.

[2] Prior to 1981, women in common-law unions were considered married when fertility rates were calculated; since 1981, they have been considered unmarried. Because the proportion of women living common law was very small until the 1980s, this change did not affect the overall trend.

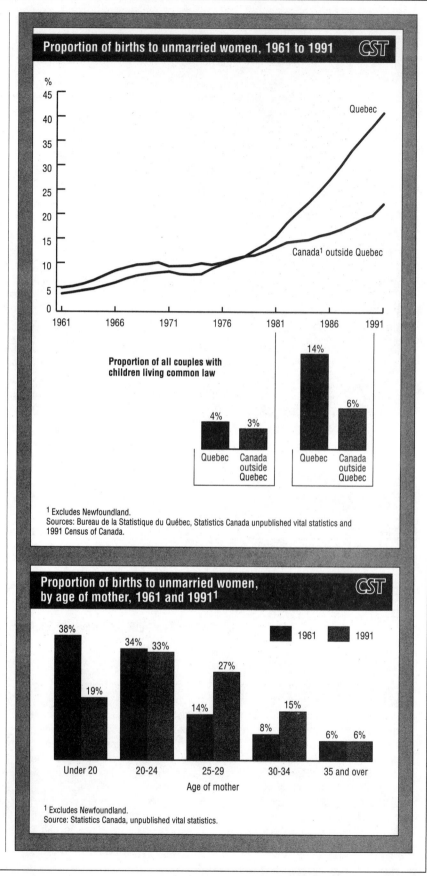

Proportion of births to unmarried women, 1961 to 1991 CST

Quebec

Canada[1] outside Quebec

Proportion of all couples with children living common law

4% Quebec
3% Canada outside Quebec

14% Quebec
6% Canada outside Quebec

[1] Excludes Newfoundland.
Sources: Bureau de la Statistique du Québec, Statistics Canada unpublished vital statistics and 1991 Census of Canada.

Proportion of births to unmarried women, by age of mother, 1961 and 1991[1] CST

1961   1991

Under 20: 38% / 19%
20-24: 34% / 33%
25-29: 14% / 27%
30-34: 8% / 15%
35 and over: 6% / 6%

Age of mother

[1] Excludes Newfoundland.
Source: Statistics Canada, unpublished vital statistics.

CANADIAN SOCIAL TRENDS BACKGROUNDER

Trends similar in other industrialized nations Canada is not the only industrialized nation to experience a major increase in non-marital childbearing. Sharp increases also occurred in the United States, France and the United Kingdom. In these three countries, around 10% of births in 1970 were to unmarried women. Like Canada, proportions in these countries rose slowly through the 1970s and more sharply during the 1980s. By 1989, the proportion of non-marital births in each of these countries was over 25%.

However, this pattern is not found in all industrialized societies. In Japan, for example, the proportion of births outside marriage has remained very low. In 1989, only 1% of Japanese births occurred to unmarried women, a proportion unchanged since 1970.

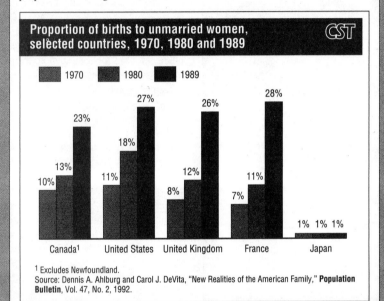

Proportion of births to unmarried women, selected countries, 1970, 1980 and 1989

1 Excludes Newfoundland.
Source: Dennis A. Ahlburg and Carol J. DeVita, "New Realities of the American Family," **Population Bulletin**, Vol. 47, No. 2, 1992.

Proportion of births to unmarried women, by birth order, 1990[1]

	1st child	2nd child	3rd child	4th child
		%		
Prince Edward Island	32	15	6	7
Nova Scotia	35	18	14	15
New Brunswick	36	17	13	12
Quebec	47	29	20	15
Ontario	21	10	8	10
Manitoba	33	20	19	26
Saskatchewan	37	19	20	25
Alberta	29	14	13	17
British Columbia	28	17	15	17

1 Comparable data for Newfoundland was unavailable.
Source: Statistics Canada, Catalogue 91-209E.

women aged 25-29, the non-marital fertility rate doubled to 50 per 1,000 in 1991 from 22 per 1,000 in 1976.

Similarly, among women aged 30-34, the non-marital fertility rate increased to 37 from 16 per 1,000. Among teens, on the other hand, non-marital fertility has been rising slowly but steadily since the early 1960s. In 1991, there were 24 births per 1,000 unmarried women aged 15-19, up from 17 per 1,000 in 1976.

Highest proportion of births outside marriage in Quebec Among the provinces, Quebec had the highest proportion of births to unmarried women in 1991 – 41%. In contrast, Ontario had the lowest proportion, with only 17% of births in 1991 occurring to unmarried women. Proportions in the remaining provinces ranged from 31% in Saskatchewan and 30% in New Brunswick to 24% in both Alberta and Prince Edward Island.

Unmarried women in Quebec were also more likely than those in all other provinces, except Saskatchewan, to have had a child in 1991. That year, 42 of every 1,000 unmarried women in Quebec had given birth. In Saskatchewan (46 per 1,000) and Manitoba (40 per 1,000), non-marital fertility rates were also very high. Unmarried women in Ontario, on the other hand, were the least likely to have given birth (22 per 1,000 unmarried women). In the remaining provinces, rates ranged from 29 to 34 for every 1,000 unmarried women.

Third and fourth births outside marriage more common in Quebec, Saskatchewan and Manitoba In 1990, 29% of women in Quebec having their second child were unmarried. In the other provinces, however, proportions were much lower, ranging from 20% in Manitoba to 10% in Ontario. Similarly, in 1990, 20% of Quebec women having their third child were unmarried. Again, proportions were much lower in the other provinces, with the exception of Manitoba and Saskatchewan. Proportions of women having their third child outside of marriage ranged from 20% in Saskatchewan and 19% in Manitoba to 8% in Ontario and 6% in Prince Edward Island.

Of the few women who had a fourth child, the proportion who were unmarried in 1990 was higher in all four

Western provinces than in Quebec and the other provinces. Among the Western provinces, proportions ranged from 26% in Manitoba to 17% in Alberta. Proportions in the remaining provinces ranged from 15% in Quebec and Nova Scotia to 7% in Prince Edward Island.

Non-marital fertility related to emergence of common-law unions During the 1980s, when the proportion of births outside of marriage doubled, the proportion of couples living common law also

rose sharply. In addition, as with growth in the proportion of non-marital births, increases in the prevalence of common-law unions were more dramatic in Quebec than in the other provinces.

By 1991, Quebec couples with children under age 18 were more than twice as likely to be living common law (14%) as those in all other provinces combined (6%). Also that year, the proportion of births outside of marriage in Quebec (41%) was almost double that of provinces outside of Quebec (22%). Such

large differences are a recent phenomenon, however, having emerged only in the last decade. In 1981, the proportion of couples with children living common law in Quebec (4%) was about equal to that in the other provinces (3%). Similarly, there was little difference between the proportion of births outside of marriage in Quebec (16%) and in the other provinces (13%).

Although vital statistics records contain only information on the legal marital status of mothers, some evidence of the growing proportion of births to common-law couples in Quebec is recorded on birth certificates. According to the Bureau de la Statistique du Québec, between 1976 and 1991, around 5% of all births were to unmarried women who listed the father as unknown. Over the same period, the proportion of all births that were to unmarried women who listed the father as known increased to 37% from 5%.

The fact that relatively high proportions of women are having more than one child outside of marriage in Manitoba and Saskatchewan is also likely related to common-law unions. Within these provinces, there are large communities of Aboriginal peoples, among whom unions outside of legal marriage have always been common.[3] However, the proportions of all couples living common law in Manitoba (9%) and Saskatchewan (8%) were less than the national proportion (11%) in 1991.

In Ontario, where the proportion of births to unmarried women is the lowest in the country, the proportion of couples living common law is also low. In 1991, 8% of couples in Ontario were living common law, up only slightly from 5% in 1981.

[3]Jean Dumas, **Report on the Demographic Situation in Canada, 1992**, Statistics Canada Catalogue 91-209E.

Marilyn Belle is a Lecturer and **Kevin McQuillan** is an Associate Professor of Sociology, both with the University of Western Ontario.

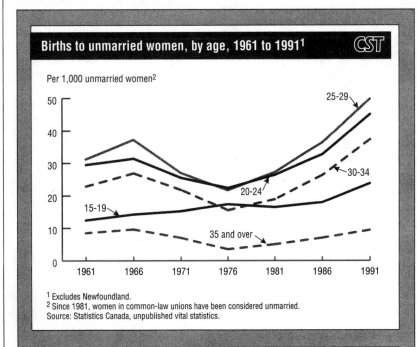

Births to unmarried women, by age, 1961 to 1991[1] CST

Per 1,000 unmarried women[2]

25-29
30-34
20-24
15-19
35 and over

[1] Excludes Newfoundland.
[2] Since 1981, women in common-law unions have been considered unmarried.
Source: Statistics Canada, unpublished vital statistics.

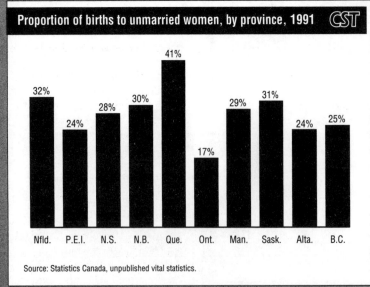

Proportion of births to unmarried women, by province, 1991 CST

Nfld.	P.E.I.	N.S.	N.B.	Que.	Ont.	Man.	Sask.	Alta.	B.C.
32%	24%	28%	30%	41%	17%	29%	31%	24%	25%

Source: Statistics Canada, unpublished vital statistics.

1994 International Year of the Family
Année internationale de la famille

UNIT 2: WOMEN, MARRIAGE AND THE FAMILY

Family Indicators For Canada

Statistics Canada collects a variety of information on Canadian families. Now you can find a selection of family indicators (including provincial indicators) on the World Wide Web, at http://www.statcan.ca/.

❑ A **census family** refers to a now-married couple or a couple living common law (with or without never-married sons and/or daughters of either or both spouses/partners), or a lone parent of any marital status, with at least one never-married son or daughter living in the same dwelling.

❑ An **economic family** refers to a group of two or more persons who are living together in the same dwelling, and who are related by blood, marriage (including common-law relationships) or adoption.

❑ A **private household** is made up of a person or a group of persons (other than foreign residents) who occupy a private dwelling and do not have a usual place of residence elsewhere in Canada.

TRENDS AND PROJECTIONS

| | Observed | | Projected[2] | |
	1981	1991[1]	2001[3]	2011[3]
Census families				
Number of census families	6,324,975	7,356,170	8,728,300	9,885,600
Decade change – %		16.3	18.7	13.3
Number of husband-wife families	5,610,970	6,401,455	7,474,600	8,389,700
Decade change – %		14.1	16.8	12.2
% of total census families	88.7	87.0	85.6	84.9
Number of lone-parent census families	714,010	954,705	1,253,700	1,495,900
Decade change – %		33.7	31.3	19.3
% of total census families	11.3	13.0	14.4	15.1
• Male lone parents	124,180	168,240	241,500	299,600
• Decade change – %		35.5	43.5	24.1
• % of all lone parents	17.4	17.6	19.3	20.0
• Female lone parents	589,830	786,470	1,012,200	1,196,300
• Decade change – %		33.3	28.7	18.2
• % of all lone parents	82.6	82.4	80.7	80.0
Households				
Number of households with one or more census families	6,231,490	7,235,230	8,475,300	9,592,600
Decade change – %		16.1	17.1	13.2
Number of households with no census family	2,050,045	2,783,035	3,749,300	4,579,500
Decade change – %		35.8	34.7	22.1
Persons living alone	1,681,130	2,297,060	2,950,100	3,559,800
Decade change – %		36.6	28.4	20.7
% of total households	20.3	22.9	24.1	25.1
Average household size	2.9	2.7	2.6	2.5

[1] For the first time, the 1991 Census included non-permanent residents in its population coverage. Users should take this into consideration when comparing data from 1991 with those from previous censuses.
[2] Series "B" projection. See **Projections of Households and Families for Canada, Provinces and Territories,** Statistics Canada, Catalogue no. 91-522-XPB.
[3] Data for 2001 and 2011 are adjusted for net census undercoverage, while the 1991 data are not. The percentage change for 1991-2001 is therefore overstated.
Source: Statistics Canada, Catalogue nos. 91-522-XPB, 92-904-XPB, 93-106-XPB, 93-311-XPB and 93-312-XPB.

ECONOMIC FAMILIES

% of economic families with both
    spouses employed in 1993   50.2

% of husband-wife economic families with
    both spouses employed in 1993   60.0

% of economic families with children under age 16 in
    which the female head or spouse was employed in 1994   61.4

% of economic families in 1994 with
    pre-school children (under age 6)   20.8

Unemployment rate in 1994   10.4
- Economic family members   10.1
- Unattached individuals
    (*living alone or not related to anyone in the dwelling*)   11.8

1994 economic family income
- Average $54,153
- Median (*half of families have incomes above
    and half below this amount*) $48,091

*Families who spent 60% or more of their total income on food,
shelter and clothing (significantly more than the 40% spent by the
average Canadian family) were considered to have low incomes.*

% of economic families with low income in 1994   13.5

% of children under age 18 living in low-income
    economic families in 1994   19.5

Source: Statistics Canada, Catalogue nos. 13-207-XPB, 13-215-XPB, 13-569-XPB
and 71-529-XPB.

CENSUS FAMILIES

	1981	1991
Number of census families	6,324,975	7,356,170
% of population in private dwellings living in census families	86.6	84.4
Average census family size	3.3	3.1
% of census families without children at home	31.8	35.1
% of census families headed by lone parents	11.3	13.0
% of census families that are common-law couples	5.6	9.9
% of census families that are empty-nest couples	17.2	20.8
Number of children (of any age) in census families	8,666,685	8,800,735
Average number of children per census family	1.4	1.2

Average time spent on unpaid work in 1992
by parents aged 25 to 44:
- Married fathers employed full time   3.2 hours/day
- Married mothers employed full time   4.8 hours/day
- Married mothers not employed   7.9 hours/day

Source: Statistics Canada, Catalogue nos. 89-544-XPB, 93-106-XPB, 93-312-XPB
and 93-320-XPB.

VITAL STATISTICS

	1981	1991
Live birth rate (per 1,000 population)	15.3	14.9
Average age of mother at first birth	24.8	26.5
Marriage rate (per 1,000 population)	7.8	6.4
Average age of women at first marriage	23.6	26.2
Average age of men at first marriage	25.7	28.2
Total marriages	190,082	172,251
Remarriages as a % of total marriages		
• Brides	17.9	22.6
• Grooms	20.0	23.4
Divorce rate (per 1,000 population)	2.8	2.7

Source: Statistics Canada, Catalogue nos. 82-553-XPB, 84-210-XPB, 84-212-XPB,
84-213-XPB, and unpublished data.

Canada's caregivers

by Kelly Cranswick

We live in a society in which social support networks are increasingly being put to the test. The number of seniors has more than doubled in the past 25 years, and most of them are living longer; for example, women born in 1941 can expect to live four years longer than those born in 1921. This growing population of older Canadians with greater life expectancy has increased the caregiving responsibilities of families, especially offspring. Recent changes in the health care system and social services have put further pressure on the caregiving capabilities of families; for instance, shorter hospital stays and greater use of outpatient treatment have increased the need for care at home. These new demands occur at a time when the majority of women — traditionally the primary caregivers — now participate in the labour force. As such, Canadians face the burden of multiple responsibilities to employers, their own spouse and children, and to parents, relatives or friends requiring care.

Many people provide care without any sense of obligation, while others may view it as a duty, as a sacrifice, or as a necessity if formal structures are no longer available. Regardless of the reasons for becoming a caregiver, the responsibility entails a significant commitment and can be intense and time-consuming. Caregiving tasks fall into two categories: "instrumental activities," such as preparing meals, doing housework, doing yard work or providing transportation; and "personal care" activities, such as bathing, dressing or toileting.[1] Meeting these demands often necessitates adjustments to the life of the caregiver, and may affect the time the caregiver spends with family and friends, personal time, or the priority given to paid employment and household responsibilities. This article looks at the unpaid, informal care being provided by Canadians to people with long-term health problems — that is, any condition or physical limitation lasting, or expected to last, more than six months. It focuses on who these caregivers are, and how well they are coping.

[1] A second type of care covered by the 1996 GSS is *caring about*. Caring about involves a psychological connection between people; for example, by providing emotional support, keeping someone's spirits up or giving reassurance and encouragement. Caring about can also include checking up on someone, either by visiting or telephoning, to ensure he or she is all right.

Defining care with the General Social Survey

This article uses data from the 1996 General Social Survey (GSS) on social and community support. Between February and December 1996, the survey interviewed almost 13,000 Canadians aged 15 and over living in private dwellings in the ten provinces. Data on caregiving refers to help provided by respondents in the 12 months preceding the survey interview. The GSS collected data on both formal and informal caregiving. Informal care is defined as the performance of tasks by family and friends, without pay, that helps maintain or enhance people's independence; since 86% of caregivers were providing informal care, it is the focus of this article.

Please note that this analysis of caregiving relationships does not take into account the amount of time spent providing care. Research using data collected by the 1996 GSS on the actual time devoted to caregiving will provide further insights into caregiving.

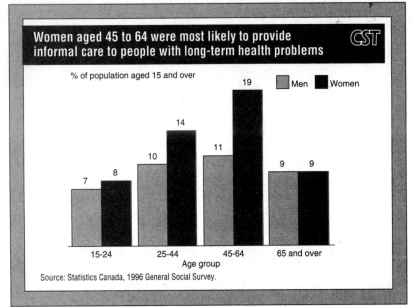

Women aged 45 to 64 were most likely to provide informal care to people with long-term health problems

% of population aged 15 and over

Source: Statistics Canada, 1996 General Social Survey.

Who are the caregivers? While much caregiving is still done by women, many men also provide help to people with long-term health problems — 10% of men compared with 14% of women. There is a concentration of caregivers in the 45 to 64 age group — 19% of women and 11% of men — which is to be expected, since the data indicate that many people of this age group were providing help to elderly parents. However, it should also be noted that a considerable proportion of seniors aged 65 and over provided care to their spouses, friends and neighbours.

Having paid work outside the home did not prevent people from providing support when the need was there, as 15% of employed women and 10% of employed men were caregivers. Among unemployed people, 16% of women and 12% of men combined their job search activities with caregiving duties. About 15% of women who worked in the home were also caregivers.

Having a family seemed to have little impact on caregiving. Sixteen percent of women living with their spouse and children were caregivers, as were 14% of those living with their spouse only. A somewhat smaller proportion of women living with their children only (12%) provided care to someone with a long-term health problem. Roughly one in ten men were caregivers, regardless of their living arrangements.

So who are the caregivers? No one specific "type" of person seems more likely than another to become one. It appears that people provide care when their help is required, regardless of the responsibilities they already shoulder. Most caregivers already have many obligations, with the majority being married with children and having work commitments outside the home.

Who are they helping? People caring for others with long-term health problems or physical limitations can be faced with widely differing sets of tasks depending on the situation. For example, the help needed by an elderly parent may be quite different than that required by a child with a developmental disability or by a terminally ill friend or relative. A caregiver may be called on to assist with instrumental tasks, such as cooking or cleaning, or with personal care, such as bathing or dressing.[2]

Almost half of assistance with instrumental activities was given to parents and parents-in-law (47%). About 24% of care involved help to friends,[3] 13% to members of the extended family and 5% to spouses. Close to two-thirds of the help with personal care was given to parents (46%) and spouses (16%); friends (13%) and children (5%) received less than one-fifth of personal care. This finding is not surprising due to the intimate nature of these tasks, and supports the view that family becomes more important than friends when help is needed for such personal activities as dressing and using the washroom.[4, 5]

[2] "Instrumental activities" is defined as help with at least one of the following activities: childcare; meal preparation and clean-up; house cleaning, laundry and sewing; house maintenance and outside work; shopping for groceries and other necessities; providing transportation; banking and bill-paying.

[3] "Friends" also includes neighbours, co-workers and ex-partners.

[4] Eric G. Moore, Mark W. Rosenberg et al., *Growing Old in Canada*. Statistics Canada, Catalogue no. 96-321-MPE, No. 1, 1997, p. 46.

[5] Leroy O. Stone, 1993. "Social consequences of population ageing: The human support systems dimension." *Proceedings of International Population conference.* Montreal; International Union for the Scientific Study of Population. 3: 25-34.

Most informal care to people with a long-term health problem was given to parents CST

% of care given (by relationship to caregiver)		
	Instrumental tasks	Personal care
Total	**100**	**100**
Spouse	5	16
Child[1]	3	5
Parent[1]	47	46
Sibling[1]	6	5
Extended family	13	11
Friend[2]	24	13
Other	1	--

-- Sample too small to be released.
[1] Also includes those related by marriage or adoption, eg. stepchild, mother-in-law, brother-in-law.
[2] Also includes neighbours, co-workers and ex-partners.
Source: Statistics Canada, 1996 General Social Survey.

Caregivers generally feel positive about their activities CST

	Never	Rarely/ Sometimes	Nearly always	Don't know/ Not stated	Total
			(%)		
How often do you feel ...					
you don't have enough time for yourself, because of the time you spend helping people?					
Women	55	31	12	--	100
Men	65	25	9	--	100
Total	59	29	11	1	100
others help you more often than you help them?					
Women	64	26	9	--	100
Men	63	29	6	--	100
Total	63	27	8	2	100
stressed between helping others and trying to meet other responsibilities for family or work?					
Women	41	40	18	--	100
Men	55	32	12	--	100
Total	46	36	15	2	100
by helping others, you simply give back what you have received from them?					
Women	21	27	50	3	100
Men	25	27	45	--	100
Total	22	27	48	3	100
angry when you are around the person(s) you are helping?					
Women	75	19	3	2	100
Men	82	14	--	--	100
Total	78	17	3	2	100
by helping people, you simply give back some of what life has given you?					
Women	15	22	60	3	100
Men	15	26	56	3	100
Total	15	24	58	3	100

-- Sample too small to be released.
Source: Statistics Canada, 1996 General Social Survey.

How do caregivers feel? Whether it is viewed as a completely voluntary activity, as one's duty, a sacrifice, or a necessity, some significant costs can be associated with caring for someone with a long-term health problem. These can include negative feelings the caregiver may harbour, disruptions to the caregiver's life or economic costs.

Respondents were asked a set of questions intended to assess how they felt about their caregiving responsibilities. When asked, 59% of caregivers said they rarely felt that helping others meant that they did not have time for themselves, and 11% said they nearly always felt that way. When the question focussed on the impact caregiving had on their families, almost half of caregivers (46%) rarely felt stressed about helping others while trying to meet family and work responsibilities, while 15% reported nearly always feeling that way. In both instances, women were more likely than men to feel pressed for time.

Some questions tapped the feelings caregivers had towards the person they were helping. The majority (64%) of caregivers nearly always felt that helping others strengthened their relationship with them; in contrast, 13% rarely felt that way. Most caregivers only rarely felt angry when they were around the person they were caring for and only 3% nearly always felt angry. While higher proportions of women than men felt anger, both women and men were equally likely to experience the positive feelings of a strengthened relationship. This finding may reflect the type of caregiving being performed by women; as the data suggest, they are doing the more demanding tasks such as personal care. However, when asked how often they wished someone else would take over their caregiving duties, 63 % of caregivers said they did so only rarely, and only 4% reported that they nearly always wished for such relief from their responsibilities.

Caregivers were also asked to state, overall, how great a burden it was to be caring for others. More than half (56%) did not feel at all weighed down by their duties, while about 5% felt "quite a bit" or "extremely" burdened. This response, in particular, suggests that caregivers not only give help, but do so willingly. Although a higher proportion of women than men felt burdened, on the whole differences between men and women were minimal.

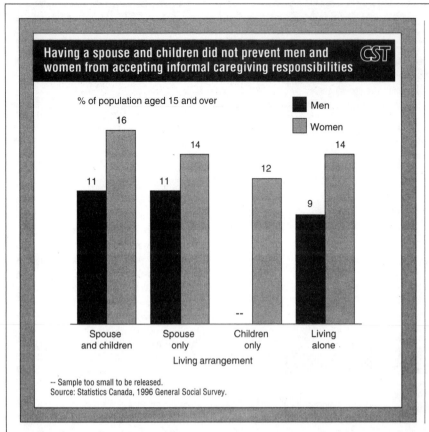

Having a spouse and children did not prevent men and women from accepting informal caregiving responsibilities

% of population aged 15 and over

■ Men
▨ Women

Living arrangement	Men	Women
Spouse and children	11	16
Spouse only	11	14
Children only	--	12
Living alone	9	14

-- Sample too small to be released.
Source: Statistics Canada, 1996 General Social Survey.

People care, but at what cost? Less subjective than feelings are the changes that caregiving responsibilities can have on a person's life. According to the 1996 GSS, 45% of caregivers said they had modified their social activities because they were helping someone, and about 25% had altered their vacation plans. About 12% of caregivers reported that they or the person they were caring for had relocated in order to be in closer proximity to one another, while 6% of caregivers had actually moved in with the person they were assisting.

Some caregivers interrupted their education and work plans. Approximately 6% of caregivers postponed plans to enrol in an education program, while caregivers with paid work reported even more substantial changes in their lives. Half of employed caregivers (55% of women and 45% of men) stated that their caregiving duties affected their work, citing instances of coming to work late or leaving early (34% of women and 31% of men) or having to miss at least one day of work (34% of women and 24% of men). Possibly more significant

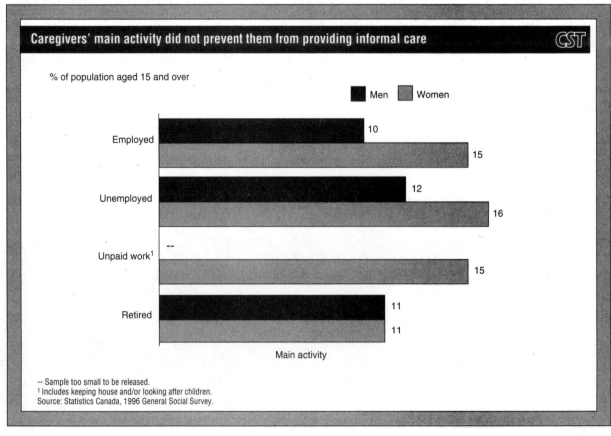

Caregivers' main activity did not prevent them from providing informal care

% of population aged 15 and over

■ Men
▨ Women

Main activity	Men	Women
Employed	10	15
Unemployed	12	16
Unpaid work[1]	--	15
Retired	11	11

-- Sample too small to be released.
[1] Includes keeping house and/or looking after children.
Source: Statistics Canada, 1996 General Social Survey.

Summary Among the many social changes facing Canadian society, one of the most important is the need for informal care for people with long-term health problems. The findings of the 1996 GSS indicate that many Canadians already provide such help, and that they do so without resentment. While the majority of caregivers feel very positive about their activities and report few hardships, the demands on some can have considerable consequences, altering the routine of their home and work lives and, in some instances, causing some degree of financial hardship. Further analysis should help to identify measures that will allow caregivers to provide support to their family and friends with greater ease.

women. But, when asked what, if anything, might make it easier to cope with the demands of providing care, about half of the caregivers said they needed nothing. Many others suggested potential sources of help, however.

Almost one in seven caregivers (15%) wished someone would occasionally take over their duties, with an equal proportion of women and men feeling this way. Since many people incurred extra expenses, 15% of women and 16% of men caregivers reported that financial compensation for their unpaid work would help them to continue. This finding suggests that there is a group of caregivers whose duties are taking an economic toll on their families.

Knowledge was also regarded as important, with 14% of women and 12% of men wanting information on the nature of long-term illnesses and disabilities. Information on how to be an effective caregiver was also important to both women (14%) and men (10%). An equal proportion of men and women believed that counselling for caregivers would be beneficial (5%).

Kelly Cranswick is an analyst with Housing, Family and Social Statistics Division, Statistics Canada.

Most caregivers experienced some disruption in their lives

% of caregivers who agree that helping others caused them...

	Total	Men	Women
to make changes in social activities	45	44	47
to change holiday plans	25	25	26
to postpone plans to enrol in an educational or training program	6	5	7
to have repercussions at work	50	45	55
to move in with person being helped	6	5	7
to move closer to person being helped	12	9	15
to change sleep patterns	29	26	31
to incur extra expenses	44	46	42
to affect health	21	12	27

Source: Statistics Canada, 1996 General Social Survey.

was the financial cost of providing help to someone with a long-term health problem; 44% of caregivers reported that they had incurred extra expenses in the previous 12 months because of their responsibilities.

Without question, the most severe alterations to caregivers' lives were the changes in their own health status: 29% of caregivers reported that their sleep patterns had changed and 21% said that their health had been affected. The impact on health showed marked gender differences, with women more than twice as likely to report that their health had been affected.

What help do the caregivers need?
While most caregivers did not have negative feelings about their responsibilities, many experienced substantial changes in their lives. This was especially true for

TRENDS in contraceptive sterilization

Compared with other industrialized nations, voluntary sterilization for contraceptive purposes is remarkably widespread in Canada. By 1995, some 3.3 million couples had
undergone a vasectomy or tubal ligation in order to end their ability to have children.
The prevalence of this practice, the early age at which it is often performed, and its
generally irreversible nature have had a significant effect on women's fertility rates
and the size of families. This article outlines the changing patterns of male and female
sterilization between 1984 and 1995, and examines some of the characteristics of couples
who choose this option.

by Alain Bélanger

Almost half of couples of childbearing age are sterile In 1995, approximately 4.6 million Canadian couples, nearly half of all couples in which the woman was aged 15 to 49, were sterile. This total includes couples in which one or both partners were sterile from natural causes, as well as those who were sterilized for medical or contraceptive reasons. Data from the 1995 General Social Survey (GSS) show that natural and medical sterility is more widespread among women than men. In 1995, some 250,000 women were sterile from natural causes compared with 106,000 men. The difference was even more pronounced for those who underwent sterilization for medical reasons: 857,000 women compared with 58,000 men.

On the other hand, sterilization for contraceptive purposes has recently become more common for men. By 1995, approximately 1.8 million men had undergone contraceptive sterilization compared with 1.5 million women. These figures reveal significant changes in attitudes and behaviour over the last few decades. The most striking feature of the trend in contraception during the 1984 to 1995 period was, without doubt, the steady increase in the proportion of vasectomies and a corresponding decrease in tubal ligations.

Sterilization appeals to older couples Because sterilization procedures are virtually irreversible, very young couples, who are less likely to have completed their family, tend not to undergo them. Generally, couples where the woman is between 25 and 29 are the youngest to opt for this procedure. As of 1995, about 10% of couples in this age range had chosen this method. Once people reach their thirties, the percentage of those who opt for sterilization increases rapidly: from 26% of couples in which the woman was between 30 and 34, to nearly 45% by ages 35 to 39. By the end of a woman's reproductive cycle, between ages 45 to 49, nearly half (49%) of couples had chosen this option.

Whether the man or the woman undergoes contraceptive sterilization depends, to a large extent, on which generation the partners belong to. Among couples who underwent this procedure, 45% of men whose partner was between 45 and 49 had a vasectomy, whereas this proportion rose to 66% among couples in

which the woman was aged 25 to 29. It appears that the younger generation of men are more inclined to assume their share of responsibility for contraceptive sterilization.

Two children the norm It is after the birth of the second child that the use of sterilization as a contraceptive method becomes a major phenomenon. The proportion of couples in which one of the

CANADIAN SOCIAL TRENDS BACKGROUNDER

What you should know about this study

Data in this article come from the 1995 General Social Survey (GSS), which is the first national survey since the 1984 Canadian Fertility Survey to ask questions on birth control practices. Men and women between the ages of 15 and 50, regardless of marital status, were asked to respond to the contraceptive methods part of the survey. Of the 5,300 respondents who met these criteria, almost 2,250 confirmed that they were currently using some method of contraception. Pregnant women, men whose partner was pregnant at the time of the interview, and couples in which one of the partners was sterile as a result of natural or medical conditions, were excluded from the interview.

Contraceptive sterilization includes tubal ligation and vasectomy. The GSS distinguishes between persons who have had an operation for contraceptive purposes, those who have been sterilized for medical reasons, and those who are sterile without surgery. This article focuses on those who have had the operation for contraceptive reasons.

The use of contraceptive sterilization has almost doubled over the past 20 years

| | % of married women aged 18 to 49 using method | | |
Contraceptive method	1976[1]	1984	1995[2]
Natural methods	**9.5**	**4.3**	**1.9**
Periodic abstinence	6.1	3.0	0.8
Withdrawal	3.4	1.3	1.0
Barrier methods	**14.8**	**13.5**	**16.8**
Condom	6.0	10.8	15.7
Diaphragm	2.2	1.4	0.6
Douche, jelly	2.5	0.7	0.2
Others	4.1	0.6	0.3
Pill and intra-uterine devices	**45.2**	**23.0**	**25.2**
Pill	39.2	15.0	20.8
IUD	6.0	8.0	4.4
Sterilization	**30.5**	**59.3**	**56.1**
Tubal ligation	--	41.7	30.0
Vasectomy	--	17.6	26.1

-- Figures not available.
[1] Aged 15 and over.
[2] Includes women in common-law relationships.
Sources: C. Guilbert-Lantoine (1990). "The contraceptive revolution in Canada." *Population*, vol. 45 (2), pp. 361-398; Statistics Canada, 1995 General Social Survey.

partners has undergone a vasectomy or tubal ligation rises from 14% for couples with only one child to 47% for those with two; it levels off at 51% for couples with three or more children.

The widespread use of sterilization is one of the contraceptive tools which has allowed for the emergence of a smaller and relatively uniform family size across Canada. In sharp contrast with earlier generations, the two-child family is increasingly becoming the norm. The proportion of ever-married women aged 45 to 49 with only two children grew from 23% in 1981 to 40% in 1991, while the percentage with five or more decreased from 22% to 6%.[1]

Married couples more likely to choose sterilization Except in the youngest age groups, married and common-law couples practice contraception in similar proportions, implying comparable fertility patterns and family sizes. The methods they use, however, differ. In particular, common-law couples where the woman is 25 or over tend to favour birth control pills, whereas married couples in the same age group choose sterilization as a means of contraception. Among the youngest (20- to 24-year-olds), common-law couples practiced contraception more often than married couples, at 86% versus 70%.

Vasectomy less common among foreign-born men Ontario, Quebec and British Columbia, the three most populous and urbanized provinces, have the highest proportions of couples who do not use any type of contraception. These are also the provinces which have received the largest numbers of recent immigrants. Results of the 1995 GSS suggest that the contraceptive practices of immigrants are considerably different than the practices of those born in Canada. While 20% of Canadian-born couples used no contraceptives, the corresponding percentage was 31% for those born in Europe or the United States and 35% for those from other countries.

Sterilization practices, particularly for men, vary significantly as well between Canadian and foreign-born couples. The proportion of couples in which the man underwent a vasectomy was much lower among non-Western foreign-born persons than among those born in Canada: 7% versus 25%. It appears that cultural norms (as approximated by place of birth) are most likely responsible for these differences. According to the GSS, men from non-Western cultures are nearly four times less likely to undergo vasectomies than those born in Canada. Since the proportion of immigrants is highest in Ontario, it is not surprising to find that male sterilization rates were lowest in this province.

Method of sterilization varies with education Although the proportion of people using contraception does not vary markedly with educational attainment, the choice of method does. By 1995, for example, couples in which the respondent had a high school diploma only were nearly twice as likely to opt for female sterilization as those who had earned a college or university degree: 29% versus 15%. Interestingly, the difference was much less pronounced in the case of male sterilization. The proportion of couples who decided on vasectomies ranged between 23% and 24% regardless of whether the highest level of educational attainment was a high school diploma or a university degree.

By 1995, one-third of Canadian couples had opted for sterilization as a contraceptive method ⒸⓈⓉ

Age Group	Total number of couples	% of couples where one partner had contraceptive sterilization	% of couples where man had vasectomy
	'000	%	%
25-29	1,432	9.6	6.3
30-34	2,193	26.2	16.5
35-39	1,960	44.9	25.2
40-44	1,739	45.8	23.6
45-49	1,735	49.0	22.2
Total	**9,825**	**33.2**	**17.9**

Source: Statistics Canada, 1995 General Social Survey.

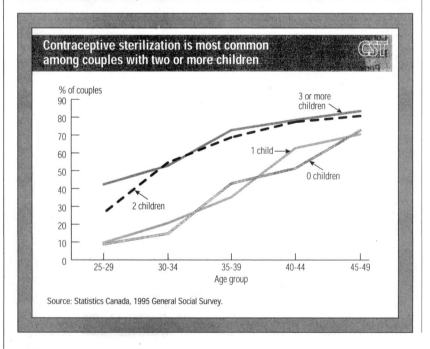

Contraceptive sterilization is most common among couples with two or more children ⒸⓈⓉ

Source: Statistics Canada, 1995 General Social Survey.

---

[1] Data are provided for 1981 and 1991 because fertility questions are only asked on the decennial censuses, the most accurate source for this type of information.

Changes in contraceptive methods over time

Canadian women have come a long way in managing their fertility. Before 1969, both the sale of contraceptives and the dissemination of information regarding contraceptive methods were prohibited under the Criminal Code.[1] As a result, until not so long ago, "natural" methods were the primary, and often only, means of birth control available. In contrast, today's couples have a wide range of reliable contraceptives at their disposal. Which ones they use depends on factors such as age, education, health concerns, ease of use, cost, marital status and the number of children the couple already have.

Between 1976 and 1995, significant changes occurred in the choice of contraceptives. The use of barrier methods increased, that of medical ones plummetted and natural methods nearly disappeared. In 1976, for example, 10% of married women reported using periodic abstinence or withdrawal as a means of birth control.[2] By 1984, that proportion had fallen to 4% and by 1995, to 2%.

Among the medical methods available, the birth control pill has gained ground at the expense of the intra-uterine device (IUD). Between 1984 and 1995, the proportion of married women using the pill increased by over a third, while the share of those who used the IUD fell by nearly half.

Finally, the use of condoms also gained popularity, rising from 6% in 1976 to 16% in 1995. In contrast, the use of diaphragms and spermicides has steadily declined until it practically disappeared by 1995. The increased popularity of the condom may be partly due to its prophylactic advantages in preventing sexually transmitted diseases, particularly AIDS, and men's apparent willingness to take greater responsibility for birth control.

[1] Liberalization of contraceptive use preceded changes in the law.

[2] Guilbert-Lantoine, C. (1990). "The contraceptive revolution in Canada". *Population.* Vol. 45 (2), pp. 361-391.

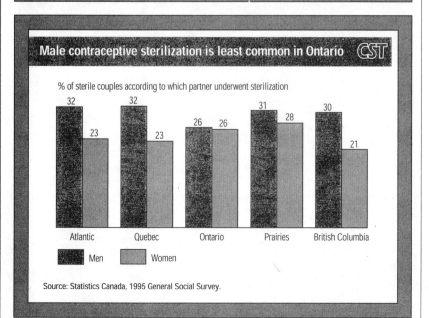

Male contraceptive sterilization is least common in Ontario

% of sterile couples according to which partner underwent sterilization

	Atlantic	Quebec	Ontario	Prairies	British Columbia
Men	32	32	26	31	30
Women	23	23	26	28	21

Source: Statistics Canada, 1995 General Social Survey.

Sterilization choices differ between religious groups Catholics and Protestants, the two largest religious groups in Canada, report virtually identical choices in the use of contraceptives. It is mainly members of "other religions" (for example, Jews, Moslems, Hindus, Buddhists, Sikhs) and those with no religious affiliation who diverge from both the two dominant groups and each other. For example, the proportion of couples who do not use contraception is over twice as high among followers of "other religions" (36%) than among couples with no religious affiliation (15%). Catholics and Protestants fall roughly midway between the two. Similarly, the use of sterilization is much less widespread among couples reporting "other religions"; approximately one-fourth of these couples are sterilized for contraceptive purposes, compared with nearly half of Catholics, Protestants and those with no religious affiliation.

Conclusion Contraception plays an important role in the lives of couples who are able to have children. Being able to decide when to start a family, how many children to have and when, enables people to better plan the birth of their children. And when the time comes, they are able to end their reproductive years through sterilization.

In Canada, more than in other industrialized countries, the contraceptive revolution coincided with the drop in the fertility rate which followed the baby boom. While the populations of many European countries began to exhibit low fertility levels as early as the 1920s and 1930s, fertility in Canada did not decline significantly until the early 1960s. While the advent of truly effective and accessible contraceptives — including sterilization — has enabled couples to better manage their fertility, these methods were not in themselves responsible for the decision to have fewer children, or indeed any children at all. Rather, social and economic changes lie at the root of both the drop in desired family size and the low birth rate of contemporary times.

Alain Bélanger is a senior analyst with Demography Division, Statistics Canada.

CHILDREN IN LOW-INCOME FAMILIES

by Garnett Picot and John Myles

Employment earnings of workers under age 35 have declined substantially since the late 1970s. Although most children under age 15 live in families headed by young adults, the proportion of children living in low-income families was relatively stable through the 1980s, rising and falling with the business cycle. Had declining earnings been the only factor at work, the percentage of children in low-income families would have risen substantially. However, rising transfer payments to families helped keep the incidence of children living in low-income families stable. Moreover, changes in family and labour market behaviour have counter-balanced the effect of declining earnings. Today's parents are having fewer children and are having them later in life. Education levels are higher than in the past, and dual-earner families are more common.

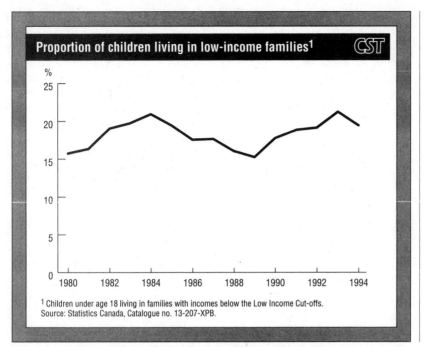

Proportion of children living in low-income families[1]

%

[Line graph showing percentage on y-axis from 0 to 25, years on x-axis from 1980 to 1994. The line starts around 16% in 1980, rises to about 21% in 1984, dips to about 15% in 1989, then rises to about 21% in 1993, ending around 19.5% in 1994.]

[1] Children under age 18 living in families with incomes below the Low Income Cut-offs.
Source: Statistics Canada, Catalogue no. 13-207-XPB.

CANADIAN SOCIAL TRENDS BACKGROUNDER

Measuring low income

This article uses a measure of low income known as the "0.5 median income cut-off." The approach examines the distribution of family income based on the "Adult Equivalent Adjusted" (AEA) income for each economic family.[1] To calculate the AEA family income, the first adult in the family is given a weight of 1.0 while other members are assigned weights of 0.4 or 0.3, depending on the family composition. The number of "adult equivalents" in the family is simply the sum of these weights. The per capita AEA family income is the total family income divided by the number of "equivalent" adults in that family. In this manner, the efficiencies that can be gained in larger families from sharing the costs involved in running a household are taken into account.

Next, the median AEA family income is determined (the point where half of families have incomes above that value and half have incomes below). Families with incomes less than one-half of this median value (the 0.5 median income cut-off) are considered to have a low income.

This article also employs a measure of low income more widely used at Statistics Canada known as Low Income Cut-offs (LICOs). Based on 1992 spending patterns, families below the LICOs spent at least 60% of their income on food, shelter and clothing, and were therefore considered to have a low income. In comparison, the average Canadian family spent only 40% of their income on these items.

[1] An economic family is a group of two or more people who live in the same dwelling and are related to each other by blood, marriage, common law or adoption. Family income includes federal and provincial income taxes and all government transfers.

• For more information, see Wolfson, M. and J. Evans, **Statistics Canada's Low Income Cut-offs: Methodological Concerns and Possibilities**, Statistics Canada, Analytical Studies Branch, Product no. 72N0002.

Proportion of children in low-income families stable Fluctuations in the percentage of children under age 18 who lived in low-income families can be attributed to changes in the business cycle through the 1980s and early 1990s. The percentage of children below Statistics Canada's Low Income Cut-offs (LICOs) rose during recessions and declined during expansions. There was, however, no long-term trend, either upward or downward.

The percentage of children in low-income families was higher in 1993 than during the recession of the early 1980s. It is, however, too early to tell whether or not an upward long-term trend began in the 1990s, as more years of data are needed. In any case, there was no upward trend in the proportion of children living in low-income families, during the 1980s.

Measuring low income using the 0.5 median income cut-off tells a similar story. In 1991, 17% of Canadian children under age 7 lived in families that had less than one-half the median family income, a slight increase from 16% in 1973. Among older children aged 7 to 14, however, the rate dropped to 14% in 1991, from 19% in 1973. Overall, the incidence of children living in low-income families did not change significantly over this period.

Employment earnings have been falling among young and low-wage workers Earnings among young adults began to fall in the late 1970s, and this decline accelerated during and immediately following the recession of the early 1980s. Shifts in the earnings of young men illustrate this decline. After adjusting for inflation, the annual earnings of men aged 25 to 34 working full time all year fell 10% between 1979 and 1992. Among those aged 17 to 24, the decline was 19%.

Employment earnings constitute the largest proportion of overall family income. In addition, the majority (60%) of young children under age 7 lived in households where the highest earner was under age 35.

Consequently, one might have expected the rate of low income among children to have risen as the earnings of younger adults fell. As outlined above, however, this did not happen and rates of children living in low-income families remained quite stable.

The drop in earnings among young workers is part of a larger story regarding the widening gap between low- and high-wage earners. For example, lower paid workers experienced greater declines in earnings than did other workers throughout the 1980s. Focusing on those working full time all year, the lowest paid (the one-fifth of workers with the lowest annual earnings) saw their earnings fall 15% between 1975 and 1993, while earnings changed little among higher paid workers. This increased polarization of earnings has been among the most significant economic developments of the past two decades.[1]

Despite significant changes in the distribution of labour market earnings, however, the distribution of overall family income has remained remarkably stable. Although the trend among younger workers has been towards lower employment earnings, the prevalence of low incomes (employment earnings plus income from other sources) among young families has followed the ups and downs of the business cycle, in part because government transfers to families have increased, and in part because of changes in family composition.

Government transfers grew as employment income fell among young families with children Between 1973 and 1991, as employment earnings declined for many families, government transfers[2] became an increasingly important source of income, especially for families with children. By 1991, transfers accounted for nearly two-thirds of the

after-tax income of low-income families, up from just over one-third in 1973.

In those low-income families with young children under age 7, the share of after-tax income from government transfers rose to 63% in 1991, up from 45% in 1981, and from 36% in 1973. Most of this increase in transfer payments came from the Child Tax Credit and from Social Assistance.

Transfer payments played a significant role in keeping the incidence of low income among children stable. In the absence of transfer payments and taxes, the proportion of children under age 7 in low-income families would have risen to 28% in 1991, up from 20% in 1981. However, the actual rate of low income among these children (including the impact of transfers and taxes) rose much

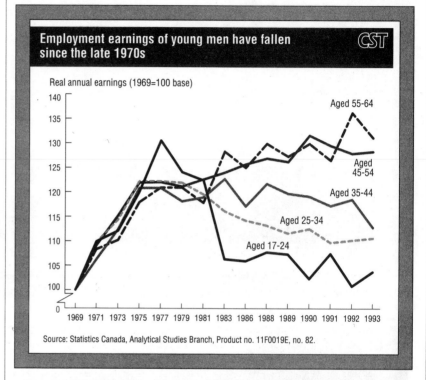

Employment earnings of young men have fallen since the late 1970s

Real annual earnings (1969=100 base)

Aged 55-64
Aged 45-54
Aged 35-44
Aged 25-34
Aged 17-24

Source: Statistics Canada, Analytical Studies Branch, Product no. 11F0019E, no. 82.

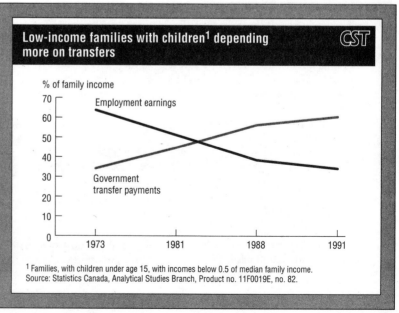

Low-income families with children[1] depending more on transfers

% of family income

Employment earnings

Government transfer payments

[1] Families, with children under age 15, with incomes below 0.5 of median family income.
Source: Statistics Canada, Analytical Studies Branch, Product no. 11F0019E, no. 82.

[1] For more information, see Morissette, R., J. Myles and G. Picot, "Earnings Inequality and the Distribution of Working Time in Canada," **Canadian Business Economics**, Spring 1994; and Morissette, René, **Why Has Inequality in Weekly Earnings Increased in Canada?**, Statistics Canada, Analytical Studies Branch, Product no. 11F0019E, no. 80.

[2] Government transfers include family and youth allowances, Old Age Security, Guaranteed Income Supplement, Canada and Quebec Pension Plans, Unemployment Insurance benefits, Social Assistance, federal and provincial tax credits, and other government transfers.

more modestly, to 17% from 15% over the same period. The pattern was similar for families with children aged 7 to 14. Thus, increases in transfer payments off-set declines in earnings and contributed to a relatively stable incidence of low income among children.

Changing family structure has had a major impact on low income among children Transfer payments are not the only reason for the relative stability in the prevalence of low income among children in the face of declining earnings. The families in which children live today are very different from those of a decade or two ago. Parents are having fewer children, and are having them later in life. Also, parents are generally better educated, and mothers are more likely to

be in the labour force. The cumulative effect of these changes helped stabilize the incidence of low income among children.[3]

• *Fewer children* The proportion of families with two or fewer children increased from 60% to 70% between 1973 and 1991. Smaller families are at lower risk of low income because there are fewer people sharing resources.

• *Having children later* The age at which parents have children has also increased. The proportion of children in families in which the highest earner was under age 26 dropped to 11% in 1991 from 18% in 1973. Since family income tends to be higher among older workers, children born to older parents are relatively better off.

• *Parents are better educated* Parents are also better educated than in the past, again increasing their earnings potential. The proportion of children in families where the highest earner had at least some postsecondary education rose to over 40% in 1991 from 25% in 1973.

• *More dual-earner families* The share of children in families with two or more adult earners rose dramatically to 62% in 1991 from 38% in 1973. This rise in the number of dual-earner families increased the earnings of families and reduced the risk of low income among children.

• *More lone-parent families* In contrast, children living with only one parent are more likely to be in a low-income situation. The proportion of children living in economic families with only one adult rose to 11% in 1991 from 5% in 1973. However, the other changes in family characteristics – particularly the trend toward more dual-earner families and the lower number of children per family – have more than offset the impact of the rising number of lone-parent families.

Demographic changes tended to reduce low income among children These changes in family characteristics (fewer children, having them later in life, higher education levels of parents, more dual-earner families and more lone-parent families) reduced the incidence of low income among children under age 7 by nearly 4 percentage points between 1973 and 1991.[4] For children aged 7 to 14, changing family characteristics had an even more significant effect. It is estimated that these changes in family composition reduced the incidence of low income among this age group by 7 percentage points. Without these changes, the incidence of low income would have risen.

Transfers and demographics resulted in stability If employment earnings had

[3] For more information, see Dooley, M., "The Demography of Child Poverty in Canada, 1973-1986," **Canadian Studies in Population**, vol. 18(1), 1991.

[4] This estimate was derived using a statistical technique known as logistic regression analysis decomposition. For more information, see Statistics Canada, Analytical Studies Branch, Product no. 11F0019E, no. 82.

declined in isolation, the percentage of children in families with low income would have risen between 1973 and 1991. There are two main reasons why this did not happen: rising transfer payments to families through the 1980s and changes in the characteristics of families with children.

Financial pressure on Canada's social safety net may result in reductions of overall transfers and an increased emphasis on targeting such transfers on the basis of need. Whether changes in family characteristics, in particular the increase in the number of dual-earner families, will off-set any future declines in employment earnings of young families

remains to be seen. It also remains to be seen whether employment earnings among young and low-wage workers will continue to decline as they did through the 1980s and early 1990s.

Thus, there is considerable uncertainty over future trends in the three factors (employment earnings, transfer payments and changing family structure) that resulted in relatively stable proportions of children in low-income situations over the past two decades. Given the significant changes taking place both in the labour market and in Canada's social transfer system, continued careful monitoring of trends in low income and their underlying causes is needed.

• For more information, see Picot, G. and J. Myles, **Social Transfers, Changing Family Structure and Low Income Among Children**, Statistics Canada, Analytical Studies Branch, Product no. 11F0019E, no. 82.

Garnett Picot is Director of the Business and Labour Market Analysis Division, Statistics Canada, and **John Myles** is Professor of Sociology, Florida State University.

CANADIAN SOCIAL TRENDS BACKGROUNDER

A work disincentive effect?

Some have suggested that increases in social transfers actually encourage low employment earnings (resulting in more children living in low-income situations). By providing an alternative to the labour market, it is argued, the welfare state creates disincentives for individuals and families to work and encourages dependency. Although a work disincentive almost certainly exists, the issue is one of magnitude. It is highly unlikely that any work disincentive effect would be large enough to explain the declines in employment income among young families outlined in this article.

Studies examining the effects of transfer payments in Canada, and elsewhere, conclude that changes in the system of taxation and social transfers have only modest effects on labour supply.[1] Furthermore, declining employment earnings among young people are not unique to Canada. In fact, similar declines have occurred in most Western countries, despite vastly different social security systems. The United States experienced comparable changes in the distribution of earnings, even though work disincentives in that country were being reduced through the 1980s as the transfer system was eroded.

After almost a decade of work in this area, researchers have moved away from the view that the transfer system explains declining earnings among younger and low-wage workers. Instead, attention is turning to the demand side of the labour market, the effects of changing trade patterns and the introduction of new technologies.

Thus, it is unlikely that work disincentive effects of transfer programs were the major cause of declining earnings for most young parents. It is much more likely that the transfer system responded to changing labour market conditions.

[1] For more information, see Blank, R., **Social Protection vs. Economic Flexibility, Is There a Trade-Off?**, Chicago Press, 1994; and Hum, D. and W. Simpson, **Income Maintenance, Work Effort and the Canadian Mincome Experiment,** Economic Council of Canada, 1991.

The Impact Of Family Structure On High School Completion

by Judith A. Frederick and Monica Boyd

Over the past several decades, there has been an unsettling increase in the number of Canadian children living in lone-parent families. According to the Census, just under 1.8 million children — almost one in five — lived in a lone-parent family in 1996, up 19% from 1991. Considerable research has established that children growing up in lone-parent families can be disadvantaged throughout their lives, compared to children from two-parent families. Not surprisingly, Canadians are concerned about the impact of this trend on current and future generations.

One of the principal reasons for this disadvantage is that children from lone-parent families are more likely to leave secondary school without finishing. High school graduation is a critical turning point in the life course, since drop-outs are the most vulnerable members of the labour force. This article uses the 1994 General Social Survey to examine the high school graduation rate of Canadian-born adults aged 20 to 44 who were living in a lone-parent family at age 15.[1] Immigrants are not included in the study because educational systems can differ substantially between countries; and adolescent and older Canadians are not included because, for different reasons, they are less likely to have secondary school completion.

Families with two biological parents most likely to produce high school graduates Growing up in a family with both biological parents has definite advantages for both young women and young men. Among Canadian-born adults aged 20 to 44, more than 80% of those from two-parent biological families completed high school, compared with about 71% of those from lone-parent families.[2] Those who lived in blended or step-parent families at age 15 also reported a 70% graduation rate, meaning they were just as likely as those from lone-parent families to have an incomplete education. The reasons for this remain unclear; it may be that the possible economic advantage of having a stepparent is offset by the stress created by another change in family structure.[3]

The GSS results also clearly suggest that parental education (and the concomitant implications for family income) plays an influential role in the children's educational outcomes. The best-case scenario for finishing high school is growing up with two biological parents who have a high school diploma or more.[4] Nearly all adults aged 20 to 44 (94%) from this type of family are also high school graduates. The rate drops for adults from two-parent biological families in which only one parent had a high school diploma (88%) and slips further for those from lone-parent families with high school completion (86%). However, the most telling story is in families where parents do not have high school graduation: only 71% of adults who lived with both biological parents at aged 15, and 59% of those who lived with one parent, finished high school. These results suggest that while children may face significant disadvantages if their parents have a low level of education, the effect may be exacerbated in lone-parent families: the stress surrounding the family breakup, the virtually inevitable drop in family income, the unwillingness or inability of the absent parent to finance education, can all affect the academic success of children.

Summary The 1994 GSS findings add weight to the view that family structure

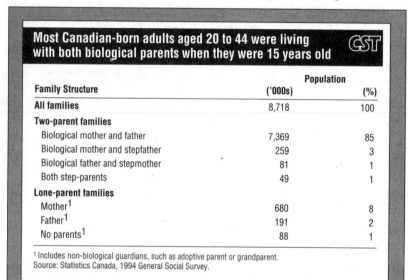

Most Canadian-born adults aged 20 to 44 were living with both biological parents when they were 15 years old CST

Family Structure	Population ('000s)	(%)
All families	8,718	100
Two-parent families		
Biological mother and father	7,369	85
Biological mother and stepfather	259	3
Biological father and stepmother	81	1
Both step-parents	49	1
Lone-parent families		
Mother[1]	680	8
Father[1]	191	2
No parents[1]	88	1

[1] Includes non-biological guardians, such as adoptive parent or grandparent.
Source: Statistics Canada, 1994 General Social Survey.

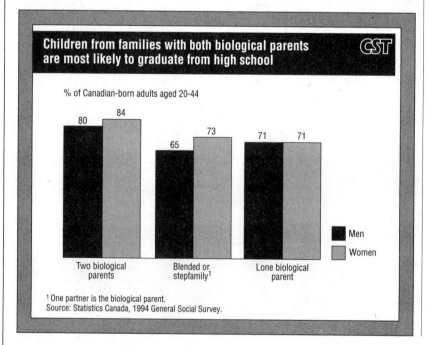

Children from families with both biological parents are most likely to graduate from high school CST

% of Canadian-born adults aged 20-44

	Men	Women
Two biological parents	80	84
Blended or stepfamily[1]	65	73
Lone biological parent	71	71

[1] One partner is the biological parent.
Source: Statistics Canada, 1994 General Social Survey.

[1] The 1994 General Social Survey (GSS) on education, work and retirement collected data from nearly 11,000 Canadians aged 15 and over living in private households in the ten provinces. It also gathered information about the type of family the respondent was living in at the age of 15.

[2] Sample sizes for father-headed families are too small for meaningful analysis; therefore, all lone-parent families have been aggregated.

[3] Researchers are unsure whether blended and step-parent families should be considered similar to two-parent biological families (the income effect) or to lone-parent families (the stress effect).

[4] There are too few blended and stepparent families to include in the analysis related to parents' education.

Why are children from lone-parent families less likely to graduate?

Researchers disagree about the reasons why different family structures produce different educational outcomes for the children. The dominant theories, however, relate the differences between children to the reduced income, lack of a role model and stress that are more common in lone-parent families.

One of the oldest explanations is the theory of household production, which argues that since lone-parent families have fewer resources, they have less time, money and energy to devote to the child's education. A variant on this is the theory of economic deprivation, in which low income is identified as the problem; although lone-parent families accounted for just under 15% of all families in Canada in 1996, they made up over one-half of all families below the low income cut-offs.[1] As well, some researchers claim that the stigma of low income may undermine the child's schooling.

A third group of hypotheses addresses the issue of the absent father. These theories posit that children need a male role model in their lives to thrive. It argues that the family is the key institution for socializing young children and two parents can provide more attention, help and supervision to foster the necessary skills for educational success. Some researchers also suggest that the stress created by the conflict surrounding the breakup of the family, or the reconstitution into a blended family, subverts academic achievement.

And some analysts dispute the idea that family structure plays a role at all in the different outcomes of children from lone-parent compared with two-parent families. The no-effect hypothesis, for example, claims that the differences arise entirely from factors such as the education and occupation of parents.

[1] Sample sizes are too small to test whether respondents from lone-parent families left school in order to help the family financially; however, GSS data for *all* respondents show that the most common reasons were financial (26%) and preferring work to school (22%). Somewhat different results were reported by the 1991 School Leavers Survey: men dropped out because they preferred work to school (28%), while women most often cited boredom (22%). For further information, see Sid Gilbert and Bruce Orok, "School Leavers," *Canadian Social Trends*, Autumn 1993.

plays a significant role in determining whether a child will graduate from high school. The debate will continue over the cause-and-effect connections between family structure and children's educational attainment, although many topics lend themselves to further research — the relationship with the parent or stepparent, the discipline and support offered by parents, and parental involvement with the child's schooling. Most of these issues can only be addressed by longitudinal surveys of child development outcomes, such as the National Longitudinal Survey of Children and Youth. In the meantime, researchers have offered recommendations for offsetting the disadvantages observed among children from lone-parent families, including programs that allow young adults to finish high school, providing affordable day care and after-school programs, and providing job training and skills upgrading to women.[5]

[5] For example, see Garry D. Sandefeuer, Sara McLanahan, Roger A. Wojtkiewics, "The Effects of Parental Marital Status during Adolescence on High School Graduation," *Social Forces*, September 1992, Vol. 71, no.1, pp. 103-121. Sheila Fitzgerald Krein, "Growing up in a Single Parent Family: The Effect on Education and Earnings of Young Men," *Family Relations*, 1986, Vol. 35, pp. 167.

Judith A. Frederick is a senior analyst with Housing, Family and Social Statistics Division, Statistics Canada and **Monica Boyd** is professor of sociology at Florida State University.

Parents' education affects the likelihood that their children will complete high school

% of Canadian-born adults aged 20-44

Two parent
- Men: 94 / 85 / 66
- Women: 94 / 90 / 75

One parent
- Men: 85 / 61
- Women: 86 / 57

Legend:
- Both high school or more
- One high school or more
- No high school

Note: Parent is the biological parent.
Source: Statistics Canada, 1994 General Social Survey.

GETTING AHEAD IN LIFE

does your *parents income* count?

It is increasingly suggested that the current generation of young Canadians will not be as well-off as their parents. While older workers are worried about financing their retirement, younger workers are concerned about finding secure, well-paid employment. Diminishing opportunities could affect the ability of the younger generation to support themselves and their families.

The study of intergenerational equity addresses the social and economic issues that arise from changing relations between older, younger and future generations as our society ages. As a series of studies addressing various aspects of these relations has recently been published by Statistics Canada in a volume entitled Labour Markets, Social Institutions, and the Future of Canada's Children. Selected findings from two chapters are excerpted here. Each article addresses separate but related aspects of transfers between generations, focusing on how parents' educational and labour market background contribute to their children's long-term prospects as adults.

– Ed.

by **Miles Corak**

Parents hope their children will become successful and self-sufficient adults. But raising children is a complicated affair, and a child's fortune in life is determined not only by parenting strategies, but also by the support available in the community, the resources offered by the state, and sometimes just plain luck. That being said, a prime role in the eventual labour market outcomes of children is often attributed to money.

If the role of money in the process were simple, then every dollar — no matter where it came from and who received it — should have the same impact on a child's employment earnings in adulthood. But this article shows that a dollar is not a dollar is not a dollar, and strongly suggests that the sources of a parent's income influence the employment outcomes of their grown-up children. First, the adult earnings of all children are compared to see how much they are affected by the income of parents and of the neighbourhood; then, the adult earnings of children from very-low-income families are studied to learn if they are influenced by the same factors.

All dollars are not created equal If only money matters to a child's labour market outcomes, then it should not matter where the dollar comes from — whether from paid work, self-employment, assets, government transfers, or any other source. However, if a dollar from one source has a different effect than a dollar from another, other factors are probably at work. Thus, an effective way to evaluate the role of money in children's labour market success as adults is to examine the composition of their parent's income (in this case, the father's income).

The source of the father's income is strongly associated with the adult incomes of children. Children had significantly higher market incomes as adults if their fathers had self-employment income than if they did not — almost $1,200 for sons and $850 for daughters in 1994. If fathers had received Unemployment Insurance (UI) benefits, the effect was just as dramatic but in the opposite direction: sons' incomes were $1,400 and daughters' $870 lower than those of children whose fathers who had not received UI.

A father with asset income provided the most significant advantages for his children. After accounting for all other factors, sons whose fathers had some income from assets earned over $3,100 more than those whose fathers had no assets, and daughters earned almost $2,700 more. These are very substantial amounts, but what may be even more significant is that the actual dollar amount of the father's asset income seems much less important than its presence. In fact, children's adult incomes rise by only an average $28 for every $1,000 increase in their father's asset income; for example, someone whose father had $10,000 in asset income would enjoy a market income that was only $252 higher

CANADIAN SOCIAL TRENDS BACKGROUNDER

What you should know about this study

This analysis is based upon income tax information reported by a cohort of about 285,000 young men and women aged 28 to 31 in 1994. The total market income of these young adults was related to the incomes of their fathers and mothers in 1982, when they (the children) were 16 to 19 years of age and still living at home. The analysis excludes families headed by single mothers and taxfilers not residing in an "urban" community in 1982. All monetary values are presented in 1986 constant dollars.

Estimates of the degree of association between parent and child incomes took account of (controlled for) neighbourhood median income, the province of residence, and a number of individual and family characteristics, including the number of residential moves experienced during the five-year period 1978 and 1982 (as determined by examining the addresses on the father's income tax returns). However, the effects of some socio-demographic factors that are also known to influence labour market experiences — such as parental education, immigrant status and occupation — cannot be controlled for because the information is not available from tax records.

Total income: all income derived from market activities (wages and salaries, self-employment, pension, investment and interest income) and any government transfers (such as UI benefits, social assistance, family allowance and so on). Data for parents is total income.

Total market income: all income derived from market activities. The income of adult children excludes government transfers because the children's labour market outcomes can only be measured by examining their earnings from market-based sources (employment and investments).

Asset income: net income from interest and investments, net income from real estate, dividends from Canadian corporations, and taxable capital gains/losses. Corrections are made for changes in tax laws so that parent-child incomes can be legitimately compared through time.

Neighbourhood: area in which all individuals have the same first three characters in their postal codes (Forward Sortation Area, or FSA). A "high" income neighbourhood has a median income in the top 25% of all neighbourhoods nation-wide, and a "low" income neighbourhood has a median income in the bottom 25%.

Income decile: a scale for measuring the distribution of the population according to income; in this case, the population of taxfilers was ranked from lowest to highest income and divided into ten equal parts. The 10% of people with the lowest incomes are in the bottom decile, the 10% with the highest incomes in the top decile, and so on.

($280 – $28) than a person whose father had $1,000 in asset income.

So why might the simple presence of asset income, as opposed to its amount, have such an effect? Asset income includes interest on bank deposits, and since interest rates were very high during the late 1970s and early 1980s (the prime rate exceeded 19% in 1981), even relatively small savings would have generated some interest income. Yet having any amount of asset income may also indicate that parents consider it important to plan for the future, a quality that may be passed on to their children and contribute to their labour market success later in life.

Fathers' income has greater effect on sons' than daughters' earnings Not only do varying sources of income have different effects on an adult child's labour market success, but so does the parent who earns it. For every $1,000 increase in the father's income, the adult child's market income increased by about $91 for sons and about $47 for daughters. In contrast, sons and daughters did equally well

as the mother's income rose — about $80 to $90 per $1,000 increase.

There are two possible explanations for this finding. The first focuses on the father's role and suggests that a high-earning father has a stronger effect on sons than on daughters by encouraging the pursuit of income.[1] The second keys on the mother's role and suggests that mothers may be more likely to treat children of each gender equally when making spending decisions, and if women have higher incomes, they probably have greater discretion over spending. This interpretation is based on studies that show household spending differs depending on which parent receives the income, and that control over the family's spending is important for child outcomes.[2]

Community ties matter The affluence of the neighbourhood in which children, especially boys, spend their early teens is positively associated with their incomes as adults. For every $1,000 increase in the median income of the neighbourhood, adult incomes increased by about $370

for sons, and by $72 for daughters. There are a number of reasons why high-income neighbourhoods may improve the labour market outcomes of children. They may offer a more well-developed physical infrastructure — higher quality schools, recreation facilities, and social institutions — as well as the kind of network or peer group effects sometimes called "social capital"[3] — that is, the set of norms or standards that exist at the community level and help to reinforce the parents' goals for their children. An alternative interpretation is that parents will select a neighbourhood with the qualities they prefer if they can afford to choose the community where they raise their children. The type of neighbourhood may thus reflect the parents' choices and priorities for their children's future, rather than being a causal factor in its own right.

If community networks and relationships are important for children, then the more frequently these are broken, the greater the consequences for incomes in adulthood. The adult children of fathers who moved once during their teens earned about $550 less than those whose fathers stayed in the same neighbourhood; children whose fathers moved three or more times earned about $2,000 less.

Do different dollars also matter to low-income children? Clearly, different dollars produce different effects for the "average kid." Does the same hold true for low-income children? To address this question, adult children's labour market success is assessed by measuring the income mobility of children from low-income families: did they do better, as adults, than their parents by moving into higher deciles of the income distribution?

In a world of equal opportunity, the labour market outcomes of adult children would not depend upon their family

Adult children had substantially higher market incomes if their fathers had some asset income CST		
	Market income of adult child changed by $...	
	Sons	**Daughters**
Father's income		
If father reported income from		
Self-employment	1,157	850
Assets	3,107	2,698
Unemployment Insurance	-1,442	-865
For every $1,000 increase in father's income from		
Paid work	91	47
Self-employment	76	50
Assets	28	28
Unemployment Insurance	-10	-23
For every $1,000 increase in		
Mother's income	90	82
Median income of neighbourhood	368	72
For every residential move		
One	-544	-554
Two	-1,059	-1,282
Three or more	-2,134	-1,819

Source: Statistics Canada, Longitudinal Administrative Databank.

[1] Martha S. Hill and Greg J. Duncan (1987). "Parental Family Income and the Socioeconomic Attainment of Children." *Social Science Research*. Vol. 16, pp. 39-73.

[2] Shelly J. Lundberg, Robert A. Pollack, and Terence J. Wales (1997), "Do Husbands and Wives Pool Their Resources?" *Journal of Human Resources*. Vol. 32, pp. 463-80. Shelley Phipps and Peter Burton (1992), "What's Mine is Yours? The Influence of Male and Female Incomes on Patterns of Household Expenditure." Working Paper No. 92-12, Department of Economics, Dalhousie University.

[3] James S. Coleman (1988). "Social Capital in the Creation of Human Capital." *American Journal of Sociology*. Vol. 94 Supplement, pp. S95-S120.

background. Ideally, a child with a very-low-income father (bottom 10% of the income distribution) would have an equal chance of entering any income decile; that is, the child would be just as likely to become a very-high-income earner (10%) as a very-low-income-earner (also 10%).

But in fact, children of very-low-income fathers were more likely to follow in their fathers' footsteps than to improve their own position in the income distribution. About 15% of sons also found themselves in the bottom decile, and another 14% moved up by only one decile. The figures for daughters were very similar, at 14% and 11% respectively. Only about 6% of sons and daughters of very-low-income fathers managed to reach the top 10% of the income rankings. (In contrast, over 20% of sons and daughters born to fathers in the top decile also occupied the top decile, and less than 7% fell all the way to the bottom.) These patterns suggest that low-income in one generation is associated with low-income in the next, with children of very-low-income families most likely to end up at the bottom of the income hierarchy.

A father's sources of income had a clear effect on their adult children's incomes. Children were less likely (12 to 13%) to remain in the bottom income decile if their father had some self-employment income than if he did not (15 to 16%), while children whose father received UI benefits were more likely to remain there (15 to 16%) than if he did not (13 to 14%).

However, the most striking result is the improvement in income mobility if a father reported some asset income: only 12% of sons remained in the bottom decile, compared with over 17% of those whose fathers had no income from assets. For daughters, the pattern was very similar, at 11% compared with 17%. This finding would seem to strengthen the suggestion made earlier about the personal attributes that having asset income imply: although these fathers were in the bottom 10% of the income distribution, having a total annual income of less than $15,000 (1986 constant dollars), they were able to set aside some amount of money in anticipation of the future.

The community has as great an effect on a low-income child as on the average child. Children of very-low-income fathers living in high-income neighbourhoods tended to do better. This was especially true in the case of sons; only 12% remained in the bottom income decile if they grew up in a high-income community, compared with 16% if they were raised in a low-income neighbourhood. For daughters, the difference was slight, at 14% and 15% respectively.

Since a "good neighbourhood" can have such a positive effect, it is not surprising to find that moving is generally detrimental to a child's adult earnings. If children with very-low-income fathers moved at least once during the period 1978 to1982, between 16% and 17% also ended up with very low adult incomes; if they did not move, between 13% and 14% remained in the bottom decile.

Summary Money does matter to the eventual labour market success of children. But how it is obtained, by whom, and where, also matter. Why should this be so? The findings presented here underline the complex nature of the processes that determine the type of job and level of income a child will have, a process that involves both the family and the community.

The contrasting effects of the different sources of a parent's income may reflect the parent's personal attributes (which are not observable with conventional data sets). This may be particularly so in the

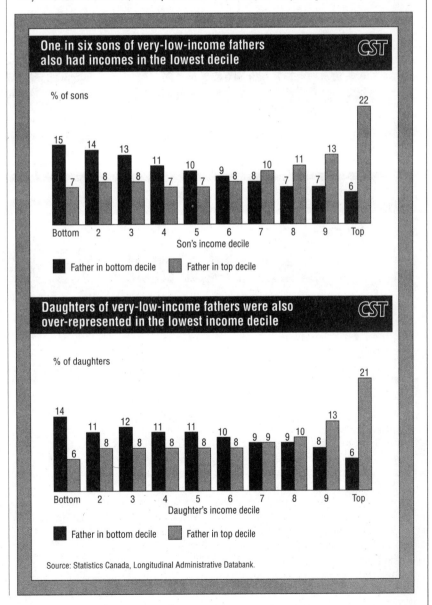

One in six sons of very-low-income fathers also had incomes in the lowest decile

% of sons

Son's income decile

■ Father in bottom decile   ▨ Father in top decile

Daughters of very-low-income fathers were also over-represented in the lowest income decile

% of daughters

Daughter's income decile

■ Father in bottom decile   ▨ Father in top decile

Source: Statistics Canada, Longitudinal Administrative Databank.

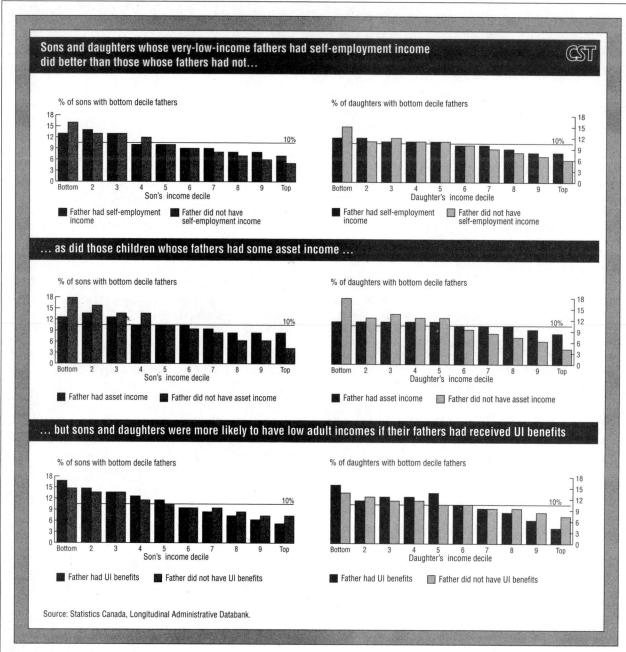

Sons and daughters whose very-low-income fathers had self-employment income did better than those whose fathers had not...

CST

% of sons with bottom decile fathers

Son's income decile

■ Father had self-employment income   ■ Father did not have self-employment income

% of daughters with bottom decile fathers

Daughter's income decile

■ Father had self-employment income   ▨ Father did not have self-employment income

... as did those children whose fathers had some asset income ...

% of sons with bottom decile fathers

Son's income decile

■ Father had asset income   ■ Father did not have asset income

% of daughters with bottom decile fathers

Daughter's income decile

■ Father had asset income   ▨ Father did not have asset income

... but sons and daughters were more likely to have low adult incomes if their fathers had received UI benefits

% of sons with bottom decile fathers

Son's income decile

■ Father had UI benefits   ■ Father did not have UI benefits

% of daughters with bottom decile fathers

Daughter's income decile

■ Father had UI benefits   ▨ Father did not have UI benefits

Source: Statistics Canada, Longitudinal Administrative Databank.

case of asset income, which is so strongly associated with the adult children's incomes. A recent study has argued, for example, that a parent's integrity, responsibility, and a good work ethic — all of which are valued by employers — also contribute to positive child outcomes, regardless of the parent's income.[4]

The future prospects of children are also influenced by the community in which they live, although the neighbourhood may reflect attributes such as stability in the child's family, rather than being an independent influence.

These findings, however, simply underscore the complex nature of raising self-sufficient and financially successful children. While a child's labour market success is influenced by the economic resources available to the parents, other factors both in the family and in the community play a role — quite possibly a central role. As every parent knows, when it comes to children, more than money matters.

[4] Susan E. Mayer (1997), *What Money Can't Buy: Family Income and Children's Life Chances*, Cambridge: Harvard University Press, p. 2.

• This article is adapted from "How to Get Ahead in Life: Some Correlates of Intergenerational Income Mobility in Canada," *Labour Markets, Social Institutions, and the Future of Canada's Children*, Statistics Canada, Catalogue Number 89-553-XPB.

Miles Corak is senior economist in the Analytical Studies Branch, Statistics Canada.

CST

does your *parents* *education?* count

Education is an important determinant of one's position in society, affecting a person's participation in the community and likely success in the labour market. The inherited intellectual capital of the family – forged over the years by generations of family members' achievements at school and work – often plays a large role in a child's educational achievement. It can contribute directly to a child's education by providing a more or a less supportive environment for learning, and can contribute indirectly by paving the way for a higher level of educational attainment. This article assesses the role of inherited intellectual capital in children's acquisition of postsecondary education.

by Patrice de Broucker and Laval Lavallée

Most adults aged 26 to 35 have as much or more education than their parents[1]

	Child's level of education		
	Higher	Same (%)	Lower
Parent's education			
Total	51	34	16
Did not complete secondary	84	15	--
Completed secondary	40	46	--
Postsecondary	--	45	40

-- Sample too small to produce reliable estimate.
[1] Parent with highest level of educational attainment.
Source: Statistics Canada, 1994 International Adult Literacy Survey.

Educational attainment has improved over generations

Educational mobility – that is, the difference in educational attainment between parents and their children – is common in Canada. In 1994, about half (51%) of Canadian respondents aged 26 to 35 reported having a higher level of education than their parents (upward mobility), just under 34% had the same level, while the rest (16%) had less formal schooling.

Because the upward trend is dominant, the average level of educational attainment in Canada has been rising over time. The lower the level of one's parents' education, the greater the scope for increasing one's own level, and so the rate of upward mobility accelerates. For example, 84% of 26- to 35-year-olds whose parents had not completed secondary school had gone further in their own education. Compulsory school attendance has had a significant influence on this achievement.

The rise in the general level of education throughout society has improved the intellectual capital available to the next generation. However, it remains true that the higher the parents' level of education, the more likely that the child will pursue further studies. Young adults aged 26 to 35 were close to three times more likely to earn postsecondary credentials if their parents had a postsecondary education than if their parents had not completed high school.

CANADIAN SOCIAL TRENDS BACKGROUNDER

What you should know about this study

This article uses data from the International Adult Literacy Survey (IALS) for Canada, conducted among 5,660 individuals in 1994.[1] It examines the likelihood that an adult has completed a postsecondary education (college or university), given their inherited intellectual capital. The analysis focuses on young adults aged 26 to 35 because most have completed their initial education and are at the beginning of their careers (sample size of 1,010, representing a population of about 5 million Canadians). Where a comparison over time is illuminating, the young adults are compared to older adults aged 46 to 55 (sample size of 658, representing 3.3 million Canadians). The older cohort is chosen because it is on average 20 years, or an "educational generation," older and is still in the labour market. Since this study is concerned about the most recent level of education attained, the negligible percentage of those respondents still in school was excluded from the analysis.

The size of the sample restricts the analysis to only four levels of education for children (incomplete secondary, secondary, postsecondary non-university, and university) and three for their parents (incomplete secondary, secondary, and postsecondary). This may result in some blurring of the extent of educational mobility. For example, a child with a university degree will be defined as having more education than a parent who also has a university degree (since postsecondary for parents includes both college and university); similarly, a child with a college diploma will be defined as having the same educational attainment as a parent with a university degree.

Inherited intellectual capital: in this study, it is represented by the education of the parent with the highest level of educational attainment (mother or father) and the socio-economic status of the father's occupation.

Socio-economic status of occupations (SES): an index that measures the "importance" of an occupation relative to others. It is calculated for 21 groups of occupations based on three variables: the average level of education of workers, the average income and the percentage of women in the occupation.[2] The index ranges from a low of 25 (Fishing occupations) to a high of 62 (Natural science and Teaching occupations). In-between lie such occupations as Management, Social Science and Medicine (56 to 57), Mining and Machining (41 to 42) and Clerical and Sales (37 to 38).

[1] For more information about the IALS and its findings, see "Adult Literacy in Canada, the United States and Germany," *Canadian Social Trends*, Winter 1996.

[2] The calculation is based on the method developed by Bernard R. Blishen, William K. Carroll and Catherine Moore, "The 1981 Socio-economic Index for Occupations in Canada," *Canadian Review of Sociology and Anthropology*, Vol. 24, no. 4; 1987.

Fathers with high-status occupation have a positive effect Parents also contribute to their child's education by passing on attitudes and expectations, providing encouragement and opportunities to learn, helping outside the classroom, standing as positive role models and so on. These elements of the family's intellectual capital arise not only from the parents' education but also from their life experience. If a parent's education is important to a child's educational attainment, what role might his occupation play? Specifically, might fathers with higher status occupations have children with higher educational qualifications?

Indeed, the data strongly suggest that the socio-economic status (SES) of the father's occupation is associated with their children's educational attainment. Men with low levels of education whose children have postsecondary credentials had, on average, higher status occupations. For example, the average SES score for fathers who had not finished high school was 35; but the SES was 39 for those whose children had a university degree, and only 33 for those whose children had not completed high school.[1] In contrast, fathers with a good education who worked in an occupation with below-average status for their level of schooling were more likely to have children with lower educational attainment.[2]

Creating an environment for education achievement The International Adult Literacy Survey (IALS) data cannot directly address how intellectual capital may be inherited, but they do offer some hints. Intellectual capital can be transmitted through the use of educational "investment strategies" that parents use to encourage their children to learn. The IALS does capture data on a number of activities that may be considered useful proxies for the parents' desire to further their children's education: buying books for their children, setting aside time to read and limiting time spent watching television.

By and large, parental support of children's education reproduces the parents' own educational background. The strongest relationships are between education, reading and academic performance. Parents with a college or university education are more likely to buy books for their children, perhaps because they often have higher incomes and can afford to purchase books; while less affluent families may borrow books for their children from the library. However, parents with a university degree have a much greater probability of reading to children, and this habit is not necessarily linked to income levels.

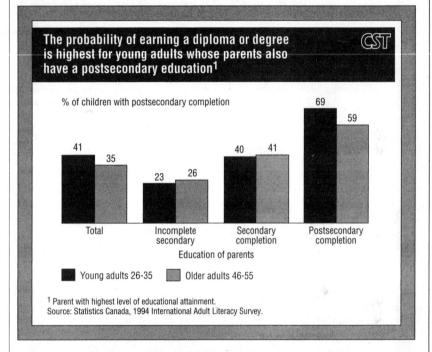

The probability of earning a diploma or degree is highest for young adults whose parents also have a postsecondary education[1]

% of children with postsecondary completion

	Total	Incomplete secondary	Secondary completion	Postsecondary completion
Young adults 26-35	41	23	40	69
Older adults 46-55	35	26	41	59

Education of parents

■ Young adults 26-35   ■ Older adults 46-55

[1] Parent with highest level of educational attainment.
Source: Statistics Canada, 1994 International Adult Literacy Survey.

Whatever their own education, fathers in higher status occupations were more likely to have children with high education[1]

	Child's level of education				
	Total	Incomplete secondary	Secondary completion	Post-secondary, non-university	University
Father's average SES score[2]					
Did not complete secondary	35	33	36	35	39
Completed secondary	42	38	40	43	45
Postsecondary	48	44	48	47	50

[1] Includes all respondents for whom data are available.
[2] Value for lowest SES = 25, highest SES = 62.
Source: Statistics Canada, 1994 International Adult Literacy Survey.

[1] The values for socio-economic status of the fathers's occupation ranged from a low of 25 to a high of 62. With only 37 points' difference between the lowest and the highest SES, a difference of 6 points is quite substantial.

[2] Unfortunately, the sample size is too small to perform this analysis for both cohorts separately to see whether the influence of the father's occupation has changed over time. However, results of the regression analysis (see "Factors that influence years of schooling") would suggest that its importance has declined.

No group of parents seems more inclined than any other to limit the time spent watching TV, but TV time would be reduced by other activities (such as reading) without any need for parental intervention. About one child in two starts reading before entering Grade 1, regardless of the parents' education; this is probably the result of experiences that cut across the educational background of parents, such as daycare, junior kindergarten or educational television programs. However, parents with university are least likely to have children who are behind at school.[3]

Factors that influence years of schooling

A number of factors can influence the educational attainment of children. These factors include gender, parents' highest level of educational attainment, father's occupation, mother's participation in the paid workforce, and immigrant status. The table below shows the effect of some of these characteristics — measured in terms of the difference in average years of formal schooling — when the influence of all other factors is taken into account.

The higher level of education that used to be enjoyed by men — men aged 46 to 55 had over two-thirds of a year more formal schooling than women their age — has disappeared among younger adults. Although gender may no longer matter, parental education does: young adults aged 26 to 35 whose parents did not complete high school have one less year of schooling than those whose parents graduated from high school.

A man's occupation has a strong effect on the years of education his children receive, and the impact was much greater on older than younger adults. Compared with 46- to 55- year olds whose fathers were skilled agricultural workers, others in this age group had almost 6 years more schooling if their fathers had been professionals, and 3.5 years more if their fathers had been managers. In the next generation (aged 26 to 35), the advantage had dropped to less than two more years for children of professionals and just over one more year for children of managers. Meanwhile, people whose mothers had worked for pay acquired about half (aged 46 to 55) to one (aged 26 to 35) more year of education than those whose mothers had not been not employed outside the home.

Impact of various factors on number of years of education [1]

	Young adults 26-35	Older adults 46-55
	(Average number of years)	
Base number of years of education	12.8	11.9
Male	-0.1	0.7
Female	--	--
Parent's education[2]		
Incomplete secondary	-1.0	-1.4
Secondary completion	--	--
Postsecondary	1.2	-0.4*
Father's occupation		
Armed Forces	4.3	-1.4*
Manager	1.3	3.5
Professional	1.9	5.9
Technician	0.2*	3.0
Clerk	1.2	3.4
Service worker	-0.1*	1.7
Skilled agricultural worker	--	--
Craft worker	-0.8	1.3
Plant & machine operator	-0.6*	0.9
Elementary occupations	-1.1	0.7*
Never worked	3.0*	0.0
Mother's labour force status		
Mother worked	0.9	-0.5
Mother did not work	--	--
Region		
Outside Canada	-0.9	0.7*
Atlantic	-0.1*	-1.5
Quebec	-0.4*	-2.3
Ontario	--	--
West	-0.5	0.1*

-- sample too small to produce reliable estimate.
* Not statistically significant.
[1] Reference group shown in italics. Values for all other groups in the category are shown compared to the reference group.
[2] Parent with highest level of educational attainment.
Source: Statistics Canada, 1994 International Adult Literacy Survey.

It seems that parents with higher levels of education are more likely to set their children on the path to educational success. However, this finding should be interpreted with caution, because the data were collected only for children aged 6 to 18 years, and provide no information about the final outcomes of parents' educational strategies, that is, whether the children completed a post-secondary education.

Summary It does appear that parental education plays a significant role in children's ability to match or improve upon their parents' educational attainment. Most probably, this occurs because the learning environment in the home reflects the parents' own academic background. However, it seems that a parent with little formal schooling but a high socio-economic status occupation can also see his children earn high level educational qualifications. This finding suggests that parents provide a sound learning environment for their children — extracurricular activities, books, lessons and so on[4] — if they can afford to do so.

In other words, financial stability is an important agent in the transmission of intellectual capital.

If the family cannot transmit intellectual capital, is the education system able to provide equal educational opportunities to all? An education policy is a powerful instrument to influence human capital formation, but other public policies that recognize the link between low education and low income also play an important role. Such programs could help young low-income parents to complete their higher education, find adequate day care facilities, obtain career counseling and integrate into the labour market.

Recently, a Canadian university advertised on a commercial billboard with these words:

> *Not everyone inherits the family business. No one's about to hand you your future.*

Rather, to a large extent, it seems that your future is in the hands of your parents.

[3] Defined as being at least two years behind the normal grade for their age.

[4] See "The social context of school for children," *Canadian Social Trends*, Winter 1997.

• This article is adapted from "Intergenerational Aspects of Education and Literacy Skills Acquisition," *Labour Markets, Social Institutions, and the Future of Canada's Children*, Statistics Canada, Catalogue Number 89-553-XPB.

Patrice de Broucker is chief of Integration, Analysis and Special Projects, Centre for Education Statistics, Statistics Canada, and **Laval Lavallée** is a consultant with Vestimetra International Inc.

WHEN PARENTS REPLACE TEACHERS:
THE HOME SCHOOLING OPTION
by Jacqueline Luffman

At the start of every school year, a number of children do not head off to the classroom. Instead, they stay with a parent who will be teaching them at home what others learn at school. Despite the fact that registered home schoolers still only account for a small percentage of school age children, their number has increased every year since the early 1980s. These increases may be the result of more parents home schooling, or of better coverage of home schoolers by education ministries. Home schooling is especially active and growing in the Western provinces, particularly in Alberta and British Columbia. Increased public acceptance and the introduction of more flexible legislation may have contributed to this growth.

UNIT 2: WOMEN, MARRIAGE AND THE FAMILY

In most cases, parents home school for religious, moral or pedagogical reasons.[1] This arrangement is ideal for those who wish to incorporate their beliefs and values into the curriculum, who are concerned that not enough learning takes place in the classroom, and who prefer their child to learn in a non-formal, family setting. According to supporters of home schooling, the benefits for children are many: they may, for example, learn at their own pace, pursue special interests, make the most of individual strengths and weaknesses, and avoid the competition and peer pressure of the classroom. Home schooling may also be the solution for a child who, for whatever reason, does not fit in a regular classroom and is falling behind academically, socially or both.

Critics, however, are quick to point out areas of concern: the average parent's ability to cover all areas of the curriculum, the availability of appropriate program materials and the potential absence of social interaction. And although every province monitors home schoolers for compliance with the Education Act, no province has regulations regarding the qualification of parents to teach.

Different regulations in different provinces All provinces exempt children from attending public schools provided parents can prove that the child receives satisfactory instruction at home or elsewhere. Typically, parents must register their children for home schooling with a local school board or school in their area. In Alberta and the Northwest Territories — the only two jurisdictions where some funding is guaranteed to parents who home school — home educational plans must be approved. In all other provinces, guidelines are issued for the preparation of these plans but approval is not required.[2]

Because registration requirements and tracking of home schoolers vary across Canada, reliable estimates on the number of home-educated students are difficult to come by. In addition, for a variety of reasons (most of which have to do with fear of interference), not all parents who home school their children register with the province.[3]

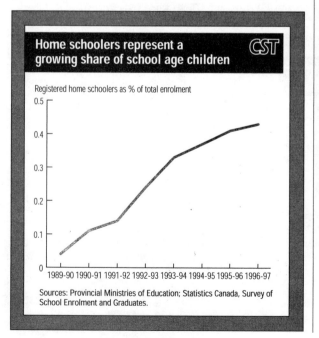

Home schoolers represent a growing share of school age children

Registered home schoolers as % of total enrolment

Sources: Provincial Ministries of Education; Statistics Canada, Survey of School Enrolment and Graduates.

CANADIAN SOCIAL TRENDS BACKGROUNDER

What you should know about this study

One of the most challenging aspects of home schooling research relates to the difficulty of identifying home schoolers. There are no statistical portraits or analyses, Statistics Canada does not collect information on this topic, and little is known about the characteristics of home schooling families. Because reliable data on the number of home schoolers are not available, estimates from various sources must be used when analyzing this population. The numbers relating to home schoolers presented in this article were derived mainly from ministry officials in each province, with the exception of Quebec, where these figures are not collected.

Definitions

Home schooling, home educating or home-based education: occurs when a child participates in his or her education at home rather than attending a public, private or other type of school. Parents or guardians assume the responsibility of educating their child and may develop their own curriculum guidelines.

Instruction which takes place at home because of health, disability or location, and which remains under the direction of public education authorities, is considered school-based instruction and not home schooling.

Home schooler or home-based learner: a student who receives instruction through a home-based education program without attending a formal school.

Registered home schooler: a home schooler whose parent or guardian has notified a school, school board or provincial ministry of their intention to home educate their child.

Home-based educational plan: provincial curriculum guidelines that parents must follow when educating their children at home. In some provinces, parents are required to submit an educational plan proving that their curriculum complies with the learning objectives of provincial legislation.

[1] D.S. Smith. 1993. *Parent-generated home study in Canada: the national outlook, 1993.* Westfield, N.B. : Francombe Place.

[2] For full details of provincial requirements, see "A profile of home schooling in Canada", *Education Quarterly Review*, Winter 1997, Catalogue 81-003-XPB, Statistics Canada.

[3] Brian, Ray. 1994. *A nationwide study of home education in Canada: Family characteristics, student achievement and other topics.* Salem, Oregon: National Home Education Research Institute. Of the 762 families in this study, 8% did not comply with legal requirements for notification of home schooling.

This suggests that a number of home schooling families remain invisible and, as a result, official counts of registered home schoolers typically underestimate the actual numbers. For example, according to provincial ministries of education, in 1996-97, registered home schoolers totaled approximately 17,500 or about 0.4% of total enrolment.[4] In contrast, home schooling organizations have placed the number of students studying at home at 30,000 to 40,000, or approximately 1% of total student enrolment.[5]

The popularity of home schooling varies widely by province

	1995-96		
	Total [1] enrolment	Registered home schoolers	Home schoolers as % of total enrolment
	'000		
Newfoundland	111	54	0.1
Prince Edward Island	25	80	0.3
Nova Scotia	168	290	0.2
New Brunswick	138	241	0.2
Quebec	115	--	--
Ontario	219	2,916	0.1
Manitoba	223	926	0.4
Saskatchewan	213	1,113	0.5
Alberta	548	7,058	1.3
British Columbia	654	4,801	0.7
Yukon	6	44	0.7
North West Territories	18	--	--
Canada	**5,440**	**17,523**	**0.4**

-- Figures not available.
[1] Includes public, private, federal, as well as visually and hearing impaired students.
Sources: Statistics Canada, Catalogue no. 81-229-XPB; Provincial Ministries of Education.

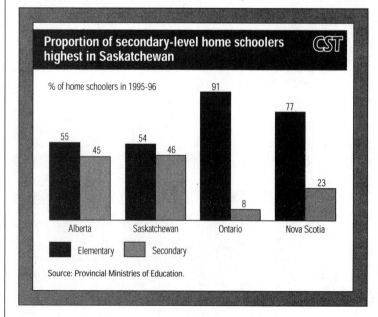

Proportion of secondary-level home schoolers highest in Saskatchewan

% of home schoolers in 1995-96

	Alberta	Saskatchewan	Ontario	Nova Scotia
Elementary	55	54	91	77
Secondary	45	46	8	23

Source: Provincial Ministries of Education.

Majority of home schoolers at elementary level Alberta, Saskatchewan, Ontario and Nova Scotia are the only provinces where data on the grade level of home schoolers are available. These data show that an average of over 60% of children studying at home were elementary students in 1995-96; however, this proportion varied quite substantially, ranging from 52% in Saskatchewan to 91% in Ontario.

Although data on educational level are not collected by the other provinces and territories, it seems reasonable to assume that in the rest of the country, most children educated at home are elementary school students as well. Generally, home schooling at the high school level is more difficult, as parents need to have a wide range of advanced subject matter knowledge to cover the curriculum. In addition, teenagers usually want to participate in social or extra-curricular activities, which are not as easy to provide in a home environment. Nonetheless, the number of registered secondary-level home schoolers has grown between 1993-94 and 1995-96. Perhaps fuelling this growth are school board policies that allow home schoolers use of library and other resources; provinces where these special arrangements are available tend to have higher proportions of high school-level students studying at home.

Conclusion With the help of regionally based support groups and national organizations, the home schooling movement has been gaining momentum over the last 12 years. But, home schooling is not for everyone. Relatively few parents are able to invest vast amounts of time, effort and energy into teaching their children at home. Fewer still have the required knowledge — particularly at the secondary level — and instructional capability necessary to carry out the job well. Those who do, however, feel that they are raising healthy, well-adjusted children in a positive, family-oriented environment.

Over the past decade, home schooling has shed its image as a social or educational aberration. As a result, or perhaps because of it, the proportion of students who, during these years, received their education at home has grown steadily. Because home schooling remains for some a viable alternative to traditional school-based learning, it is, and will continue to be, an important issue in education.

[4] Excludes home schoolers in Quebec, where the Ministry of Education does not collect figures on registered home schoolers.

[5] Priesnitz, Wendy and Heidi Priesnitz. (1990) *Home based education in Canada — An investigation.* Canadian Home Schoolers. St. George, Ontario: Alternative Press.

• This article is based on "A profile of home schooling in Canada," *Education Quarterly Review*, Winter 1997, Catalogue 81-003-XPB, Statistics Canada.

Jacqueline Luffman is an analyst at Statistics Canada.

Working Arrangements and Time Stress

by Janet E. Fast and Judith A. Frederick

Meeting the competing demands of paid work and family roles is a challenge for an increasing number of Canadians. In recent decades, women's labour force activity has increased markedly while men have become somewhat more involved in family and domestic roles. As a result, many people experience conflicts between job and family responsibilities, mostly due to lack of time or energy (or both) to successfully meet all demands. Studies have shown that this work-family conflict can lead to increased stress, poorer health, lost income and missed job advancement opportunities for employees; for employers, it can result in greater absenteeism, higher work-force turnover and lower productivity.

When asked how their workplaces could be made more "family friendly," many Canadians have suggested that they would benefit from working arrangements that allow greater flexibility in the scheduling of hours and the location of the workplace.[1] Specific working arrangements that were mentioned include flexible work schedules, compressed work weeks, part-time work, work-at-home arrangements and job sharing. But do employees' "family-friendly" work arrangements actually help them to balance their paid work and family demands? The 1992 General Social Survey (GSS) provides a first glimpse of the way working arrangements might be related to at least one outcome of work-family conflict – perceived time stress.

Prevalence of various working arrangements differs Three characteristics of working arrangements appear to affect workers' ability to balance work and personal demands and so affect their level of perceived time stress. They are the number of hours worked, the time when hours are worked and the place where hours are worked.[2] Respondents were asked if their working arrangements included any flexibility or departure from the norm – 40 hours per week spread over five weekdays at the employer's place of business. Seven alternate work arrangements were identified: self-employment, part-time employment (less than 30 hours per week), shift work (other than a regular daytime shift), flextime (employees choose when they begin and end their work day), flexplace (employees work some of their regular paid work hours at home), compressed work week (employees work extended hours each day in order to work fewer days per week) and on-call work (employees are obliged to work when specifically requested – nurses, teachers, workers in commodity sales).

Some of these work arrangements are more common than others. Only 9% of respondents worked compressed weeks,

[1] J.L. MacBride-King, **Work and family: Employment challenge of the '90s**, Ottawa: The Conference Board of Canada, November 1990; Ontario Women's Directorate & Camco Inc., **Work and family: Flexible working arrangements**, Toronto, October 1991.

[2] Berna J. Skrypnek and Janet E. Fast, "Work and family policy in Canada: Family needs, collective solutions," **Journal of Family Issues**, vol. 17, no. 6, Fall 1996.

CANADIAN SOCIAL TRENDS BACKGROUNDER

General Social Survey

The General Social Survey (GSS), conducted annually since 1985, gathers data on social trends and policy issues of current or emerging interest.[1] It covers all persons aged 15 and over residing in Canada, excluding residents of the Yukon and Northwest Territories and full-time residents of institutions. Each cycle of the GSS covers one of five subject areas – health and social support, time use, personal risk, education and work, and family – each of which is repeated every fifth cycle. This study uses data from the second GSS on time use (Cycle 9). Over 9,800 respondents were interviewed between January and December in 1992. The sample used in this study consists of 5,060 respondents aged 15 and over, whose main activity in the twelve months preceding the survey was working at a job or business.

Measuring perceived time stress Respondents to the 1992 GSS were asked a set of ten questions intended to measure their perceptions of time stress. The number of positive responses to these questions represents an overall measure of time stress, with scores ranging from zero (no positive responses) to ten (positive responses to all of the questions). Scores of seven or higher are considered to indicate "high" perceived time stress.

☐ 1. Do you plan to slow down in the coming year?

☐ 2. Do you consider yourself a workaholic?

☐ 3. When you need more time, do you tend to cut back on your sleep?

☐ 4. At the end of the day, do you often feel that you have not accomplished what you had set out to do?

☐ 5. Do you worry that you don't spend enough time with your family or friends?

☐ 6. Do you feel that you're constantly under stress to accomplish more than you can handle?

☐ 7. Do you feel trapped in a daily routine?

☐ 8. Do you feel that you just don't have time for fun any more?

☐ 9. Do you often feel under stress when you don't have enough time?

☐ 10. Would you like to spend more time alone?

[1] Starting in 1998, with the third survey on time use, the GSS will be conducted every two years rather than every year.

while 36% had a flextime arrangement. Also, many respondents had multiple alternate work arrangements. For example, among part-time workers, 25% were self-employed, 46% had flextime arrangements and 33% did on-call work. Similarly, of those who were self-employed, 76% also worked flextime and 60% had flexplace arrangements. In addition, 41% of those with flextime also worked some regular hours at home and 42% of on-call employees worked flextime.

The prevalence of alternate working arrangements differs for men and women. Men were more likely than women to be self-employed (21% versus 14%, respectively), to have flextime (40% and 30%) and to work on call (25% and 19%). There were also some variations in the prevalence of work arrangements depending on the presence of children, especially for women. Women with children were more likely than women without children to work part time (32% versus 23%, respectively), to be self-employed (17% versus 12%), to have flextime (26% versus 18%) and to have flexplace working arrangements (27% versus 16%). Parents were somewhat less likely to work shifts than other men and women.

Parents more time stressed than workers without children Family responsibilities appear to be closely related to time stress. Parents with children under age 19 living at home were more likely to report high levels of time stress than those without dependent children, though the difference was much greater for women than for men. In 1992, 27% of mothers and 18% of fathers reported high time stress, compared with only 17% of childless women and 13% of childless men. The higher rate for women may reflect the fact that although the labour force activity of men and women is increasingly similar, women still retain primary responsibility for family care and domestic work.[3] Interestingly, the age of the youngest child had no significant effect on the level of perceived time stress reported by employed parents.

Some common working arrangements did not affect perceived time stress If some workers are adopting alternate work arrangements in an attempt to find more time for themselves or their families, then some work schemes are not meeting their expectations. Three of the seven alternate work arrangements identified – self-employment, flexplace and shift work – were not related to workers' time stress. In fact, similar proportions of men and women reported high levels of time stress, whether or not they had one of those arrangements. This was true even when the effect of other factors (such as occupation and children) were taken into account. Some working arrangements, however, did seem to be related to levels of perceived time stress.

For many, part-time work reduces time stress About 19% of full-time workers were highly time stressed, compared with just 11% of part-time workers. This held true for both men and women; in fact, women working full time were twice as likely as those working part time (24% versus 12%) to report high levels of perceived time stress. Meanwhile, high time stress was almost three times more common among men working full time (16%) as among those working part time (6%).

For many women, working part time presents a strategy for balancing employment and family demands. According to the Labour Force Survey, many women who choose to work shorter hours do so for family-related reasons.[4] General Social Survey data suggest that working part time is a fairly successful strategy for alleviating time stress. However, part-time workers have made some economic concessions that their counterparts in full-time jobs have not. Part-time work is often marginalized, low-wage work lacking benefits such as extended medical, dental and pension plans; for example, only 27% of part-time workers have employer-sponsored pension plans, compared with 54% of full-time workers. Since the personal incomes of part-time workers are lower than those of full-time workers, families with at least

Percentage of employees with alternate working arrangements CST

| Working arrangement | All employees | Men | | | Women | | |
		All men	With children	Without children	All women	With children	Without children
				%			
Part-time	12	5	2	7	22	26	18
Self-employed	18	21	20	22	14	17	12
Flextime	36	40	40	40	30	32	29
Flexplace	22	23	24	21	21	27	16
Compressed work week	9	9	9	9	9	8	10
On-call work	22	25	26	23	19	20	19
Shift work	23	25	22	26	21	19	23

Percentages do not total to 100 as some respondents' work arrangements included more than one category.
Source: Statistics Canada, 1992 General Social Survey.

one part-time earner tend to have lower household incomes than those in which both partners work full time. Furthermore, personal self-esteem, independence and decision-making power within the family are often related to the individual's ability to contribute to the family's income.

It is widely believed that it is more acceptable for women to cut back on their paid work hours to meet family obligations and that it is more acceptable for men to accommodate their family life to the demands of their jobs. The reason for this "division of responsibilities" is partly financial: men's contribution to the family income is greater, on average, than women's (56% versus 31% in 1994). Men and women need equal freedom to choose the combination of work and family involvement that best suits them. The evidence presented here suggests that part-time work may help both men and women deal effectively with time stress. However, men are much less likely than women to adopt this strategy.

Women with flextime less time stressed... In 1992, almost one-third (30%) of employed women had a flexible work schedule, and they were less likely to be highly time stressed than women without flextime (18% versus 23%, respectively). Although an even larger proportion of men (40%) had flexible work schedules, flextime did not reduce their perceived time stress (15%).

Flexibility in the workplace, especially flexibility with respect to starting and finishing times, is believed to be important for workers trying to manage work and family responsibilities.[5] Indeed, a somewhat larger proportion of women with children than those without were working flextime (32% versus 29%, respectively). Such an arrangement may provide an opportunity for parents to share the twice daily peak demand periods of getting children off to school in the morning, and picking them up and preparing supper in the evening. And, in fact, flextime does appear to be an effective stress reliever, at least for women.

[3] For more information, see J.A. Frederick, **As time goes by...Time use of Canadians**, Statistics Canada, Catalogue no. 89-544-XPE.

[4] See Ron Logan, "Voluntary part-time workers," **Perspectives on Labour and Income**, Autumn 1994, Statistics Canada, Catalogue no. 75-001-XPE.

[5] Women's Policy Office, "Women and men in the workplace: A discussion of workplace supports for workers with family responsibilities," 1993 Paper presented at the 12th Annual Conference of Ministers Responsible for the Status of Women.

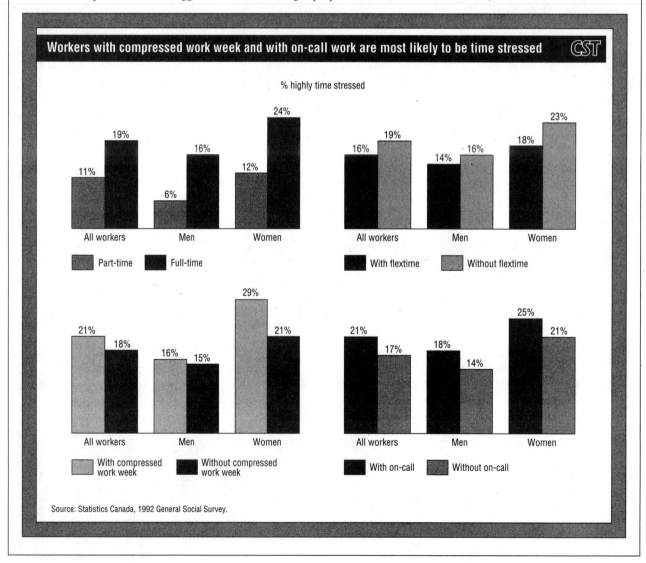

Workers with compressed work week and with on-call work are most likely to be time stressed CST

% highly time stressed

Part-time / Full-time

With flextime / Without flextime

With compressed work week / Without compressed work week

With on-call / Without on-call

Source: Statistics Canada, 1992 General Social Survey.

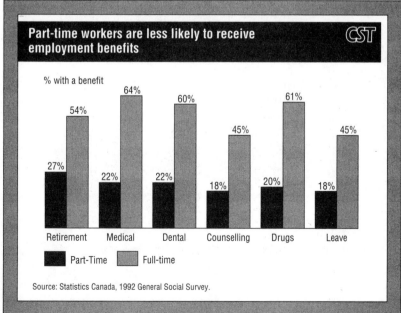

Part-time workers are less likely to receive employment benefits `CST`

% with a benefit

Benefit	Part-Time	Full-time
Retirement	27%	54%
Medical	22%	64%
Dental	22%	60%
Counselling	18%	45%
Drugs	20%	61%
Leave	18%	45%

■ Part-Time　■ Full-time

Source: Statistics Canada, 1992 General Social Survey.

Yet proportionally fewer women than men have this arrangement. This raises the question of whether access to flextime and other "family-friendly" work arrangements is related to more specific characteristics of employment, such as occupation and full- or part-time work status.

...while those with compressed work weeks more time stressed Even though compressed work weeks have been promoted as a "family-friendly" working arrangement, women using this arrangement are more likely to experience a high level of time stress than women without this work arrangement. Women working extended daily hours in exchange for fewer work days (29%) were more likely to be highly time stressed than women who did not work extended hours (21%). In contrast, compressed work weeks did not influence the proportion of men who reported being highly time stressed; in fact, the stress levels were consistent with most of the other alternate work arrangements.

Many household tasks, such as meal preparation and child care, cannot easily be delayed or re-scheduled. Considering the greater responsibility women have assumed for meeting family demands, a longer day on the job probably makes dealing with peak stress times – morning and after work – even more stressful. There may also be pressure on women to accomplish more at home on their "day off," since many household tasks are continuous and repetitive, making it difficult to say that the work is finished. Perhaps that is why so few women (9%) use this working arrangement.

On-call work associated with higher perceived time stress for men On-call work is not a work arrangement that has been touted as "family friendly," but it appears to be a common experience among Canadian workers. In 1992, 25% of men and 19% of women respondents did some on-call work. Men with on-call jobs were more highly time stressed than those without (18% versus 14%), while differences for women were not statistically significant.

It should not be surprising to find that on-call workers report such high levels of time stress. Not only is on-call work especially incompatible with caring for children (whose needs may be difficult to cover at short notice), but it probably interferes with personal time and family plans more often than other work arrangements.

Not an issue for workers alone This study has focused on the relationship between people's working arrangements and their levels of perceived time stress.

For ease of discussion, this article has reported only the results of direct comparisons between workers who did, and those who did not, use alternative work arrangements. However, these findings are supported even when the effects of other factors are controlled for. For example, employees with flextime arrangements reported considerably less time stress than people who did not

work flextime, even if they were very similar in terms of other characteristics. The analysis controlled for factors such as presence of children, occupation, industry of employment, and additional alternate work arrangements they might have had (for example, working part time as well as flextime).

Working arrangements have implications for employers as well as employees. Employers may face higher recruitment and training costs and increased payroll taxes if more employees opt for part-time work. Similarly, they may have to spend more on computer and communications equipment for employees who adopt a flexplace working arrangement. On the other hand, part-time workers may receive fewer benefits, thus lowering employers' costs, while more telecommuting may also reduce the need for costly office space. Similarly, enabling employees to better balance their paid work and family demands may reduce employer costs by reducing absenteeism and workforce turnover. Clearly, costs and benefits for both employers and employees must be considered when making any decisions about workplace policies that relate to working arrangements.

Dr. Janet E. Fast is an associate professor with the Department of Human Ecology, University of Alberta. **Judith A. Frederick** is a senior analyst with the General Social Survey, Housing, Family and Social Statistics Division, Statistics Canada.

CANADIAN SOCIAL TRENDS BACKGROUNDER

National Child Care Survey

The National Child Care Survey (NCCS) was conducted by Statistics Canada in partnership with the National Daycare Research Network in September and October 1988. A supplement to the monthly Labour Force Survey, it covered households with a child or children under the age of 13. The information gathered addressed most aspects of child care arrangements made by the parent with primary responsibility for arranging child care, 94% of whom were women.

The NCCS offers a valuable insight into the working arrangements that employed parents would *prefer* to have, as opposed to the ones they *actually* have. As such, these findings complement the issues raised in this article. Only one-third (34%) of employed parents with primary responsibility for child care wanted to work full time; the majority (53%) would have preferred to work part time, while 13% wished they did not have to work at all. Perhaps because neither of these options was feasible (73% of parents worked full time), a large minority of parents (39%) wanted to change their work schedules. When asked to select only one child-related benefit their employers could provide that would best support them as parents, nearly one-quarter of working parents (23%) identified child care facilities in the workplace and another one-fifth (19%) cited flexible work hours.

The NCCS also found that parents' employment characteristics were related to their access to family-supportive workplace benefits and arrangements. Parents in skilled occupations (professionals, semi-professionals and technicians) had greatest access to part-time work and job-sharing, while flexible work schedules and paid family responsibility leave were most often available to senior and middle managers. Part-time workers had more access to flexible hours but less to paid leave, suggesting that these parents may be trading paid benefits (such as family leave, or employer-sponsored "top-up" of Unemployment Insurance maternity benefits) for the opportunity to work fewer or more flexible hours.

A series of analytical reports based on the NCCS data is available from Statistics Canada. Data in this Backgrounder were drawn from **Workplace Benefits and Flexibility: A Perspective on Parents' Experiences**, Statistics Canada, Catalogue no. 89-530-XPE. This report focuses on parents' knowledge and opinions of workplace arrangements that would help them harmonize work and family life.

The Crowded Nest: Young adults at home

by Monica Boyd and Doug Norris

B ecoming an adult involves many changes in a teen-ager's life. Leaving high school, going to college or university, getting a full-time job, becoming economi-cally self-sufficient, getting married — all these are commonly accepted indicators of being an adult. Since these changes often go hand in hand with leaving the parental home, many people also think of "moving out" as being part of the transition to adulthood.

Throughout most of the twentieth century, most people viewed the steps to adulthood as sequential and irre-versible. Today, however, these changes are not one-time-only events that occur in sequence. Young Canadians may stay in school and live with a partner, rather than first completing school and then legally marry-ing. They also may find jobs and subsequently, or simultaneously, return to school. And they may continue to live with their parents, or move out and then move back in, throughout these schooling, employment and family-building years.

According to Canadian censuses, the proportions of young adults who lived with their parents fell between 1971 and 1981, following the general twentieth century trend toward non-familial living arrangements for the young and the older generations. Since then, however, the transition to adulthood has become more dynamic and young adults are now more likely to live with parents. This article uses census data from 1981 to 1996 to examine the growing phenomenon of young adults living at home.

Young adults now more likely to live with their parents
Since 1981, the percentage of young adults in their twen-ties and early thirties living in the parental home has been increasing. In 1996, 23% of young women aged 20 to 34 lived at home, up from 16% in 1981. Over the same period, the percentage of young men the same age residing in the parental home rose to 33% from 26%. Most of the increase

took place from 1981 to 1986 and from 1991 to 1996, both periods of economic recession and slow recovery.

The growing propensity to live at home was common to both unmarried and married young adults. In 1996, nearly half (47%) of unmarried women aged 20 to 34 lived with parents, up from 44% in 1981. More than half of young unmarried men also resided in the parental home, about the same as in 1981. Despite a brief decline from 1986 to 1991, by 1996, the percentages of young unmarried adults living with their parents were the highest in 15 years.

In Canada and other industrial countries, young couples are usually expected to establish residences separate from those of their parents; as a result, not many young adults in common-law or legal marriages reside with their parents. Nevertheless, in 1996 a higher percentage of young married adults (including common-law) were living in the parental home than in 1981. Unlike their unmarried counterparts, the proportion of married young adults living with their parents has risen steadily over the past 15 years.

Young adults living at home are older and the majority are men

One of the most notable shifts in the characteristics of young adults living at home is that they are older. In 1981, only about one-quarter of unmarried women and men living with their parents were aged 25 or over; by 1996, the percentages had risen to 33% and 40%, respectively.

Changes were even more pronounced for young adults who were married, jumping from 52% of women and 64% of men in 1981, to 69% and 78% in 1996.

Many other studies in Canada and the United States have found that the living arrangements of young adults differ considerably by gender. Smaller percentages of young women live at home, which researchers speculate may be partly explained by gender roles. Parents may more closely supervise the social lives of their daughters than their sons, so that women may feel they have more independence living elsewhere. Researchers also suggest that, because they are more involved in household tasks as teenagers, young women may be better able to take care of themselves in terms of cooking, cleaning and laundry skills.[1]

Differences in the way families assign chores to men and women may also deter young women from living with their parents. When at home, young women report spending more hours doing housework than young men, whereas

1. Boyd, Monica and Edward T. Pryor. 1989. "The Cluttered Nest: The Living Arrangements of Young Canadian Adults," *Canadian Journal of Sociology*, 15: 462-479. DaVanzo, Julie and Francis Kobrin Goldscheider. 1990. "Coming Home Again: Returns to the Parental Home of Young Adults," *Population Studies*, 44 : 241-255. Ward, Russell A. and Glenna Spitze. 1992. "Consequence of Parent-Adult Child Co-residence: A Review and Research Agenda," *Journal of Family Issues*, 13: 553-572.

CST — The proportion of young adults living at home has been rising over the past 15 years

| | Percent living with parents | | | | | | | |
| | Unmarried | | | | Married* | | | |
	Total	20-24	25-29	30-34	Total	20-24	25-29	30-34
Women								
1981	44	60	27	18	1	3	1	1
1986	46	64	32	18	2	3	2	1
1991	44	63	33	19	2	5	2	1
1996	47	67	36	19	3	7	4	2
Men								
1981	55	69	40	28	2	3	2	1
1986	57	72	45	30	2	4	2	1
1991	53	71	44	29	3	6	3	1
1996	56	74	48	32	4	9	5	3

* Married includes legal marriages and common-law relationships.
Source: Statistics Canada, Censuses of Population.

UNIT 2: WOMEN, MARRIAGE AND THE FAMILY

young men are more likely to pay room and board.[2] Another explanation could be that women outnumber men as lone parents, since the presence of children dampens the likelihood of young women living with parents.

Education, labour markets and marriage are factors at work

The growing tendency of young adults aged 25 and over to co-reside with their parents suggests that fundamental changes are occurring in the living arrangements of young Canadians. And indeed, this increase has coincided with significant social and economic changes. Starting in the 1960s, the expansion of colleges and universities has led to higher rates of enrollment, extending young people's adolescence and their dependence on their parents. The economy likewise has gone through several business cycles, recording prolonged boom times but also periods of severe recession, when young people generally experience higher rates of unemployment than older adults.

Fluctuations in living arrangements and in school enrollments of young adults are sensitive to labour market conditions.[3] The upswing in young unmarried adults living at home between 1981 and 1986 coincided with a severe recession in the early 1980s. A more prolonged recession occurred in the early 1990s, and was followed by increased percentages of young adults at home in 1996. Economic downturns do not mean that young adults automatically either stay in the parental home or move back in. But living with parents can be one of the ways in which young adults respond to unemployment, relatively low wages or low incomes while attending school.

In 1996, for example, 71% of unmarried women aged 20 to 29 who were full-time students lived at home, as did 66% of unmarried men with incomes of only $10,000 to $14,999 a year. These patterns are consistent with other studies which suggest that co-residency is a strategy for minimizing the household expenditures of young adults. But it also may represent an economic strategy for the family. When living together, parents and children can share

---

CST Full-time students were most likely to live at home

Percent of young adults aged 20-29 living at home				
	Unmarried		Married	
	Women	Men	Women	Men
All	**55**	**63**	**5**	**6**
School attendance				
Full-time	71	76	6	7
Part-time	52	64	5	6
Not attending	45	56	5	6
Labour force status				
Not in labour force	52	69	6	9
In labour force	56	62	5	6
Employed	56	61	4	5
Unemployed	58	68	7	8
Income				
Less than $5,000	69	75	6	10
$5,000-9,999	65	70	6	9
$10,000-14,999	47	66	5	8
$15,000-19,999	43	61	4	7
$20,000-29,999	42	54	4	6
$30,000-39,999	34	43	3	4
$40,000 or more	27	33	2	3

Note: Because the proportion of 30- to 34-year-olds living with parents is quite small, data are presented for the population aged 20 to 29 only.

Source: Statistics Canada, 1996 Census of Population.

2. Ward, Russell A. and Glenna Spitze. 1996. "Gender Differences in Parent-Child Coresidence Experiences," *Journal of Marriage and the Family*, 58: 718-725.

3. Boyd, Monica and Doug Norris. 1995. *The Cluttered Nest Revisited: Young Adults at Home*. Working Paper Series 94-127, Center for the Study of Population and Demography, Florida State University. Card, David and Thomas Lemieux. Forthcoming. "Adapting to Circumstances: The Evolution of Work, School and Living Arrangements Among North American Youth," in *Youth Unemployment and Employment in Advanced Countries*, David Blanchflower and Richard Freeman (eds.). University of Chicago Press for the National Bureau of Economic Research.

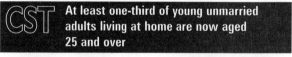

CST At least one-third of young unmarried adults living at home are now aged 25 and over

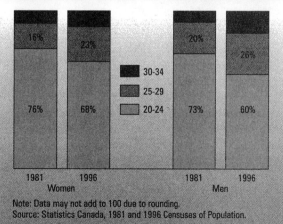

Note: Data may not add to 100 due to rounding.
Source: Statistics Canada, 1981 and 1996 Censuses of Population.

resources and adopt economies of scale with respect to food and shelter costs.[4] It should also be noted that there can be a cultural component to such living arrangements, since rates of co-residence with parents are greater for some ethnic and immigrant groups than for others.[5]

CST What might have been

Noteworthy as they are, the increases in the percentages of young adults living at home would be even greater if the age structure of this population had not changed over the period. Between 1981 and 1996, the age profile of the population aged 20 to 34 became older, resulting in proportionately fewer young adults in their early twenties and proportionately more in their late twenties and early thirties. Since children tend to move away from home as they get older, the aging of the young adult population has artificially reduced the overall percentage of 20- to 34-year-olds living at home. If the age profile had been the same in 1996 as in 1981, young adults would be even more likely to be living at home with their parents — 26% of all young women and 36% of all young men.

Percent of young adults aged 20 to 34 living with parents (age standardized)*

	Unmarried	Married
Women		
1981	44	1
1986	47	2
1991	47	3
1996	50	4
Men		
1981	55	2
1986	59	2
1991	57	3
1996	60	5

* Age standardization is a technique adopted when the age profile of a population (in this case, those aged 20 to 34) has changed significantly and might affect the results of comparisons over time. The population in this study has been standardized to the 1981 age distribution, using sex specific age distributions for unmarried women and men.

Source: Statistics Canada, Censuses of Population.

A final factor underlying the increasing percentage of young adults co-residing with parents is that they are remaining unmarried longer. Since the mid-1970s, the rate of first (legal) marriage has declined and the average age at marriage has increased. Women marrying for the first time were on average about three years older in 1996 than in 1981 — 27 versus 24 years. Similarly, men married at the more mature age of 29, compared with 26. And although the drop in legal marriage has been somewhat offset by an increase in common-law marriages, the percentage of young adults who are unmarried rose substantially between 1981 and 1996: from 35% to 45% for women, and from 45% to 56% for men.

Summary

Many young Canadian adults live with parents not just in their late teenage years but also throughout their twenties and early thirties. Interpretations of this phenomenon vary. One view assumes that living apart from the family of origin signals the successful transition to adulthood, alongside other indicators such as completion of education, employment, marriage and childbearing. From this perspective, the continued presence of adult children in the parental home is unusual.

Yet a more general lesson from the 1980s and 1990s emphasizes the fallacy of holding a narrow image of family life. The forms of Canadian families are diverse and constantly changing over the life cycle of their individual members. From this perspective, young adults live at home because this arrangement ultimately benefits them in making other types of transitions from adolescence to adulthood.

4. Grisgby, Jill S. 1989. "Adult Children in the Parental Household: Who Benefits?" *Population Studies*, 44: 241-255.

5. Boyd, Monica. 1998. *Birds of a Feather: Ethnic Variations in Young Adults Living at Home*. Working Paper Series 98-140. Center for the Study of Population and Demography, Florida State University.

Monica Boyd is the Mildred and Claude Pepper Distinguished Professor of Sociology and a Research Associate, Center for the Study of Population, and Demography Florida State University. She also is a Visiting Research Scholar at Statistics Canada, 1998-1999. **Doug Norris** is Director, Housing, Family and Social Statistics Division, Statistics Canada.

Under one roof: Three generations living together

by Janet Che-Alford and Brian Hamm

In contemporary Canadian society it is rare to find grandparents, parents and children living together. In the vast majority of cases, grandparents live in one home, while their children and grandchildren live in another. This "intimacy-from-a-distance" relationship, which largely reflects both grandparents' and parents' mutual preference for privacy and independence, has become somewhat like a prescribed norm. It is, therefore, not surprising to find that in 1996, three-generation households represented less than 3% of all family households in Canada.

Nonetheless, the number of three-generation households has risen 39% over the past decade, from some 150,000 in 1986 to more than 208,000 in 1996, a rate of increase more than twice that of all family households. This article uses census data to examine the characteristics of three-generation households in 1986 and 1996. It also explores why some families may be more likely than others to settle into an arrangement where grandparents, parents and children live under the same roof.

Over half of three-generation households have one grandparent

Canada's 208,000 three-generation households take many different shapes and forms. In 1996, the most common arrangement consisted of a home shared by one grandparent, two parents and any number of children — 31% of three-generation households fell into this category. The next two most common arrangements were those centred around a single parent and children, but while one grandparent rounded out the first type of family (some 24% of three-generation families), two grandparents were present in the second (24%). Finally, in 21% of cases, three-generation households were made up of two grandparents, two parents and children.

Although many people might believe that extended family living is more common in rural Canada, the vast majority of three-generation households (80% in 1996 and 74% in 1986) live in cities. The urban concentration of these households is no different than that of the general population.

The provincial distribution of three-generation households also resembles that of the general population. The majority of these households were found in Ontario (44%), British Columbia (16%) and Quebec (16%), which taken together accounted for 76% of the nation's three-generation households in 1996, up from 70% in 1986. However, as a percentage of all households, they were most common in Newfoundland (just over 4%) and least common in Quebec (less than 2%).

Asian immigrants contribute to rise in three-generation households

The provincial distribution of households reveals strong associations between three-generation households and the immigrant population. Overall, nearly half of all three-generation households in Canada were headed by immigrants.[1] This average, however, masks some widely varying scenarios; in both British Columbia and Ontario, immigrants headed every six out of ten three-generation households, while the proportion was closer to four out of ten in Alberta and just three out of ten in Quebec.

Through successive waves of arrivals over the years, immigrants have come to account for a substantial share (17%) of Canada's population. Since the 1970s, the overall number of immigrants from the United Kingdom and Europe has declined, while the number of those from Asia has increased. Three-generation families are part of

---

1. Census respondents are asked to identify a reference person or "head" for their household and then to describe the relationship of each household member to this individual.

---

this trend. In 1996, more than one out of five family households (22%), and nearly half of three-generation households (46%), were headed by immigrants. Among immigrants who arrived between 1986 and 1996, Asians made up the majority (75%) of three-generation household heads.

The gain of Asian immigrants may explain, at least in part, the rising number of three-generation households in Canada

---

This gain of Asian immigrants may explain, at least in part, the recent rise of three-generation households in Canada. People born in Asia are more culturally accustomed to live in a large, extended family system. And because most Asian immigrants are recent arrivals, they are more likely to uphold the traditions of their country than immigrants who have been in Canada longer.

Family re-unification may also have contributed to the increase of three-generation households. Indeed, between 1986 and 1996, family re-unification accounted for more than 30% of all immigrants.[2] The arrival of an elderly parent joining the family of

an adult child can add to the pool of three-generation households.

40% of three-generation households include someone with an activity limitation

Health is one of the key factors affecting people's living arrangements. This is particularly so when one's ability to perform specific household tasks (such as getting in and out of bed, cutting food, walking up and down the stairs) is compromised. The loss of functional independence is often a reason for a person to live with others, very often with relatives. According to the 1996 Census, 40% of three-generation households included someone with an activity limitation. The majority (over 70%) of these activity limitations had lasted, or were expected to last, at least six months. Three-generation households were also likely to have more than one family member with a disability; in 1996, for example, 13% of these households included two or more persons with limitations compared with 6% of all family households.

---

2. Citizenship and Immigration Canada. *Landed Immigrant Data System*.

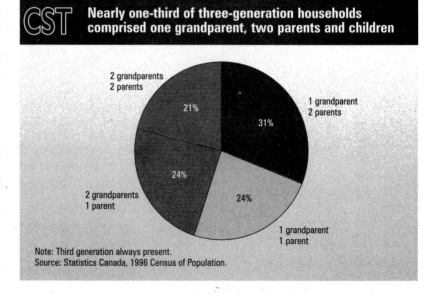

CST **Nearly one-third of three-generation households comprised one grandparent, two parents and children**

2 grandparents 2 parents — 21%

1 grandparent 2 parents — 31%

2 grandparents 1 parent — 24%

1 grandparent 1 parent — 24%

Note: Third generation always present.
Source: Statistics Canada, 1996 Census of Population.

Because older people are generally more susceptible to chronic health conditions, physical ailments and activity limitations, it is often assumed that grandparents account for the high proportion of persons with disabilities in three-generation households. However, 1996 Census data do not confirm this view. Indeed, they suggest that members with activity limitations were just as likely to belong to the younger as the older generation; for example, in 1996, 37% came from the oldest and 38% from the middle generation, with children accounting for the remaining 25%. The pattern was nearly identical in 1986, when the first and second generations each accounted for 38% of household members with limitations. It appears, then, that three-generation households act as family support systems for all members with disabilities, young or old.

Three-generation households pool resources for higher family incomes and larger homes

Pooling resources among family members can help secure shelter payments and reduce economic hardship. The 1996 Census asked each household to report who paid the rent or mortgage, taxes, electricity, and other expenses for the dwelling. These persons were labelled "household maintainers." It is reasonable to assume that if more than one maintainer is reported in a household, income pooling has taken place.

According to census data, households with multiple maintainers were quite common; about 45% of all family households and 48% of three-generation households had more than one maintainer. But it is in the case of three or more maintainers that major differences between households can be observed. While the probability of having three or more maintainers was 13% in three-generation households, it was only 2% in all family households (and only slightly higher, 3%, in family households with three or more persons). It appears that pitching in for shelter payments among extended kin is quite an acceptable arrangement in three-generation households.

Three-generation households were also more likely to have multiple income recipients. In 1996, over 80% of these households had at least three income recipients compared with less than one-quarter of all family households. As a result, three-generation households had higher average incomes: $66,000 versus $57,000 for all family households. However, since these households also had more members, averaging five persons per household compared with three for all family households, their per capita

	Three-generation households		All family households	
	No.	%	No.	%
Total households	208,500	100	7,841,000	100
With a person with activity limitation	82,700	40	1,594,200	20
Long-term	58,700	28	1,226,700	16
Not long-term	24,000	12	367,500	5
No person with activity limitations	125,800	60	6,246,800	80

CST Three-generation households were more likely to have a member with an activity limitation...

... and to have multiple income recipients

Number of income recipients in the household

	Three-generation households		All family households	
None	35	0	8,140	0.1
One	2,800	1	1,052,075	13
Two	36,620	18	4,866,980	62
Three	77,905	37	1,233,845	16
More than three	91,100	44	679,955	9

Note: Numbers may not add to 100 due to rounding.

Source: Statistics Canada, 1996 Census of Population.

income ($13,000) turned out to be lower than that of all family households ($19,000). And if per capita income is used as a proxy for economic well-being, then members of three-generation households were considerably less well off than their counterparts in other families. However, pooling of resources does allow for economies of scale, which have the effect of raising the standard of living.

Like other family households, the majority of those with three generations (69%) lived in single detached houses in 1996 and most (77%) owned their homes. About one-third were mortgage-free. Unlike all family households, however, almost two-thirds of three-generation households (61%) lived in houses with more than seven rooms. But because they tend to have more members than the average household (five versus three), despite their larger accommodations, three-generation households ended up with less room per person. Considering that their houses were larger, it is not surprising that average shelter costs — for both owned and rented accommodation — were higher for three-generation families.

Grandparents help families cope financially

It is interesting to identify which generation in three-generation families contributes to household maintenance. In households with only one maintainer, that maintainer was most often the grandparent: in 59% of cases in 1986 and 55% in 1996. In situations where there were multiple maintainers, the contribution of grandparents for shelter payments was also considerable. At least one grandparent helped out with household payments in about 55% of three-generation households in 1991 and 54% in 1996.[3]

From these figures it is clear that, over the past decade, grandparents have played a key role as contributors to shelter payments in three-generation households. This period coincides with a time when structural changes in the economy eroded the ability of many young families to be economically self-sufficient. The financial contribution of grandparents may have alleviated the harsher aspects of tough economic circumstances.

Summary

Despite a general preference for nuclear family households, some Canadians have settled into a living arrangement involving three generations — an arrangement which became much more common between 1986 and 1996. With current trends to longer lives, aging populations, and high levels of immigration, three-generation households will likely continue to increase in number, possibly at an even faster rate. Increased longevity will result in more families with three or perhaps four generations living at the same time; older Canadians, particularly women, will likely spend more years in family roles such as grandparenthood. Many generations living together could have positive or negative implications for family life. On the one hand, it may generate new kinds of stresses on families' needs and obligations; on the other, it could signal inter-generational cohesion and family resilience.

Janet Che-Alford is a senior analyst and **Brian Hamm** is an analyst with Housing, Family and Social Statistics Division, Statistics Canada.

---

3. Information on multiple maintainers was not collected in 1986.

Widows Living Alone

by Irwin Bess

The death of a spouse can be very stressful, particularly for many older women who may have devoted most of their lives to their husband, children and home. They are suddenly alone — often for the first time ever — and in addition to the emotional adjustment, they also have to decide about new living arrangements. With many years of life ahead, widows have a number of options such as living on their own, sharing a home with family or friends, or moving into a seniors' residence.

According to the 1995 General Social Survey, 75% of Canada's 887,000 widows aged 65 and over lived alone. Most of these widows had left home before age 25 to marry and have children. They remained married to the same man for an average of 39 years, and were widowed at the average age of 63. As of 1995, most (82%) had been widowed for at least four years. This article examines some of the characteristics that appear to predispose widowed women to live on their own, with particular emphasis on the extent of their contact with family and friends.

Half of senior widows still live in the home once shared with their husband

Although the majority of widows have at least one son or daughter, most do not live with their children.[1]

Living with family may provide emotional and economic support, but it raises a number of other practical questions such as the widow's involvement in day-to-day decisions about household and family activities, and the effect on her friendships, lifestyle and privacy.[2] Thus, a widow may feel that sharing a home would jeopardize her independence while increasing the likelihood of conflicts with her children, many of whom have children of their own.

This argument finds some support in the 1996 General Social Survey (GSS), which found that three in four Canadian widows aged 65 and over

---

1. Connidis, Ingrid Arnet. 1989. *Family Ties and Aging*. Toronto: Butterworths.

2. According to the 1996 General Social Survey, 17% of widows living with a married son or daughter felt that they had little to no control over day-to-day decisions affecting their lives, while less than 4% of those living alone felt that way.

(about 661,000) lived by themselves. Another 11% (about 95,000) lived with an unmarried adult son or daughter, while a further 11% shared a home with a married adult child and their families. The remainder (36,000) lived with siblings, other relatives or friends.

Some researchers contend that newly widowed women should not leave the home they shared with their husband for at least one year, since its many family memories and traditions can provide stability and emotional security; but they also warn that the therapeutic value of living alone in the family home may diminish over time and delay the transition to independence.[3] Nevertheless, slightly more than half (53%) of widows living alone in 1995 still occupied the home they had shared with their husband, and the large majority of these women (92%) had been widowed for more than three years. Homeowners were particularly well-grounded in their neighbourhood: among widows living by themselves, those who owned the family home had resided there for an average of 29 years, while widows in rental housing once shared with their husband had lived there for about 12 years.[4]

After the death of their husband, widows may see less of other couples with whom they previously had close contact; similarly, they may sense increasing emotional distance from their husband's friends and family as the years pass. For example, when respondents to the 1996 GSS were asked how many relatives they felt close to emotionally (excluding their children), widows living alone reported an average of only four relatives, compared to an average of six for married women. To compensate for the diminution of their previous social network, widows who live alone may look to strengthen their emotional ties with friends.

Three-quarters of senior widows living alone said they felt most close emotionally to a neighbour

---

Supportive relationships are key to dealing with the changes wrought by widowhood.[5] Whether continued residency in the family home helps or hinders long-term adjustment to widowed life, staying in the neighbourhood can help to maintain these relationships. Living alone is often balanced by frequent social contact, and senior widows seem to depend on a network of other women their own age. About one-half of widowed women living on their own in 1996 had a strong attachment to four or more friends; in fact, three-quarters of senior widows living alone said they felt most close emotionally to a neighbour. Being close friends with a neighbour allows frequent social contact, help with household tasks and emotional support during stressful times. Homeowners were likely to have more close friends than widows who rented, probably reflecting the length of time most had lived in the same residence.

Children and grandchildren living nearby may also provide a stable source of support for widows on their own.[6] According to the GSS, well over half (59%) of widows living by themselves in 1995 reported at least one adult child residing within 10 kilometres and almost one-fifth had a child within 50 kilometres. Although daily visits from a son or daughter were more common for widows in only fair or poor health (28%) than for those in good to excellent health (17%), weekly visits were equally frequent regardless of health status (43% and 45%, respectively).

Who is most likely to live alone?

A number of factors are significantly associated with a widow's living arrangement at age 65 and over. A statistical technique called logistic regression estimates the likelihood that, when the

---

3. Hartwigsen, Gail. 1987. "Older Widows and the Transference of Home," *International Journal of Aging and Human Development* 25, 3.

4. Over one-half (55%) of widows living alone in 1995 owned their dwelling.

5. Lopata, Helena Z. 1996. *Current Widowhood: Myths and Realities*. Thousand Oaks: Sage Publications.

6. Martin Matthews, Anne. 1987. "Widowhood as Expectable Life Event," in *Aging in Canada*, Victor W. Marshall (ed.), Toronto: Fitzhenry and Whiteside.

CST What you should know about this study

The General Social Survey (GSS), conducted since 1985, gathers data on social trends and policy issues of current or emerging interest. It covers all persons aged 15 and over residing in private households in the ten provinces. This study uses data primarily from the 1995 GSS, which focused on the family, marital histories and contact with children. Analysis is based upon over 600 female respondents representing 887,000 women age 65 and over in private households who were widows at the time of the interview. Additional analysis was supported by data from the 1996 GSS focusing on community and social support, as well as data from the 1996 Census.

The odds of a widow living alone instead of with others are strongly linked to health, age and children

Current age	
65 to 69	*1.0*
70 to 74	1.0
75 to 79	1.7*
80 and over	3.7
Age at widowhood	
Before age 65	*1.0*
Age 65 to 74	3.0
Age 75 and over	1.2*
Number of living children	
Had raised no children or has no living children	*1.0*
One or two	0.2
Three or more	0.1
Experience living alone before age 60	
Never	*1.0*
For at least three consecutive months	8.9
Occupying residence previously shared with husband	
No	*1.0*
Yes	1.0*
Health status	
Fair to poor	*1.0*
Good	2.1
Very good to excellent	2.5
Limited in amount of physical activity can do at home	
No	*1.0*
Yes	1.3*
Income	
Above $20,000	*1.0*
$10,000 to $20,000	0.5*
Less than $10,000	0.2

Note: Reference group shown in italics. An odds ratio close to 1.0 for the comparison group means there is little or no difference between widows in the comparison group and the reference group, when the effects of other factors shown in the table are controlled for.

* Not statistically significant.

Source: Statistics Canada, 1995 General Social Survey.

effects of other factors are controlled for, widows with certain characteristics will live alone as opposed to living with family or friends.

Many people assume that widows who live alone tend to be younger seniors. This is not the case. In fact, the odds that widows aged 80 and over would live alone was close to four times greater than those for widows aged 65 to 69, perhaps because the older group has lost other kin with whom they might have lived.

A woman's age at the time of her husband's death also influences the likelihood of living alone in the senior years. Women who lost their husband between the ages of 65 and 74 are three times more likely to live by themselves than women who lost their husband before they were 65. This finding supports other research which has found that women widowed younger in life may adjust to widowhood differently.[7] Women experiencing their husband's death at a younger age may still have dependent children at home. Also, women widowed early in life may not be able to benefit from a social network that could support them living independently, since they are probably the first of their friends and acquaintances to be widowed.

The overwhelming majority of widows who do not live alone are sharing a home with their adult sons or daughters, so there is a strong relationship between kin and living arrangement. Depending on the number of children they have, widows with children were only 10% to 20% as likely to be living by themselves as childless widows.

Although living independently requires some basic physical capability — taking care of personal needs, moving about in the home, and so on — having some activity limitations did

7. McPherson, Barry. 1990. *Aging as a Social Process: An Introduction to Individual and Population Aging*. Toronto: Butterworths.

not affect the likelihood that a widow would live on her own, after controlling for other factors. However, general overall health was an important determinant; the odds were over twice as great for widows in good to excellent health as for those whose health was fair to poor.

Widows now in their senior years tend to be an economically vulnerable group because most did not work outside the home during their married life; in fact, two-thirds of their children reported in the 1995 GSS that their mother had never been employed in the paid workforce while they were growing up. Many widows rely on public pension plans, survivor benefits or income support programs. Not surprisingly, the odds of living alone are lowest among widows with low incomes: compared with widows whose total annual personal income was over $20,000, those with an income below $10,000 were only one-fifth as likely to be living on their own.

The experience of living alone before being widowed may be yet another predictor. A widow will have many accomplishments to her credit, including raising her children, volunteer work and/or career. However, many had never lived by themselves for three consecutive months or more.[8] Compared with these widows, the odds of living alone at 65 and over were nine times greater for those who had lived on their own before age 60.

Summary

Becoming a widow often forces older women to weigh the advantages and disadvantages of sharing a home against those of living by themselves. Certainly, living on one's own can be a lonely and difficult experience at times. But the majority of widowed women aged 65 and over do live on their own, perhaps because they have strong support networks: many of them have lived in the same home for a long time and have close relationships with friends and their adult children. The belief that older widowed women living by themselves are isolated from supportive social relationships appears to be mistaken.

8. According to the 1995 General Social Survey, about 23% of senior widows who were living with others had never lived alone for 3 months or more.

Irwin Bess is an analyst with Statistics Canada.

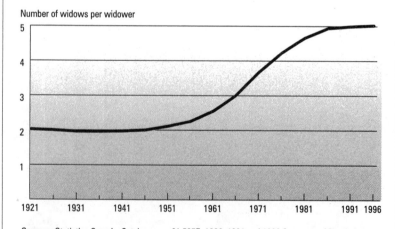

CST Widowers

Men represent a small proportion of all senior widowed persons. In 1996, only 11% of senior men, compared with about 46% of senior women, were widowed. Over the century, the gap between the number of widowed women and men aged 65 and over has widened substantially, from about two widows for every widower to about five to one by 1996 (887,000 women and 164,500 men in private households). The rising ratio is due to a combination of factors, including greater female life expectancy and age differences at marriage (according to the 1995 GSS, widows had been about five years younger than their husbands).

Number of widows per widower

Sources: Statistics Canada, Catalogue no. 91-535E, 1990; 1991 and 1996 Censuses of Population.

UNIT 3

WORK, LIFE STYLE, AND SOCIAL PROBLEMS

Skill Deficits Among The Young

by Sid Gilbert and Jeff Frank

Advancing technology has made adaptability a key component of success in the workplace. And while young people need the technical knowledge provided by an education to succeed in the job market, generic skills are also highly valued by employers. Some of these skills, such as literacy and numeracy, are formally taught by the education system. Others are acquired through experience and upbringing, including oral and written communication; thinking skills such as creativity, critical thinking and problem-solving; and "soft skills" such as interpersonal abilities, learning and team work.

These generic skills are maintained and improved with practice, and young people who rarely use them may face a more difficult transition from school to work. Indeed, they may also be vulnerable over the long-term, since having weaker generic abilities may make it harder to adapt to the changing requirements of the job market. This article focuses on the key factors associated with infrequent use of basic skills, and then examines the role of educational attainment in the application of these skills.

CST — What you should know about this study

Conducted by Statistics Canada on behalf of Human Resources Development Canada, the 1995 School Leavers Follow-up Survey (SLF) continued an ongoing survey of young people's lives as they finish their education and enter the workforce. The first survey, the 1991 School Leavers Survey (SLS), was designed to determine high school leaving rates ("drop-out" rates), and to compare young people who had successfully completed high school (graduates) with those who were still attending (continuers) and those who had left school before graduating (leavers). The SLS collected information from almost 9,500 young people aged 18 to 20 living in private dwellings in the ten provinces.

In 1995, the SLF revisited over 6,000 of the original respondents, now aged 22 to 24, to focus on school-to-work transitions of young adults by gathering information on education and work activities beyond high school. This article examines the generic skills respondents possessed, as measured by the frequency with which they performed these skills activities. Although this measure of skill use should not be interpreted as a direct indicator of proficiency, it is assumed that a skill performed frequently is less likely to be lost. Nevertheless, people may not use some of their skills because of the nature of their work, schooling or personal circumstances.

Skill sets: Skills were grouped into six categories, or sets: reading, writing, numeracy, communication, learning, and group or team work.

Skill use: Respondents were asked about the frequency with which they used the six basic skill sets during the 12 months preceding the survey. There was no restriction on the context in which these skills may have been used, allowing respondents to include activities at work, at school or in their personal life. For each of the six skill sets, respondents were asked four questions about the frequency with which they performed various skill-related activities. Responses ranged from never (least frequent) to more than three times a week (most frequent).

Self-assessment of ability: Respondents were asked to rate their abilities for each of the six skill activities on a scale of one to ten, that is, from very basic to very advanced.

Odds ratios: In this article odds ratios are used to assess whether, all other things being equal, people with a specific characteristic (say, employed) are more or less likely to report infrequent use of skills than a benchmark group of people (say, unemployed). An odds ratio close to 1.0 means there is little or no difference in skill use between the groups, but an odds ratio of 0.5 means the odds of low skill use are only half as high for the comparison group as for the benchmark group.

What factors are associated with having insufficient skills?

Who is most likely to have a low level of skill use? Using a statistical technique called odds ratios, which examines the relationship between frequency of skill use and some key socio-economic characteristics, six skill sets were analyzed: reading, writing, numeracy, verbal communication, learning, and group or team work.

Three factors — education, employment and student status — were consistently related to the low use of all six skill sets. For example, infrequent use of skills was associated with relatively low levels of education. In contrast, having a job or attending college or university decreased the odds of reporting low skill use. These findings suggest that without appropriate environments conducive to using

their skills, some young people risk losing the generic skills they already have, or may fail to develop new ones.

Even though women are widely believed to have better developed "soft skills," the analysis shows that after controlling for selected factors gender did not play an important role in low skill use. For instance, men are no more likely than women to report that they rarely read or use verbal

CST — Odds of rarely using basic skills are much higher for high school leavers

| | \multicolumn{6}{c}{Never or seldom used skills} |
	Reading	Writing	Numeracy	Verbal communication	Learning	Team work
Education						
School leaver	1.9	2.7	1.4	2.3	1.4	1.7
Not school leaver	*1.0*	*1.0*	*1.0*	*1.0*	*1.0*	*1.0*
Employment status						
Employed	1.1*	1.1*	0.7	0.6	0.8	0.6
Not employed	*1.0*	*1.0*	*1.0*	*1.0*	*1.0*	*1.0*
Student status						
Postsecondary student	0.4	0.4	0.8	0.8	0.7	0.8
Not postsecondary student	*1.0*	*1.0*	*1.0*	*1.0*	*1.0*	*1.0*
Gender						
Male	1.0*	1.3	0.4	1.0*	0.8	0.7
Female	*1.0*	*1.0*	*1.0*	*1.0*	*1.0*	*1.0*
Family structure						
Lone parent	1.0*	1.1*	1.0*	1.2	0.9	1.1
Two parents	*1.0*	*1.0*	*1.0*	*1.0*	*1.0*	*1.0*
Socio-economic status[1]						
Lower	1.3	1.4	1.0*	1.2	1.1*	1.1*
Higher	*1.0*	*1.0*	*1.0*	*1.0*	*1.0*	*1.0*

Note: Benchmark group shown in italics. An odds ratio of close to 1.0 for the comparison group means there is little or no difference in skill use between the comparison and the benchmark groups, when the effects of other factors shown in the table are controlled for.

* Not statistically significant.

1. Measured using mother's level of education as a proxy.

Source: Statistics Canada, School Leavers Follow-up Survey, 1995.

communication. On the other hand, they are considerably less likely than women to demonstrate low use of numeracy and teamwork skills.

Not unexpectedly, being a school leaver (not completed high school) was associated with low skill use, most notably in the areas of writing, reading and verbal communication. What seems more surprising, given conventional wisdom, is that after controlling for other factors, there were only very modest positive relationships between low skill use and living in a lone-parent family or a family with lower socio-economic status.

But how important was education?
The odds-ratio analysis shows that education is by far the most important predictor of a young person's skill use, but different patterns exist at different levels of education. Infrequent skill use was quite common among high school leavers, ranging from 55% for team work to 88% for verbal communication. As might be expected, high

> *Low skill use is only modestly associated with living in a lone-parent family, or in a family with lower socio-economic status.*

school graduates had higher levels of skill use than school leavers. Even among these young people, though, skills were not used frequently: the proportion of graduates who never or seldom used skills ranged from 37% for reading to 73% for verbal communication skills. Interestingly, the skill-use patterns of graduates with high school only more closely resembled those of leavers than of graduates who went on to further education.

How do youth rate their skills?
When asked to rate their skills, there was some noticeable dissonance between self-assessment and frequency of skill use, especially among

CST Literacy skills "mismatch" in the Canadian workplace

According to the 1994 International Adult Literacy Survey (IALS), about three-quarters of Canadian workers report there is a reasonable fit between their job requirements and their literacy skills (reading, writing and numeracy). Nevertheless, a significant number of people are a literacy "mismatch" with the work they do: one in five had higher level skills than were demanded by their job (literacy surplus), and as many as one in ten had insufficient skills to do their jobs adequately (literacy deficit).

Certain groups of workers are more likely to have a literacy surplus. Since the level of literacy among young Canadians is high, and yet many have difficulty finding satisfactory employment, it was not surprising that 16- to 24-year-olds were most likely (33%) to have a literacy surplus.

Among other factors, the extent of a worker's interaction with co-workers seems to influence literacy fit. Workers with limited or no supervisory responsibilities, the self-employed and those who worked part-time or in temporary jobs were more likely to find that their literacy skills were under-used. Jobs with these characteristics are often held by young people.

Having high literacy skills and not using them could have serious long-term consequences not only for individuals, but also for the overall level of human capital in the Canadian labour force. Analysis of the IALS data provides some support for the "use it or lose it" hypothesis, showing that under-using literacy skills in the workplace has a negative, if small, effect on literacy.

● For more information, see Harvey Krahn, and Graham Lowe, *Literacy Utilization in Canadian Workplaces*. Human Resources Development Canada, National Literacy Secretariat and Statistics Canada. Catalogue no. 89-552-MPE.

	Never or seldom used skills					
	Reading	Writing	Numeracy	Verbal communication	Learning	Team work
				%		
High school leavers	58	82	58	88	64	55
High school graduates	37	58	51	73	55	41
no post-secondary education	56	77	58	80	61	48
with some postsecondary	41	65	51	75	58	43
with university degree	24	37	47	61	53	31
with other postsecondary completion	42	63	49	74	54	39
Postsecondary students	21	41	47	70	50	40

CST High school leavers and high school only graduates have similar rates of low skill use

Source: Statistics Canada, School Leavers Follow-up Survey, 1995.

those with less education. The self-assessments were more positive than the frequency of skill use would indicate. Also, high school graduates with no further education were less likely than leavers to rate their skills as low, even though their skill use patterns were quite similar. University graduates and postsecondary students were least likely to view their skills as being only basic.

Summary

Young people were most likely to use basic skills infrequently if they had less than high school completion. They were also more likely to rate their abilities as low-level. These findings suggest that in an increasingly well-educated society, which demands a wide array of formal and informal skills, young people without postsecondary training face, and know they face, a difficult transition from school to work.

In contrast, young people with postsecondary qualifications assessed their abilities highly, even though their use of basic skills was lower than might be expected. This may indicate that although they possess the necessary skills, they are not yet employed in jobs that require them to exercise their abilities to the fullest extent. In other words, people in their 20s are still very much in the midst of maturing from students into workers.

• This article is adapted from *High School May Not Be Enough: An Analysis of Results from the School Leavers Follow-up Survey*. 1995. Human Resources Development Canada, Catalogue No. SP-105-05-98E and Statistics Canada, Catalogue No. 81-585-XPE.

Sid Gilbert is Director of the Centre for Educational Research and Assessment, University of Guelph, and **Jeff Frank** is a senior analyst with the Centre for Education Statistics, Statistics Canada.

Search for success: Finding work after graduation

by Warren Clark

Postsecondary graduates may have different priorities when they start looking for that first job after graduation. The main intention of many is to find a job that helps pay off their student debt. In fact, most recent graduates say they entered their program to learn job skills and to make a good income. For some, the ideal situation might be well-paying part-time employment, which would allow them to balance the demands of work and family, or a job where they could be their own boss.

Previous research has revealed a strong relationship between field of study, students' expectations and employment outcomes. This article examines what recent graduates looked for in a job and what contributed to their success in finding that first job: special skills, job search methods, or field of study.

What's important in a job is high pay

Graduates have certain expectations of what they want in a job. For many who graduated in 1995, finding a job with high pay was the most important. On their list of criteria for selecting a job, 21% of college and 13% of bachelor's degree graduates rated high pay as number one. Job location ranked second, liking the work ranked third and having a job related to their field of study ranked fourth for both groups of graduates.

High pay and job security may be particularly important to graduates with high student loans. At the bachelor's level, those with large student loans (more than $20,000) were more likely than graduates who did not borrow at all to consider a high-paying job as most important (18% versus 13%). College graduates, on the other hand, reported

CST — 1995 graduates were least successful finding full-time work and high level jobs

Two years after graduation	Class of 1982	Class of 1986	Class of 1990	Class of 1995
Working full-time			%	
College	77	82	76	70
Bachelor's	71	73	72	66
Working full-time in high level jobs[1]				
College	51	54	56	47
Bachelor's	78	77	77	73

1. Six highest categories of the Pineo-Carroll-Moore socio-economic classification of occupations including self-employed and employed professionals, semi-professionals, technicians, and senior and middle managers.

Source: Statistics Canada, National Graduates Survey, 1997.

that a job with high pay was their most important criterion regardless of the extent of their student loan indebtedness at graduation.

People at different stages in their lives and careers seek different qualities in a job. Although high pay remained the most important characteristic of a job for graduates at all ages, graduates over age 40 placed less importance on pay than those in their early 20s. Job location was very important to both college and university graduates in all age groups, though women university graduates under 40 placed a higher importance on job location than those aged 40 and over. Married women, especially those with children, placed less importance on a high-paying job than men or single women. When people have children, family-friendly job characteristics become more significant, while the importance of other job qualities may decline. For example, job location was more important to married women with children under age 5 than it was for women without children, for women with older children or for men. And while women university graduates placed almost as much importance on liking their work as they did on job location, when they had young children, the priorities changed. With men university graduates, marriage seemed to change their view of the importance of liking their work.

Single university men judged liking their work to be as important as job location, while their married counterparts placed much less importance on it. However, for college graduates, the importance of liking the kind of work they did, did not vary in the same way.

Networking most effective in finding first job

Learning about a job opening through friends, relatives, co-workers or associates was the most successful way of finding a first job. Perhaps one reason for this is that acquaintances can share information about jobs and about who is hiring. In addition, they can provide direct referrals to employers or people who know more about jobs of interest. In a sense, networking expands the circle of people helping with the job search. In a small U.S. survey, for example, referrals from current employees were considered extremely important by employers.[1] It is therefore no surprise that nearly one-third

---

1. In a survey of 192 employers during the summer of 1997, 77% of employers considered referrals from current employees important or extremely important in finding new employees. Richard Fein. 1998. "Traditional or Electronic Tools: How Do People Get Hired?" *Journal of Career Planning and Employment* 58, 4: 40-43.

CST   High pay was the most important job selection criterion for 1995 graduates

Criteria considered when selecting a job	College			Bachelor's		
	Total	Men	Women	Total	Men	Women
	(Importance score 0 to 3)					
High salary/pay	1.53	1.61	1.47	1.34	1.43	1.28
Job location	0.80	0.76	0.84	0.73	0.69	0.75
Like the kind of work	0.57	0.56	0.59	0.67	0.63	0.70
Job is in my field of study	0.45	0.47	0.44	0.52	0.45	0.56
Uses and develops my skills and abilities	0.32	0.30	0.34	0.44	0.39	0.48
Job security	0.28	0.33	0.24	0.17	0.20	0.14
Career advancement	0.27	0.36	0.21	0.37	0.45	0.32
Able to work with people	0.24	0.19	0.28	0.20	0.18	0.22
Feeling of accomplishment	0.17	0.17	0.17	0.32	0.34	0.31
Job allows flexibility	0.16	0.13	0.18	0.13	0.12	0.14
Well respected or prestigious occupation	0.10	0.11	0.09	0.07	0.08	0.07

Note: Graduates identified the three most important criteria they would consider when selecting a job. A value of 3 was assigned to criterion selected as the most important, a 2 for the second most important, a 1 for the third most important and a value of 0 for those criteria that were not in the top three. An importance score was calculated by averaging the values assigned across all graduates for each job selection criterion.

Source: Statistics Canada, National Graduates Survey, 1997.

During the summer of 1997, Statistics Canada, in partnership with Human Resources Development Canada, interviewed 43,000 people in the National Graduates Survey of 1995 Graduates (NGS). This sample represented more than 295,000 Canadians who had graduated from trade/vocational, college and university programs during 1995. Interviewers asked respondents about their education, training and labour market experiences during the two years immediately following graduation. They also asked graduates about how they found their first job after graduation, difficulties they may have had looking for a job, and what they considered important in a job.

The results presented in this article are for college graduates (graduates from publicly-funded community colleges, technical institutes, hospital schools of nursing and radiology, and similar institutions) and for graduates from bachelor's degree programs. Undergraduate certificates and diplomas, and first professional degrees (e.g., medicine, dentistry, veterinary medicine and law) are excluded from the bachelor's degree group. About 11,000 college and 11,500 bachelor's graduates were interviewed. The terms bachelor's and university are used interchangeably in the text to indicate graduates from bachelor's degree programs.

First post-graduation job: The first job graduates had after graduation. It includes jobs that may have started before graduation but continued after graduation.

Difficulty with job search tasks: Graduates indicated how difficult job-search activities for their first post-graduation job had been. On a four-point scale, responses ranged from no difficulty (0) to great difficulty (3).

of college (33%) and bachelor's (32%) graduates found their first job through friends or family.

Unsolicited calls or visits to employers helped one-sixth (17% of college and 18% of bachelor's) of graduates find their first job. A person using this method of finding work may have to make many unsuccessful calls or visits before finding a job. It needs high motivation and good interpersonal skills, but cold-calls made to the right person at the right time are likely to turn up jobs listed nowhere else.[2]

Many people start their job search by looking through want ads because it is easy to do and newspapers contain lists of specific openings that are frequently updated. However, the wide circulation of newspapers ensures much competition. Moreover, some sources say that over 80% of job openings are not advertised in newspapers.[3] According to the 1997 NGS, only about one in seven (14%) graduates found their first job after graduation through newspaper ads.

Previous employers may be a valuable source of information about new jobs. About 10% of graduates found their first job through this method. Although campus placement offices are often valuable sources of career information, only about 9% of graduates found their first job using them. Even fewer (3% of college and 4% of bachelor's) found their first job with the help of public or private employment agencies and less than 1% via the Internet.[4]

Many graduates experienced trouble in their job search
Searching for employment after graduation involves a lot of hard work for most new graduates. About one-quarter of college and bachelor's graduates had great difficulty finding a first job that paid enough, while one-third of bachelor's and one-quarter of college graduates had great difficulty finding one related to their field of study.[5]

One-sixth of graduates also had problems finding a job in the location of their choice. Newfoundland graduates had the most trouble, with 38% of college and 30% of bachelor's graduates experiencing great difficulty finding a job in the right location. In the other Atlantic provinces, about 24% of college and between 22% and 26% of bachelor's graduates had similar trouble. In contrast, only in Alberta and British Columbia did less than 15% of college and bachelor's graduates report great difficulty finding work in a place where they wanted to live.

Uncertainty about long-term goals can hamper a job search, and many university graduates — particularly in the humanities and social sciences — had trouble deciding what they wanted to do after graduation. Fourteen percent of bachelor's graduates reported having great difficulty making up their minds compared with 7% of college graduates. And the younger these graduates were, the higher their level of indecision.

The actual leg work involved in finding job openings was very difficult for about 7% of graduates. Although job interviews can be a problem for new job seekers, 51% of college and 45% of bachelor's graduates reported having no trouble in doing well during interviews for their first job.

Most college (69%) and bachelor's (61%) graduates had no difficulty writing résumés and letters of introduction, or completing job applications.

Age played a role in the problems encountered in the job search. Generally older graduates (over age 30) had less difficulty finding job openings than younger graduates (under age 22). Graduates of all ages reported finding a job that paid enough among their most difficult tasks, but older bachelor's graduates found it easier than young bachelor's graduates. In contrast, college graduates of all ages reported the same degree of difficulty in finding a well-paying job.

Graduates in some fields had a much less difficult job search experience than others; the health professions, sciences and technologies field was one of these. Many health-related fields have restrictive entrance requirements with very limited numbers of spaces, thereby controlling the number of graduates entering the labour market. Bachelor's graduates from these fields had the least trouble of all university graduates deciding what they wanted to be, knowing how to find jobs, finding jobs related to their field of study and finding a job that paid enough. For them, finding a job in the desired location was the hardest task, although still less difficult than for other fields. College graduates from health-related fields enjoyed similar experiences but also had more difficulty than other college graduates finding a job where they wanted to live.

Previous work experience most useful in finding a job

In 1995, 17% of college and 7% of bachelor's graduates had completed their studies through a co-op program. About half of the college and two-thirds of the bachelor's co-op graduates said that their co-op experience was helpful in finding a job after graduation. Even more graduates indicated that previous work experience had been helpful. Although over 80% of graduates had participated in career counselling or job search courses, only about 18% of college and 13% of university participants found them useful in finding a job.

Volunteering helps some find employment

Some graduates found their way into the paid workforce through volunteer activities. During the two years after graduation (1995 to 1997), about 54% of bachelor's and 39% of college graduates had done volunteer work, although women were more likely to do so than men. Over half of the volunteers reported that their volunteer activities were related to their field of study. About 39% of both college and bachelor's volunteers felt their activities had helped a great deal in developing positive work attitudes and about one third indicated they had helped greatly in developing work skills. About 13% of college and 18% of bachelor's volunteers indicated that these activities were a great help in finding a job. However, volunteers were less likely to be working full-time in June 1997 than those who did not volunteer; perhaps some graduates hoped to obtain work experience through volunteering if their employment prospects were not promising.

> *Bachelor's graduates had more difficulty deciding what to do after graduation than college graduates*

CST — Over one in four graduates reported great difficulty in finding a well-paying job

	College	Bachelor's
	%	
Finding a job that paid enough	28	27
Finding a job related to my field of study	25	33
Finding a job where I wanted to live	17	16
Knowing how to find job openings	7	8
Deciding what I wanted to be	7	14
Performing well in job interviews	2	2
Completing job applications, writing résumés or letters of introduction	1	1

Source: Statistics Canada, National Graduates Survey, 1997.

2. Wagner, Judith O. 1992. "Job Search Methods." *ERIC Digest No. 121*, ERIC Clearinghouse on Adult, Career, and Vocational Education. Columbus.

3. Student Employment Network. 1999. *The 1999 Canada Student Employment Guide*. Toronto, p.31.

4. Although the Internet now provides numerous resources to post job openings and résumés, it was still in its infancy when 1995 graduates were seeking their first jobs.

5. Bachelor's graduates from the humanities and related fields, social sciences, agriculture and biological sciences and technologies had the greatest difficulty in finding a job related to their education.

The first post-graduation job

By the time the class of 1995 was interviewed in June 1997, 95% had found their first post-graduation job. On average they had held 2.1 jobs between graduation and June 1997, but one in sixteen had held five or more jobs. Young workers typically show their quest for a good career with frequent job moves, while more experienced graduates move less often.[6] Graduates aged 20 or 21 went through 2.3 jobs on average; 7% had had five or more jobs. Meanwhile those aged 40 and over had had about 1.5 jobs, with only 2% reporting five or more jobs in the previous two years.

Graduates who accepted their first job because it was the only one they could find tended to stay in that job for a period averaging 21 or 22 months. In contrast, first jobs selected for other reasons (better pay, more opportunities for advancement, curiosity about the work) lasted an average of 31 or 32 months.

Some graduates began their first post-graduation job long before they graduated, and in some cases before they began their program: 6% of college and 8% of bachelor's graduates had been working at their first post-graduation job for five or more years before they graduated. About one-third of bachelor's graduates in this group were over age 30 working full-time in professional, semi-professional, senior or middle management, or technician jobs while pursuing part-time studies. Another 39% were under age 30 working as semi-skilled or unskilled labourers. About 29% of college graduates who started five years or more before graduation were in high level jobs.

Other graduates started working while they were at university or college. Among graduates with jobs that began one to four years before graduation (early starters), over half were in clerical, sales and service occupations: in other words, the type of part-time jobs that many students use to help finance their education. In contrast, graduates starting their first post-graduation job after graduating were more likely to be in professional or technical jobs. Early starters were more likely to stay in the same job than graduates who started to work after graduation. In fact, more than 70% of early starters had the same job one year after graduation, but only 47% of bachelor's and 52% of college graduates who had started their first job within three months of graduation were still in that job 12 months later.

> Graduates who accepted their first job because it was the only one they could find stayed in that job an average of 21 or 22 months

Summary

Many colleges and universities now offer job search seminars and workshops to help students find employment. These activities seem to have paid off in that the class of

CST Over half of 1995 graduates began their first job within three months of graduation						
	College			Bachelor's		
	Total	Men	Women	Total	Men	Women
First post-graduation job began...				%		
5 or more years before graduation	6	5	6	8	6	9
1 to 4 years before graduation	12	11	13	13	12	13
Less than 1 year before graduation	9	9	9	9	10	9
Less than 3 months after graduation	32	33	31	27	29	26
3 to 5 months after graduation	11	11	11	14	14	14
6 to 11 months after graduation	10	10	10	9	9	9
12 to 23 months after graduation	12	14	11	13	13	13
2 or more years after graduation	3	3	3	3	3	3
No job yet as of June 1997	6	5	6	5	5	6

Source: Statistics Canada, National Graduates Survey, 1997.

UNIT 3: WORK, LIFE STYLE AND SOCIAL PROBLEMS

1995 had little difficulty filling out job applications, writing résumés and letters of introduction. But few found their first job with the help of career counselling; in fact, networking with friends, family members and acquaintances remains the most successful method of finding a first post-graduation job. For graduates in both college and university, high pay was the single most important criterion for choosing a job. Many found a first job in a professional or technical occupation, but turnover was high. Those who had started their first job back in the days when they were still in school were least likely to leave it, while more recent job starters were more keen to switch. Both college and bachelor's graduates experienced the greatest difficulty in finding work that paid enough.

6. Lankard Brown, Bettina. 1998. *Career Mobility: A Choice or Necessity? ERIC Digest No. 191*, ERIC Clearinghouse on Adult, Career and Vocational Education.

Warren Clark is an analyst with Housing, Family and Social Statistics Division, Statistics Canada.

University graduates at college

by Warren Clark

Though most university graduates with bachelor's degrees go from school to work, those who continue their studies usually enroll in a master's or a professional program soon after graduation. Others, however, pursue studies at community colleges or technical institutes. During the 1990s, full-time postsecondary enrolment at Canada's publicly-funded colleges grew. Part of this growth was the result of young people with bachelor's degrees hoping to improve their career prospects by learning more job-specific skills at the college level.

According to the 1997 National Survey of 1995 Graduates, about 46% of people who had earned a bachelor's degree in 1995 had gone back to school within two years of graduating.[1] About 5% of bachelor's graduates entered a college program.[2] The evidence suggests that in subsequent years, even more members of the class of 1995 will pursue a college education. In an earlier group of university graduates, the class of 1990, the percentage who had enrolled in college programs after graduation doubled from 6% in 1992 (two years after graduation) to 13% in 1995 (five years after).

That university graduates may wait several years before enrolling in a college course is also suggested by data from other sources. The 1998 Adult Education and Training Survey shows that university attendance drops off quickly after age 24. In 1997, 41% of young bachelor's degree-holders under age 25 were still enrolled at university; the proportion fell to 14% of those aged 25 to 34, and stood at 6% for those aged 35 to 44. In contrast, the attendance rates of bachelor's graduates enrolled in college programs, although small (3%), remained steady from age 25 to age 44.

College attendance of bachelor's graduates on the rise
In recent years, the percentage of university graduates who subsequently obtain a college diploma (within five years of university graduation) has doubled, from 3% of the Class of 1982 to 7% of the Class of 1990. This growth suggests that more young university graduates are supplementing their education with additional, and perhaps more marketable, skills obtained at college.

CST What you should know about this study

It is often difficult to assess the school-to-work transition of graduates who pursued additional studies within two years of graduation. At that time, many have had only a brief opportunity to find a full-time, high-paying, high-level job. For this reason, the 1995 Follow-up of 1990 Graduates Survey (FOG) was used to compare the labour market experience of two groups of graduates five years after graduation: the 2% of bachelor's graduates who obtained a college diploma within two years of getting their bachelor's[1] and the 36% of bachelor's graduates who did not pursue further studies after graduation. Statistics Canada conducted this survey of nearly 31,000 university, college and trade/vocational graduates during 1995, on behalf of Human Resources Development Canada.

1. Bachelor's graduates who obtained a college diploma within two years of obtaining their bachelor's degree would have had nearly three years to find a good job by the time they were interviewed for the FOG survey.

---

1. Includes graduates who have taken at least 20 hours of instruction between graduation and survey interview in 1997.

2. College programs include postsecondary level programs at community colleges, Colleges of Applied Arts and Technology (CAATs), CEGEPs, technical institutes, non-degree granting colleges of art, hospital schools of nursing or radiology, and private business schools.

UNIT 3: WORK, LIFE STYLE AND SOCIAL PROBLEMS

1990 bachelor's graduates from the social sciences (16%), health professions, sciences and technologies (15%) and agriculture and biological sciences (14%) were the most likely to pursue further studies at college. Even 10% of engineering graduates pursued a college education, usually taking business, computer science or engineering technology courses. Of 1990 university graduates continuing to college, most chose programs in commerce, management or business administration (22%), data processing or computer science (14%), nursing (9%) or medical lab technologies (8%).

The reasons cited by those who continue their education at the college level are usually labour market-related: to find a job, to get a better one or to improve their performance in their current job.

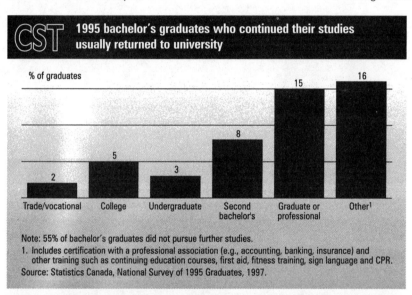

1995 bachelor's graduates who continued their studies usually returned to university

% of graduates

Note: 55% of bachelor's graduates did not pursue further studies.
1. Includes certification with a professional association (e.g., accounting, banking, insurance) and other training such as continuing education courses, first aid, fitness training, sign language and CPR.
Source: Statistics Canada, National Survey of 1995 Graduates, 1997.

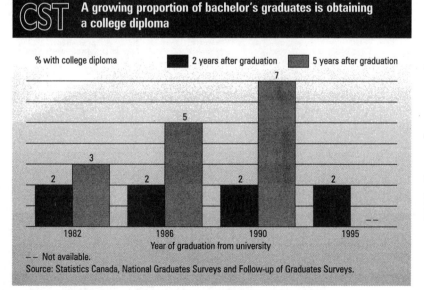

A growing proportion of bachelor's graduates is obtaining a college diploma

% with college diploma ■ 2 years after graduation ■ 5 years after graduation

Year of graduation from university
–– Not available.
Source: Statistics Canada, National Graduates Surveys and Follow-up of Graduates Surveys.

Does a college diploma help university graduates?

Many factors influence a young university graduate's success in the labour market: field of study, previous work experience, the demand for labour and job search skills. After accounting for differences in age, sex, field of study and previous education, 1990 bachelor's graduates who had obtained a college diploma by mid-1992 were just as likely to have a high income (top quartile) and a high-level job by 1995 as graduates who did not pursue further studies.[3] Also, the odds of working full-time were about 1.4 times higher for bachelor's graduates who had received a college diploma than for those who did not pursue any studies after graduation.

Although these results indicate that a college education may be helpful to some university graduates, there is no doubt that a university degree is much more valuable to college graduates. College graduates who subsequently obtained a bachelor's degree were much better off in the labour market than their college-educated colleagues who did not pursue further education. After accounting for several socio-demographic and education factors,[4] the odds of being in the top income quartile were about 1.6 times higher, of being in a high-level job about 2.1 times higher and of working full time about 1.9 times higher than those of college graduates who did not pursue further studies.

3. High-level job refers to the six highest categories of the Pineo-Carroll-Moore socioeconomic classification of occupations including self-employed and employed professionals, semi-professionals, technicians, and senior and middle managers.

4. Age, sex, marital status, presence of children under age 5, field of study and education before entering the program.

Warren Clark is an analyst with Housing, Family and Social Statistics Division, Statistics Canada.

"*I feel* overqualified *for my job...*"

T he Canadian population has become more highly educated in the last 25 years: between 1971 and 1996, the percentage of adults with more than a high school education more than doubled from 21% to 50%, while the proportion with a university degree tripled from 5% to 15%. At the same time, many jobs are demanding more sophisticated and technically complex skills, as shifts in Canada's industrial structure and rapid advances in information technologies raise the basic skill requirements of the workplace. It may seem odd that, in a time when an internationally competitive economy needs highly skilled workers, many well-educated workers feel that their education and experience exceed the demands of the job. Nonetheless, many well-educated Canadians feel they are overqualified for their jobs.

This article cites data from the 1994 General Social Survey (GSS) and focuses on Canadian workers who have graduated from a university or community college.[1] Workers were asked: "Considering your experience, education and training, do you feel that you are overqualified for your job?" Although respondents did not identify their reasons for describing themselves as overqualified, well-educated workers may feel overqualified if they take jobs requiring lower levels of skill; if their skill set does not match the requirements of the job market; or if their job expectations remain unmet.

[1] Includes university and college graduates who were employed at the time of the survey and whose main activity during the previous year was working at a job or business.

by Karen Kelly, Linda Howatson-Leo and Warren Clark

One in five well-educated Canadians felt overqualified for their jobs In 1994, there were 4.4 million employed Canadians — 39% of all workers — with a university or community college certificate, diploma or degree. More than one-fifth (22% or just under 1 million) of these workers felt overqualified for their jobs. Twenty-seven percent of those with an earned doctorate, master's or diploma above the bachelor's level felt overqualified, compared with just over one-fifth of those with a bachelor's/first professional degree[2] (22%) or a community college diploma (21%).

Postsecondary graduates in jobs that may not require postsecondary education are more likely to feel overqualified. For example, in 1994, 23% of university and community college graduates were employed as clerical, sales or service workers, and 37% of them felt overqualified for their jobs. When the effects of other demographic and socio-economic factors are held constant, the odds of feeling overqualified was at least twice as great for graduates working in clerical, sales and service jobs as for those in management or professional jobs.

Women more likely than men to feel overqualified In 1994, one in four women with a university or community college education felt overqualified for their jobs, compared with one in five male graduates. While it is true that women are more likely to work in service and clerical positions,[3] the difference in men's and women's assessment of their jobs can only partially be explained by their differing occupational profiles. All other factors being equal, the odds of feeling overqualified were 1.3 to 1.6 times greater for women than men. One possible explanation is that more women than men may accept jobs with lower-level requirements in order to balance family demands and earning an income; for example, taking a retail sales job because it allows them to work part-time.

Young adults feel over-educated for their jobs According to the GSS data, some of the most highly qualified young graduates have difficulty finding jobs that they believe match their educational credentials and experience. This belief was most frequently reported by young graduates aged 20 to 29 with a bachelor's/first professional degree (37%). Bachelor's graduates in their twenties may have felt overqualified because almost 30% of them held clerical, sales, service, or blue collar positions, whereas the likelihood that older graduates held such jobs was much lower. But even after accounting for other factors, including occupation, the odds of feeling overqualified were 1.8 times greater for bachelor's degree-holders aged 20 to 29 than for those aged 35 to 44 or 55 to 64.

A somewhat smaller proportion of community college graduates in their twenties (25%) felt overqualified for their job, even though they were more likely to be employed in the type of occupations in which university graduates felt most overqualified. This seems to suggest that college graduates found jobs more closely matching their skills and expectations. All other factors being held constant, the odds of feeling overqualified were about half as great for young college graduates as for those aged 55 to 64.

[2] Includes first professional degrees in medicine (MD), dentistry (DDS, DMD), veterinary medicine (DVM), law (LLB), optometry (OD), and divinity (MDIV), and one-year B.Ed after a bachelor's degree.

[3] In 1994, women who had completed university or community college were three times more likely than men to have a clerical or service job (24% versus 8%).

A high proportion of postsecondary graduates work in clerical, sales, service or blue collar jobs — CST

Educational attainment	Felt over-qualified	Type of job held when interviewed		
		Management, professional	Clerical, sales, service	Blue collar
	(%)	(% distribution by occupation)		
Postsecondary graduates	22	64	23	13
Community college certificate or diploma	21	46	30	24
Undergraduate diploma or certificate	23	58	32	10
Bachelor's or first professional degree	22	78	17	5
Master's degree, earned doctorate[1]	27	83	12	5

[1] Includes university diplomas or certificates above a bachelor's degree.
Source: Statistics Canada, 1994 General Social Survey.

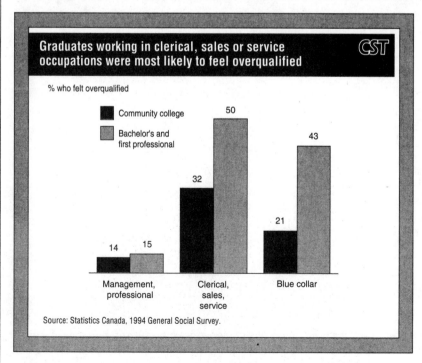

Graduates working in clerical, sales or service occupations were most likely to feel overqualified — CST

% who felt overqualified

- Community college
- Bachelor's and first professional

	Management, professional	Clerical, sales, service	Blue collar
Community college	14	32	21
Bachelor's and first professional	15	50	43

Source: Statistics Canada, 1994 General Social Survey.

Influences on feeling overqualified for a job are complex

The 1994 GSS asked respondents if they felt they were overqualified for their current job, given their education, training and experience. A wide range of factors can influence a person's answer to that question; for example education, current occupation, earnings, age, sex and work history. Of course, other factors that were not collected by the GSS may play a significant role in determining people's opinion of their job such as job expectations, relationships with co-workers and supervisors, skill requirements, and skill resources.

A simple model has been developed to illustrate the relationship between feeling overqualified and socio-demographic characteristics. The table below shows how great an effect various socio-demographic characteristics had on workers' belief that they were overqualified for their job. It presents the odds that a group of workers with a certain characteristic will feel overqualified relative to the odds that a bench mark group of workers will feel overqualified (odds ratio) when all other variables in the analysis are held constant. The bench mark group is shown in boldface for each characteristic. For example, the odds ratio for college graduates in blue collar jobs is 3.4; this indicates that the odds they feel overqualified for their job is 3.4 times greater than college graduates in managerial or professional occupations (bench mark category), after the influence of all other variables shown in the table has been removed. A number of variables — for example occupation, income and field of study — interact together. The model has not accounted for these interactions in order to simplify the description of the results.

Odds ratio for feeling overqualified for a job

Socio-demographic characteristics		Odds ratio	
		College	Bachelor's and first professional
Age	20-29	0.4	1.8
	30-34	0.4	1.3
	35-44	0.4	1.0
	45-54	0.5	1.8
	55-64	**1.0**	**1.0**
Sex	**Men**	**1.0**	**1.0**
	Women	1.3	1.6
Field of study	**Education, recreation, counselling**	**1.0**	**1.0**
	Commerce, management and business administration	1.0	1.7
	Engineering and applied science	--	2.0
	Engineering and applied science technologies and trades	0.2	--
	Fine and applied arts, humanities, social sciences	0.7	1.3
	Health professions, sciences and technologies	0.6	--
	Math and physical sciences	--	1.6
Occupation	**Management, professional**	**1.0**	**1.0**
	Clerical, sales or service	2.4	4.9
	Blue collar	3.4	4.6
Employment income	Less than $15,000	3.3	5.9
	$15,000 to less than $50,000	1.4	4.9
	$50,000 or more	**1.0**	**1.0**
Lost job in last 5 years	Yes	1.5	1.0
	No	**1.0**	**1.0**
Job tenure	for every year of job tenure	0.96	0.95

-- Sample too small to be released.
Source: Statistics Canada, 1994 General Social Survey.

What is an odds ratio?

To help understand what an odds ratio means and how to interpret it, the following example using hypothetical numbers might be instructive. If there were 20 men who felt overqualified for their job and 80 who did not feel overqualified, then the odds of feeling overqualified are 20÷80=0.25. This implies that for every 100 men who do not feel overqualified, there are 25 who do feel overqualified.

An odds ratio expands on this concept by measuring the strength of association between two variables. The value of an odds ratio can range from zero to infinity, where an odds ratio of 1 indicates there is no association between the variables being studied. For example, the odds ratio could compare the odds of feeling overqualified for women to the odds of feeling overqualified for men. An odds ratio of 1 means there is no association between gender and feeling overqualified for the job, but an odds ratio of greater than 1 means that women are more likely to feel overqualified than men. Similarly, when the odds ratio is less than 1, women are less likely than men to feel overqualified. So if 25 women felt overqualified for their jobs and 75 didn't, the odds of women feeling overqualified is 25÷75=0.33. Returning to the example for men, the odds ratio of women feeling overqualified relative to men is 0.33÷0.25 = 1.32.

Some labour market observers believe that some young well-educated Canadians are unable to find meaningful work and therefore this group is more likely to feel overqualified. Also, young people have little previous work experience and are perhaps judging the job as inadequate before its real nature (and full responsibilities) have become apparent; when fully initiated into the job, the young worker may assess it differently.

This suggestion seems to be supported by the GSS, which shows that workers in transition (i.e., those with short job

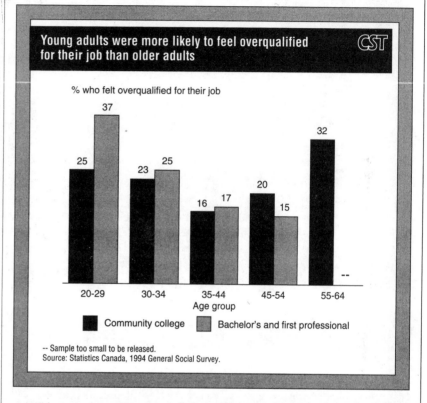

Young adults were more likely to feel overqualified for their job than older adults CST

% who felt overqualified for their job

Age group	Community college	Bachelor's and first professional
20-29	25	37
30-34	23	25
35-44	16	17
45-54	20	15
55-64	32	--

-- Sample too small to be released.
Source: Statistics Canada, 1994 General Social Survey.

Feelings of overqualification varied by field of study CST

Field of study	College	Bachelor's and first professional degree
		%
Total	**21**	**22**
Education, recreation, counselling	30	18
Fine and applied arts, humanities, social sciences	24	27
Commerce, management and business administration	33	26
Engineering and applied science[1]	--	24
Engineering and applied science technologies and trades[2]	10	--
Health professions, sciences and technologies	14	--
Mathematics and physical sciences	--	20

-- Sample too small to be released.
[1] University level engineering and applied science programs.
[2] Technology and trades programs in engineering and applied science field.
Source: Statistics Canada, 1994 General Social Survey.

tenure), regardless of age, were more likely to feel overqualified than workers who had long-term employment in the same job. In 1994, one in three of those who had been in their job for less than two years felt their qualifications exceeded the job's requirements, compared with one in six of those with five or more years of job tenure.

Previous job loss affects perceptions of current job In 1994, 16% of college graduates who were working at the time of the GSS had lost a job at least once in the previous five years. The odds of feeling overqualified were 1.5 times higher for these workers than for those who had not lost a job. Interestingly, job loss had a greater influence on older graduates feeling overqualified, even though younger graduates were more likely to have experienced a job loss during this period. Older workers often have a more difficult time than younger workers in finding new employment at the same level of skill, knowledge and authority associated with their previous job. Also, if some people had depleted their financial reserves and were forced to take employment simply to make ends meet, their higher rate of discontent with their current job is understandable.[4]

Feelings of overqualification varied by field of study The 1994 GSS shows that workers who had completed college programs in engineering and applied science technologies and trades (10%)[5] and health professions, sciences and technologies (14%)[6] were least likely to feel overqualified. Evidently, most of them had found jobs that matched their expectations. On the other hand, the workers most likely to feel they had more qualifications than the job needed were graduates of college programs in commerce, management and administration (33%).

CANADIAN SOCIAL TRENDS BACKGROUNDER — CST

I want a good job when I graduate

Finding a job consistent with their educational attainment is an important goal for young people. They expect to receive a sufficiently high return on their investment in education to compensate for their costs and foregone income while they were studying. Without stable work, young people may be deprived of the material and social benefits of a job; without rewarding work, they may feel dissatisfied with their job, have poor relationships with co-workers, low job motivation, a high rate of job turnover and lower psychological well-being.[1] The lack of stable and rewarding work may also inhibit other social transitions such as formation of separate households, marriage, and a sense of self and maturity.[2]

The belief that they are overqualified for the job may change as young graduates adapt to the work environment and family priorities. A study of recent graduates in the United States found that the most important characteristics of a job when a young person first started working were very achievement-oriented – challenge and diversity, opportunities for technical or managerial career advancement, and a high degree of authority for their project. After some work experience, however, factors related to quality of life — such as time to reflect on the job, work schedules and benefits — became increasingly important.[3]

[1] Borgen W.A., N.E. Amundson and H.G. Harder, "The experience of underemployment," *Journal of Employment Counselling*, Vol. 25, December 1988; and J. Hersh, "Education match and job match," *Review of Economics and Statistics*, Vol. 73, No. 1.

[2] Hartnagel T.F. and H. Krahn, "Labour market problems and psychological well-being: A panel study of Canadian youth in transition from school to work," *British Journal of Education and Work*, Vol. 8, No. 3, 1995.

[3] Cotterman R., "How recent graduates view their jobs," *Research Technology Management*, Vol. 34, No. 3, May-June 1991.

[4] Daniel C. Feldman, "The nature, antecedents and consequences of underemployment," *Journal of Management*, Vol. 22, No. 3, 1996.

[5] Examples of training programs in engineering and applied science technologies and trades at the community college level include computer science technology, microcomputer and information systems, architectural technology, earth resources technology, drafting, survey and photogrammetric technology.

[6] Examples of training programs in health professions, sciences and technologies at the community college level include nursing, X-ray medical technology, dental assistant and pharmacy assistant.

A 1992 survey of people who had graduated in 1990 found that bachelor's/ first professional graduates in general arts and science, humanities, social science or fine and applied arts were most likely to report that their job did not require a post-secondary qualification.[7] The 1994 GSS found that graduates from these fields were the most likely bachelor's graduates to feel overqualified (27%). About a quarter of bachelor's/first professional graduates from commerce, management and business administration or engineering and applied science also reported the same feelings.

Low employment income has a strong effect on workers' opinion of job
Almost half (47%) of university and community college graduates who earned under $15,000 in 1994 felt their skills and knowledge exceeded the requirements of the job, while only 11% with earnings over $50,000 felt that way. This finding is not unexpected, nor is it surprising that the impact of low earnings is particularly marked for university graduates. After holding all other factors constant, the odds of feeling overqualified were 5.9 times greater for university graduates with earnings under $15,000 than for those making over $50,000; among workers with community college, the odds were 3.3 times higher for low-earners.

Summary Canadians have become more highly educated in the last 25 years while new jobs require increasingly higher levels of education. Nonetheless, 1994 survey data show that over one-fifth of Canada's well-educated workers feel they are overqualified for the job they are doing. People generally prefer to have jobs appropriate to their education and experience; finding such a match, however, may be difficult and some workers may accept jobs that require less skill and knowledge than they possess.

The advancement of information technology may have contributed to the problem. Computers in the workplace first displaced people processing relatively simple information and working in highly paid manual jobs. Computers now have the processing capabilities to replace some of the human labour of people in the well-paid white collar jobs that were traditionally held by postsecondary graduates.[8] The result has been the disappearance and "deskilling" of some white collar jobs. Consequently, well-educated workers may feel overqualified if they remain in a deskilled job, while those who do not have the training now needed in the fast-growing fields of high-skilled knowledge jobs may be forced into lower level jobs. However, almost half the workers who believe they are overqualified for their job are under 35, and their feelings may change as they acquire more work experience, obtain better jobs or adjust their expectations.

[7] Don Little and Louise Lapierre, *The Class of 90: A compendium of findings from the 1992 National Graduates Survey of 1990 Graduates*, Human Resources Development Canada and Statistics Canada, Catalogue no. MP43-366/1996E, 1996.

[8] Michael Dunkerley, "The jobless economy? Computer technology in the world of work," Polity Press, 1996, p. 33.

Karen Kelly and **Linda Howatson-Leo** are analysts in the Housing, Family and Social Statistics Division, Statistics Canada and **Warren Clark** is an analyst with *Canadian Social Trends*.

CST

THEIR OWN BOSS

by Arthur Gardner

The Self-employed in Canada

SELF-EMPLOYMENT CAN INVOLVE WORKING AS A professional, a business owner/operator, an artist, a tradesperson or a child-care giver. Often, being self-employed requires extensive education and training, or expertise in a particular field gained through years of work experience. In addition, having access to the capital necessary to start a business is sometimes a prerequisite for self-employment. There are many self-employment opportunities, however, that do not involve such extensive requirements.

Self-employment can offer many benefits, including a great degree of flexibility in work arrangements. It can also be a highly lucrative prospect. For some, however, self-employment does not offer the same advantages as working for someone else. Self-employed people who work independently, for example, have lower average incomes than other workers. In addition, the self-employed generally have no recourse to unemployment insurance, have no company-sponsored health or other benefits and must plan for their own retirement. Being self-employed can also involve long hours and hard work, and many self-employed people work well past normal retirement age. For some, however, this is a matter of choice.

Self-employment has decreased over the long term Despite increases between 1981 and 1991, total self-employment in Canada declined dramatically in the past 60 years, from 25% of all workers in 1931 to 10% in 1991. This was largely because employment in agriculture, where self-employment was particularly high, declined as a proportion of all employment. In 1991, only 4% of all Canadian workers were in agriculture, down from 30% in 1931. Moreover, the rate of self-employment in agriculture dropped slightly during this period to 50% from 57%.

Over the same period, self-employment in industries other than agriculture remained relatively stable. In 1991, 8% of the non-agricultural labour force were self-employed. This was higher than the proportion in 1971 (7%), but lower than that in 1931 (9%). The remainder of this article focuses on the 1.2 million people who identified themselves on the 1991 Census as being self-employed in non-agricultural industries.

Self-employed more likely to employ others now than in the past The self-employed can either be "employers" who have people working for them or "independent workers" who do not. The proportion of the self-employed with people working for them (employers) has almost doubled since the 1930s. In 1991, nearly one-half (570,800) of those self-employed in non-agricultural industries reported being employers, up from one-quarter in 1931.

This reflects several overlapping factors. The number of businesses in manufacturing and construction has been growing. These businesses normally require more than one person to operate. In addition, operation of businesses in many resource-based industries, including fishing and forestry, has changed. Work in these industries is now more often done by "companies" of workers than by individuals. Also, the number of skilled, independent tradespeople (such as shoemakers or cabinetmakers) has declined. These people may find it difficult to compete with the manufacturing capabilities of larger companies.

Self-employed tend to be older than other workers The self-employed are an older population than the rest of the labour force. Less than two-thirds of self-employed people were either aged 15 to 34 (27%) or 35 to 44 (33%). In contrast, three-quarters of other workers were either aged 15 to 34 (49%) or 35 to 44 (26%). The average age of self-employed people with others working for them was slightly higher (43) than that of the independently self-employed (42). Other workers (that is, employees working for another person or company) were somewhat younger, with an average age of 36 in 1991.

It is not surprising that the self-employed are older given that occupations associated with self-employment often require years of work experience, training or both. Also, older people are more likely than younger adults to have access to the capital required to start and run a business.

Self-employed work longer hours... The self-employed, particularly those who have others working for them, work longer hours than do other workers. Employers worked an average of 47 hours per week in 1991, while independently

self-employed people worked an average of 40 hours per week. Other workers, in comparison, worked 37 hours per week on average.

Self-employed people who had others working for them had a lower rate of part-time work (9%) than did workers who were not self-employed (20%). Independent workers, however, were most likely to work part-time (25%).

...and tend to defer retirement The self-employed are more likely to work to a later age in life than other workers. About 17% of employers and independent workers were aged 55 and over, compared with 10% of other workers. Similarly, about 5% of the self-employed were aged 65 and over, while this was the case for only 1% of other workers.

This tendency can be attributed to several factors. For example, although Registered Retirement Savings Plans (RRSPs) and other methods of saving are commonplace, the absence of structured pension plans for the self-employed can lead some to continue working past the point at which they may have liked to end their careers. On the other hand, with the flexibility that being one's own boss affords, and given the absence of predefined company retirement rules, the self-employed person may be able to work

to a later age and ease more gradually into retirement, choosing reduced work hours and greater reliance on employees.

Most self-employed are men, but women's share is growing The self-employed work force is predominantly male, with men making up three-quarters of employers and two-thirds of independent workers in 1991. Women's share of self-employed workers, however, has grown substantially, particularly in the past decade. In 1931, women accounted for 19% of independent workers and 4% of employers. Even as late as 1981, women made up just 26% of the independently self-employed and 17% of employers. By 1991, these proportions had increased to 34% and 24%, respectively.

Similar to the overall situation among women and men in the labour force, self-employed women are more likely than self-employed men to work part-time. In 1991, 31% of self-employed women worked part-time, compared with 11% of self-employed men. Many women may choose part-time employment because of the flexibility in work arrangements that this type of work can offer.

An educated work force In 1991, 24% of employers and 18% of independent workers had a university degree. In

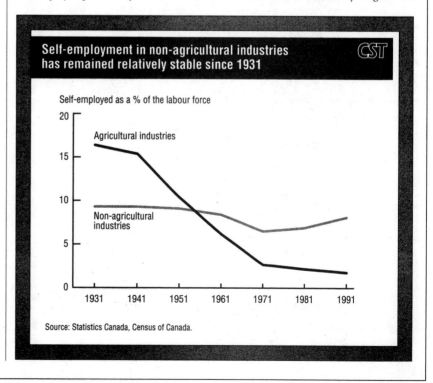

Self-employment in non-agricultural industries has remained relatively stable since 1931 CST

Self-employed as a % of the labour force

Agricultural industries

Non-agricultural industries

Source: Statistics Canada, Census of Canada.

Most common occupations, 1991			CST
	Occupation	Number	%
Self-employed employers			
Men	Sales supervisors	34,845	8.1
	General managers	33,095	7.7
	Sales and advertising	26,925	6.2
	Construction foremen/women	22,535	5.2
	Physicians	19,285	4.5
	Lawyers	18,805	4.4
	Other managers	15,860	3.7
	Accountants/auditors	12,685	2.9
	Services management	12,545	2.9
	Carpenters	10,185	2.4
	Other	224,975	52.1
	Total	**431,740**	**100.0**
Women	Sales supervisors	18,085	13.0
	Bookkeepers/accounting clerks	11,050	7.9
	Sales and advertising	9,540	6.9
	Barbers/hairdressers	7,855	5.6
	Services management	6,630	4.8
	Other managers	6,105	4.4
	Secretaries/stenographers	5,825	4.2
	Food and beverage supervisors	5,585	4.0
	General managers	5,390	3.9
	Physicians	4,870	3.5
	Other	58,130	41.8
	Total	**139,065**	**100.0**
Independently self-employed			
Men	Sales clerks and sales	31,840	8.3
	Carpenters	23,835	6.2
	Truck drivers	21,445	5.6
	Motor vehicle mechanics	10,445	2.7
	Taxi drivers	9,725	2.5
	Sales/advertising managers	8,420	2.2
	Accountants/auditors	8,225	2.1
	Painters	8,215	2.1
	Construction foremen/women	8,160	2.1
	General managers	8,000	2.1
	Other	246,640	64.1
	Total	**384,950**	**100.0**
Women	Child care	21,745	11.0
	Sales clerks and sales	19,435˙	9.8
	Barbers/hairdressers	17,440	8.8
	Bookkeepers/accounting clerks	10,615	5.4
	Fine arts teachers	6,460	3.3
	Sales/advertising managers	4,665	2.4
	Writers and editors	4,490	2.3
	Secretaries/stenographers	4,405	2.2
	Painters/sculptors	3,805	1.9
	Product/interior designers	3,805	1.9
	Other	101,000	51.0
	Total	**197,865**	**100.0**

Source: Statistics Canada, 1991 Census of Canada.

comparison, this was the case for only 15% of other workers. A large proportion of self-employed people are in professional occupations that require a university degree (such as doctors, dentists, lawyers or engineers). The proportion of self-employed people who had not graduated from high school (25%) was slightly lower than that for other workers (27%).

Immigrants more likely to be self-employed Overall, 11% of immigrant workers were self-employed in 1991, compared with 8% of those who were Canadian born. Only among immigrants who arrived between 1986 and 1991 was self-employment less common (7%) than among the Canadian-born population. Recent immigrants may not yet have had the time to acquire the capital and business contacts necessary to establish a business.

Both immigrant men and women are more likely to be self-employed than are those born in Canada. In 1991, 15% of immigrant men and 7% of immigrant women were self-employed, compared with 10% and 5% of Canadian-born men and women. In addition, at all ages and across all industries, immigrants were consistently more likely than Canadian-born people to be self-employed.

Dentists most likely to be self-employed Some occupations, particularly certain professional occupations, tend to have high concentrations of self-employment. For example, 83% of dentists and 76% of osteopaths and chiropractors were self-employed in 1991. Denturists (68%), optometrists (65%), and physicians and surgeons (60%) also had high rates of self-employment. Other occupations with large proportions of self-employed workers included painters and sculptors (71%), and fishing captains (60%).

Occupational patterns differ for men and women For the self-employed with others working for them, two trade occupations (construction foremen, 5% and carpenters, 2%) were among the top 10 occupations for male employers, while no trade occupations were common among female employers. The most common occupations among women employers were sales supervisors (13%), followed by bookkeepers and accounting clerks (8%).

UNIT 3: WORK, LIFE STYLE AND SOCIAL PROBLEMS

These occupations, however, are common among women workers in general.

Among the independently self-employed, sales representatives, tradespeople and child-care givers are the most common occupations. In 1991, independently self-employed men were concentrated in sales (8%), carpentry (6%) and truck driving (6%). Independently self-employed women, on the other hand, were most often in child care (11%), sales (10%) and barber or hairdressing occupations (9%). In addition, four occupations of an artistic nature were among the 10 highest ranked occupations for independently self-employed women: fine arts teachers; writers and editors; painters, sculptors and related artists; and product and interior designers.

Higher employment incomes among self-employed employers As a group, the self-employed earn more on average than do other workers. This is not true, however, for independently self-employed workers, who earn less on average than do workers who are not self-employed. Employers, those self-employed people who have others working for them, have the highest employment incomes among the three categories of worker. Across all of these worker categories, men had higher employment incomes than did women.

Among those who worked full-time for at least 40 weeks during 1990, self-employed men who had people working for them had an average employment income of $51,300, compared with $38,300 for men who were not self-employed. Independently self-employed men earned less on average ($32,000) than either of these groups.

This pattern is the same for women. Among those working full-time for at least 40 weeks of the year, self-employed women who employed other workers earned $29,100 on average. Women who were not self-employed had an average annual employment income of $25,300.

As was the case with men, independently self-employed women had the lowest employment incomes ($19,300) among the three categories of women workers. Female independent workers were most likely to work as child-care givers, in sales positions or as barbers/hairdressers – jobs which are not the highest-paying among the self-employed.

Self-employed professionals had highest employment income On average, self-employed professionals who employ other workers have higher incomes than self-employed employers in all other types of occupations. Among those who worked full-time for at least 40 weeks of the year, physicians and

surgeons had the highest average employment income ($121,600), followed by dentists ($100,100) and lawyers ($96,900). In contrast, common employer occupations with relatively low average annual incomes included supervisors of food and beverage preparation services ($25,400) and services management occupations ($29,100).

Among occupations most common to independently self-employed people, child-care givers had the lowest incomes. Independently self-employed child-care givers who worked full-time for at least 40 weeks in 1990 earned an average of $10,400. Other common self-employment occupations with relatively low incomes included independent barbers and hairdressers ($17,700), sales people ($23,100), motor vehicle repairers ($23,400), and bookkeepers and accounting clerks ($23,500).

Self-employed are a diverse and growing group The self-employed are not a homogenous group, but rather include people with diverse backgrounds who work in a range of occupations. At one extreme, self-employed professionals are well educated with high average annual incomes. These self-employed people often have others working for them. At the other extreme are those who work on their own, in relatively low income occupations.

Self-employment in non-agricultural industries has increased steadily since 1971. With high unemployment rates, and with businesses, governments and other public sector organizations increasingly seeking to streamline operations, it is unclear to what extent people who become self-employed today do so by choice or by necessity.

Arthur Gardner is an analyst with Labour and Household Surveys Analysis Division, Statistics Canada. For more information, see **The Self-Employed** from the *Focus on Canada* series, Statistics Canada Catalogue 96-316.

CST

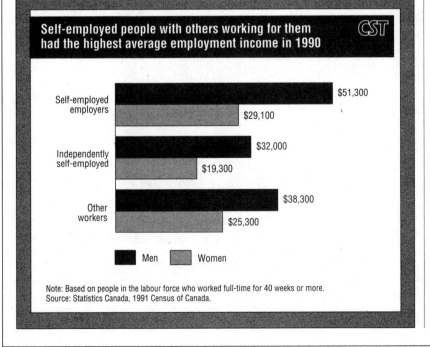

Self-employed people with others working for them had the highest average employment income in 1990   CST

	Men	Women
Self-employed employers	$51,300	$29,100
Independently self-employed	$32,000	$19,300
Other workers	$38,300	$25,300

Note: Based on people in the labour force who worked full-time for 40 weeks or more.
Source: Statistics Canada, 1991 Census of Canada.

Projections of People with Work Disabilities, 1993 to 2016

people with work disabilities to account for 8% of the population aged 15 to 64 by 2016 People with work disabilities comprise one of the four designated groups under the *Employment Equity Act.* According to Statistics Canada's medium-growth projections of people with disabilities,[1] if current age-specific rates of disability continue, this population is expected to reach 2 million by 2016, up from 1.4 million in 1993. As a proportion of the working-age population, those with a disability will grow to 8% by 2016, from 7% in 1993.

Number of people with work disabilities growing at a faster rate... The growth rate of people with work disabilities is expected to be higher than that of the population without disabilities. The average annual growth rates of people with work disabilities is projected to be 2% between 1996 and 2001, and 0.8% between 2011 and 2016. In comparison, the average growth rates for people without disabilities for the two periods are projected to be 1.4% and 0.5%, respectively.

The projected number of people with work disabilities is the result of the interaction between two factors: the projected general population and age-specific disability prevalence rates. The projected population is based on the 1993 preliminary estimates adjusted for net census undercoverage, non-permanent residents and returning Canadians. Disability prevalence rates were estimated from data in the 1991 Health and Activity Limitation Survey (HALS) and were assumed to be the same throughout the projection period.

• For more information, see **Projections of Persons with Disabilities (Limited At Work/Perception), Canada, Provinces and Territories, 1993-2016**, Statistics Canada, Catalogue no. 91-538-XPE. Also available are **Projections of Population with Aboriginal Ancestry, Canada, Provinces/Regions and Territories, 1991-2016**, Statistics Canada, Catalogue no. 91-539-XPE, and **Projections of Visible Minority Population Groups, Canada, Provinces and Regions, 1991-2016**, Statistics Canada, Catalogue no. 91-541-XPE. These publications are available from your nearest Statistics Canada Reference Centre or call 1-800-267-6677.

...due to population aging The likelihood of having a work disability is higher among older people. Thus, population aging will result in older people accounting for a growing share of the working-age population with disabilities. By 2016, 60% of people with work disabilities will be aged 45 to 64, up from 48% in 1996.

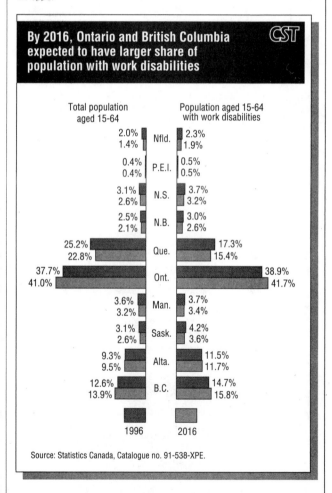

By 2016, Ontario and British Columbia expected to have larger share of population with work disabilities

Total population aged 15-64		Population aged 15-64 with work disabilities	
2.0% 1.4%	Nfld.	2.3% 1.9%	
0.4% 0.4%	P.E.I.	0.5% 0.5%	
3.1% 2.6%	N.S.	3.7% 3.2%	
2.5% 2.1%	N.B.	3.0% 2.6%	
25.2% 22.8%	Que.	17.3% 15.4%	
37.7% 41.0%	Ont.	38.9% 41.7%	
3.6% 3.2%	Man.	3.7% 3.4%	
3.1% 2.6%	Sask.	4.2% 3.6%	
9.3% 9.5%	Alta.	11.5% 11.7%	
12.6% 13.9%	B.C.	14.7% 15.8%	

1996   2016

Source: Statistics Canada, Catalogue no. 91-538-XPE.

[1] The projections of the population with work disabilities include people aged 15 to 64 who indicated that they were limited in the kind or amount of work they perform, due to a long-term physical condition or health problem.

Plugged into the Internet

by Paul Dickinson and Jonathan Ellison

Have you ever wondered why your neighbours' phones are always busy? It may be because they are surfing the Internet. More and more Canadians are now using the Net to stay in touch with each other, to bank, to shop, to research a topic for a school project, to browse for information, to play games, or to make travel plans. Conquering the limitations of geographic location, the Internet could change the lives of people as much as the telephone did in the early 20th century and television in the 1950s and 1960s.

Whether it will improve or harm participation in community life and social relationships is yet to be seen. But like it or not, the Internet is here to stay. In 1998, there were 4.3 million households in Canada (36% of all households) in which at least one member used computer communications regularly. This compared with 3.5 million households in 1997.[1] Household members may access the Internet from many locations: a child or teenager at school, a public library or a friend's house; a mother or father at work; a student at the university residence or perhaps at a cybercafé.

Ultimately, many people obtain access to the Internet from home. In fact, people were just as likely to use the Net from home as from the workplace, with home–use showing the largest growth between 1997 and 1998. Furthermore, those who used the Net at home did so frequently: 95% more than once a week.

E-mail most popular use of the Internet at home

Without doubt, e-mail was the most widely used application of home users: 86% households plugged into the Internet used e-mail. The advantages of communicating electronically are many. In seconds, messages can be sent around the world to family members, friends or business colleagues. Digital photos can be appended to mail messages, thus making distribution of family photos easy. E-mail enables employees to work at home and still stay in contact with a central office, thereby reducing commuting time and providing a more family-friendly work environment. E-mail also keeps people with similar interests in

---

1. Households stating that they had ever used computer communications rose to 46% in 1998 from 38% in 1997.

touch: they can share information about a hobby, distribute special interest newsletters, or provide personalized editions of the daily news.

The Internet also has a wealth of information on nearly every topic imaginable. Government agencies, universities and colleges, libraries, banks, newspapers and magazines, businesses and maybe even your neighbours have web sites describing their products, services, programs, interests and opinions. It is little wonder, then, that searching for information, and general browsing, were the second and third most common uses of the Internet for home users.

Although Internet shopping is becoming more popular, only one in 10 Internet-using households made purchases via computer at home (3% of all households). This low level of e-commerce may reflect consumer concerns over the security of credit card transactions on the Internet or perhaps the need by some consumers to see, feel or smell goods before they decide to buy.

CST Well-educated, high-income households were most likely to use the Internet

	Households using the Internet	
	1997	**1998**
	%	
All households	29	36
Household income		
Bottom quartile	12	13
Second quartile	18	24
Third quartile	33	42
Top quartile	54	65
Education level of household head		
Less than high school graduation	9	13
High school graduation/some postsecondary/postsecondary[1]	31	37
University degree	60	68
Age of household head		
Less than 35	38	45
35 to 54	39	47
55 to 64	21	28
65 and over	6	7
Family type		
One person household	16	20
Single family, without children under 18	28	34
Single family, with children under 18	38	48
Multi-family household	44	46

1. College or trade/vocational diploma or certificate.

Source: Statistics Canada, Household Internet Use Survey.

High-income households more likely to use the Internet

The use of computer communications is closely related to the socioeconomic status of the household. In 1998, the highest regular Internet use (65%) was among individuals living in households in the top income quartile and among households where the head had a university degree (68%). In contrast, Internet use was far lower in the bottom quartile (13%), and in households where the head had not graduated from high school (13%). Members of the top income and education households were more likely to use the Internet at work, school, public libraries and other places (as well as at home) than persons living in households with lower income or less education. Nevertheless, even among households in the lowest income quartile, Internet use grew, with 7% using it at home, 6% at school, 4% at work and 3% at a library in 1998.

Younger generation more connected

As with other household technologies, Internet use varies not just with income but also with the generations.[2] Overall, Internet use was highest among households headed by a 35- to 54-year-old (47%). This is in part because middle-aged households have higher incomes. In the bottom three income quartile groups, households headed by someone under age 35 led in Internet use. After accounting for income differences,

2. Howatson-Leo, L. and A. Peters. 1997. "Everyday technology: Are Canadians using it?" *Canadian Social Trends*, Autumn 1997.

young households and households with children under age 18 were more likely to be users of computer communications than older or childless households.

Other research shows that the biggest computer and Internet user in a family is most likely to be a teenager.[3] This may be because young people have the most free disposable time. At the same time, parents may view Internet access as a way of preparing their children for the future and providing them with an advantage over peers who don't have access.[4] Yet some parents are fearful that their children will give out personal information, view sexually explicit material or become isolated from other people.[5]

In contrast to high use in young households, only 7% of households headed by a senior used the Internet. Many seniors, at risk of social isolation after retirement and with the onset of physical disability, could benefit from access to Internet communities. However, most seniors did not use computers as younger adults and therefore did not acquire basic computer skills. In addition, many may be resistant to computer technologies and may not recognize the possible usefulness of the Internet.

Internet use highest in Ottawa

More than half of Canada's households are located in the 15 largest census metropolitan areas (CMAs) of the country. People living in these areas are generally more connected than those from smaller urban areas and rural communities. Ottawa[6] is the most connected CMA, even though its Internet use did not change between 1997 and 1998. The population's high average levels of education and household income contribute to Ottawa's leadership in this area, as do the presence of the high-tech industry and the federal government, which provide Internet access to many of their employees. Household use of the Internet in all of the other large CMAs increased during the year, with the growth being particularly large in Calgary, Halifax, Victoria, Hamilton

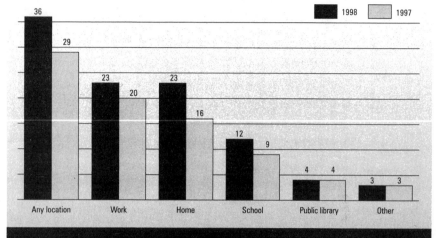

CST Internet use is growing fastest at home …

% of all households with regular user

■ 1998 ☐ 1997

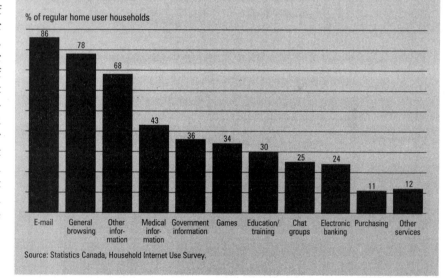

… and e-mail and general browsing are the most common uses

% of regular home user households

Source: Statistics Canada, Household Internet Use Survey.

3. Tapscott, D. 1998. *Growing up Digital: The Rise of the Net Generation*. New York: McGraw-Hill. p. 48; and ACNielsen. 1998. *The ACNielsen Canadian Internet Survey '98*. (http://www.acnielsen.ca/sect_internet/internet_en.htm).

4. Haddon, L. 1999. *European Perceptions and Use of the Internet*. Paper for the conference Usages and Services in Telecommunications, Arcachon, 7-9 June 1999.

5. Turow, J. 1999. *The Internet and the Family: The View from Parents, the View from the Press*. The Annenberg Public Policy Center of the University of Pennsylvania, report no 27. (http://appcpenn.org/appc/reports/rep27.pdf).

6. Includes only the Ontario component of the census metropolitan area of Ottawa-Hull.

% of households using Internet regularly

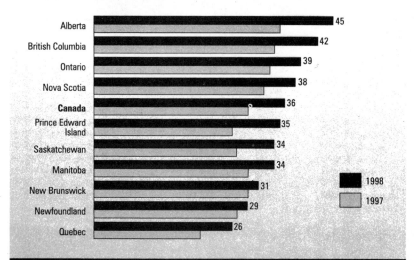

Province	1998
Alberta	45
British Columbia	42
Ontario	39
Nova Scotia	38
Canada	36
Prince Edward Island	35
Saskatchewan	34
Manitoba	34
New Brunswick	31
Newfoundland	29
Quebec	26

■ 1998
▨ 1997

... and may be high in Ottawa[1] because of the presence of government and high-tech industries

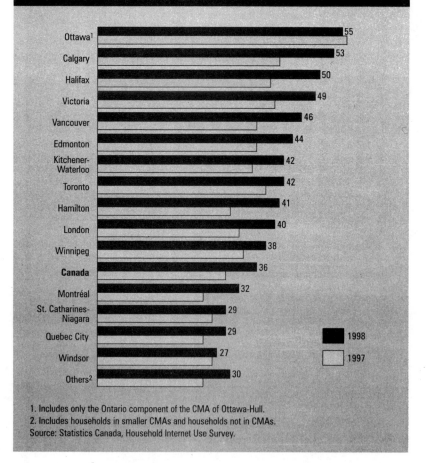

CMA	1998
Ottawa[1]	55
Calgary	53
Halifax	50
Victoria	49
Vancouver	46
Edmonton	44
Kitchener-Waterloo	42
Toronto	42
Hamilton	41
London	40
Winnipeg	38
Canada	36
Montréal	32
St. Catharines-Niagara	29
Quebec City	29
Windsor	27
Others[2]	30

■ 1998
□ 1997

1. Includes only the Ontario component of the CMA of Ottawa-Hull.
2. Includes households in smaller CMAs and households not in CMAs.
Source: Statistics Canada, Household Internet Use Survey.

and London. In addition, Internet access at schools increased everywhere, while access at public libraries grew in most locations.

• This article is adapted from "Getting connected or staying unplugged: The growing demand for computer communications services," *Service Indicators*, Volume 6, No. 1, Statistics Canada, Catalogue 63-016-XPB. 1st Quarter 1999.

Paul Dickinson is a consultant who teaches economics at McGill University, Montréal, and **Jonathan Ellison** is an analyst with Science, Innovation and Electronic Information Division, Statistics Canada.

The Persistence of Christian Religious Identification in Canada

by Reginald W. Bibby

Organized religion in Canada is approaching the next millennium with fewer participants and considerably less influence than it had fifty years ago. About forty years ago, more than half of Canadians attended church services every week; today, that proportion has dropped to less than one-quarter.[1] But despite their declining participation in religious life, most Canadians (87% in 1991) still think of themselves as Catholic, Protestant, or members of other faiths.

This article addresses the paradox of religious affiliation in the absence of religious involvement. Using the 1991 Census (the most recent census to collect data on religion), the analysis focuses on the role that the family and assimilation play in the perpetuation of religious identification.

[1] For a summary of some of the findings on religion's impact socially and individually, see Reginald W. Bibby, **Fragmented Gods**, Toronto: Stoddart, 1987; and **Unknown Gods**, Toronto: Stoddart, 1993.

Parents the key source of religious identification In 1991, 85% of married couples (including common-law) belonged to the same religious group. This tendency is important to religious identification because people who marry partners of the same faith are inclined to pass that faith on to their children. Between 94% and 99% of couples, depending on the faith, reported that their children had the same religious identification. Similarly, parents who do not identify with any religion generally reported that their children had no religion. Thus, when both parents belong to the same faith, religious identification (and non-identification) tends to pass from one generation to the next. In the few exceptions to the rule, parents usually indicated that their children described themselves as having no religion.

Children in interfaith marriages often have their mother's religion Interfaith marriage, including common-law unions, is the principal contributor to differences

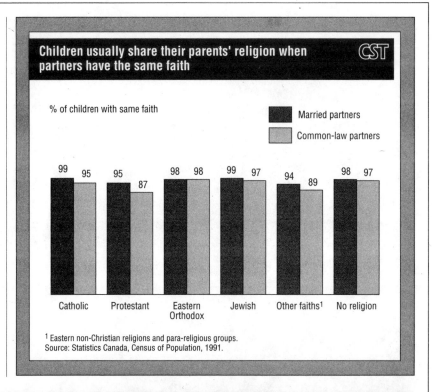

Children usually share their parents' religion when partners have the same faith

% of children with same faith

■ Married partners
▨ Common-law partners

	Married	Common-law
Catholic	99	95
Protestant	95	87
Eastern Orthodox	98	98
Jewish	99	97
Other faiths[1]	94	89
No religion	98	97

[1] Eastern non-Christian religions and para-religious groups.
Source: Statistics Canada, Census of Population, 1991.

CANADIAN SOCIAL TRENDS BACKGROUNDER

Untangling religious identification and religiosity

In the 1960s, social scientists turned away from the simple, nominal-level measure of religious group identification such as the census question on religion. Instead, they began to focus on more sophisticated objective and subjective measures of "religiosity" – such as beliefs, experiences, and knowledge.[1] Today, however, it is clear that identification with a religious group has importance apart from beliefs, attendance and perceived personal commitment. The sheer tendency to identify with a religious tradition – to remain what might be called an "affiliate" – appears to have some important cultural, psychological, and emotional meanings that need to be understood more clearly.[2]

Research on the meaning of "identification" in Canada is still in its early stages. One recent attempt to broach this subject, the *Project Canada* survey of 1995, found that "affiliates" of religious groups are not inclined to adopt other religions. Most attach importance to their identification. The survey also found that affiliates would consider being more involved in the activities of their religious groups if they found it worthwhile for themselves or their families.[3]

Despite their limitations, census data on affiliation are potentially valuable because they help to shed light on the nature, sources, and consequences of religious identification. Census data on religion were first captured in 1871 and have been collected in every decennial census since then. The most recent information available is from the 1991 Census. Respondents were asked to specify "the religion" of each person in the household, even if they were not a practising member of that faith. If they wished, respondents could answer "no religion." Information about children refers to never-married sons and daughters living at home with their parents at the time of the census, and therefore covers primarily younger children rather than adult children. (In 1991, 83% of children living with their parents were under the age of 20.)

[1] See Charles Y. Glock and Rodney Stark, **Religion and Society in Tension**, Chicago: Rand-McNally, 1965; Will Herberg, **Protestant, Catholic, Jew**, New York: Doubleday, 1960; and Gerhard Lenski, **The Religious Factor**, New York: Doubleday, 1961.

[2] For a discussion of the possible significance of identification, see Bibby, **Unknown Gods**, 1993.

[3] Reginald W. Bibby, **The Bibby Report: Social Trends Canadian Style**, Toronto: Stoddart, 1995.

in religious identification between parent and child. In these marriages, which accounted for 15% of unions in 1991, the key issue is not whether one partner converts to the other's faith, but how the children are raised. And here the pattern is clear: when couples of different religions marry or cohabit, the women tend to raise their children in their own tradition, including not having religion.

Catholics and Protestants tend to gain affiliates when marital relationships cross religious lines, while other religious groups and those professing "no religion" usually lose adherents. The reason for this is fairly straightforward: since there are relatively large numbers of Catholic and Protestant women, they bring large numbers of offspring to their religions when they marry men from different faiths or with no religion. The only exception to this "mirroring of mothers" pattern occurs when women of other faiths marry outside their religious groups. In these interfaith marriages, the women are more inclined to raise their children in their husband's tradition rather than their own.

The same basic pattern is found when one marriage partner reports that he or she has no religion. But since it is usually the men who report having "no religion" (74% in 1991), and since it is most often mothers who pass on their religion, the majority of children (56%) of these inter-faith marriages had a religious affiliation (almost all Catholic or Protestant). Here again, mothers' propensity

Children of interfaith marriages are most likely to have the same faith as their mothers — CST

Religion of				Religion of Children					
Mother	Father	No. of Couples[1]	No. of Children	Catholic	Protestant	Eastern Orthodox	Jewish	Eastern non-Christian	No religion
							%		
Catholic	Protestant	259,130	324,590	70	11	– –	– –	– –	9
	Eastern Orthodox	12,735	14,920	54	1	39	– –	– –	6
	Jewish	3,070	3,480	38	2	– –	25	– –	35
	Eastern non-Christian	7,600	10,370	57	1	– –	– –	21	20
	No religion	82,745	106,525	67	3	– –	– –	– –	30
Protestant	Catholic	254,105	320,940	42	44	– –	– –	– –	14
	Eastern Orthodox	10,300	11,540	2	55	29	– –	– –	14
	Jewish	3,555	3,720	2	38	– –	26	– –	34
	Eastern non-Christian	5,735	7,520	1	45	– –	– –	26	28
	No religion	126,935	145,900	1	58	– –	– –	– –	41
Eastern Orthodox	Catholic	8,625	9,380	62	4	28	– –	– –	7
	Protestant	6,595	6,560	4	47	36	– –	– –	13
Jewish	Catholic	2,055	2,310	28	1	1	45	– –	25
	Protestant	2,520	2,740	1	23	– –	52	– –	24
Eastern non-Christian	Catholic	3,195	3,865	58	4	– –	– –	12	26
	Protestant	3,220	3,500	2	42	– –	– –	26	29
	No religion	4,415	6,035	3	5	– –	– –	22	70
No religion	Catholic	35,050	44,630	40	3	– –	– –	– –	57
	Protestant	35,115	38,630	2	27	– –	– –	– –	71
	Jewish	1,225	1,365	2	6	– –	29	– –	62
	Eastern non-Christian	2,365	3,165	5	4	– –	– –	22	70

[1] Includes husband-wife couples with and without children living at home.
– – Estimate not reliable enough to publish.
Source: Statistics Canada, Census of Population, 1991.

to raise their children in their own faith appears to ensure the continued flow of adherents to the Catholic and Protestant religions.

Generally speaking, most smaller religious groups are losing some of their children to the mainstream Christian traditions, or to no tradition at all. For example, the 1991 General Social Survey shows that although one-third (32%) of Canadians of non-European ancestry born outside Canada identified with non-Christian faiths, only one-tenth (10%) of those born in Canada did so. The only notable exception to the general rule of assimilation is Judaism, which appears to hold its own in interfaith marriages.

Only one in thirty-three identify with major non-Christian religions Despite the stimulus of immigration from countries where other major world religions are predominant, faiths other than Christianity are not making significant inroads in Canada. Overall, the proportion of people claiming affiliation with Eastern non-Christian religions – such as Islam, Buddhism, Hinduism, and

Sikhism – comprised less than 3% of the population in 1991. Generally speaking, members of faiths that comprise less than 1% of the population often find that their children befriend, date, and marry people from other cultural and religious groups.

Most adherents of the Eastern non-Christian religions (67% in 1991) are immigrants, mainly from the Middle East and Asia. In contrast, a relatively small proportion of Catholics and Protestants (both 13% in 1991) are immigrants.

"New religions" have few affiliates Contrary to media reports and popular anecdotes, very few Canadians describe themselves as adherents of "new religions." In 1991, less than 30,000 Canadians (about one in 1,000) identified as members of para-religious groups like Scientology, New Age, Pagan, Theosophical, Metaphysical and other faiths. The persistence of identification with traditional religions suggests that Canada has an extremely tight religion "industry" dominated by Catholic and Protestant organizations. New "entries" find the going extremely tough.

CANADIAN SOCIAL TRENDS BACKGROUNDER CST

No religion? A call for caution

In the 1991 Census, 12% of Canadians reported that they had no religious affiliation, a three-fold increase from 4% in 1971. The Yukon and British Columbia had the highest proportion of people with no religious affiliation (more than 30%) and Quebec, Prince Edward Island, and Newfoundland the lowest (less than 5%).

The growing percentage of Canadians claiming to have "no religion" should be interpreted with caution for two reasons. The first is that the 1971 Census was the first in which respondents were able to answer "no religion" to the religious identification question; the second reason is demographic, since 81% of people with "no religion" in 1991 were under the age of 45. However, having no religious affiliation may be a temporary situation: about one-third of Canadians with "no religion" were not married, and almost half did not have children. Research suggests that many will turn to religious traditions when they want to secure "rites of passage" such as marriage and the baptism of children.[1] When they do, many will adopt the religious identities of their parents, which for most people means remaining Catholic or Protestant.

[1] See Bibby, **Unknown Gods**, 1993.

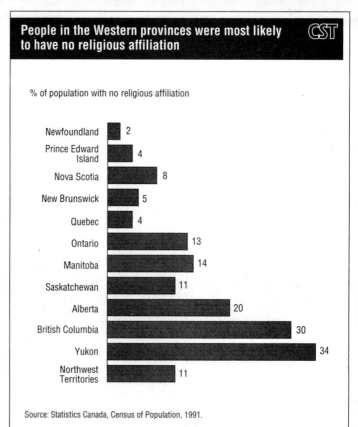

People in the Western provinces were most likely to have no religious affiliation CST

% of population with no religious affiliation

Province	%
Newfoundland	2
Prince Edward Island	4
Nova Scotia	8
New Brunswick	5
Quebec	4
Ontario	13
Manitoba	14
Saskatchewan	11
Alberta	20
British Columbia	30
Yukon	34
Northwest Territories	11

Source: Statistics Canada, Census of Population, 1991.

The Religious Paradox The net result of these patterns of socialization and assimilation is that the vast majority of Canadians (82% in 1991) identify with the numerically-dominant Catholic and Protestant traditions. Secularization may have drastically reduced personal participation and the influence of the Christian churches in Canada. But socialization and assimilation appear to perpetuate the ties with those two dominant traditions. The vast majority of Canadians in the 1990s "think" they are Catholic or Protestant, and "think" they are raising Catholic or Protestant children. An increasing number of people are arriving from countries where other world faiths predominate. But other world religions are having difficulty growing in Canada, both because they are unable to attract converts and because their children tend to join Christian groups.

Ironically, many Canadians seem to want little to do with organized religion, precisely at a time when research (and popular culture) suggests they have unmet spiritual needs and are fascinated by supernatural phenomena. Such conditions would seem to be ideal for religions that have traditionally had something to say about spiritual and supernatural matters.

Reginald W. Bibby, PhD, is a professor of sociology at the University of Lethbridge.

Are children going to religious services?

by Frank Jones

One important decision that parents must make when raising their families concerns the religious or spiritual education of their children. It can also be one of the most contentious, both between parents who may not share the same faith or beliefs about child-rearing, and sometimes between parents and educational authorities.

So what do we know about children's religious observance? Is it true that few Canadian children attend church, Sunday school, or other places of worship? Are children in some faith communities more likely to attend than others? Do children have to sacrifice sports, music lessons, or club activities in order to participate in religious activities?

Using data from the National Longitudinal Survey of Children and Youth (NLSCY), conducted first in 1994-95, this article addresses some of these questions about the religious observance of children under 12 years.

One in three children attend religious services regularly

Over one-third, 36%, of Canada's children under 12 years of age attended religious services at least once a

CST What you should know about this study

This article is based on data from the 1994-95 National Longitudinal Survey of Children and Youth (NLSCY).[1] The NLSCY is conducted by Statistics Canada every two years on behalf of Human Resources Development Canada. It is designed to develop a clearer understanding of the factors that contribute to a child's development over time.

The 1994-95 NLSCY collected data on more than 22,500 children from newborn to 11 years, living in private households in the ten provinces (excluding Aboriginal children on reserves). Information was gathered about the children and their families in an interview with the "person most knowledgeable" about the child; at school, teachers and principals evaluated the child's scholastic development; and 10- to 11-year-olds were asked about their experiences with family, friends and school. Information will be collected about the same children every two years until they reach adulthood.

Child: a person under the age of 12. Not all data were collected for all children; for example, information about involvement in supervised activities was not captured for children under the age of four.

Person most knowledgeable (PMK): In 98% of cases, the PMK was the child's parent, usually the mother; therefore, this article uses "mother" or "parent" as a synonym for PMK.

Regular attendance: attendance at religious services at least once a month during the year preceding the survey.

1. The 1996-97 NLSCY does not include information about religion and religious observance.

month, and the majority were weekly participants. A further 22% attended less frequently, but did go at least once during the year. The vast majority of children were accompanied by a parent, most often the mother.

Regular attendance (weekly or monthly) varied considerably depending on the child's age, sex, region of residence and religious affiliation. It generally increased until children were eight years old, and then began to stabilize.[1] Girls were somewhat more likely to be regular attendees (38%) than boys (34%). Children living in Atlantic Canada had the highest regular attendance rate, 52%, while those in Quebec had the lowest, 19%.

Religious affiliation accounted for the largest differences in children's regular participation in religious services. The highest weekly attendance occurred among children in the Jehovah's Witness (90%), smaller Christian denominations (64%), and Baptist (60%) communities. Most people would not be surprised at these figures, since many regard these as conservative faith communities. On the other hand, children in what many observers consider the mainline faith communities, such as Anglican and United Church, reported the lowest weekly attendance rates (18%).

Non-attendance tended to be highest in the faith communities where weekly attendance was lowest. Islam was an exception: a high proportion of Muslim children attended Islamic religious services weekly (44%), but they also recorded the highest rate of non-attendance (39%) during the year preceding the survey.

Mother and family are important factors in child attendance

Because mothers are often most responsible for their children's informal education,[2] it is not surprising that their education and labour force activity are associated with the child's attendance at religious services.[3] What may surprise, though, is the nature of the relationships.

First, regular attendance rates for children increased with the educational attainment of the mother. The rate climbed from 30% for children whose mothers had less than high school graduation, to 40% for those whose mothers had a university degree. This finding would seem to contradict a widespread perception that less well-educated people are more likely to participate regularly in religious services. But the NLSCY results support an earlier study which found that families

CST **Over one-third of children attend religious services regularly,[1] and most are accompanied by a parent...**

	Frequency of attendance			
	Weekly	**Monthly**	**Occasionally**	**Not at all**
			%	
Child	23	13	22	42
Parent attends with child[2]	81	77	90	100

... but their attendance varies widely with their religious affiliation

Roman Catholic	22	18	31	29
United Church	18	18	30	34
Anglican	18	16	30	36
Presbyterian	39	10	23	29
Lutheran	29	18	29	24
Baptist	60	10	12	17
Islam	44	--	--	39
Jehovah's Witness	90	--	--	--
Other[3]	64	10	--	16

Note: Sample sizes for children in the Eastern Orthodox, Jewish, Buddhist, Hindu and Sikh faith communities were too small to produce reliable estimates.

-- Sample too small to yield reliable estimates.

1. Attends weekly or monthly.

2. Person most knowledgeable attends at least as often as the child.

3. Smaller, mainly Christian faith communities.

Source: Statistics Canada, National Longitudinal Survey of Children and Youth, 1994-95.

1. One study found that children's attitudes to religious education (e.g., Sunday school) change between the ages of 8 and 15, although attitudes to school do not. Francis, L. J. 1987. "The decline in attitudes towards religion among 8- 15-year-olds," *Educational Studies* 13, 2:125-134.

2. R. Bibby argues that the mother is most influential in the child's religious identification. "The persistence of Christian religious identification in Canada," *Canadian Social Trends*, Spring 1997.

3. A study using Australian data suggests that women's lower workforce participation is a more important explanatory factor than their traditional child-rearing role when accounting for women's greater religious observance. De Vaus, D. and I. McAllister. 1987. "Gender differences in religion: a test of the Structural Location Theory," *American Sociological Review* 52, 4: 472-581.

with higher socioeconomic status are more likely to take their children to church, although children from families with lower socioeconomic status tend to hold more positive attitudes towards Christianity.[4]

Second, one might expect that mothers working full-time are less likely to take their children to religious services because of increased time pressures. This finds some support in the data: only about one-third (35%) of children whose mothers worked full-time attended religious services regularly, compared with 43% of children whose mothers worked part-time. The attendance rate of children whose mothers had no paid work at all was almost identical to that for children of full-time working mothers (34%); however, mothers without paid work are more likely to be caring for very young children, who may not be considered old enough to benefit from going to religious services.[5]

The size and structure of the family also influence the likelihood of attending religious services. Children in families with both biological parents were much more likely to attend regularly (38%) than children in lone-parent families (28%) and step-parent families (31%). The number of children also affects regular attendance, with children from larger families being much more likely to attend services at least once a month. While

4. Francis, L. J., Paul R. Pearson and D. W. Lankshear. 1990. "The relationship between social class and attitude towards Christianity among 10- and 11-year-old children," *Personality and Individual Differences* 11, 10: 1019-1027.

5. An American study in the 1970s found that having pre-school-aged children reduces parental attendance, while having school-aged children increases it. Azzi, C. and R. Ehrenberg. 1975. "Household allocation of time and church attendance," *Journal of Political Economy* 83, 1: 27-56.

CST Regular attendance rates among children increase with the mother's educational attainment

| | Child attends religious services | | |
	Regularly	Occasionally	Not at all
		%	
Education			
Less than high school	30	20	50
High school	34	24	42
Some postsecondary	36	22	42
College	36	22	42
University	40	22	38
Labour force status			
Not in paid labour force	34	20	46
Works part-time	43	20	37
Works full-time	35	24	41

Source: Statistics Canada, National Longitudinal Survey of Children and Youth, 1994-95.

CST Children who attend services regularly are more likely to participate in other supervised activities

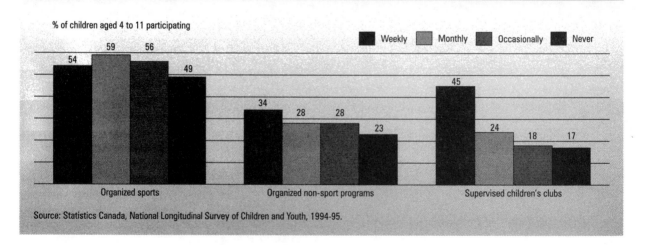

Source: Statistics Canada, National Longitudinal Survey of Children and Youth, 1994-95.

24% of children in one-child families attended services, 52% of children in families with four or more children did so. This may simply reflect the fact that large families are more likely to have older children, and that parents who want to take one child to religious services will probably take the whole family.

Does religious attendance reduce children's other activities?

Frequent attendance at religious services does not reduce the likelihood that children aged 4 to 11 will also participate in organized sports, in non-sport programs such as music lessons, or in clubs such as brownies or cubs. In fact the opposite is true: regular attendees were most likely to engage in each of these three types of activities. For example, 54% of children who attended services weekly, and 59% who attended monthly, were enrolled in weekly sports programs, compared with 49% of 4- to 11-year-olds who did not attend religious services at all. The differences are even greater for participation in supervised boys and girls clubs — 45% of weekly attendees and 17% of non-attendees. This finding is not unexpected, since many parents probably view their children's participation in organized activities as an informal education that teaches values complementary to those learned at home and reiterated in religious services.

Summary

Well over one-third of Canada's children under 12 attend religious services at least once a month. Participation increases with age and the educational attainment of the child's mother. Mothers working in the paid labour force are more likely to bring their children to a place of worship than are mothers who do not work outside the home, and single mothers are less likely to do so than married mothers. And rather than reducing involvement in sports, music lessons, or supervised clubs, attendance at religious services increases the likelihood of being involved in these other activities.

Frank Jones is a senior analyst with Labour and Household Surveys Analysis Division, Statistics Canada.

Who Gives to Charity?

by Jeffrey Frank and Stephen Mihorean

Since the early 1990s, demand for social and community services has grown; many factors — such as the aging of the population and changes in the structure of the family — have contributed to increased pressure on the social safety net. At the same time, governments at all levels have cut back spending on many social programs. Charities have traditionally filled the gaps left by government social programs, but many charitable organizations are under financial pressure as well. Government funding has declined while donations by individuals have levelled off. In addition, the number of charities operating in Canada has risen since the 1960s, further increasing competition for donors' generosity. As a result, charities are exploring new ways of soliciting contributions, while lobbying for changes to tax laws that would encourage charitable donations.

Who gives to charity? Previous analyses have illustrated quite clearly that people who contribute to charitable organizations tend to be older and to have higher incomes.[1] After describing general trends, this article demonstrates that there are also some notable regional differences in the amounts given by those who donate to charity, along with a variety of other determining factors, including the presence of children, family type and language. Nevertheless, economic factors, generally thought to drive the amount of charitable giving, explain only a small portion of donors' behaviour. Thus, a variety of "human" factors, not captured in the analysis, are likely the keys to the complex process that results in the different amounts of charitable giving.

Number of registered charities has increased dramatically In less than thirty years, the number of registered charities in Canada has more than tripled. As of December 1995, 74,000 charitable organizations were registered with Revenue Canada, up from about 22,500 in 1967. Religious organizations accounted for the largest proportion of registered charities in 1995 (42%), followed by welfare-related organizations (17%), education-related charities (16%), organizations that provide benefits to the community (15%) and health organizations (6%). The largest proportion of registered charities were located in Ontario (35%), followed by Quebec (19%), British Columbia (13%), Alberta (11%) and Saskatchewan (6%).

Charities rely heavily on governments for funding Of the $86.5 billion in revenue taken in by registered charities in 1993, 57% came from governments, mostly at the provincial level. Receipted donations from individuals accounted for 7.6% of these registered charity revenues, while those from corporations made up only 1%. Other sources of revenue for registered charities include fees, investment income, unreceipted donations, gifts from other charities and other income.

Thus, charities rely heavily on governments for the funding needed to do their work. As governments proceed with their programs of fiscal restraint, contributions made by individuals take on greater importance. In fact, the Canadian Centre for Philanthropy estimates that for every 1% cut in government grants and transfers to charities, a 5.8% increase in individual donations would be needed to keep overall funding constant.[2]

Giving to religious organizations has declined According to Statistics Canada's Survey of Family Expenditures, 71% of households gave an average of $513 to charities in 1992. That year, 61% of households gave an average of $210 to non-religious charities, while 38% gave an average of $628 to religious organizations. A decade earlier the proportion of households giving to religious organizations was

[1] See Daniela Lucaciu, "Charitable Donations," **Canadian Social Trends**, Summer 1992.

[2] David Sharpe, **A Portrait of Canada's Charities**, Canadian Centre for Philanthropy, 1994.

CANADIAN SOCIAL TRENDS BACKGROUNDER

Registered charities defined

For an organization to have charitable status with Revenue Canada, it must be registered. A registered charity must be a nonprofit organization established for the relief of poverty, the advancement of religion, the advancement of education, or other purposes beneficial to the community as a whole in a way which the law regards as charitable. Under federal law, at least 80% of registered charities' expenditures must be devoted to their mandated activities. They may engage in nonpartisan political activities that are consistent with their charitable purpose, provided these activities account for no more than 10% of their overall expenditures.

In 1995, there were 74,000 registered charities in Canada: 91% were charitable organizations, 5% public foundations and 4% private foundations. Charitable organizations generally receive funds for use in their own charitable operations, while public and private foundations generally disburse funds to support the charitable activities of other organizations. Registered charities do not pay taxes and have the right to issue official receipts to individuals and companies that donate money or other gifts. These receipts can then be used by contributors to receive federal charitable donation tax credits.

Federal charitable donation tax credit

The federal charitable donation tax credit is meant to be an incentive for Canadians to give to charity. Up to 20% of a person's net income can be claimed as a deductible donation. Taxpayers receive a tax credit equal to 17% of the first $200[1] donated to charity and 29% on the remaining amount. A charitable donation of $300, for example, would result in a $63 federal tax credit. Charitable contributions can be combined with those of a spouse and accumulated over a maximum period of five years. By combining claims in this way, the amount above $200 earns the higher tax credit.

Furthermore, charitable donations reduce the provincial tax owed. In Quebec, charitable donations can also be claimed on the provincial tax form. Elsewhere, the provincial tax calculation is based on the amount of federal tax payable.

Not everyone, however, takes advantage of these tax breaks. The Canadian Centre for Philanthropy calculates that, in 1993, for every $100 that individuals gave to charities, tax receipts worth $80 were issued and only $43 were claimed by taxpayers. The reasons for this are many: some donors may not understand the purpose of charitable tax receipts, others may lose or overlook their receipts when completing their tax returns, and still others may opt not to claim their donations. As will be shown, economic factors explain only a small part of the size of a donation, suggesting that donors may be driven more by humanitarian concerns than by the promise of a tax break.

[1] This was changed from 17% on the first $250 in 1993.

higher (43%), while the proportion giving to other charitable organizations was the same (61%).

The decrease in giving to religious organizations corresponds with a decrease in the proportion of Canadians reporting a religious affiliation on the census. In 1991, 13% of Canadians had no religious affiliation, up from 7% in 1981. It also corresponds to declining attendance at religious services or meetings. According to the General Social Survey, the proportion of people aged 15 and over attending services at least once a month dropped to 33% in 1994 from 43% in 1985.

Number of charitable donors and total amounts donated have levelled off The Small Area and Administrative Data Division of Statistics Canada maintains information provided by Revenue Canada based on personal income tax returns. According to this information, the number of taxfilers who donate to charity has levelled off since 1991. Between 1984 and 1991, the number of donors increased to 5.5 million from 3.9 million. By 1994, the number had dropped to 5.3 million. This drop is more evident when the number of donors is expressed as a percentage of all taxfilers. In 1991, 30% of taxfilers claimed a charitable donation; by 1994 this proportion had declined to 27%.

Similarly, the total amount donated by individuals to charitable organizations has also levelled off in recent years. Total donations increased to $3.4 billion in 1994, up 33% from $2.5 billion in 1984 (after taking inflation into account). Over the 1984 to 1994 period, the average charitable donation remained relatively stable, ranging between $573 and $653 (in 1994 dollars); in 1994, the average donation was $634.

Proportion of donors and amounts donated vary by region The proportion of taxfilers who claimed a charitable donation in 1994 varied by province and territory. This proportion ranged from nearly 32% in Prince Edward Island to less than 16% in the Northwest Territories. The median donation of those who received a charitable tax credit also varied, ranging from $250 in Newfoundland to $100 in Quebec.

Dividing median donation by donors' median income provides a rough indicator of charitable giving. However, this indicator includes only donations claimed on tax forms, and only those people who donated in this way are being considered. Using this measure, donors in Newfoundland were most generous, giving 0.9% of their income to charity. The median donation in Quebec, meanwhile, represented only 0.3% of donors' median income. Charitable donations reported on income tax returns have historically been lower in Quebec than in other parts of Canada. This issue is addressed further in the final part of this article.

Characteristics of donor families help explain how much they give The remainder of this article presents the results of a statistical analysis of several factors affecting the amount that families and non-family persons donate to charity. Only those families and non-family persons that reported making a charitable donation on their income tax returns in 1993 were included. Individual taxfilers

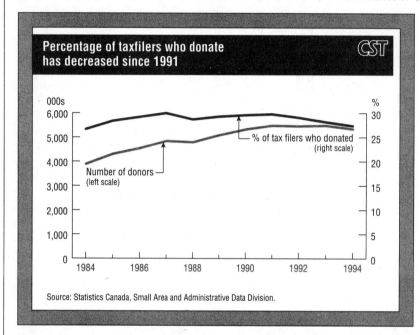

Source: Statistics Canada, Small Area and Administrative Data Division.

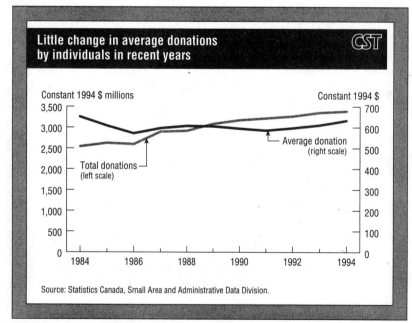

Source: Statistics Canada, Small Area and Administrative Data Division.

from the same family were grouped together, not only because families function as an economic unit, but because donations can be combined with those of a spouse and claimed on one return.

Previous analyses of individual taxfiler data indicate clearly that it is largely income that makes someone a charitable donor. This finding, however, should be reviewed from two perspectives: how well it explains whether or not someone donates, and how big a factor it is in explaining the amount of the donation. When the entire taxfiling population is examined, income explains most of the difference between donors and non-donors. When one looks at only those who have donated to charity (as this study does), income is still a significant predictor of the amount donated. However, income is not the dominant characteristic explaining the donation amount, as it is with the explanation of who is a donor. Region, the presence of children, family type, age of the oldest taxfiler, and the language used for filing returns also had a statistically significant impact on the amounts given by donating families and non-family persons. Overall, these factors were able to explain 15% of the difference between the donations of particular contributing families and non-family persons and the average amount given by donors.

• Age affects charitable donations across the country The age of the oldest person in the family was universally related to the amount donated to charity. The age effect was greatest in Ontario where each additional year of age resulted in about $16 in additional donations. For example, a family in Ontario contributed $160 dollars more when the oldest member was aged 60 than when the oldest member was aged 50, all other things being equal. Each additional year of age resulted in an increase in charitable donations of nearly $15 in the Atlantic provinces, $13 in Quebec, $10 in British Columbia and $10 in the Prairie provinces.

• Income most important in the Atlantic provinces and in Quebec Not surprisingly, income also had a statistically significant impact on the amount donated to charity in each region of the country. In Ontario, the Prairie provinces and British Columbia, every additional $1,000 of income resulted

Proportion of individuals who donate, size of donations and incomes of donors in 1994 vary by area				
	Donors	**Median donation/ median income**	**Median donation of donors**	**Median income of donors**
Province/territory	%	%	$	$
Newfoundland	22.6	0.9	250	27,100
Prince Edward Island	31.7	0.8	220	26,900
Nova Scotia	27.0	0.6	190	31,400
New Brunswick	25.6	0.7	220	30,200
Quebec	25.1	0.3	100	33,000
Ontario	29.5	0.5	170	36,100
Manitoba	31.0	0.6	170	30,400
Saskatchewan	29.8	0.8	220	29,300
Alberta	27.8	0.5	160	34,700
British Columbia	24.8	0.5	160	35,200
Yukon Territory	19.3	0.3	130	44,100
Northwest Territories	15.7	0.3	170	56,600
Census metropolitan area				
St. John's	22.8	0.6	210	33,200
Halifax	30.9	0.4	150	35,700
Saint John	29.3	0.6	190	34,200
Chicoutimi-Jonquière	24.0	0.3	100	34,800
Montréal	25.3	0.3	100	35,000
Québec	31.5	0.2	70	34,900
Sherbrooke	25.9	0.5	140	31,200
Ottawa-Hull (Que.)	28.2	0.2	60	38,000
Trois-Rivières	21.9	0.4	120	33,800
Hamilton	31.7	0.5	190	37,100
Kitchener	32.3	0.6	190	34,000
London	32.4	0.5	180	35,900
Oshawa	31.6	0.3	140	41,900
Ottawa-Hull (Ont.)	35.1	0.3	140	42,200
St. Catharines-Niagara	31.4	0.6	190	34,100
Sudbury	28.3	0.3	130	39,400
Toronto	27.3	0.4	160	37,400
Thunder Bay	30.1	0.4	140	35,500
Windsor	33.0	0.5	200	39,400
Winnipeg	32.8	0.5	150	32,200
Regina	32.9	0.5	170	34,400
Saskatoon	29.7	0.6	200	33,100
Calgary	29.8	0.4	140	37,900
Edmonton	28.7	0.4	140	35,500
Vancouver	25.7	0.4	160	36,100
Victoria	30.5	0.5	160	35,400

Source: Statistics Canada, Small Area and Administrative Data Division.

in, on average, between $9 and $14 in additional contributions to charity. The effect of income was even greater in the Atlantic provinces and in Quebec where an increase of $1,000 of income resulted in about a $20 increase in donations.

• *Presence of children resulted in lower charitable donations* In Quebec, families without children and non-family persons had charitable donations that were $322 higher, on average, than those of families with children. In Ontario, non-family persons and families without children contributed $158 more than did families with children and in Atlantic Canada the difference was $240 more. In other parts of the country, the impact of the presence of children was less noticeable.

• *Family composition important in some areas but pattern varies* The impact of family composition on how much donors gave to charity was found to vary in different regions. For example, in Atlantic Canada, a lone-parent family (when all else was equal) gave $500 more than average, while husband-wife families with two filing spouses gave $218 more than average. The pattern was reversed in the Prairies, where husband-wife families with two filing spouses resulted in $517 in additional contributions, compared with $337 above the average for lone-parent families. There were also regional variations in the amounts associated with the same family type. For example, being a husband-wife family with one filing spouse meant giving $306 more than average in Atlantic Canada and $519 more in the

CANADIAN SOCIAL TRENDS BACKGROUNDER

A model of charitable donations made by families and non-family persons in Canada

A statistical technique known as multiple linear regression was used to try to explain why some families and non-family persons give more than the average donation and why others give less. Several independent variables were combined to try to account for changes in a dependent variable, in this case, the amount donated to charity. The independent variables are those factors that contribute to variation in the dependent variable. Independent variables included in this study were income, the presence of children, family type, age of the oldest taxfiler and the language used for filing returns.

Only those families and non-family persons that donated money to charity and claimed their donation on their tax return were included in the analysis. Family donation is the sum of all charitable donations made by each family member or the donations of a non-family person. Total family income is the sum of the total incomes of each family member or the individual income of non-family persons.

The following table shows the average effect of particular variables on family donation, when all other variables in the analysis are held constant. Only those results which were statistically significant are presented.

Effect of certain variables on family donations

Characteristics of families and non-family persons	Atlantic	Quebec	Ontario	Prairies	British Columbia
			$		
Increase per thousand dollars of total family income	19.35	21.80	14.26	9.06	10.08
Increase per year of age of oldest family member	14.84	12.81	15.77	9.66	9.83
Increase when no children present compared with families with children	239.74	321.68	157.87	22.38	1.09
Increase (or decrease) compared with average family donations:					
Husband/wife families with two filing spouses	218.45	-112.57	–	517.65	–
Husband/wife families with one filing spouse	306.14	-135.77	–	519.49	–
Common-law family	–	–	–	–	–
Lone-parent family	499.99	–	–	336.51	–
Non-family person	381.71	–	–	426.69	–
English language	209.56	395.50	241.25	–	–

Results presented here are statistically significant (p < 0.05).
Source: Statistics Canada, Small Area and Administrative Data Division, 1993 T1 Family File, based on tax returns filed in the spring of 1994.

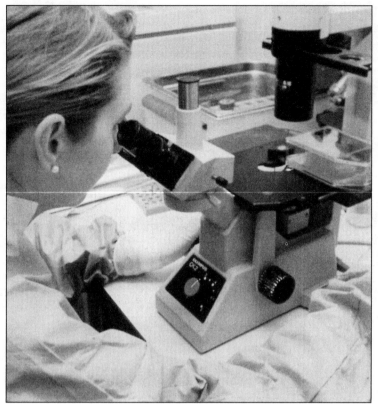

Influences on donating complex The variables available from tax forms do not capture the full complexity of factors affecting the decision to make a charitable donation or the amount of that donation. For example, varying exposure to requests for donations, family traditions, life experiences, and innumerable social and psychological factors can affect the decision to make a contribution. In this sense, this research is preliminary in that only variables found on the tax form were available for this analysis and there is no accounting of the "human" factors involved.

Even so, further work could be done using tax-filer information from Statistics Canada's Small Area and Administrative Data Division. Differences between families that donate and those that do not could be examined using a similar method to the one used in this study. The effect of the interaction between different variables on donations should also be analyzed. For example, the effect of having children changes from one region to another, indicating an interaction between region and the presence of children. In addition, families' donating behaviour over time could be tracked using taxfiler information from the Small Area and Administrative Data Division's Longitudinal Administrative Database.

Prairies. In Quebec, this type of married-couple family was associated with contributions that were $136 less than average.

• *Tax returns filed in English tend to report higher charitable donations* Language appears to be related to the amount donated to charity. Its effect is most noticeable in Quebec, where returns filed in English reported nearly $400 more than average in charitable donations. This language effect was also statistically significant in Ontario ($241) and in the Atlantic provinces ($210).

It is possible that the marketing activities of charitable organizations may not be adequately adapted to the linguistic and cultural characteristics of a Francophone audience. Certainly, the amount given to charity is related to the number of times that one is asked to give, and to the effectiveness of those requests. Quebec has a small share of registered charities relative to its population. Most charities in Canada operate out of predominantly English-speaking parts of the country. In addition, many charities are headquartered outside of Canada and operate mainly, or only, in English. This may explain at least some of the language effect uncovered in this analysis.

The lower amounts donated by Francophones may, paradoxically, be associated with the traditionally strong role of the Catholic Church in charitable activities, particularly in Quebec. Most Francophones identified themselves as Catholics (94% on the 1991 Census). However, church attendance has declined, according to the General Social Survey. By 1994, only one-third of all Catholics in Quebec attended church at least once a month, compared with one-half of Catholics in the rest of Canada. This would, therefore, limit the Church's access to a large proportion of its potential contributors.

Jeffrey Frank was an Editor with **Canadian Social Trends** and is now with Education, Culture and Travel Division, Statistics Canada. **Stephen Mihorean** is a research analyst with the Small Area and Administrative Data Division, Statistics Canada.

PR PR II

by Jean-Pierre Corbeil

Participation in amateur sport is one of the ways Canadians keep physically active and challenge their abilities. It is also an important facet of this country's culture and identity, and contributes to the social life of Canadian communities.

Young men are much more likely to regularly participate in sport than are young women. This gender difference exists within all age groups, though the gap narrows with age. Also, Canadians who participated in organized sport during their school years are more likely than others to remain physically active later in life. Nonetheless, many sport activities are enjoyed by Canadians of all ages, both men and women.

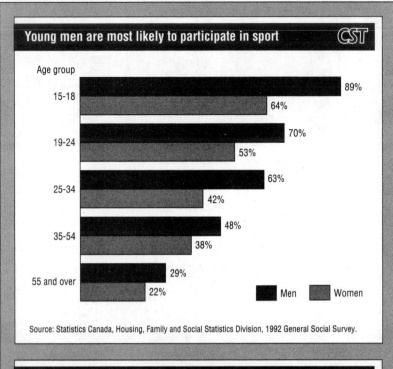

Young men are most likely to participate in sport CST

Age group

15-18	89% (Men), 64% (Women)
19-24	70% (Men), 53% (Women)
25-34	63% (Men), 42% (Women)
35-54	48% (Men), 38% (Women)
55 and over	29% (Men), 22% (Women)

■ Men ■ Women

Source: Statistics Canada, Housing, Family and Social Statistics Division, 1992 General Social Survey.

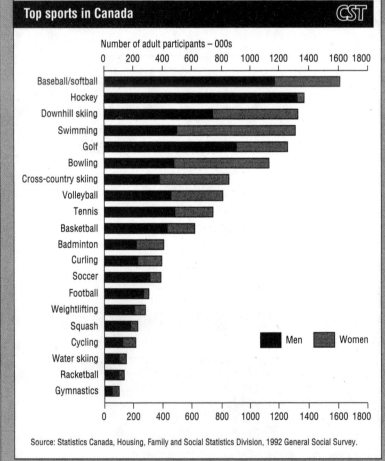

Top sports in Canada CST

Number of adult participants – 000s

Baseball/softball, Hockey, Downhill skiing, Swimming, Golf, Bowling, Cross-country skiing, Volleyball, Tennis, Basketball, Badminton, Curling, Soccer, Football, Weightlifting, Squash, Cycling, Water skiing, Racketball, Gymnastics

■ Men ■ Women

Source: Statistics Canada, Housing, Family and Social Statistics Division, 1992 General Social Survey.

45% of Canadians active in sport

According to the 1992 General Social Survey (GSS), 9.6 million Canadians aged 15 and over (45%) indicated that they regularly participated in one or more sports. Regular participation involves taking part in any sport at least once a week during a season or a certain period of the year.

Sports that were individually categorized on the survey include those funded by Sport Canada, such as baseball and softball, hockey, downhill skiing, swimming, golf and bowling. These sports are extremely popular, each with over 1 million adult Canadians taking part. In addition, about one-quarter of people who reported being regularly active in sport were involved in other physical activities such as jogging, recreational cycling or aerobics.

Sport most popular among youth, but many sports are lifetime activities

Given that most young people are still in school where they have many opportunities to engage in sport, it is not surprising that they had the highest sport participation rate. In 1992, 77% of people aged 15-18 participated regularly, compared with only 53% of those aged 25-34, and 25% of those aged 55 and over.

Basketball, volleyball, hockey, baseball/ softball, and, to some extent, downhill skiing tend to be younger people's sports. For example, 74% of people who played basketball and 65% of those who played volleyball were under age 25. On the other hand, people of all ages were involved in bowling, cross-country skiing, golf, tennis and curling. About two-thirds of cross-country skiers (64%), golfers (65%) and curlers (66%) were aged 35 and over.

Most sports dominated by men

Overall, men were much more likely to participate in sport (52%) than were women (38%). The gender gap was greatest among teenagers, but narrowed considerably with age. In 1992, 89% of men aged 15-18 and 64% of women that age were active in sport. Among people aged 55 and over, however, 29% of men and 22% of women participated regularly in sport.

Men made up the majority of participants in about three-quarters of the sports recognized by Sport Canada that had 40,000 or more regular participants. Hockey was almost completely male-dominated, with men accounting for 97% of Canada's 1.4 million adult hockey players. Men also formed a substantial majority (over 70%) of those playing rugby, football, soccer, squash, racquetball, baseball/softball and golf, and those doing weightlifting.

Women outnumbered men in only a few sports, and in only two did women make up more than 70% of participants. Almost all figure skaters were women (97%), as were 74% of equestrians. Total involvement in these two sports was relatively low, however, with 46,000 and 44,000 participants, respectively. Other sports in which women accounted for the majority of participants included swimming (62%), bowling (58%) and cross-country skiing (56%).

More sport participation among those with higher incomes Being active in sport can be expensive because of equipment, coaching or facility costs. It comes as no surprise, therefore, that adults with higher household incomes were more likely to take part in sport than those with lower incomes. Among people in households with an annual income of $80,000 or more, 63% were sport participants, compared with only 31% of those with household incomes less than $20,000.

People in higher income households were more likely to downhill ski, to play golf, tennis, hockey, and to some extent, baseball/softball. Income had less impact, however, on participation in cross-country skiing, volleyball, basketball, curling and bowling.

Sport preferences vary across the country Adults in British Columbia were the most likely to regularly participate in sport (53%), followed by those in Quebec (49%) and Nova Scotia (47%). At 36%, the participation rate in Newfoundland was the lowest among the provinces.

The sports with the most participants – baseball/softball and hockey – were prevalent across most of the country. Many of the other top sports, however, owed much of their popularity to high participation rates in particular regions. For example, people in Quebec, Alberta and British Columbia, provinces with a variety of major downhill ski resorts, were the most likely to downhill ski. Quebec

residents were also the most likely to cross-country ski.

Golf was most popular in each of the Western provinces. Residents of British Columbia, followed by those in Quebec,

were most likely to play tennis. Swimming was also most prevalent in these two provinces.

Basketball was most common in Newfoundland, with Saskatchewan having the

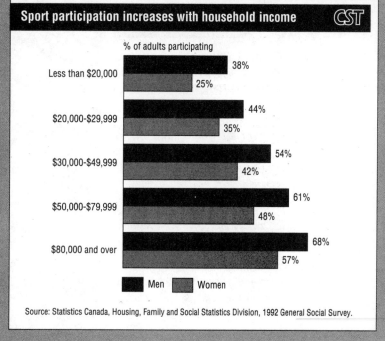

Sport participation increases with household income   CST

% of adults participating

Income	Men	Women
Less than $20,000	38%	25%
$20,000-$29,999	44%	35%
$30,000-$49,999	54%	42%
$50,000-$79,999	61%	48%
$80,000 and over	68%	57%

■ Men ▨ Women

Source: Statistics Canada, Housing, Family and Social Statistics Division, 1992 General Social Survey.

1992 General Social Survey

The primary source of data for this article was the 1992 General Social Survey (GSS) on time use. This survey (Cycle 7 of the GSS) collected data on time use, unpaid work and participation in sport and cultural activities on a monthly basis from January to December 1992. Nationally, a total of 9,815 people aged 15 and over completed the 30-minute telephone interview. This represented a 77% response rate.

Questions on sport participation were sponsored by Sport Canada, Department of Canadian Heritage. Sport participation in this article was determined on the basis of responses of people aged 15 and over to the following question:

❑ *"During the past 12 months did you regularly participate in any sports such as – volleyball, bowling or skiing?"*

Those who said yes were asked about the specific sports in which they participated. Questions about participation in organized sport were also included.

Many sports, including those funded by Sport Canada in 1992-93, were separately categorized. Other activities, however, such as hiking, fishing, jogging, aerobics and cycling for transportation or recreation, were not separately identified, but were included in the calculation of overall rates of sport participation.

Sports funded by Sport Canada, 1992-93

The Department of Canadian Heritage, through Sport Canada provides funding to many of the amateur sports popular in this country. These sports are:

❑ *Amputee Sport, Archery, Badminton, Baseball, Basketball, Biathlon, Blind Sport, Bobsleigh, Bowling, Boxing, Canoeing, Cricket, Cross-Country/Nordic Skiing, Curling, Cycling, Diving, Downhill/Alpine Skiing, Equestrian, Fencing, Field Hockey, Figure Skating, Football, Freestyle Skiing, Golf, Gymnastics, Handball, Hockey, Judo, Karate, Kayaking, Lacrosse, Lawn Bowling, Luge, Modern Pentathlon, Nordic Combined Skiing, Orienteering, Racquetball, Rhythmic Gymnastics, Ringette, Rowing, Rugby, Sailing/Yachting, Shooting, Ski Jumping, Soccer, Softball, Speed Skating, Squash, Swimming, Synchronized Swimming, Table Tennis, Team Handball, Tennis, Track and Field, Volleyball, Water Skiing, Waterpolo, Weightlifting, Wheelchair Sport, Wrestling.*

next highest participation rate. In addition, Saskatchewan had the highest rate of volleyball players.

Curling was concentrated in the Prairie provinces, especially Saskatchewan. Bowling, on the other hand, was particularly favoured in New Brunswick and Nova Scotia.

Organizations an important factor in amateur sport Almost half (46%) of adult Canadians active in sport participated in at least one sport through a club, a league or an organization. The proportion was highest in Saskatchewan (66%) and lowest in Quebec (33%).

Curling (95%), karate (89%) and rugby (84%) were the three sports with the highest proportion of people participating through a club, community program or sport organization. In contrast, cross-country skiing (9%), downhill skiing (11%) and swimming (17%) were least likely to be pursued through an organization.

People who participated in sport at school were more likely to remain physically active During their school years, 60% of Canadians had been involved in organized school sport. Over one-half (52%) of adults who had taken part in school sport in their youth reported participating regularly in sport in the year before the survey, compared with only 37% of those who had not.

Consistent with the overall gender gap in sport participation, men (68%) were considerably more likely than women (53%) to have played school sports. Among people who had participated in sport during their school years, 58% of men and 44% of women were still regularly active, compared with 44% of men and 33% of women without a history of school sport.

Many Canadians do not have time to participate in sport Overall, 55% of Canadians aged 15 and over indicated they did not regularly take part in sport. Among non-participants, 73% gave at least one reason for not taking part in sports. Over one-third (37%) of these people cited a lack of time. Other commonly reported reasons were no interest (26%), health (19%), age (15%) and disability (5%).

Lack of time was the reason mentioned most often by non-participants between 19 and 54 years of age. Those aged 19-34 were the most likely to say they lacked the time to participate regularly in sport – about 63% of men and 55% of women. Lack of interest was the most common reason among teenaged non-participants. Among those aged 15-18, 50% of men and 45% of women reported a lack of interest in sport as a reason for not participating. Not surprisingly, people aged 55 and over who did not take part in sport were most likely to mention age (39%) and health (35%) reasons.

Jean-Pierre Corbeil was an analyst with the Housing, Family and Social Statistics Division, Statistics Canada when he wrote this article. For additional information, contact Sport Canada, Department of Canadian Heritage.

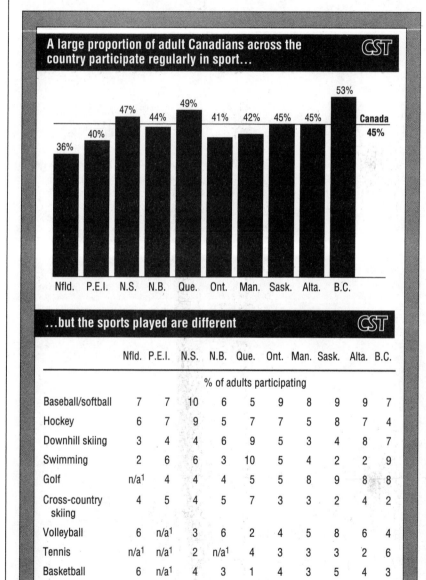

A large proportion of adult Canadians across the country participate regularly in sport... CST

Nfld.	P.E.I.	N.S.	N.B.	Que.	Ont.	Man.	Sask.	Alta.	B.C.
36%	40%	47%	44%	49%	41%	42%	45%	45%	53%

Canada 45%

...but the sports played are different CST

	Nfld.	P.E.I.	N.S.	N.B.	Que.	Ont.	Man.	Sask.	Alta.	B.C.
	\% of adults participating									
Baseball/softball	7	7	10	6	5	9	8	9	9	7
Hockey	6	7	9	5	7	7	5	8	7	4
Downhill skiing	3	4	4	6	9	5	3	4	8	7
Swimming	2	6	6	3	10	5	4	2	2	9
Golf	n/a[1]	4	4	4	5	5	8	9	8	8
Cross-country skiing	4	5	4	5	7	3	3	2	4	2
Volleyball	6	n/a[1]	3	6	2	4	5	8	6	4
Tennis	n/a[1]	n/a[1]	2	n/a[1]	4	3	3	3	2	6
Basketball	6	n/a[1]	4	3	1	4	3	5	4	3
Bowling	4	5	10	13	4	6	6	6	4	4
Curling	n/a[1]	n/a[1]	n/a[1]	2	n/a[1]	1	6	10	4	2

[1] Data suppressed due to high sampling variability.
Source: Statistics Canada, Housing, Family and Social Statistics Division, 1992 General Social Survey.

CST

The Leisurely Pursuit of Reading

Recent discussion about the literacy of Canadians has centred mainly on the importance of strong literacy skills to meet the demands of new technology, productivity and global competitiveness. This emphasis has focused the debate exclusively on the economic dimension of literacy. But because reading is one of society's main conduits of culture, knowledge and entertainment, strong literacy skills can also enhance a person's quality of life. To provide some measure of this aspect of literacy, this article briefly describes the reading habits of Canadian adults outside the workplace.

by Susan Crompton

Literacy requirements not as high for reading at home Some level of literacy is necessary to complete common everyday household chores and activities such as paying bills, following a recipe and doing home repairs. However, data from the International Adult Literacy Survey (IALS) suggest that these reading tasks are generally not as demanding as those at work. Because people at all but the lowest level of literacy (Level 1) were engaged in everyday reading tasks with similar frequency, IALS researchers concluded that Level 2 ability is adequate for most ordinary literacy tasks outside the workplace.[1]

Although dealing with bills, catalogues or recipes may demand little in the way of literacy skills, reading "for fun", that is, reading undertaken as a leisure activity, seems to require a higher level of skill. This can be seen in the most common leisure-time literacy activity, reading the newspaper. The majority of Canadians aged 16 and over (87%) read a newspaper at least once a week. However, a newspaper is not a homogeneous entity: it consists of multiple sections designed to appeal to multiple interests. According to the IALS, some sections — advertisements, local news, sports, horoscopes, TV list-ings and advice columns — are read with almost equal frequency by people at all literacy levels (except Level 1). For example, people at Level 2 are no less likely to read the sports section than people at Level 4/5. But people at the highest literacy level are most likely to read those sections containing more complex information: national and international news, editorials, articles on health and lifestyle, and book or movie reviews.

People at the higher literacy levels were also more likely to report engaging in literacy activities outside the workplace. Nevertheless, many people at Level 1 reported reading a newspaper (70%) or book (30%) at least once a week, and a significant minority write letters (19%) or visit a library (10%) at least once a month. Given these findings, it seems reasonable to assume that people with weak literacy skills do not forego reading altogether — they simply read at a lower level of complexity. This interpretation is supported by data on reading habits from the 1992 General Social Survey.

[1] *Reading the Future: A Portrait of Literacy in Canada,* Statistics Canada/Human Resources Development Canada/National Literacy Secretariat, Catalogue no. 89-551-XPE.

Who reads for fun?[2] On an average day in 1992, about 4 in 10 Canadians aged 25 and over (39%) spent some of their leisure time reading books, magazines or newspapers. Adults with higher education levels were more likely to read during their leisure time — about half of university graduates (51%) reported leisure-time reading compared with only one-third (33%) of Canadians without a high school diploma. Given the strong link between education and literacy skills, this difference in leisure-time reading habits is not surprising. Interestingly, women at almost all educational levels were slightly more likely than men to be readers.

Older Canadians were most likely to take time to read: 56% of those aged 65 and over, compared with 43% of those aged 45 to 64 and only 30% of those aged 25 to 44. This reflects the fact that seniors have more time available for recreational activities — 7.7 hours per day in 1992, compared with 5.4 hours for Canadians under 65.

What do people read? Men and women exhibit distinctly different reading preferences. On an average day in 1992, men were moderately more inclined to read newspapers — 29% versus 23% of women — while women were almost twice as likely to read books — 20% compared with 11% of men. This marked difference between the sexes holds across all educational levels. The types of books favoured by men and women also differ substantially, with 60% of women book-readers reporting that the last book they had read was fiction, compared with only 45% of men.

Different age groups also exhibit different choices. On an average day in 1992, 26% of Canadian adults aged 25 and over read newspapers and 16% read books. But those aged 45 and over were very keen consumers of news, being twice as likely to read a newspaper as a book. In contrast, 25- to 44-year-olds were only moderately more likely to choose a newspaper (17%) than a book (13%) for their leisure-time reading.

How much time do readers spend reading? People who read during their leisure time devote a substantial amount of time to the printed word: readers aged 25 and over are immersed in books, magazines and newspapers for almost an hour-and-a-half a day — an average of 84 minutes. Because seniors have more leisure time, they spend much more time

CANADIAN SOCIAL TRENDS BACKGROUNDER · CST

Defining literacy

This article uses data from the 1994 International Adult Literacy Survey (IALS) and the 1992 General Social Survey (GSS) on time use. In the past, literacy measures divided people into two very separate categories — the literate and the illiterate — and usually used highest level of schooling to make the distinction. In contrast, the IALS defined literacy as the ability to understand and use printed and written documents in daily activities to achieve goals, and to develop knowledge and potential. As such, literacy was measured as a continuum of successive levels of skill; this continuum was separated into five levels, with the lowest level being "Level 1" and the highest "Level 5."[1]

The IALS assessed adult literacy skills in three areas: prose, document and quantitative skills. All three areas concern the information-processing skills of respondents — that is, the ability to locate, integrate, construct and generate information — but the emphasis is somewhat different for each type. *Prose literacy* measures the skills needed to understand texts seen in everyday life, such as newspaper articles or instruction manuals; *document literacy* assesses the skills needed to understand forms such as job applications or transportation schedules, maps, tables and graphs; and *quantitative literacy* describes the numeracy skills needed for such tasks as balancing a chequebook or verifying an invoice. Only prose literacy is of interest in this study.

Data on reading as a leisure activity, presented in the second half of this article, were drawn from the 1992 GSS on time use. The GSS did not collect data on literacy skills, but for purposes of this analysis, level of educational attainment has been used as a proxy for literacy. The table below — presenting the IALS prose literacy level by educational attainment — shows that education is correlated with literacy skills.

[1] For more information, see *Reading the Future: A Portrait of Literacy in Canada,* Statistics Canada/Human Resources Development Canada/National Literacy Secretariat, Catalogue no. 89-551-XPE.

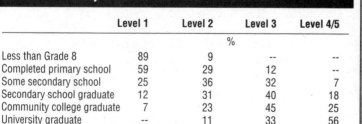

The prose literacy skill of Canadians aged 16 and over is closely linked to their level of education · CST

	Level 1	Level 2	Level 3	Level 4/5
		%		
Less than Grade 8	89	9	--	--
Completed primary school	59	29	12	--
Some secondary school	25	36	32	7
Secondary school graduate	12	31	40	18
Community college graduate	7	23	45	25
University graduate	--	11	33	56

-- Amount too small to be expressed.
Source: Statistics Canada/Human Resources Development Canada/National Literacy Secretariat, Catalogue no. 89-551-XPE.

[2] Youths aged 15 to 24 were excluded from the analysis of reading habits because they are still students, and their inclusion may skew the two categories for incomplete education, that is "less than high school" and "some postsecondary."

reading than younger adults. Readers aged 65 and over spend 109 minutes on this leisure activity, compared with 82 minutes for readers aged 45 to 64 and only 70 minutes for those aged 25 to 44.

The data also show that readers at all educational levels are equally dedicated to their habit. It is true that people with lower levels of education are, presumably because their literacy skills are weaker, less likely to be readers; but those who do read devote just as much time to it as readers with higher levels of education. For example, readers with less than high school spend an average of 87 minutes per day on leisure-time reading, while university graduates dedicate 82 minutes.

The average reader aged 25 and over devotes the same amount of time each day — about 38 minutes — to newspapers and books, for a total of 76 minutes or 90% of daily reading time; magazines account for about 8 minutes. And although men and women who read spend the same amount of time on this activity, women dedicate the majority of their reading time to books, while men dedicate their time to newspapers.

While women's preference for reading books seems unrelated to their educational level, men's interest does seem to be linked to education. Male readers with no more than high school devote less than one-quarter of their leisure-time

reading to books, while those with post-secondary and university education devote well over one-third.

Summary Almost 40% of adult Canadians spend almost an hour and a half of their leisure time each day immersed in the pleasures of the printed word. Yet reading for fun should be considered more than a diverting form of entertainment. The International Adult Literacy Survey found strong evidence that literacy is maintained and strengthened through practice — like a muscle, if it is not used regularly, it atrophies. Reading during their leisure hours probably helps people to retain or improve their literacy skills, especially if

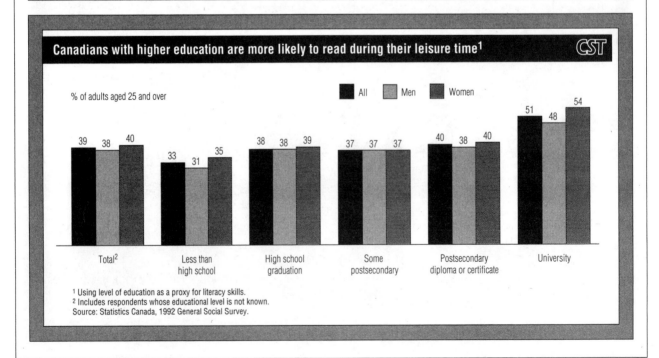

Level 2 literacy skills seem to be adequate for most everyday reading tasks outside the workplace CST

% of Canadians aged 16 and over who read... at least once a week

	Letters or memos	Reports, articles, magazines or journals	Manuals or reference books, including catalogues	Diagrams or schematics	Bills, invoices, spreadsheets or budget tables	Directions or instructions for medicines, recipes or other products
Level 1	32	41	24	5	34	37
Level 2	51	67	49	15	52	53
Level 3	55	69	53	21	60	54
Level 4/5	59	78	55	23	69	62

Source: Statistics Canada/Human Resources Development Canada/National Literacy Secretariat, Catalogue no. 89-551-XPE.

Canadians with higher education are more likely to read during their leisure time[1] CST

% of adults aged 25 and over

Legend: All | Men | Women

	All	Men	Women
Total[2]	39	38	40
Less than high school	33	31	35
High school graduation	38	38	39
Some postsecondary	37	37	37
Postsecondary diploma or certificate	40	38	40
University	51	48	54

[1] Using level of education as a proxy for literacy skills.
[2] Includes respondents whose educational level is not known.
Source: Statistics Canada, 1992 General Social Survey.

UNIT 3: WORK, LIFE STYLE AND SOCIAL PROBLEMS

A rough ride for Canada's book and periodical publishers

Canadian periodical publishers faced rough times during the first half of the 1990s. Between 1990-91 and 1994-95, the number of titles published fell by 7% while total annual circulation dropped by 3 million copies. Over the same period, the number of full-time employees in the industry slipped by 3%, while part-time positions dropped 8% to 1,600. However, revenues averaged about $860 million per year, and profits showed steady growth, reaching almost 8% of total revenues by 1994-95.

The book publishing industry also underwent a period of decline in the early 1990s. Between 1990-91 and 1993-94, book publishers increased the total number of their titles by 23% but net sales in Canada remained flat, full-time employment dropped 7%, and pre-tax profits dipped to just over 5%. In 1994-95, however, the industry's outlook improved considerably as before-tax profits rose to almost 7%, with 71% of firms reporting profits, suggesting that recessionary pressures accounted for the industry's poor performance in the early years of the decade.

• For more information, see *Canada's Culture, Heritage and Identity: A Statistical Perspective.* Statistics Canada, Catalogue no. 87-211-XPB, 1997.

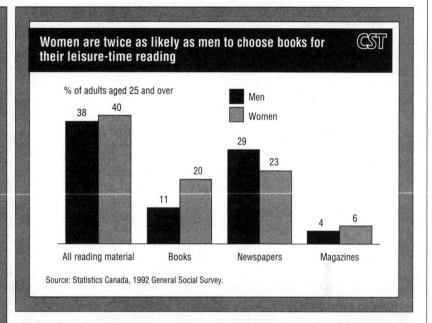

Women are twice as likely as men to choose books for their leisure-time reading CST

% of adults aged 25 and over

■ Men
▨ Women

	Men	Women
All reading material	38	40
Books	11	20
Newspapers	29	23
Magazines	4	6

Source: Statistics Canada, 1992 General Social Survey.

Readers spend almost 1.5 hours of their leisure time reading, regardless of their level of educational attainment CST

Level of education[1]	Minutes per day spent reading by readers			
	Total	Books	Newspapers	Magazines
Men aged 25 and over	**83**	**29**	**48**	**7**
Less than high school	88	21	62	5
High school graduation	75	16	49	10
Some postsecondary	84	37	40	6
Postsecondary diploma or certificate	80	33	39	8
University	84	32	46	6
Women aged 25 and over	**84**	**45**	**30**	**9**
Less than high school	86	43	34	8
High school graduation	81	42	29	9
Some postsecondary	88	52	27	9
Postsecondary diploma or certificate	87	45	33	9
University	79	46	25	7

[1] Using level of education as a proxy for literacy skills. See table in Backgrounder: Defining literacy for distribution of literacy skills by educational attainment.
Source: Statistics Canada, 1992 General Social Survey.

they do not read a great deal on the job. Reading outside the workplace — whether the sports page, a celebrity pro-file, a whodunnit — contributes to Canadians' ability to participate more fully in the social, cultural and economic life of their community.

• For more information, see "Adult Literacy in Canada, the United States and Germany," *Canadian Social Trends*, Winter 1996; and *Reading the Future*, Statistics Canada/Human Resources Development Canada/National Literacy Secretariat, Catalogue no. 89-551-XPE.

Susan Crompton is Editor-in-Chief of *Canadian Social Trends.*

Youth and Crime

by Kathryn Stevenson, Jennifer Tufts, Dianne Hendrick and Melanie Kowalski

It is what every parent dreads. The phone rings. It's the police. They ask you to collect your child, who has just been charged with a criminal offence. Fortunately, very few parents receive such a phone call: contrary to popular belief, youth crime is neither widespread, nor is it rising. Just the opposite, in fact. In 1997 less than 5% of young Canadians aged 12 to 17 (approximately 121,000 youths) were charged with a federal statute offence. And the rate of youths charged has been declining steadily since 1991.

Nonetheless, some young people do get into trouble with the law. What happens in the life of a child that leads to criminal activity? Although experts disagree about motivations for crime and delinquency, most would agree that the risk of becoming involved in antisocial behaviour varies with both personality and social conditions. The first part of this article examines young offenders and their crimes; the second explores current theories about the causes of youth crime in the context of Canada's social and economic landscape.

Theft most common charge

Young people are most commonly charged with theft. In 1997 nearly half of youths charged (49%) were involved in property crime,[1] most often theft, and break and enter. Violent offences,[2] including assault and robbery, were much less frequent, accounting for about 18% of young people charged, while "other" Criminal Code and "other" federal statute offences made up the remainder of charges. In comparison, in 1987 a larger proportion of youths were charged with property crimes (67%) and a smaller proportion with violent crimes (9%) and all other offences.

The total number of criminal charges against youths increased between 1987 and 1991, peaked in that year and then began to decline. By 1997 the rate was virtually the same as it was in 1987. In contrast, the violent crime rate for youths doubled (102%) over the decade. Some experts, however, question whether these figures indicate a real rise in violent crime or simply changing attitudes, resulting in an increase in the reporting of crime, particularly common

CST What you should know about this study

Most of the data in this article come from the Uniform Crime Reporting Survey (UCR) and the Revised Uniform Crime Reporting Survey (UCRII). In operation since 1962, the UCR is a nationally representative survey that records the number of criminal incidents reported to police. It collects information on the number of persons charged by sex and by an adult/youth breakdown. Incidents that involve more than one infraction are recorded under the most serious violation. As a result, less serious offences are undercounted.

The Revised Uniform Crime Reporting Survey (UCRII) was developed in 1984 (and has since been conducted concurrently with the UCR) to provide detailed information on criminal incidents. Information collected by the UCRII includes the age and sex of the accused and the victim, the relationship of the victim to the accused, injuries sustained during a violent incident, location of the incident, and the presence of a weapon. The 1997 data, collected from 179 police departments in six provinces (New Brunswick, Quebec, Ontario, Alberta, Saskatchewan and British Columbia), represented about 48% of the national volume of crime. These data are not nationally representative.

---

1. Property offences consist of unlawful acts to gain property, but do not involve the use or threat of violence against a person.

2. Violent offences involve the use of, or threatened use of, violence against a person.

assault.[3] For example, more aggressive "zero tolerance" strategies have meant that students involved in a schoolyard fight, who would previously have been disciplined by the school principal, are now more likely to be dealt with by the police and to become "justice statistics."

Common assault, major assault and robbery constitute the majority of violent crimes, with common assault being by far the most frequent. On the other hand, the number of youths charged with homicide (54 youths in 1997)

represents a very small proportion of young people charged with a criminal offence (about 2 in 100,000). Over the last 10 years, the actual number of youths charged with homicide fluctuated considerably and ranged from a low of 36 in 1987 to a high of 68 in 1995.

16- to 17-year-old boys are most likely to be charged

According to police data, the peak age for involvement in criminal activity differs for boys and girls. Girls aged 14 to 15 are most likely to be charged, while boys accused of crimes tend to be 16 to 17 years old. But while criminal activity continues as boys age, among girls it begins to decline at around 16 years.

The majority of young people involved in crime are boys (78% in 1997), although the gap between the sexes has been narrowing over the past decade (in 1987, 84% of youths charged were boys). Compared with 10 years before, the total charge rate in 1997 was 7% lower for boys and 38% higher for

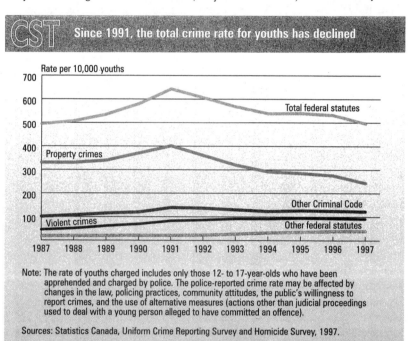

Since 1991, the total crime rate for youths has declined

Rate per 10,000 youths

Total federal statutes

Property crimes

Other Criminal Code

Violent crimes

Other federal statutes

1987 1988 1989 1990 1991 1992 1993 1994 1995 1996 1997

Note: The rate of youths charged includes only those 12- to 17-year-olds who have been apprehended and charged by police. The police-reported crime rate may be affected by changes in the law, policing practices, community attitudes, the public's willingness to report crimes, and the use of alternative measures (actions other than judicial proceedings used to deal with a young person alleged to have committed an offence).

Sources: Statistics Canada, Uniform Crime Reporting Survey and Homicide Survey, 1997.

3. Common assault is the least serious form of assault and includes pushing, slapping, punching, and face-to-face verbal threats. In contrast, major assault involves carrying, using or threatening to use a weapon against someone or causing bodily harm, or in the most serious case, maiming, disfiguring or endangering the life of a person.

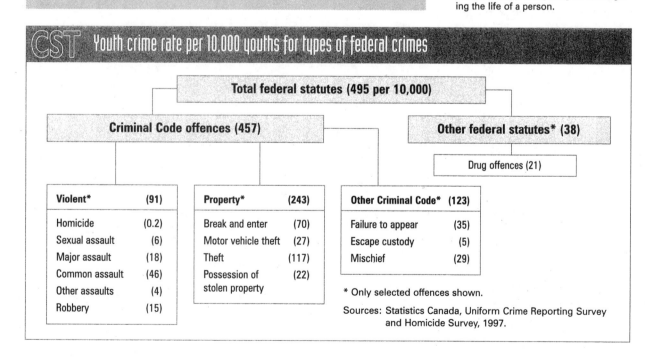

Youth crime rate per 10,000 youths for types of federal crimes

Total federal statutes (495 per 10,000)

Criminal Code offences (457)

Other federal statutes* (38)

Drug offences (21)

Violent*	**(91)**
Homicide	(0.2)
Sexual assault	(6)
Major assault	(18)
Common assault	(46)
Other assaults	(4)
Robbery	(15)

Property*	**(243)**
Break and enter	(70)
Motor vehicle theft	(27)
Theft	(117)
Possession of stolen property	(22)

Other Criminal Code*	**(123)**
Failure to appear	(35)
Escape custody	(5)
Mischief	(29)

* Only selected offences shown.

Sources: Statistics Canada, Uniform Crime Reporting Survey and Homicide Survey, 1997.

girls. In the area of violent crime, the rates increased for both boys and girls, but much faster for girls: 85% versus 179% over the past decade. However, in 1997 the actual rate of girls charged with violent crime (47 per 10,000) was still substantially lower than that for boys (133 per 10,000).

Boys and girls tend to be involved in similar types of offences. The three most common crimes for young men were theft under $5,000, break and enter, and common assault. Young women were also most often charged with theft under $5,000, followed by common assault, and failure to appear in court.

Repeat offenders account for over 4 in 10 youth court cases

In 1996-97, over 40% of cases dealt with by youth courts involved repeat offenders (youths with prior convictions) of whom 21% had one prior conviction, 10% had two and 11% had three or more. A previous study on recidivism, conducted in 1993-94, yielded very similar results, implying that repeat offenders represent a substantial proportion of youths involved with the justice system. This situation has not changed substantially over the past few years.

Like first-time offenders, repeat offenders are brought to court most often for property offences (59%). In terms of specific offences, however, repeat offenders are more likely to be involved in more serious infractions. For example, possession of stolen property represented 17% of all property offences for repeat offenders and 12% for first-time offenders. In contrast, the less serious crime of theft under $5,000 accounted for 31% of all property offences for repeat offenders and 35% for first-time offenders. The same patterns held true for violent offences.

CST Victims of youth violence are usually other young people

When youths commit a violent act, other youths — young men in particular — are their most likely victims. In 1997, more than half (56%) of all victims of youth violence were other youths, 34% were adults while the remaining 10% were children under 12 years. Some 62% of victims were male; boys aged 12 to 17 accounted for 36% of all victims.

Most victims of youth violence know their assailant. Police data from 1997 show that 74% of victims knew the perpetrator in some way. For the majority (57%) of victims, the accused was an acquaintance, for 13% the accused was a family member, and for 4% of victims the accused was a close friend. Common assault was the crime most frequently perpetrated against both male and female victims. However, major assault and robbery were the second and third most common violent crimes against male victims, while females tended to be victims of sexual assault and major assault.

The vast majority of victims of violent youth crime do not sustain serious physical injuries. In 1997, 49% of victims reported that no injuries resulted from the incident and about 47% suffered minor injuries that did not require medical attention. Some 5% of victims experienced major injuries (medical attention was required), while 0.1% died.

Most youth violence occurs in a public place, such as a parking lot or public transportation. In 1997, 35% of victims were assaulted in a public place, 26% in private homes, 22% in schools, and 17% in commercial places and public institutions. The location of youth violence varied depending on the type of offence. Homes tended to be the predominant setting for sexual assaults and homicides, while public areas were most often the sites for robbery, major assaults and common assaults.

	Victims		
Offence	**Total**	**Female**	**Male**
		%	
Common assault	53	57	51
Major assault	18	13	21
Robbery	14	8	17
Sexual assault	8	16	3
Homicide	0.1	0.1	0.1
Other*	7	6	8

Note: Excludes 21 victims (0.2%) whose sex was unknown.

* Includes all other violent offences.

Source: Statistics Canada, Revised Uniform Crime Reporting Survey, 1997.

Repeat offenders are also more likely to be charged with multiple offences. Youths facing multiple charges per case are assumed to be more criminally active than those having only one charge per case. In 1996-97, half of first-time offenders were charged with multiple charges compared with 62% of offenders with one prior conviction, 69% with two and 72% with three or more prior convictions. Young men were more likely than young women to be repeat offenders: 43% versus 32%.

Both personality and society play a part in youth crime

Most experts agree that the risk of becoming involved in criminal activities is influenced by personal as well as social factors. Biological or genetic predisposition, alcoholism and drug abuse, mental illness, family structure, low income, dropping out of school, and unemployment are just a few of the factors that have been linked to young people's involvement in crime. In a recent public opinion survey, the majority of respondents felt that poor parenting and broken homes were the most important factors contributing to involvement in crime, followed by illegal drugs, a lenient justice system, poverty, low moral standards, unemployment, violence on television and lack of discipline in schools.[4]

Economic disadvantage, coupled with difficult family circumstances, is a common explanation for delinquency. Children living in low-income households can be affected by low-quality housing and transient, run-down neighbourhoods. Parental frustration may lead to substance abuse and violence in the home,[5] which in turn may place children at risk of becoming involved with a delinquent peer group and potentially criminal activity. Indeed, according to the National Longitudinal Survey of Children and Youth (NLSCY), children in low-income households are at risk of indirect and physically aggressive behaviour that may persist from early childhood through adolescence.[6]

In 1996, more than 20% of children under 18 (1.5 million) lived in a low-income family. At the same time, some 17% of children were cared for by a lone parent. As many lone-parent families are economically disadvantaged, children growing up in these households may be especially vulnerable. NLSCY findings suggest that children from lone-parent families are at greater risk of emotional, behavioural, academic and social problems than children from two-parent families.[7] However, data from this source also indicate that good parenting practices act to counter the impact of low income and negative peer pressure.[8]

Social bonds may help to prevent criminal behaviour

Delinquency is often explained by the absence of strong bonds to society. People who are "bonded" tend to have strong attachments to others who conform to society's goals and who participate in conventional work, education and leisure activities. A young person's ties to parents, teachers, community leaders and conforming peers are important sources of informal control that can help monitor leisure time and discourage criminal behaviour.[9]

4. Environics Research Group. 1998. *Focus Canada Environics 1998-1*. Ottawa: Environics.

5. Trocme, N. D. McPhee, K. Kwan Tam and T. Hay. 1994. *Ontario Incidence Study of Reported Child Abuse and Neglect*. Toronto: Institute for the Prevention of Child Abuse. Also Thompson, R.A. 1994. "Social Support and the Prevention of Child Maltreatment," *Protecting Children from Abuse and Neglect: Foundations for a New National Strategy*. G.B. Melton and F.D. Barry. (eds.) New York: Guilford.

6. Tremblay, Richard E., et al. 1996. "Do Children in Canada Become More Aggressive as They Approach Adolescence?" *Growing Up in Canada: National Longitudinal Survey of Children and Youth*. Ottawa: Human Resources Development Canada and Statistics Canada (Catalogue no. 89-550-MPE, no.1).

7. ibid.

8. Landy, Sarah and Kwok Kwan Tam. 1996. "Yes, Parenting Does Make a Difference to the Development of Children in Canada." *Growing up in Canada: National Longitudinal Survey of Children and Youth*. Ottawa: Human Resources Development Canada and Statistics Canada. (Catalogue no. 89-550-MPE, no.1).

9. Sacco, V. and L. Kennedy. 1994. *The Criminal Event*. Scarborough: Nelson Canada. p. 64.

Multiple charges were most common among repeat offenders

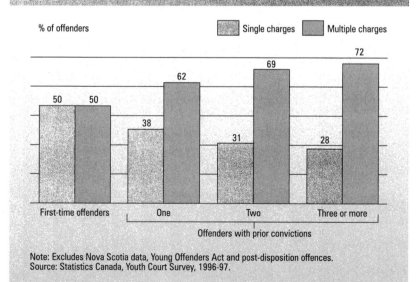

% of offenders — Single charges — Multiple charges

First-time offenders: 50 / 50
One: 38 / 62
Two: 31 / 69
Three or more: 28 / 72

Offenders with prior convictions

Note: Excludes Nova Scotia data, Young Offenders Act and post-disposition offences.
Source: Statistics Canada, Youth Court Survey, 1996-97.

In the absence of social bonds, and with exposure to norms and beliefs that support law-breaking, criminal behaviour may be quick to surface. Within certain gangs, for example, violence and other criminal behaviour are not only acceptable, but also expected. Additionally, violent behaviour can also be learned through mainstream society (for example, through easy access and widespread exposure to violence on television, movies and video games) as a response to frustration or a technique for achieving goals.[10]

Dropping out of school linked to youth crime

Lack of attachment to school may be associated with youth crime. Students who leave school before graduating do so for many reasons, including boredom, the perception that school rules are too strict, associations with non-student friends who place little value on education and, in the case of many teenage girls, pregnancy. According to the 1991 School Leavers Survey (SLS), approximately 184,000 or 16% of all 18- to 20-year-olds had left school before graduating; as of 1995, the vast majority (160,000) had not returned. Almost 40% of school leavers were under 17 years when they left and 32% had no more than a grade nine education. The rate of leaving school was considerably higher for men (18%) than for women (10%).

Youths who leave school are more likely to become involved in other high-risk behaviour associated with crime. For example, according to results from the SLS, regular consumption of alcohol was more common among school leavers than graduates (18% versus 11%) as was use of soft and prescription drugs (30% versus 16%).[11] School leavers also experience higher rates of unemployment than graduates. In 1997, unemployment rates for youths without a high school diploma were almost two times higher than the corresponding rates for high school graduates and three times higher than those of university graduates.

Higher jobless rates may contribute to crime

Unemployment may lead to criminal activity when youths have no legitimate means of earning money. Being unemployed also reduces formal involvement in community life and can lead to an abundance of unstructured time, which in turn increases the risk of becoming involved in deviant or criminal activity.

In the early 1990s, it became increasingly difficult for young Canadians to find employment. Many adult workers are hanging on to entry-level positions that have generally been available for youths. Furthermore, without job security or seniority, youths are primary targets for lay-offs during corporate restructuring. At around 22% in 1997, the unemployment rate for 15- to 19-year-olds was more than double that of the overall population. Summer jobs are also difficult to find, which, in turn, can affect job prospects after graduation. The percentage of 15- to 19-year-olds without job experience has more than doubled over the past decade, to 40% in 1997.

Summary

The risk of becoming involved in criminal activities has been associated with living in a lone-parent family, lacking adequate social bonds, belonging to a gang, dropping out of school and being unemployed. Other factors, which are much more complicated to measure, such as physical and sexual abuse, television violence and poor parenting, may also increase the chances of becoming involved in crime. In many cases, by the time youths become involved in the criminal justice system, they have already exhibited warning signs.

However, the proportion of youths charged with a crime has been declining for the past six years. In 1997, among those involved in crime, most were charged with theft under $5,000. Although the gap in crime rates between the sexes has fallen over the past decade, the majority of young people charged continue to be 16- to 17-year-old males.

• This article was adapted from *A Profile of Youth Justice in Canada*, Statistics Canada Catalogue no. 85-544-XPE.

Kathryn Stevenson, Jennifer Tufts, Dianne Hendrick and **Melanie Kowalski** are analysts with the Canadian Centre for Justice Statistics, Statistics Canada.

10. Reiss, A. and J. Roth (eds.). 1993. *Understanding and Preventing Violence*. Washington D.C.: National Academy Press.

11. See also Galambos, Nancy L. and Lauree C. Tilton-Weaver. 1998. "Multiple-Risk Behaviour in Adolescents and Young Adults." *Health Reports* 10, 2:9-20. Statistics Canada Catalogue no. 82-003-XPB.

Family characteristics of problem kids

by Kathryn Stevenson

The teacher calls about your eight-year-old son's behaviour — again. He used to be a carefree kid who had only been involved in the playground scuffles typical of young children. You thought he would grow out of it when he started school but, instead, his behaviour has become worse. Now he's getting into daily fights, steals from other children, and is frequently disruptive in class.

In 1995, about 20% of children aged 8 to 11 (173,000 children) displayed some form of inappropriately aggressive behaviour, known formally as conduct disorder. Boys were nearly twice as likely as girls to fall into this category: 26% versus 13%. Experts generally agree that children who exhibit aggressive tendencies are more likely than others to display this behaviour during their adolescence and into adulthood. In fact, recent studies have shown that 12- to17-year-old youths charged with a federal offence had frequently exhibited behaviour problems as children.[1] Policy makers and researchers believe that identifying the factors that predispose children to develop conduct disorder is, therefore, the first of many steps involved in reducing crime.

Using data from the 1994-95 National Longitudinal Survey of Children and Youth (NLSCY), this article examines the family circumstances of 8- to 11-year-old youngsters to assess the link between behaviour and certain family characteristics. Do children with conduct disorder, as many assume, live in low-income and lone-parent families? Do their parents use different child-rearing approaches than the parents of children who keep out of trouble? And does the age of the mother or the number of siblings have any effect on the child's behaviour?

Parenting style makes the most difference

One of the most important influences in young children's lives is their family environment and the bond they establish with their parents — a bond closely affected by parenting practices. Most policy makers and crime prevention organizations recognize, and people intuitively acknowledge, the link between parents' and children's behaviour. In a recent public opinion survey, 64% of Canadians felt that poor parenting and broken homes were very important factors in crime.[2] The federal Department of Justice has identified positive child development as key to preventing children's future involvement in delinquent activities as youths or adults.[3] And The National Crime Prevention Centre has stated that parenting practices that are "inconsistent,

---

1. For further information, see Sprott, J. and A. Doob. 1998. *Who Are the Most Violent 10 and 11 Year Olds? An Introduction to Future Delinquency*. Research paper no. W-98-29E. Ottawa: Human Resources Development Canada.

2. Environics Research Group. 1998. *Focus Canada Environics 1998-1*. Ottawa: Environics.

coercive or excessively permissive appear to maintain disruptive and aggressive behaviour in children. These practices, combined with insufficient monitoring, are associated with delinquency that begins before age 14 and persists into adulthood."[4]

Findings from the National Longitudinal Survey of Children and Youth support these conclusions. In fact, among all the variables examined in this study, parenting style appeared to have the strongest association with aggressive behaviour. This does not mean, however, that parents who use less-than-perfect child-rearing techniques from time to time — as all parents inevitably do — pay for their mistakes with delinquent kids. What makes the difference is the frequency with which the various parenting approaches are used.

Parents who employed ineffective, aversive, inconsistent or negative disciplining most of the time were significantly more likely to have children with behaviour problems than parents who utilized these approaches infrequently. For example, 63% of children whose parents very often used an ineffective technique exhibited conduct disorder, compared with 4%[5] of children whose parents only rarely practised this kind of parenting style. When the effects of other family variables[6] are held constant, the

3. Department of Justice Canada. 1998. *A Strategy for the Renewal of Youth Justice*. Ottawa: Standing Committee, Justice and Legal Affairs.

4. National Crime Prevention Centre. 1997. *Preventing Crime by Investing in Families: Promoting Positive Outcomes in Children 6 to 12 years old*. Ottawa.

5. Subject to high sampling variability.

6. Other variables included in this model are aversive, positive and consistent parenting styles, lone-parent versus two parent families, number of siblings, mother's age at birth of child, mother's work status and the family's socioeconomic status.

CST What you should know about this study

This article is based on data from the 1994-95 National Longitudinal Survey of Children and Youth (NLSCY). The NLSCY is conducted by Statistics Canada every two years on behalf of Human Resources Development Canada. It is designed to develop a better understanding of the factors that contribute to a child's development over time.

The 1994-95 NLSCY collected information on more than 22,500 children from newborn to 11 years living in private residences in the 10 provinces (excluding Aboriginal children living on reserves). Interviews were held with the "person most knowledgeable (PMK)" about the child (usually the mother) to gather information about the children and their families; with teachers and principals about the child's scholastic development; and with 10- to 11-year-olds themselves to learn about their experiences with family, friends and school. Information will be collected about the same children every two years until they reach adulthood.

Conduct disorder: Although there is no generally accepted and consistent definition of conduct disorder, most experts agree that it is characterized by either physical or indirect aggression against persons or property, or a severe violation of societal norms.[1] This study uses the conduct disorder scale developed by the NLSCY, which incorporates such items as frequency of fighting, threatening people and bullying other children. Following the methodology established by Offord and Lipman,[2] children who scored in the highest 10% of the scale were identified as having conduct disorder. In this article, "conduct disorder" is used interchangeably with "aggressive behaviour" or "delinquent behaviour."

Parenting practices: based on questions parents answered about interaction with their child, the NLSCY developed scales for four different parenting practice categories.

Ineffective: often annoyed with child, telling child he/she is bad or not as good as others.

Aversive:[3] raising voice when child misbehaves, using physical punishment.

Consistent: disciplining the same way for the same behaviours each time.

Positive: praising the child, playing together, laughing together.

Socioeconomic status (SES): the relative social position of a family or individual. For the NLSCY, SES was derived from the level of education of the PMK, the level of education of the spouse/partner, the prestige of the PMK's occupation, the prestige of the occupation of the spouse/partner and household income. The highest SES families were in the top quartile and the lowest SES families were in the bottom quartile.

1. Measuring conduct disorder among children is complicated by the lack of benchmark crime data and by the fact that parents may not be fully aware of their child's conduct or may be unwilling to admit their child's problem behaviour to interviewers.

2. Offord, David R. and Ellen L. Lipman. 1996. "Emotional and behavioural problems," *Growing Up in Canada: National Longitudinal Survey of Children and Youth* (Statistics Canada catalogue 89-550-MPE) Ottawa: Human Resources Development Canada and Statistics Canada.

3. In the 1996-97 NLSCY, the scoring on this category was changed to reflect better parenting practices (e.g., calmly discussing problems, not using physical punishment) and the category was renamed the "rational parenting style."

Source: Statistics Canada, *National Longitudinal Survey of Children and Youth: Overview of Survey Instruments for 1994-95* (Report no. 95-02).

Parenting style used	Children with conduct disorder %
Ineffective	
Rarely	4[1]
Sometimes	24
Very often	63
Aversive	
Rarely	7
Sometimes	22
Very often	40
Consistent	
Rarely	38
Sometimes	24
Very often	16
Positive	
Rarely	27
Sometimes	19
Very often	14

1. Subject to high sampling variability.

Source: Statistics Canada, National Longitudinal Survey of Children and Youth, 1994-95.

odds of children displaying delinquent behaviour were 36 times higher if their parents employed ineffective disciplining techniques very often rather than rarely.

Aversive parenting techniques were associated with similar child behaviour patterns. Nearly 40% of children with parents who frequently used an aversive style exhibited aggressive behaviour compared with only 7% of youngsters whose parents were rarely aversive. And when the effects of other factors were controlled for, children whose parents regularly employed aversive parenting practices were twice as likely to display conduct disorder as kids whose parents were rarely aversive.

On the other hand, consistent and positive parenting practices were associated with less aggressive behaviour in children. Among youngsters who received consistent parenting most of the time, 16% displayed conduct disorder, compared with 38% of children whose parents rarely used consistent methods. Similarly, although to a lesser extent, 14% of children whose parents interacted positively with them most of the time demonstrated delinquent behaviour compared with 27% of children whose parents adopted positive approaches only rarely. After accounting for other factors, the odds of children exhibiting conduct disorder were 1.6 times higher for those whose parents used consistent

parenting styles infrequently. The effect of positive parenting style alone was not significant when holding all other factors constant.

Staying at home full-time may not solve all problems

In order to develop strong bonds, children require consistent supervision.[7] When both parents work outside the home, they tend to have less time to spend with their children. As a result, it is generally believed that children in families where a parent (usually the mother) is at home tend to grow up more secure, better adjusted and are less likely to exhibit behaviour problems. It may come as a surprise, then, that families where the mother was at home full-time had the highest proportion of children with conduct disorder (more than one in five). It is likely, however, that other variables, such as lone-parent status, influenced this outcome because lone mothers are often not employed in the workforce. To be sure, when all other family characteristics were held constant, the mother's work status proved not to be significant.

Parental education, income and job status, collectively referred to as socioeconomic status (SES), are considered important variables influencing children's development.[8] Past studies have shown that the higher the socioeconomic status of the family, the better off the children will be. Indeed, according to the NLSCY, proportionally fewer children from the highest SES families than the lowest SES families exhibited aggressive behaviour: 13% versus 28%. When all other variables were held constant, children from these lowest SES families were twice as likely to exhibit behaviour problems as children from the highest SES families.

Many reasons may account for these patterns: high SES families have higher incomes, leading to more opportunities for children. Parents in these families also tend to be better educated and may therefore be better equipped to foster an atmosphere of learning. In addition, the neighbourhoods these families live in probably boast higher quality schools, recreation facilities and social institutions, and offer peer groups whose similar norms and standards reinforce the parents' goals for their children.[9]

Children in lone-parent families exhibit more aggressive behaviour

Lone parents have often been identified as raising children with problem behaviours.[10] Data from the 1994-95 NLSCY confirm that a larger proportion of children who lived with one parent displayed conduct disorder: about one-third of children with a lone parent demonstrated aggressive behaviour compared with less than one-fifth of those living with two parents. After holding all other factors constant, the odds of children in lone-parent families exhibiting delinquent behaviour was twice as high as the odds of those in two-parent families.

Again, complex reasons lie behind these patterns. A large percentage of lone-parent families live in low income situations. For many, enrolling their children in extra-curricular activities is simply not an option. As a result, these children may have more unstructured and unsupervised free time, and thus

---

7. Sacco, V. and L. Kennedy. 1994. *The Criminal Event*. Scarborough: Nelson Canada.

8. National Crime Prevention Centre. op. cit.

9. Corak, M. 1998. "Getting Ahead In Life: Does Your Parents' Income Count?" *Canadian Social Trends*, Summer 1998."

10. Lipman, E. L., D. R. Offord and M. D. Dooley. 1996. "What do we know about children from single-mother families? Questions and answers from the National Longitudinal Survey of Children and Youth," *Growing up in Canada: National Longitudinal Survey of Children and Youth* (Statistics Canada catalogue 89-550-MPE) Ottawa: Human Resources Development Canada and Statistics Canada.

CST Many factors influence child behaviour

The table below presents the odds of children with particular family characteristics exhibiting conduct disorder, relative to the odds that a benchmark group will do so, when all other variables in the model are held constant (odds ratio). The benchmark group is shown in italics for each characteristic. A logistic regression model was used to isolate the effect of selected family variables on the child's behaviour.

	Odds ratio
Parenting style used	
Ineffective	
Very often	36.1
Sometimes	6.7
Rarely	*1.0*
Aversive	
Very often	2.1
Sometimes	1.6
Rarely	*1.0*
Positive	
Very often	*1.0*
Sometimes	1.1 *
Rarely	1.3 *
Consistent	
Very often	*1.0*
Sometimes	0.9 *
Rarely	1.6
Number of parents in household	
One parent	2.0
Two parents	*1.0*
Number of siblings	
None	*1.0*
One	1.6
Two or more	2.6
Mother's age at birth of child	
14-20	1.1 *
21-29	*1.0*
30 and over	0.7
Mother's work status	
Full-time	1.1 *
Part-time	0.9 *
Not in paid workforce	*1.0*
Socioeconomic status of family	
Lower	2.0
Middle-lower	1.3 *
Middle-higher	1.2 *
Higher	*1.0*

* Not statistically significant.

Source: Statistics Canada, National Longitudinal Survey of Children and Youth, 1994-95.

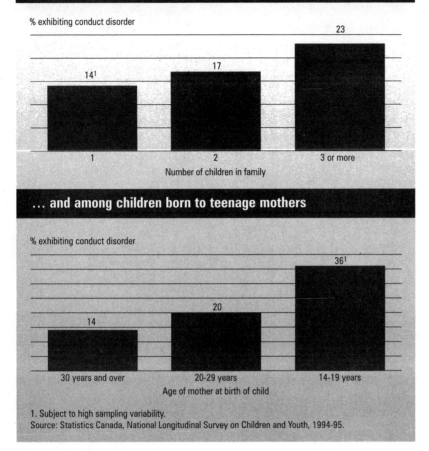

CST The percentage of children exhibiting aggressive behaviour is highest in families with three or more children ...

% exhibiting conduct disorder

14[1]
17
23

1
2
3 or more

Number of children in family

... and among children born to teenage mothers

% exhibiting conduct disorder

14
20
36[1]

30 years and over
20-29 years
14-19 years

Age of mother at birth of child

1. Subject to high sampling variability.
Source: Statistics Canada, National Longitudinal Survey on Children and Youth, 1994-95.

age, but to other variables, such as lack of support and stability, along with low income, that are often a fact of life for young mothers. When other factors were held constant, being a teenage mother had no significant effect on the child's behaviour.

Summary

There is much public debate about the relationship between family characteristics and children with conduct disorder. Results of the 1994-95 National Longitudinal Survey of Children and Youth suggest that an ineffective parenting style is the strongest predictor of delinquent behaviour in children between the ages of 8 and 11 years. In addition, aversive and inconsistent parenting techniques, lone-parent status, low socioeconomic status, and number of siblings are also associated with a higher probability of children exhibiting conduct disorder.

These findings offer a starting point for further research. The NLSCY provides policy-makers, community workers and researchers with the tools required to examine many commonly held beliefs about the factors associated with raising a child with delinquent tendencies.

Kathryn Stevenson is an analyst in Housing, Family and Social Statistics Division, Statistics Canada.

become more vulnerable to negative influences.[11] Also, parents who raise their children alone report higher levels of stress and fatigue, factors which tend to make parenting more difficult.

The number of siblings also appears to influence the child's behaviour. Children without brothers or sisters were the least likely to exhibit aggressive behaviour. As the number of siblings climbed, so did the frequency of conduct disorder, from 14%[12] of those who were lone children to 23% of those with two or more siblings. When the effect of other factors was controlled for, children with two or more siblings were 2.6 times more likely to display conduct disorder than those who had no brothers or sisters.

Finally, it seems that the younger a mother was when she gave birth, the higher the likelihood that her children will display delinquent behaviour. Nearly 36%[13] of kids born when their mother was a teenager (14 to 19 years old) exhibited conduct disorder, compared with 20% of children whose mother was between 20 and 29, and 14% of those whose mother was at least 30 years old. The higher probability that teenagers will have children with conduct disorder may not be related to

11. Canadian Centre for Justice Statistics. 1998. *A Profile of Youth Justice in Canada* (Statistics Canada catalogue 85-544-XPE)

12. Subject to high sampling variability.

13. Subject to high sampling variability.

Cases of women being stalked by ex-husbands or ex-boyfriends, and celebrities stalked by obsessed fans, have been highly publicized in Canada and the United States. Stalking, or criminal harassment, is generally defined as repeatedly following or communicating with another person, repeatedly watching someone's house or workplace, or directly threatening another person or any member of their family, causing a person to fear for their safety or the safety of someone known to them.

On August 1, 1993, Canada's first criminal harassment legislation – section 264(1) of the Criminal Code – was enacted to respond to these situations before they result in serious harm. Little data on the extent of criminal harassment is available yet, partly because the legislation is relatively new and data are not yet collected from all police jurisdictions. But the data, although somewhat limited, do allow analysis of the nature of stalking incidents in Canada.

BY REBECCA KONG

Relationship of accused to victim is key Literature on the subject suggests that one of the defining characteristics of criminal harassment is the relationship of the accused to the victim. There are various types of accused-victim relationships, meaning that the motives for this crime may vary. For example, in a marital or dating relationship, perpetrators may be motivated by their refusal to believe that the relationship has ended. In other relationships, like friendships or acquaintanceships, perpetrators may believe that their victims are equally in love with them, or that the victims might return their affections if they would only get to know the perpetrator better. The difference between "courting" and "stalking" behaviour is that stalking makes people afraid for themselves or for their friends and family.

Work-related criminal harassment occurs when a victim is harassed by a co-worker, unsatisfied client, former employee or person protesting the type of work being carried out by the victim or his/her business (e.g., abortion clinic, logging company). Criminal harassment may also occur between disputing neighbours.

Most female victims stalked by former partner According to police statistics, victims of criminal harassment are usually women who are stalked by men.[1] Data from the Revised Uniform Crime Reporting (UCR) Survey show that 80% of almost 7,500 victims during 1994-95 were female and that 88% of about 5,400 persons accused of criminal harassment were male. A large proportion of these women (57%) were stalked by an ex-husband or (ex-)boyfriend.

Research on wife assault suggests that it is not uncommon for an abusive husband or partner to continue to pursue a woman after the relationship has ended. The 1993 Violence Against

[1] Justice Canada, *A Review of section 264 of the Criminal Code (Criminal harassment)* (draft report) 1996.

CANADIAN SOCIAL TRENDS BACKGROUNDER CST

The legislation

Bill C-126, first read in the House of Commons in April 1993, was introduced in response to several highly publicized murders of women who had been killed by their estranged partners. Following on the heels of legislative reforms in the United States (where anti-stalking laws were first enacted in 1990), the Bill contains a number of reforms intended to better address family violence and violence against women.

The Bill also sought to provide better protection to victims of criminal harassment. Before the legislation was enacted, stalkers could be charged with such offences as uttering threats, intimidation, trespassing, indecent or harassing phone calls, or assault by threatening. Alternatively, persons fearing injury to themselves or their families, or damage to their property, could seek a "peace bond" or "no contact order" against the accused. However, these methods were criticized as inadequate since the accused had to have either threatened or physically harmed the victim before the authorities could take any action. Moreover, non-violent yet harassing behaviour, such as repeatedly sending gifts and letters and constantly following or watching another person, could rarely be handled by the legal tools available at the time.

Section 264 of the Criminal Code attempts to remedy these inadequacies by specifically addressing harassing behaviour and imposing more serious penalties. Under Section 264, harassment is now viewed as a hybrid offence, that is the Crown may prosecute the offence as either a summary or an indictable offence. As a summary offence, criminal harassment carries a maximum penalty of six months imprisonment and/or a fine not exceeding $2,000; as an indictable offence, it carries a maximum penalty of imprisonment not exceeding five years.

Most victims of criminal harassment were women, the majority of whom were stalked by a former partner[1] CST

Accused's relationship to victim		Total victims	Female victims	Male victims
Total	(no.)	5,023	4,046	977
	(%)	100	100	100
		%		
Husband		1.5	1.9	--
Ex-husband		31.1	38.7	--
Wife		0.1	--	0.3
Ex-wife		1.8	--	9.0
(Ex-)boyfriend		13.6	16.9	--
(Ex-)girlfriend		0.8	--	3.9
Other family		4.7	3.7	8.6
Casual acquaintance		27.9	23.5	46.1
Work relationship		4.9	3.4	11.3
Stranger		8.1	7.3	11.5
Other		1.5	0.6	5.5
Relationship unknown		4.1	4.1	3.9

-- Data not applicable.
Totals may not add due to rounding.
[1] Includes only incidents where an accused was identified. Based on a non-random sample of 130 police agencies, accounting for 43% of the national volume of crime. These data are not nationally representative.
Source: Canadian Centre for Justice Statistics, Revised Uniform Crime Reporting Survey, 1994 and 1995.

Women Survey reported that, for about 20% of women who had been in abusive relationships, the violence continued during or after the couple separated; furthermore, in 35% of these cases, the violence actually became more severe at the time of separation. Homicide statistics tell the same story, showing that women are generally at greater risk of being killed by their spouse after separation: between 1974 and 1992, women were six times more likely to be murdered by their husband after leaving him than when living with him.

Although the largest proportion of female victims were criminally harassed by a current or former partner, many were also stalked by casual acquaintances (24%), strangers (7%), other family members (4%) and persons known through work relationships (3%).

CANADIAN SOCIAL TRENDS BACKGROUNDER — CST

Crime Reporting Survey and the Adult Criminal Court Survey

The Canadian Centre for Justice Statistics (CCJS), in co-operation with the policing community, collects detailed information on police-reported criminal incidents through the Revised Uniform Crime Reporting (UCR) Survey. In 1995, 130 police agencies, which accounted for 43% of criminal incidents reported in Canada, responded to the Revised UCR Survey. However, because the participating police forces represent a non-random sample, the incidents reported are not nationally representative; in fact, over 90% of criminal harassment reports in the sample were from Quebec and Ontario. Furthermore, the majority of incidents examined in this article were reported by the largest police departments — Toronto and Montreal accounted for 30% and 25%, respectively, of stalking incidents reported.

This article draws on data from the Revised UCR Survey for the calendar years 1994 and 1995 combined, the most recent years for which criminal harassment statistics are available. Since the analysis focuses on the accused-victim relationship, meaning that the relationship of the accused to the victim must be clearly known, incidents with no victim and/or with more than one accused were dropped from the sample. The article is therefore based on records of 4,768 incidents of criminal harassment involving 5,023 victims and 4,768 accused.[1] And although stalking can involve more serious violations of the Criminal Code, harassment was the most serious offence in 96% of the incidents examined in this study.

The analysis of court cases is based on data from the seven jurisdictions that reported to the Adult Criminal Court Survey (ACCS) in 1994: Newfoundland, Prince Edward Island, Nova Scotia, Quebec, Saskatchewan, the Yukon and Northwest Territories. The ACCS provides data on federal and provincial/territorial statutes charges and municipal by-law infractions heard in adult criminal courts in Canada. This article uses the detailed information on completed charges, appearances and cases for federal statute offences. Data were collected for 972 cases involving a total of 1,110 charges of criminal harassment (a number of cases might include multiple charges of

harassment). The data reported account for only 34% of the total provincial court caseload, and the vast majority (79%) of charges in the sample originated from Quebec. Therefore, the findings should be interpreted with some caution.

Definitions of the accused-victim relationship

Husband/wife: at the time of the incident, the accused was the victim's spouse through marriage or common-law relationship.

Ex-husband/ex-wife: at the time of the incident, the accused was separated or divorced from the victim.

(Ex)-boyfriend/(ex)-girlfriend: at the time of the incident, the relationship between the accused and the victim was long-term and/or that of a close friend or intimate (excludes same-sex relationships or friendships).

Casual acquaintance: at the time of the incident, a social relationship existed that was neither long-term nor close, and includes persons known only by sight such as neighbours.

Work relationship: at the time of the incident, the workplace or business was the primary source of contact between victim and accused; the category includes co-workers, business partners, employee-customer, employee-employer, and non-commercial relationships such as student-teacher or physician-patient.

Other family: the victim and accused are related but not through marriage; for example, parents, children, other immediate family members (brothers, sisters) or extended family members.

Stranger: the victim does not know the accused.

Other: relationships not included in the previous categories, such as same-sex partners (current or former) and long-term and/or close friends of the same sex (current or former).

[1] If an incident involves two or more victims, the analysis will result in a multiple counting. For example, if a woman and her child are stalked by the woman's ex-husband, the incident and the accused will be examined under two categories: "ex-husband" and "other family." The Revised UCR Survey reported a total of 213 incidents with multiple victims and one accused.

In contrast, male victims of stalkers were most likely to be harassed by a casual acquaintance (46%); few were stalked by an ex-spouse (9%) or (ex-)girlfriend (4%). Over one in ten (11%) male victims were stalked by persons with whom they had a work relationship.

Few incidents result in injury According to data filed in police reports, few victims (5%) actually experienced physical injury and less than half a percent of stalking incidents involved a homicide or attempted murder.[2] But the general absence of physical harm does not mean that harm is not done. Police may not have known that a homicide victim had previously been stalked if the victim had never reported the harassment. And research suggests that the threat of harm alone can affect the victim's emotional and physical well-being.[3]

This reaction is not surprising, given the invasive nature of harassment and that stalkers usually follow, watch or make contact at the victim's home or place of work. Police data show that the majority of incidents occurred at the victim's home. Although workplace locations cannot be identified from police-reported data, victims being criminally harassed by someone known through work were more likely to be stalked at a corporate/commercial place or a public institution.

Victims' reactions to criminal harassment may also depend on the involvement of other offences. In fact, one in four stalking incidents was accompanied by other offences such as uttering threats, assaults, harassing phone calls, mischief, breach of probation, violating bail and breaking and entering.

Victims do not want charges laid in one in five incidents[4]
In harassment cases where the stalker was identified, the majority of the accused (70%) were charged; however, in 19% of incidents, charges were not laid because the victim was reluctant to pursue the matter. Victims involved in work relationships with their stalkers were most hesitant to lay charges (32%) as were men harassed by their ex-wives (27%). A minority of women stalked by an ex-husband or (ex-)boyfriend also preferred not to lay charges (17% and 12%, respectively), after reporting the incident to police.

A high proportion of charges are withdrawn In 1994, provincial courts in seven jurisdictions participated in the Adult Criminal Court Survey (ACCS). Data show that 23% of the harass-

[2] This finding is similar to that of Justice Canada's analysis of a sample of cases, wherein 91% of victims suffered no physical injury; and a study conducted in British Columbia found that even when victims did experience physical violence, "none suffered grievous bodily harm." Attorney General, British Columbia, 1995. *The Report of the Criminal Harassment Unit Part ii: The Nature and Extent of Criminal Harassment in British Columbia*, pp. 22-23.

[3] Kathleen G. McAnaney, Laura A. Curliss and C. Elizabeth Abeyta-Price. "From Imprudence to Crime: Anti-Stalking Laws" (1993) 68 *The Notre Dame Law Review*, page 851; and Harvey Wallace and Joy Silverman, "Stalking and Post Traumatic Stress Syndrome" (1996) LXIX *The Police Journal*, page 25.

[4] Excludes the one-quarter of incidents in which the stalker was not identified.

Most incidents of criminal harassment occurred in the victim's home[1] CST

Accused's relationship to victim	Number[2]	Total (%)	Resi- dence	Commercial/ corporate place	Street/ public transit	Public insti- tution	Parking lot	School	Open area
					%				
Total	5,023	100	69	11	10	3	2	3	1
Husband	75	100	91	3	1	1	--	1	--
Ex-husband	1,574	100	77	7	8	1	2	1	1
Wife	3	100	--	--	--	--	--	--	--
Ex-wife	88	100	78	10	3	2	1	--	2
(Ex-)boyfriend	684	100	75	11	7	1	1	2	--
(Ex-)girlfriend	38	100	87	5	3	--	--	--	--
Other family	234	100	82	6	8	1	2	--	--
Casual acquaintance	1,402	100	64	11	13	3	2	4	1
Work relationship	246	100	36	39	5	9	1	7	--
Stranger	408	100	45	16	22	7	2	3	3
Other	77	100	75	10	3	1	1	3	--
Relationship unknown	204	100	65	13	9	4	1	3	1

-- Amount too small to be expressed.
Totals may not add due to rounding.
[1] Includes only incidents where an accused was identified. Based on a non-random sample of 130 police agencies, accounting for 43% of the national volume of crime. These data are not nationally representative.
[2] Includes unknown location.
Source: Canadian Centre for Justice Statistics, Revised Uniform Crime Reporting Survey, 1994 and 1995.

An accused stalker is charged in over two-thirds of criminal harassment cases reported to police[1]

Accused's relationship to victim	Total	Cleared by charge	Cleared otherwise	
			Victim reluctant to pursue laying charges	Other [3]
			%	
Total	100	70	19	11
Husband	100	83	9	8
Ex-husband	100	75	17	9
Wife	100	--	--	--
Ex-wife	100	56	27	17
(Ex-)boyfriend	100	82	12	5
(Ex-)girlfriend	100	68	24	8
Other family	100	73	15	12
Casual acquaintance	100	64	23	13
Work relationship	100	57	32	12
Stranger	100	64	20	15
Other	100	65	17	18
Relationship unknown	100	70	24	6

Type of clearance by police [2]

-- Amount too small to be expressed.
Totals may not add due to rounding.
[1] Includes only incidents where an accused was identified. Based on a non-random sample of 130 police agencies, accounting for 43% of the national volume of crime. These data are not nationally representative.
[2] Clearance rate is 100% because an accused was identified in all incidents.
[3] Includes reasons beyond the department's control, departmental discretion and other.
Source: Canadian Centre for Justice Statistics, Revised Uniform Crime Reporting Survey, 1994 and 1995.

ment cases originally filed in provincial court were moved to a superior court. This may indicate that these cases were of a more serious nature than harassment alone; for example, 59% of criminal harassment cases involving sexual assault, and 31% of those involving assault, were transferred to superior court. The outcome of these transferred cases is unknown.

However, the data show that the outcomes of criminal harassment cases remaining in provincial court are rather different than those for minor assault, which is a similar type of charge. Although the accused in 36% of harassment cases were found guilty (including conditional and absolute discharges and guilty pleas), a full 39% of harassment cases were dropped (including withdrawn, dismissed and stayed).[5] By contrast, 57% of minor assault charges resulted in a conviction and only 27% were dropped.

While Bill C-126 clearly states that criminal harassment is a serious crime, it appears that relatively few cases are prosecuted as an indictable offence. ACCS data from the seven reporting jurisdictions show that 60% of stalkers found guilty were sentenced to probation (two-thirds for at least one year), while another 33% of convicted stalkers received a prison term (most less than six months). Cases involving a more serious violent offence in addition to a criminal harassment charge were more likely to receive a prison sentence (56%) than those in which the most serious offence was criminal harassment (19%).

Summary Legislators have responded to society's intolerance for stalking behaviour by naming it a criminal offence. However, as with any crime, legislation alone cannot prevent its occurrence. While stalking may not be new behaviour, it is "new" to the legal system. Therefore, increased knowledge of the nature and extent of criminal harassment is essential in helping agencies better understand and respond to it.

To date, statistics reported by a non-representative sample of police departments show that the majority of reported cases involve female victims, most of whom are stalked by previous partners. Yet, current statistics give only partial insight into the effect of stalking on its victims. Police and court data also show that a large number of cases are being dropped due to the victim's reluctance to take part in laying charges. As the amount of data available from police and courts increases, and as research on the issue builds, more information will be available to help deepen our understanding of criminal harassment and improve the responses of the justice system.

[5] Justice Canada's examination of a sample of criminal harassment cases found that the victim's unwillingness to participate in the court process or desire to drop charges influenced the Crown's decision whether or not to continue the prosecution.

• For more information, see *Juristat*, Statistics Canada, Catalogue no. 85-002-XPE, Vol. 16, no. 12. Also "Wife Assault in Canada," *Canadian Social Trends*, Autumn 1994.

Rebecca Kong is an analyst with the Canadian Centre for Justice Statistics, Statistics Canada.

CST

Violence against women by their spouses is widespread in Canada. According to the 1993 Violence Against Women Survey, 29% of women or 2.7 million who had ever been married or lived common law had been physically or sexually assaulted by their partner at some point during the relationship. Such assaults included only incidents where the violent partner could be charged under Canada's Criminal Code. Of women who had been abused by their spouse, 312,000 experienced the violence in the year before the survey. Many of these women, however, also suffered emotional abuse from their spouses, while still others were emotionally abused without any physical violence occurring.

Wife Assault in Canada

by Karen Rodgers

Many women assaulted by their partner reported that he used a weapon to commit the attack. As a result, a high proportion of incidents resulted in a physical injury. Despite the very violent nature of many assaults, few victims reported the incident to the police and even fewer used support services.

Wife abuse has other serious consequences beyond physical injury. Victimized women often suffer emotionally from the abuse, harbouring feelings of anger, mistrust and fear. In addition, although not necessarily victims of physical abuse themselves, children who witness violence against their mothers can be severely traumatized, and are more likely than other children to be in an abusive relationship when they are older, thus perpetuating a cycle of violence.

New partnerships have the highest rates of violence
Women who were currently in a marriage or common-law union for two years or less were more likely than others to report that their spouses had abused them in the year before the survey (8%). In contrast, 1% of women in partnerships that had lasted more than twenty years reported spousal violence.

While this is likely true because many violent relationships do not last long, another contributing factor is the age of the partners. Young women aged 18-24 were four times (12%) as likely as women overall to have reported experiencing spousal abuse in the year before the survey. A similar proportion (13%) of women whose partners were under age 25 reported being assaulted during that time.

Other factors, such as employment status, educational level and family income, generally did not have an effect on the likelihood of spousal violence in the year before the survey. The only exceptions to this were women with university-educated partners and women in very poor families. Women whose spouses had a university education were less likely than others to report spousal violence. On the other hand, women in families with household incomes below $15,000 were twice (6%) as likely as women with higher family incomes to have been physically or sexually assaulted by their spouse.

Research has suggested that women with disabilities are at greater risk of victimization.[1] According to the survey, 39% of ever-married women with a disability or a disabling health problem reported physical or sexual assault by a partner over the course of their married lives, compared with 27% of other women.

Women more likely to report violence in a past relationship Women living common law at the time of the survey were more likely (18%) than those legally married (15%) to report that their current partner had abused them at some point. Reported rates of abuse for past relationships, however, were much higher. Overall, 48% of women who previously had been married or lived common law reported that their previous partner had assaulted them.

Violence may increase following separation Sixteen percent of women who had ever been married or lived common law and whose spouse had abused them stated that the violence occurred before they were married. Rates of violence before marriage were lower among legally married women (17%) than among those living common law (28%). The violence in some marriages continued even during pregnancy: 21% of women abused by their spouse were assaulted during pregnancy. In addition, 40% of these women stated that the abuse began during their pregnancy.

Approximately one-fifth of women who experienced violence by a previous partner reported that the abuse occurred following or during separation and, in 35% of these cases, the violence increased in severity at the time of separation.

Most women victimized more than once and in several ways For almost two-thirds of women whose spouse assaulted them, the violence occurred on more than one occasion. Repeated or ongoing abuse was more often reported for previous relationships, indicating that many women leave relationships with more frequent violent incidents. Three-quarters of women who had experienced violence by a previous partner were subjected to multiple assaults, 41% on more than ten occasions. Of women currently living with an abusive partner, 39% had been violently assaulted more than once, 10% more than ten times.

Among women who had ever been assaulted by their spouses, pushing, grabbing and shoving (25%) was the most commonly reported type of violence, followed by threats (19%), slapping (15%), throwing objects (11%) and kicking, biting and hitting with fists (11%). Other less prevalent types of violence included being beaten up, sexually assaulted, choked, hit with an object and having had a gun or knife used against them. This pattern was consistent among women reporting abuse by either a current or previous marital partner. Although pushing, grabbing and shoving was the most frequently reported form of violence, only 5% of the respondents said that this was the only type of abuse that they had suffered. Similarly, just 4% of women said yes to only having been threatened by their partner. This suggests an escalation in seriousness, with threats of violence almost always followed by more serious acts.

Almost one-half (44%) of abused women had a weapon used against them. It is not surprising, therefore, that many women assaulted by their spouse suffered a physical injury (45%). Among those who were injured, the most frequent types of injury reported were bruises (90%), followed by cuts, scratches and burns (33%), broken bones (12%) and fractures (11%). Also, almost 10% of injured women stated that they suffered internal injuries or miscarriages.[2] Many injuries were severe

---

CANADIAN SOCIAL TRENDS BACKGROUNDER

Violence Against Women Survey

In recent years, the issue of violence against women has reached prominence on the agendas of all levels of governments. Between February and June 1993, under the federal government's Family Violence Initiative Program, Health Canada funded Statistics Canada's first national survey on Violence Against Women. The primary objective of the survey was to provide reliable estimates of the nature and extent of male violence against women in Canada. With assistance from victims and survivors of violence, community groups, federal and provincial government representatives, academics and other experts, Statistics Canada developed a unique method and approach to measure violence against women.

This telephone survey took into account the extreme sensitivity of the subject matter. Interviewers were trained to recognize and respond to cues that the woman might be concerned about being overheard. Telephone numbers of local support services were offered to women who disclosed current cases of abuse or who appeared to be in distress. As well, a toll-free telephone number provided women with an opportunity to call back and verify the legitimacy of the survey, or to continue the interview at a time and place more convenient to them.

Every household in the ten provinces stood an equal chance of being selected. Households without telephones could not participate, nor could women who did not speak English or French. Only 1% of the female population of the ten provinces lives in households without telephone service; in approximately 3% of the households contacted, there was a non-response due to language. A total of 12,300 women aged 18 and over were interviewed about their experiences of physical and sexual violence since the age of 16.

---

enough to require medical attention from a doctor or nurse, with approximately four-in-ten (543,000) women injured by their spouse requiring such help. In addition, one-half of abused wives who suffered physical injuries had to take time off from their everyday activities because of the assault, somewhat higher than the proportion of all abused wives (about one-third).

Given the repetitive nature of spousal violence, the extensive use of weapons and the severity of many injuries, it follows that many abused wives (about one-third) have feared for their lives at some point during the relationship. Such fear was less common in current than in previous marriages. Of women currently in a violent union, 13% (130,000) had at some point feared that their spouse would take their life, while this was the case for 45% of women who previously had lived with an abusive partner.

Men who witnessed violence against mother more likely to assault spouses
According to a recent analysis by the National Clearinghouse on Family Violence, children who grow up in homes where there is wife assault may begin to act out learned behaviour. "For boys this may mean perpetuating a cycle of violence in future relationships with women by imitating the behaviour of their fathers. In the event that girls become involved in relationships with violent men when they grow up, they may see few options for themselves to escape from the situation."[3] Given the strong relationship between witnessing violence as a child and being in an abusive marriage later in life, there are indications that the cycle of violence may continue in some families. According to the Violence Against Women Survey, 39% of women in abusive marriages reported

that their children saw them being assaulted. In addition, children are seeing very serious forms of violence.

In 52% of abusive relationships in which children witnessed the violence, women feared for their lives. Furthermore, in 61% of violent marriages in which children witnessed the abuse, the violence was serious enough to result in the woman being injured.

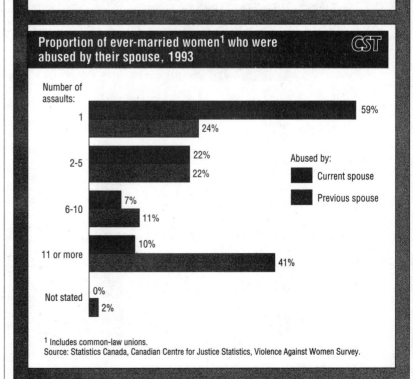

[1] Jillian Ridington. **Beating the Odds: Violence and Women with Disabilities.** Vancouver:DAWN Canada, 1989.

Bridget Rivers-Moore. **Family Violence Against Women With Disabilities.** Ottawa:The National Clearinghouse on Family Violence, Health Canada, 1993.

Dick Sobsey. "Sexual Offences and Disabled Victims: Research and Practical Implications." **Vis-a-Vis**, 6:4. Ottawa: Canadian Council on Social Development,1988.

[2] Percentages do not add to 44% because of multiple responses.

[3] Beth Allan. **Wife Abuse – The Impact on Children.** Ottawa:The National Clearinghouse on Family Violence, Health Canada, 1991.

CANADIAN SOCIAL TRENDS BACKGROUNDER CST

Many women emotionally abused Research has suggested that emotional abuse can produce lasting, harmful effects and that physical and emotional abuse often occur together. Approximately one-third of all women who had ever been married stated that their spouse was emotionally abusive, with previous partners described as more abusive than current partners. Most women (77%) who had been physically assaulted by their spouse also suffered emotional abuse. At the same time, however, many women (18%) had been emotionally abused in their marriage, even though they were not victims of physical violence.

A woman can be subjected to a variety of emotionally abusive situations by her spouse. He may insist on knowing who she is with and where she is at all times (22%); he can call her names to put her down or make her feel bad (21%); he can be jealous and not want her to talk to other men (19%); or he can try to limit her contact with family or friends (16%). In addition, he can limit her independence by not giving her access to, or even telling her about, the family income (10%).

Eighty-five percent of women who reported wife assault indicated that they were affected emotionally by the violence. The most commonly reported consequences were anger, fear, becoming more cautious or less trusting, and low self-esteem. Many women also reported being depressed or anxious, feeling ashamed or guilty, and having problems relating to men.

Proportion of ever-married women[1] who were abused by their spouse, 1993 CST

Number of assaults:

1	59% / 24%
2-5	22% / 22%
6-10	7% / 11%
11 or more	10% / 41%
Not stated	0% / 2%

Abused by:
Current spouse
Previous spouse

[1] Includes common-law unions.
Source: Statistics Canada, Canadian Centre for Justice Statistics, Violence Against Women Survey.

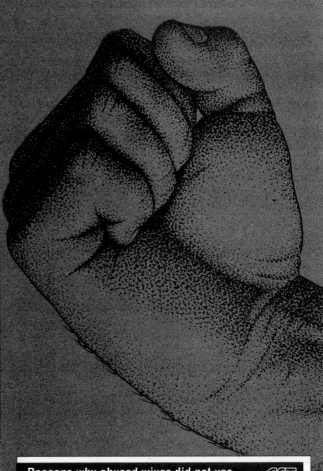

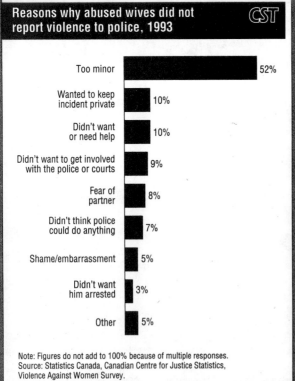

Reasons why abused wives did not report violence to police, 1993 — CST

Too minor	52%
Wanted to keep incident private	10%
Didn't want or need help	10%
Didn't want to get involved with the police or courts	9%
Fear of partner	8%
Didn't think police could do anything	7%
Shame/embarrassment	5%
Didn't want him arrested	3%
Other	5%

Note: Figures do not add to 100% because of multiple responses.
Source: Statistics Canada, Canadian Centre for Justice Statistics, Violence Against Women Survey.

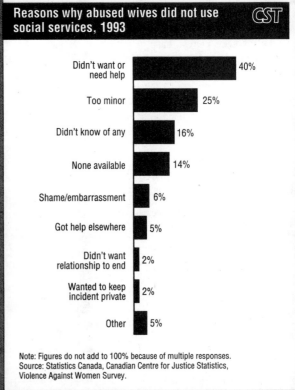

Reasons why abused wives did not use social services, 1993 — CST

Didn't want or need help	40%
Too minor	25%
Didn't know of any	16%
None available	14%
Shame/embarrassment	6%
Got help elsewhere	5%
Didn't want relationship to end	2%
Wanted to keep incident private	2%
Other	5%

Note: Figures do not add to 100% because of multiple responses.
Source: Statistics Canada, Canadian Centre for Justice Statistics, Violence Against Women Survey.

In addition, 17% of all women, regardless of whether they had ever been married, stated that, to the best of their knowledge, their father was violent toward their mother. Nine percent of currently married women and 17% of previously married women stated that their father-in-law had been violent toward their mother-in-law.

The results of this survey support the theory that children from abusive homes are at greater risk of abusing or being abused. Women with a violent father-in-law were three times (36%) more likely to have been abused by a current partner than women whose father-in-law was not violent (12%).

Women whose father-in-law abused his wife were also more likely than other women to endure repeated and more violent spousal assault. Fifty-five percent of women whose partner had witnessed violence when growing up reported being abused by that partner on more than one occasion, compared with 35% of women whose partners had not witnessed violence. Women with a violent father-in-law were more likely to be injured (37%) than those whose father-in-law was not abusive (21%). In addition, women with a violent father-in-law were more frequently beaten, choked or hit than other victims of wife assault.

Few women used support agencies Various types of social services are available to women in abusive marriages, including social services such as shelters and transition homes, crisis centres, individual counsellors, women's centres and community or family centres. However, relatively few women made use of such services. A total of 24% (683,000) of women abused by a marital partner used one or more social services. Women most frequently sought help from an individual counsellor (15%), while 8% contacted and 6% stayed at a shelter (representing 200,000 who contacted and 150,000 women who stayed in a shelter). While this survey does not examine trends over time, the increase in the availability of services for victimized women may have produced an increase in the percentage of women who have used these services in recent years.

While the use of formal social services by abused wives is fairly limited, the vast majority of women who used them found them to be helpful. Counsellors (83%) and transition houses (81%) were most often considered helpful, followed by crisis centres (77%), women's centres (73%) and community/family centres (65%).

Women who were injured by their partner (35%) or whose children had witnessed the spousal assault (38%) were twice as likely to use a social agency as those not in these situations. Women who reported the assault to the police were more likely to have contacted a social service (46%) than those who had not reported to the police (17%).

Women from abusive marriages relied most heavily on their family (45%) and friends and neighbours (44%) when they needed help. Many women (40%) also stated that these personal sources of support were the most helpful in dealing with the violent experience. Some abused wives, however, turned to other sources of help: 23% told a doctor about their experience, while 7% went to a religious leader for support.

Few incidents reported to the police In the early 1980s, mandatory domestic assault charging policies were initiated across the country to increase charging by the police and prosecution in cases of wife assault. These policies were intended to encourage women to report assault offences to the police. Nonetheless, according to the Violence Against Women Survey, relatively few women (26%) in abusive marriages reported the violence to the police.

Of abused women with children, those whose children witnessed violence against them were almost three times as likely (43%) as others (16%) to report their partner to the police. At the same time, 43% of women who indicated that they were injured at some point during the relationship had reported the abuse at least once to police, compared with only 12% of those who were never injured. In addition, women were four times more likely (42%) to report to the police if a weapon had been used against them than if this was not the case (11%). Women who suffered from repeated or ongoing spousal assault were also more likely to report to the police: 49% of women who had been abused more than ten times reported at least once to the police, compared with 6% of those who experienced only one episode.

One-half of women who contacted the police said that they were satisfied with the way the police handled the case. In 21% of reported cases, the police put the woman in touch with a community service. The police saw the victim in 84% of reported cases, but in only 28% of these cases was a charge laid. However, 79% of charges laid by the police resulted in the offender appearing in court.

Of women who reported to the police, 39% said there was nothing else that the police should have done. Another 24% stated that the police should have been more supportive and 20% felt the police should have laid a charge against the perpetrator. Police intervention decreased or stopped the violence in 45% of marriages. In 40% of reported cases, there was no change in the man's behaviour following police intervention, and in 10% of reported cases, the violence actually increased.

Many women never tell anyone According to the Violence Against Women Survey, 22% of women assaulted by their spouse never told family or friends, the police, a support agency or anyone else about the abuse they had suffered. In 18% (111,000) of these cases, the woman was injured. A similar proportion (15%) reported more than one episode of violence, and 11% had been abused on more than ten occasions. Of women who had never told anyone, 10% had at some point feared for their lives.

Women have a variety of reasons for not telling people about their abuse, including a feeling of shame or embarrassment, being too afraid of their spouse or not having anyone to turn to. Women cited very specific reasons for not reporting to the police, including that they felt that the incident was too minor (52%) or wanting to keep the incident private or not wanting help (each 10%). Similarly, there were a number of reasons why women did not go to a formal social agency for help. The primary reason given by abused wives was that they did not want or need help (40%).

Alcohol and drugs often used to cope with violence Women may use a variety of ways to cope with their partners' abusive behaviour. Approximately one-quarter of ever-married women who have lived with violence reported using alcohol, drugs or medication to help them cope with the situation. This included

12% who used alcohol, 9% who used drugs or medication, and 5% who used both alcohol and drugs or medication. Women who suffered emotional abuse as well as physical assault more frequently reported the use of alcohol or drugs to cope (31%). In addition, women who sustained an injury were more likely to use alcohol or drugs (41%). Alcohol use by women previously with a violent partner was almost twice the rate (15%) of those currently living with violence (8%). Also, women previously with a violent partner were three times (12%) more likely to have used drugs or medication than those currently with a violent partner (4%). These differences may reflect the fact that women who left a violent relationship had suffered more frequent or ongoing abuse.

In one-half of all violent partnerships, the husband was drinking at the time of the assault. The rate of wife assault for women currently living with men who drank regularly in the year before the survey (at least four times per week) was triple (6%) the rate of those whose partners never drank (2%). Women whose partners drank heavily (five or more drinks at a time) were six times (11%) as likely to be abused than those whose partners never drank.

Many women leave abusive partners, but many return Less than one-half (43%) of women who reported abuse by a spouse left him for a short while because of his abusive or threatening behaviour. A number of factors were linked to this decision. For example, 74% of women who had reported an incident to the police indicated that they had stayed apart from their partner, compared with only 32% of those who never reported to the police. Women who feared for their lives at some point during the relationship were more than twice as likely to have left their partner (72%) as those who had not had this fear (28%). Similarly, women whose children had witnessed the violence were twice as

likely to leave (60%) as those whose assault had not been witnessed by children (28%).

The majority of women who left their partner stayed with friends or relatives (77%), followed by transition homes or shelters (13%). A number of women got their own place (13%) and 5% stayed in a hotel.[4] Almost three-quarters of women who left eventually returned home.

The most common reasons why women returned home were for the sake of the children (31%), followed by wanting to give the relationship another chance (24%), the partner promising to change (17%) and a lack of money or housing (9%). Women whose partner received counselling for his abusive behaviour were more likely to return home (81%) than those whose partner did not get professional help (70%).

Conclusion The 1993 Violence Against Women Survey has shed considerable light on the extent of violence against women, including wife assault. Of

women in a current marriage, 201,000 were physically or sexually assaulted at least once by their spouse in the year before the survey.

The risk of becoming a victim of wife assault is particularly high for young women in new partnerships, and those living in lower income households – situations which often occur together. Children who witness the spousal abuse of their mother are much more likely than others to be involved in violent marriages as adults – creating a new generation of victims and abusers.

To date, many positive approaches have been taken to deal with the problem of wife assault. Since the early 1980s, police charging practices against abusive spouses have tightened. Also, additional resources have been directed to fund more shelters and other services for abused women and their children. Despite these efforts, a sizable minority of spousal assault victims suffer in silence, never reporting these acts of violence to anyone.

While most of these approaches offer help to women only after they have been assaulted, attempts have been made to address the problem before abuse occurs. The 1993 anti-stalking legislation (Bill C-126), for example, is one such measure that may reduce assaults by spouses or other men. Continuing efforts may lead to a better understanding of the circumstances surrounding abuse and how best to reduce violence against women.

[4] Percentages do not total 100% because of multiple responses if women left more than once.

Karen Rodgers is a senior analyst with the Canadian Centre for Justice Statistics, Statistics Canada.

WOMEN ASSAULTED BY STRANGERS

by Carol Strike

In 1993, Statistics Canada, with funding from Health Canada, conducted the Violence Against Women (VAW) survey as part of the federal government's Family Violence Initiative. Although the highlights of this survey were released in November 1993, since that time Statistics Canada has undertaken more detailed analyses of the survey results. The VAW survey addressed not only violence against women by men who were known to them, but also sexual and physical assaults perpetrated by male strangers. This article examines the extent and nature of women's victimization by strangers.

According to the VAW survey, 4% of women aged 18 and over (431,000) had been sexually or physically assaulted by a stranger in the year before the survey. Young women were more likely than older women to have experienced this type of an assault. Although the proportion of women assaulted by a stranger in the year before the survey was lower than the proportion assaulted by men they knew (7%), assaults by strangers are a serious concern as they can affect levels of fear and the quality of life.

Women who have been victimized by strangers are often not only physically harmed, but also suffer emotional consequences, including fear and anger, that can last long after the incident occurs. Because of the risk of an assault, even women who have never been assaulted often fear for their personal safety in many everyday situations. In response to the risk faced by women, a growing number of programs and preventative measures designed to help ensure women's safety are being organized in many Canadian communities.

Sexual and physical assaults by strangers In the 12 months before the VAW survey, 3% of women aged 18 and over (317,000) had been sexually assaulted by a stranger. Although sexual assaults can also involve physical violence, 1% of women (147,000) experienced an assault by a stranger that was strictly physical with no sexual element. Proportions were much higher when women were asked whether they had ever been sexually or physically assaulted by a stranger since the age of 16. Over 2 million women (19%) had been sexually assaulted and close to 800,000 women (8%) had been physically assaulted by a stranger at least once in their adult lives.

These incidents were all assaults chargeable under the *Criminal Code*. Sexual assault includes acts ranging from unwanted sexual touching to a sexual attack that results in wounding or maiming, or that endangers the life of the victim. Fifteen percent of women reported having been victims of unwanted sexual touching by a stranger at least once in their adult lives, and 7% said they had been violently sexually attacked. In the 12 months before the survey, 3% of women had been sexually touched by a stranger and less than 1% had been violently sexually attacked.

Physical assaults include not only the use of force, ranging from being hit or kicked to being beaten, knifed or shot, but also threats of physical harm which the victim believed would be carried out. According to the survey, 5% of women had been threatened and 4% had been physically attacked by a stranger at least once in their adult lives. During the 12 months before the survey, 1% of women had been physically threatened by a stranger and less than 1% had been physically attacked.

Younger women more likely to have been assaulted by strangers During the 12 months before the survey, women aged 18-24 were more than twice as likely to have been sexually (11%) or physically assaulted (4%) by a stranger than were women aged 25-34. Rates of sexual and physical assaults by strangers in each subsequent age group were lower. This pattern is consistent with victimization in general, as younger people of either gender are more likely than older people to be in places or situations where they are at risk.

The proportion of women who reported ever having been assaulted by a stranger during their lifetime was also higher among younger age groups. About one-quarter of women between the ages of 18 and 44 had been sexually assaulted by a stranger at least once since the age of 16. The rate for the youngest age group (18-24) was particularly high considering these women had been at risk of ever having been assaulted for the shortest period of time. In contrast, the proportions of women aged 45-54 (19%) and 55 and over (10%) who reported having ever been sexually assaulted by a stranger were much lower.

Young women were also more likely than older women to have been victims of assaults by strangers that were non-sexual in nature. About 10% of women in each age group between 18 and 44 reported having been physically assaulted by a stranger at least once since age 16, compared with 8% of women aged 45-54, and 4% of those aged 55 and over.

The lifetime assault rates for older women may be under-estimated because public perception of this type of violence has changed. Older women may have been less willing to report assaults by strangers to an interviewer, less likely to recall incidents or even less likely to have considered certain incidents as assaults. Nonetheless, the risk of violence by strangers may be higher now than in the past, partly because lifestyles have changed. In particular, young women are more likely today than in the past to be living on their own in large urban centres. Many use public transportation and are often out alone at night.

Women in British Columbia, Alberta and Ontario most likely to have been assaulted by a stranger Women living in British Columbia, Alberta and Ontario were more likely than those living in other provinces to have been assaulted by a stranger. Over one-quarter (26%) of women in British Columbia had been sexually assaulted by a stranger at least once since the age of 16, followed by 22% of women in Alberta and 20% in Ontario and Prince Edward Island. Physical assaults were also most commonly reported by women in British Columbia (11%), Alberta (10%) and Ontario (8%). Newfoundland had the lowest rates of both sexual (12%) and physical assaults (3%). This geographic pattern is consistent with that of violence against women by men who are known to the victim and with violent crime in general.

One-half of assaults by strangers occur in streets, bars or public buildings Most assaults by strangers took place in some type of public area. For example, sexual assaults most often occurred on streets (20%), at bars or dances (15%), or in public buildings (13%). Still, relatively large proportions of sexual assaults by strangers took place in a home other than the victim's (12%) or in the woman's own home (7%). Although physical assaults by strangers occurred most often on streets (44%), many took place in public buildings (15%) or at the victim's place of work (14%).

Fear, anger and physical injuries common among victims Following a personal victimization, almost all women must deal with emotions such as fear and anger. Overall, 88% of women who had been physically or sexually assaulted by a stranger reported experiencing at least one emotional effect. Among women who were physically assaulted by a stranger, 49% reported being more fearful, 40% said they were more cautious or aware, and 26% reported feelings of anger. Many sexual assault victims were also more cautious or aware (35%), angry (33%) or fearful (25%) after the incident. In addition, 11% of victims of sexual assault by a stranger reported feelings of shame or guilt.

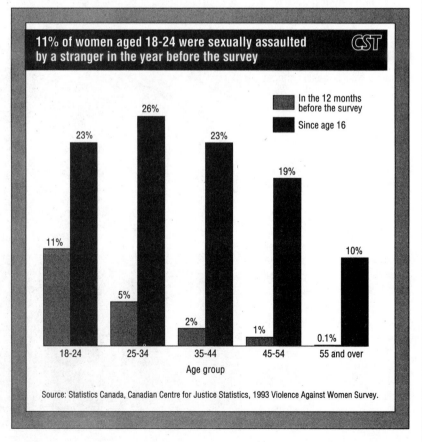

11% of women aged 18-24 were sexually assaulted by a stranger in the year before the survey CST

Legend:
In the 12 months before the survey
Since age 16

Age group	In the 12 months before the survey	Since age 16
18-24	11%	23%
25-34	5%	26%
35-44	2%	23%
45-54	1%	19%
55 and over	0.1%	10%

Source: Statistics Canada, Canadian Centre for Justice Statistics, 1993 Violence Against Women Survey.

Violence Against Women Survey

Between February and June 1993, Statistics Canada, on behalf of Health Canada, conducted a national survey (excluding the Yukon and the Northwest Territories) on male violence against women. Approximately 12,300 women aged 18 and over were interviewed by telephone about their experiences of sexual and physical violence since the age of 16, and about their perceptions of their personal safety.

This was the first national survey of its kind anywhere in the world. Most research in this area reflects the experiences of women who report violent incidents to the police or use the services of shelters and counselling services. This survey went directly to a random sample of women to ask them about their experiences, whether or not they had reported to the police or anyone else. Random selection helped ensure that the women who responded were statistically representative of all Canadian women and that the results could be generalized to the female population at large.

Measuring sexual assault Under the *Criminal Code*, a broad range of experiences, ranging from unwanted sexual touching to sexual violence that results in wounding or maiming, or that endangers the life of the victim, qualify as sexual assault. Estimates of sexual assault by strangers were derived through the following two questions:

❑ **Sexual attack –**

"Has a male stranger ever forced you or attempted to force you into any sexual activity by threatening you, holding you down or hurting you in any way?"

❑ **Unwanted sexual touching –**

"Has a male stranger ever touched you against your will in any sexual way, such as unwanted touching, grabbing, kissing or fondling?"

Incidents that met the above criteria were counted as sexual assaults whether or not they also involved physical assault.

Measuring physical assault Experiences of physical assault by men other than spouses were estimated through responses to the following questions:

"Now I'm going to ask you some questions about physical attacks you may have had since the age of 16. By this I mean any use of force such as being hit, slapped, kicked, or grabbed to being beaten, knifed or shot. Has a male stranger ever physically attacked you?

The *Criminal Code* considers threats of physical violence to be assaults, so long as they are face-to-face and the victim has a reasonable expectation that the action will occur. Responses that satisfied the following condition were also counted as physical assaults:

"The next few questions are about face-to-face threats you may have experienced. By threats I mean any time you have been threatened with physical harm since you were 16. Has a male stranger ever threatened to harm you? Did you believe he would do it?"

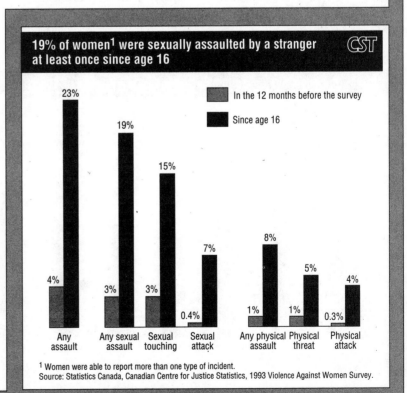

19% of women[1] were sexually assaulted by a stranger at least once since age 16

Legend:
- In the 12 months before the survey
- Since age 16

	Any assault	Any sexual assault	Sexual touching	Sexual attack	Any physical assault	Physical threat	Physical attack
In the 12 months before the survey	4%	3%	3%	0.4%	1%	1%	0.3%
Since age 16	23%	19%	15%	7%	8%	5%	4%

[1] Women were able to report more than one type of incident.
Source: Statistics Canada, Canadian Centre for Justice Statistics, 1993 Violence Against Women Survey.

Weapons, including knives, sharp or blunt objects and guns, were used in 18% of physical attacks, 16% of physical threats and 10% of sexual attacks by strangers. Perhaps partially because of the use of weapons, physical attacks by strangers were more likely to result in bodily injury (43%) than were sexual attacks (27%).

Few incidents reported to police or social services Most victims of physical (85%) and sexual assault (75%) by a stranger talked to someone, usually a family member or friend, about the incident. Relatively few assaults by strangers, however, were reported to the police: 37% of physical and only 9% of sexual assaults. Among those incidents where police were involved, about one-in-four resulted in the assailant being arrested or charged. Even fewer victims approached a social service agency for help after being assaulted. Social services were contacted after only 4% of sexual assaults.

There were a number of reasons why women who had been victimized by a stranger did not report the incident to the police. The reasons given most often included: the woman felt the incident was too minor (44%); she felt the police couldn't do anything (14%); she didn't want or need help (11%); she wanted to keep the incident private (9%); she was ashamed or embarrassed (9%); or she didn't want the police involved (9%). Reasons for not reporting the incident to the police differed by the nature of the assault. Of incidents involving threats or unwanted touching that were not brought to the attention of police, 52% were not reported because the woman felt that the incident was too minor. This reason was cited, however, in only 21% of physical and sexual attacks that were not reported to police.

Women concerned for personal safety Many women are somewhat or very worried when out alone after dark, when using public transportation alone after dark, when walking alone to their car in a parking garage, or when home alone in the evening or at night. Concern for one's personal safety generally declines with age in each of these situations. For example, 69% of women aged 18-24 stated that they were somewhat (60%) or very worried (9%) when walking alone in their area after dark. Among women aged 65 and over, 53% were concerned for their personal safety when in this situation (43% were somewhat worried and 10% were very worried). Women in large urban centres were more likely than those in small urban centres or rural areas to be concerned for their personal safety, especially in situations involving public transportation and walking alone after dark.

Women who had experienced any type of assault by a stranger tended to be more concerned for their personal safety than women who had not. Among women in general, 65% of those who had experienced an assault by a stranger worried about walking alone in their area after dark (54% were somewhat worried and 11% were very worried). In comparison, 58% of women who had not had such an experience were concerned for their safety when in this situation (51% were somewhat worried and 7% were very worried).

Among women who used public transportation and who had experienced an assault by a stranger, 81% worried when waiting for or using public transportation after dark (55% were somewhat worried and 26% were very worried). In comparison, 74% of women who had not been assaulted by a stranger were worried when in this situation (54% were somewhat worried and 20% were very worried).

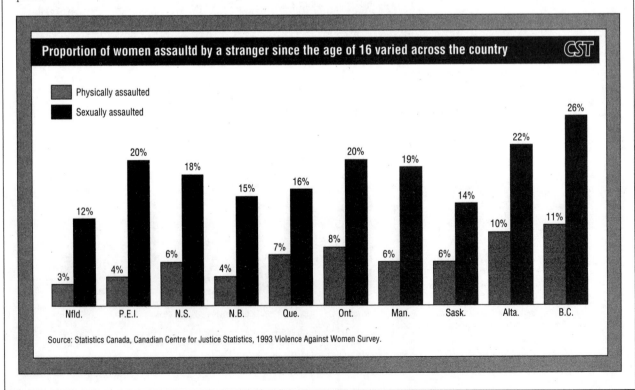

Proportion of women assaultd by a stranger since the age of 16 varied across the country CST

- Physically assaulted
- Sexually assaulted

	Nfld.	P.E.I.	N.S.	N.B.	Que.	Ont.	Man.	Sask.	Alta.	B.C.
Physically assaulted	3%	4%	6%	4%	7%	8%	6%	6%	10%	11%
Sexually assaulted	12%	20%	18%	15%	16%	20%	19%	14%	22%	26%

Source: Statistics Canada, Canadian Centre for Justice Statistics, 1993 Violence Against Women Survey.

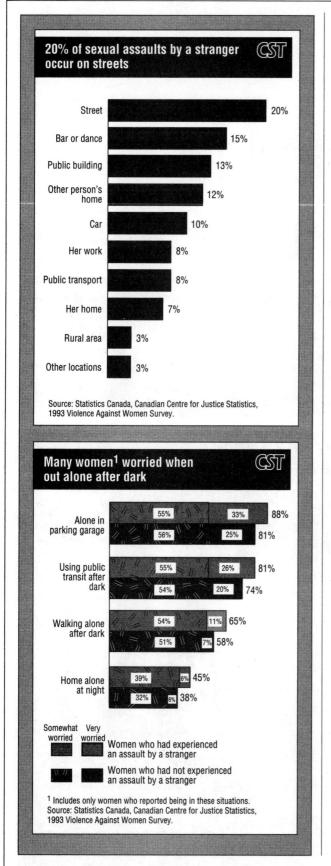

20% of sexual assaults by a stranger occur on streets CST

Location	Percentage
Street	20%
Bar or dance	15%
Public building	13%
Other person's home	12%
Car	10%
Her work	8%
Public transport	8%
Her home	7%
Rural area	3%
Other locations	3%

Source: Statistics Canada, Canadian Centre for Justice Statistics, 1993 Violence Against Women Survey.

Many women[1] worried when out alone after dark CST

Alone in parking garage: 55% / 33% = 88%; 56% / 25% = 81%

Using public transit after dark: 55% / 26% = 81%; 54% / 20% = 74%

Walking alone after dark: 54% / 11% = 65%; 51% / 7% = 58%

Home alone at night: 39% / 6% = 45%; 32% / 6% = 38%

Somewhat worried / Very worried

Women who had experienced an assault by a stranger

Women who had not experienced an assault by a stranger

[1] Includes only women who reported being in these situations.
Source: Statistics Canada, Canadian Centre for Justice Statistics, 1993 Violence Against Women Survey.

Women taking self-protective measures Women are taking action, both personally and collectively, to increase their safety. On a personal level, 17% of Canadian women reported in 1993 that they "always" or "usually" carried something to defend themselves or to alert other people. Also, 31% of women tried to avoid walking past teenage boys or young men. Among women who drove, 60% checked the back seat of the car for intruders before getting in and 67% locked the car doors when driving alone. In addition, 11% of all Canadian women had taken a self-defence course in order to improve their personal safety. Generally, women who had experienced an assault (either by a stranger or a man they knew) were more likely to state that they "always" took protective measures than were women who had not had such an experience.

Women and men are also organizing community-based programs to help increase women's safety, especially at night. Women's groups in several large cities conduct safety audits of public areas. The objective of these audits is to identify places where lighting, signs and access for persons with disabilities, could be added or changed in order to improve women's safety.[1] Women's groups in many cities, often working in conjunction with police, also hold workshops and other events in order to increase public awareness of women's safety concerns. On many university campuses, safe-walk programs have been organized to provide women with assistance after dark. In some cities, public transportation authorities have initiated programs to help improve women's safety at night. As well, many workplaces, campuses and community centres now offer training in self-defence and preventative measures.

[1] For more information on safety audits contact METRAC, 158 Spadina Road, Toronto, Ontario, M5R 2T8.

Carol Strike was an analyst with Housing, Family and Social Statistics Division when she wrote this article. For additional information, contact **Karen Rodgers**, Canadian Centre for Justice Statistics, Statistics Canada.

CST

by Karen Rodgers and Garry MacDonald

Canada's Shelters for Abused Women

*T*he number of residential facilities or shelters[1] for abused women has been steadily increasing since the 1970s, with the largest growth occurring in the 1980s. According to the 1992-93 Transition Home Survey, there were almost 400 shelters providing services for women and their children in physically or emotionally abusive situations. These facilities provide not only a secure environment for abused women and their children, but also services including general information and crisis counselling, public education and court accompaniment. In addition, women are also referred to a variety of mental health-related services, addiction programs, and medical and legal services. Despite the growing number of shelters, women who use these facilities represent only a small proportion of women abused by their partners.

Number of shelters for abused women growing On March 31, 1993, there were 371 shelters for abused women across Canada. Only 18 of these shelters existed prior to 1975, while an additional 57 began operation between 1975 and 1979. Since then, the number of residential facilities has grown rapidly, as issues of family violence and violence against women gained the attention of federal and provincial governments.

Shelters are intended to provide safe housing for women in abusive situations, and they use a variety of measures to ensure the safety of women and children who come to them. According to the Transition Home Survey, the most frequently cited security measures employed were rules for admitting non-residents, followed by an intercom system, an alarm system, steel doors, an unlisted address/phone number and security fencing.

Most residential facilities (90%) were governed by volunteer Boards of Directors with the number of members ranging between 1 and 54. However, the majority (87%) of the facilities had between 5 and 15 members. Two hundred and twenty-five facilities (68%) indicated using volunteers to help run the shelters. The average number of volunteers per facility was 15.

Shelters for abused women are, for the most part, well integrated into the communities they serve. Protocols and understandings are maintained with social agencies, medical resources, the legal community and police services. In most cases, the shelters are linked to provincial or territorial associations and many are part of established multi-agency committees.

Most facilities serve women from urban, suburban and rural areas Almost 60% of shelters indicated that they served people from more than one geographic area. The remaining facilities served women primarily in urban areas (18%), in rural/village areas (18%), those on reserves (3%) and those in suburban areas (2%). Over one-half (55%) of shelters were concentrated in the provinces of Ontario and Quebec, the two provinces that account for the largest adult female populations. The proportional distribution

1 The term "shelter" is used to refer to a wide array of residential facilities, ranging from transition homes to emergency shelters.

of provincial and territorial facilities was similar to that of women aged 15 and over, and to that of women with the highest risk of being abused (those aged 15-24 currently in a legal marriage or in a common-law union). While most women (82%) received help within their own community, others travelled a great distance to get help from a shelter. For 16% of women, their principal residence was more than 100 km from the shelter.

Wide array of services provided Services provided by shelters depend to a great extent on the needs of the victimized women and children, and can vary with the availability of services in the surrounding community. Most facilities (96%) provided general information and crisis counselling to their clients. Other in-house services included public education (90%), court accompaniment (89%), follow-up (82%) and a crisis telephone line (79%). Most facilities also were in a position to refer women with special needs to services such as mental health-related services (90%), addiction programs (89%), legal services (89%) and medical services (87%). In-house services for children most often included individual counselling (75%), child care (58%) and group counselling (54%).

Most shelters also offered assistance to non-residents by providing crisis intervention (77%), responding to information needs (64%) and court accompaniment (52%). These services were provided through telephone contact, letters, visits or walk-ins. On March 31, 1993, 577 contacts were made seeking residential services, 2,077 for non-residential services and 447 for other reasons. On that day, the number of calls to shelters ranged from 0-181, averaging 11 per facility. Between 1991-92 and 1992-93 , the number of contacts to shelters for abused women increased by 30%.

Many facilities provide for women with special needs Almost one-half of shelters accepted women who had not been physically or emotionally abused. Many facilities (over 40%) also reported that they could accommodate women with special needs, such as those who suffered from substance abuse or who required medical attention. As well, slightly less than one-quarter reported that they could accommodate women with either a serious mental health disorder or a history of being violent. Many facilities took measures to serve women with disabilities, ensuring that they had access for wheelchairs (44%), audiotapes and braille

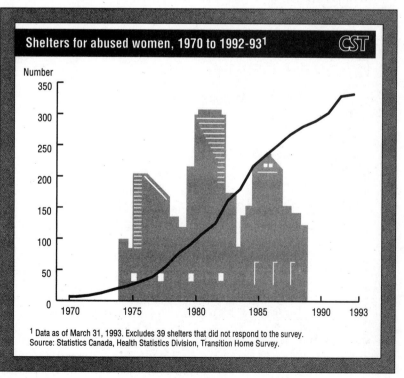

Shelters for abused women, 1970 to 1992-93¹ CST

Number

350 · 300 · 250 · 200 · 150 · 100 · 50 · 0

1970   1975   1980   1985   1990   1993

1 Data as of March 31, 1993. Excludes 39 shelters that did not respond to the survey.
Source: Statistics Canada, Health Statistics Division, Transition Home Survey.

CANADIAN SOCIAL TRENDS BACKGROUNDER CST

Types of shelters

The term shelter is used broadly to refer to all shelters or residential facilities for abused women and their children. The types of shelters are defined for the Transition Home Survey as:

Transition home – Short- or moderate-term (1-8 weeks) secure placement for abused women with or without dependent children. (288 in 1993)

Second-stage housing – Long-term (3-12 months) secure placement for abused women with or without dependent children. (22 in 1993)

Family resource centre – An Ontario initiative which provides services that are identical or similar to transition homes. Must at least provide a residential service. (11 in 1993)

Safe home network – Subsidiary, very short-term (1-3 days) placement for abused women, with or without dependent children, in private homes. (13 in 1993)

Satellite – Short-term (3-5 days) secure respite for abused women with or without dependent children. These shelters are usually linked to a transition home or another agency for administrative purposes. (4 in 1993)

Emergency shelter – Short-term respite for a wide population range, not exclusively for abused women. Some may provide accommodation for men as well as for women. This type of facility may have residents not associated with family violence but who are without a home because of some other emergency situation. (15 in 1993)

Other – All other homes/shelters for victims of family violence not otherwise classified or that did not respond to the survey. (18 in 1993)

How abused women in shelters found out about such services:

32% found out on their own

14% were referred by a social services agency

13% from a friend or relative

13% through another shelter

7% from the police

5% from a help or distress phone line

4% from a medical professional

4% through health social services

3% by another shelter user

1% through an Aboriginal organization

11% other referral source

Note: Figures do not add to 100% because of multiple responses.

material (16%), and telephone devices (TDD) (11%). In addition, 40% of facilities reported that they liaise with groups that represent people with disabilities.

Approximately one-in-five facilities served primarily Aboriginal women, while less than 10% primarily served ethno-cultural and visible minority women. In addition, 44% of the facilities offered culturally sensitive services to Aboriginal women, and 41% provided culturally sensitive services to ethno-cultural and visible minority women.

Admissions increasing In the fiscal year 1992-93, there were 86,499 admissions to the 303 facilities that responded to the survey question. Almost all of these were to transition homes (89%). An admission is the official acceptance of a women or child into a facility with the allocation of a bed, and a person may be admitted more than once during the year. Comparing facilities that responded to the survey in 1991-92 and 1992-93, there was a 2% increase in admissions.

On March 31, 1993, 3% of women living in shelters had some form of disability (including mobility, visual, hearing and other physical disabilities). This percentage is much lower than the estimated number of ever-married abused women with disabilities (24%) and of all women with disabilities (16%). Two-thirds of the residents preferred to speak English, almost one-quarter preferred French and 12% preferred to speak a language other than English or French.

Younger women less likely to use shelters According to the Transition Home Survey, the largest proportion of women residing in a shelter were aged 25-34 (43%), with only 24% aged 15-24. Women aged 55 and over accounted for only a small proportion of those in shelters in 1992-93 (3%), not surprising given their low reported rate of wife assault.

The vast majority of abused women in shelters on March 31, 1993 were seeking shelter from someone with whom they had an intimate relationship (85%). Eighty-three percent of these women indicated that their spouse or partner was the abuser, 14% of the women were abused by a former spouse or partner and 4% were abused by a current or former boyfriend.

Transition Home Survey

The federal government's Family Violence Initiative proposed a coordinated interdepartmental action plan targeting family violence on a number of different fronts. One of the objectives was to address the need for better national information on the nature and extent of family violence in Canada. In response, the Health Statistics Division (formerly Canadian Centre for Health Information) conducted a survey of transition homes to identify the services they provided and the characteristics of residents.

The 1992-93 Transition Home Survey was distributed to all transition homes, shelters, second-stage housing, family resource centres, safe home networks, satellites and emergency shelters identified as providing residential and non-residential services to victims of wife assault. The survey allowed for the collection of data on services dispensed during the previous twelve months and provided a one-day snapshot of the characteristics of the residents on a specific day. In 1992-93, there were 371 shelters for abused women. Of these, 332 facilities (89%) responded to the survey, up from the 79% response rate for the 1991-92 survey.

Violence Against Women Survey

The Violence Against Women Survey was a random telephone survey of women aged 18 and over. The survey did not include women without phones, those who spoke neither English nor French, or women living in shelters or other institutions. However, respondents included women who had used shelters or other residential facilities for abused women at some point. The definitions of violence in the Transition Home Survey and in the Violence Against Women Survey differ. The Transition Home Survey captured data on women who had gone to shelters because of a range of abuse, including physical, sexual, financial and psychological abuse as well as threats and neglect. The Violence Against Women Survey captured detailed information on the use of transition homes for only those women who were either physically or sexually abused by a current or previous spouse or common-law partner. Measures of violence for the Violence Against Women Survey were restricted to Criminal Code definitions of assault and sexual assault in order to capture "violence" as it is legally defined.

Most women stay less than 20 days On March 31, 1993, the national occupancy rate for shelters for abused women and their children was 68%,[2] but may be higher or lower at different times of the year. The most common length of stay at a facility was 11 to 20 days (39%), followed by 10 days or less (27%). The total bed capacity of the reporting facilities ranged from 2 to 80. One-third of shelters indicated that they had 10 or fewer beds, 44% had between 11 and 20, 12% had 21 to 30 and 10% had more than 30. Of the 222 facilities that reported having cribs, 88% had 5 or less.

Women who use shelters represent a small proportion of abused women According to the Violence Against Women Survey, 13% of abused women who left their spouses because of their abusive or threatening behaviour stayed in a shelter. Most women who left their spouses stayed with friends or relatives (77%), other women got their own place (13%) or stayed in a hotel (5%).

There are several reasons why abused women do not go to a formal social agency or shelter for help. The main reasons were that they did not want or need help (40%), that the incident was too minor (25%), that they were unaware of any services (16%) and that there were no services available (14%). However, 81% of women who had used a shelter said they found it to be helpful.

Women who use shelters as a safe haven from abuse are often in desperate situations. On March 31, 1993, there were 1,870 women in shelters, 80% of whom were admitted for reasons of abuse. Seventy-two percent of these women reported psychological

abuse, 69% indicated physical abuse, 44% had received threats, 28% indicated financial abuse and 22% reported sexual abuse. The remaining 20% of women sought refuge for reasons other than abuse. Approximately three-quarters of these non-abused women went to a shelter because of housing problems.

Women more likely to go to shelters when children witness violence Children witnessing violence in the home appeared to have been a factor in women's decisions to go to a shelter. According to the Violence Against Women Survey, 78% of women who stayed in a shelter indicated that at some point their children had witnessed some of the violence against them, compared with 39% of all abused women. It appears that children are witnessing very serious forms of violence. Children had witnessed violence in 52% of abusive marriages in which women had feared for their lives and in 61% in which women had been injured.

On March 31, 1993, three-quarters of women with children seeking refuge from abusive situations were admitted with their children. On that day, 1,636 children were residents in shelters, some without their mothers. Almost one-quarter of women were protecting their children from psychological abuse, 13% from physical abuse and 5% from sexual abuse. An additional 112 (7%) children were admitted to shelters for reasons not related to abuse.

[2] For some shelters, operating at 68% may mean that they are full because they included temporary beds, e.g. roll-out cots, in their total number of available beds. The range of occupancy rate by facility was from 0% to 243%. This excludes safe home networks and second-stage housing.

Almost half (45%) of all children admitted because of abuse in the home were under age 5.[3] Children aged 5-9 accounted for 32%, those aged 10-14 made up 20%, while the smallest group (3%) were aged 15-18.

Most women who use shelters have suffered injuries According to the Violence Against Women Survey, women's use of shelters was also strongly linked to the severity of the violence.[4] Over 80% of women who used shelters had suffered an injury at some point during the abusive relationship, compared with 45% of all abused women. In addition, 63% of women who stayed in a shelter had at some point been injured severely enough to seek medical attention, compared with 19% of all abused women. According to the Transition Home Survey, 26% of women in shelters on March 31, 1993 required medical attention for the most recent incident of abuse. In a further 27% of cases, it was not known whether the woman had sought any medical assistance. The Violence Against Women Survey showed that women who stayed in a shelter were more than twice as likely to have feared for their lives (85%) as all abused women (39%), and were more likely to have taken time off from their everyday activities because of the abuse (57% versus 31%).

Many women who stay at shelters report abuse to police According to the Violence Against Women Survey, 26% of all abused women reported a violent incident to the police at some time during the relationship. Of women in shelters on March 31, 1993, 30% had reported the most recent incident of abuse to the police. In over one-half of these cases, charges were laid by the police. Restraining orders were obtained in 13% of cases. In 7% of cases, the intervention of the Child Protection Services was required, and in only 2% of cases was it indicated that there was intervention by Adult Protection Services.

Most women return to abusive partners According to the Violence Against Women Survey, almost three-quarters of the women who left their abusive partner eventually returned home. The most common reason why women returned home was for the sake of the children (31%), followed by wanting to give the relationship another chance (24%), her partner promising to change (17%) and a lack of money or housing (9%). Women whose partner received counselling for his abusive behaviour were more likely to return home (81%) than those whose husband did not get such help (70%).

[3] Percentages are based on the 1,498 children for which ages were given.

[4] In the Violence Against Women Survey, the severity of the violence was measured by whether the woman was ever injured, whether medical attention was sought, whether she ever feared for her life, and whether she had to take time off from her everyday activities because of the abuse.

Karen Rodgers is a senior analyst with the Canadian Centre for Justice Statistics and **Garry MacDonald** is a senior analyst with the Health Statistics Division, both with Statistics Canada.

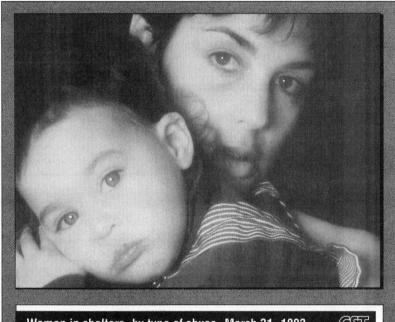

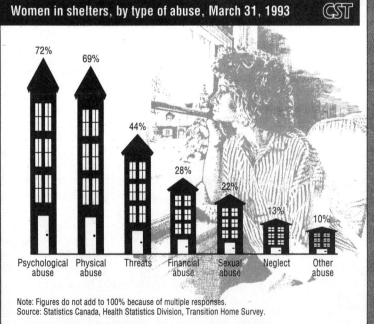

Women in shelters, by type of abuse, March 31, 1993 CST

- Psychological abuse 72%
- Physical abuse 69%
- Threats 44%
- Financial abuse 28%
- Sexual abuse 22%
- Neglect 13%
- Other abuse 10%

Note: Figures do not add to 100% because of multiple responses.
Source: Statistics Canada, Health Statistics Division, Transition Home Survey.

Street Prostitution
IN CANADA

by Lee Wolff and Dorota Geissel

S treet prostitution has become a greater concern in most large Canadian cities since the early 1980s, when residents noticed a growth in the number of visible street prostitutes.[1] In 1985, changes to Canada's prostitution laws made it more difficult to communicate publicly for the purposes of prostitution. Since then, enforcement of the laws controlling the street trade has increased dramatically.

Legislative evaluations by the Department of Justice indicated, however, that in the three years following implementation, the 1985 legislation had not been successful in suppressing the street trade in most cities. Further, laws introduced in 1988 to protect youths from sexual exploitation were found to be

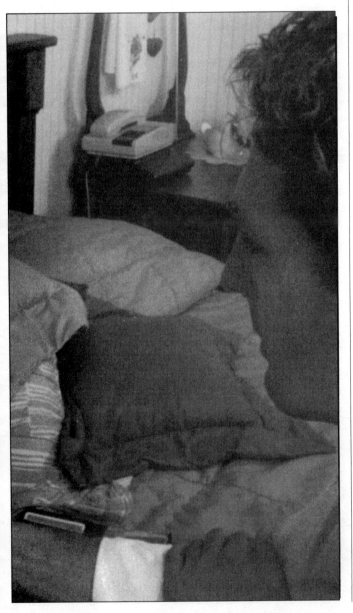

ineffective in bringing customers and pimps of youth prostitutes to justice.

While research is inconclusive, it does provide some insight into the conditions under which many enter the street trade. Some research suggests that most prostitutes enter the trade when they are very young. Factors identified as important influences on a young person's decision to prostitute include childhood sexual abuse, episodes of running away from home and the expectation of financial gain. Research findings also suggest that understanding the circumstances leading to entering prostitution may be important in developing strategies to curb the entry of youths into the street trade, and to limit the exploitive and often threatening situations many prostitutes face.

Canada's laws Prostitution among consenting adults has never been a crime in Canada, but has always been subject to very restrictive legal parameters. Throughout Canada's history, attempts to control prostitution through the Criminal Code reflect tensions between those who acknowledge the practical aspects of the trade and those who view the trade as immoral.[2]

Today, sections 210 to 213 of the Criminal Code prohibit those activities related to prostitution that are considered threatening to public order or offensive to public decency. Activities include being involved in a common bawdy house; procuring or soliciting a person to exchange sexual services for money; and communicating for the purposes of prostitution in a public place, regardless of how orderly that communication may be.

These laws, which prohibit many transactions necessarily associated with prostitution, make it very difficult to practice the trade without breaking the law. In the case of communicating, those convicted face a maximum penalty of six months in jail, a $2,000 fine, or both.

Changes in law result in wide variation in enforcement practices The nature of Canada's prostitution laws has changed, particularly over the past two decades. Canada's first Criminal Code (1892) dealt with female prostitutes on the basis of status, such as the control of vagrancy, rather than any overt act. This law prevailed for 80 years, until, in 1972, a law was introduced to control the overt act of solicitation. Since then, laws concerning the street trade have undergone significant changes, resulting in varying police enforcement practices. Indeed, over the past two decades, the annual number of prostitution offences reported by the police in Canada has ranged from under 1,000 to over 10,000.

Much of the variation in practices resulted from the unclear meaning of the 1972 soliciting law. In 1978, the Supreme Court of Canada held that for the activities of a prostitute to be criminal, the conduct had to be "pressing or persistent." Since the mere indication that sex was for sale was not illegal, the Criminal Code was rendered ineffective in reducing problems associated with the street trade. As a result, following the 1978 ruling, police enforcement of the soliciting law became minimal. The

[1] Department of Justice Canada, **Street Prostitution, Assessing the Impact of the Law: Synthesis Report**, Ottawa, 1989.

[2] C. Bagley, B. Burrows and C. Yaworski, "Street Kids and Adolescent Prostitution: A Challenge for Legal and Social Services," **Canadian Child Welfare Law: Children, Families and the State**, 1991.

UNIT 3: WORK, LIFE STYLE AND SOCIAL PROBLEMS

Sentencing patterns in Ontario and Alberta

Although prostitutes and customers in Ontario and Alberta were convicted of communicating in close to equal numbers during the early 1990s, there were differences in sentencing patterns between the two provinces.[1] Sentencing data, however, are limited because prior criminal history is not accounted for – a factor which is always considered at time of sentencing and is known to have an impact on sentence severity. Studies conducted by the Department of Justice found that, while prostitutes were sentenced more severely than customers, this was, at least in part, due to their more extensive criminal records. Another factor unaccounted for in the data is the presence of additional charges that may be associated with the communicating incident (e.g., breach of probation), and hence considered at time of sentencing.

In Ontario, communicating convictions among women often result in prison terms During the period under study, 44% of charges against women (mainly prostitutes) resulted in prison terms, followed by probation (26%), fines (22%) and absolute discharges (8%).[2] Median prison terms were 10 days and median fine amounts were $150.

Men (mainly customers) convicted of communicating in Ontario were most frequently fined (42%) or given an absolute discharge (35%). Probation (17%) and prison sentences (6%) accounted for

a much smaller proportion of charges among men. Median prison terms were 10 days and median fine amounts were $100.

In Alberta, communicating convictions among women often result in fines In Alberta, fines were the most frequent dispositions for communicating convictions among women (mainly prostitutes). During the period under study, 66% of charges against women resulted in fines, followed by prison (19%), probation (13%) and absolute discharges (2%). Median prison terms were 30 days and median fine amounts were $200.

Most convictions among men (mainly customers) in Alberta resulted in fines (89%). Probation (6%), absolute discharge (3%) and prison sentences (2%) accounted for only a small percentage of convictions against men. Median prison terms were 30 days and median fine amounts were $200.

[1] This information was obtained from the Sentencing Database Project maintained by the Canadian Centre for Justice Statistics. Data for Ontario refer to the 15-month period from June 1991 to August 1992, when 3,595 charges resulted in conviction. Alberta statistics are based on the 22-month period between January 1991 and October 1992, when 2,228 charges resulted in conviction. Court statistics were not available for other provinces where communicating offences are frequently reported.

[2] When more than one disposition is ordered on a charge, the charge is characterized by the most serious disposition. Prison sentences are the most serious of all sentences, followed by probation orders, fines and absolute discharges.

Prostitution offences, 1962 to 1992

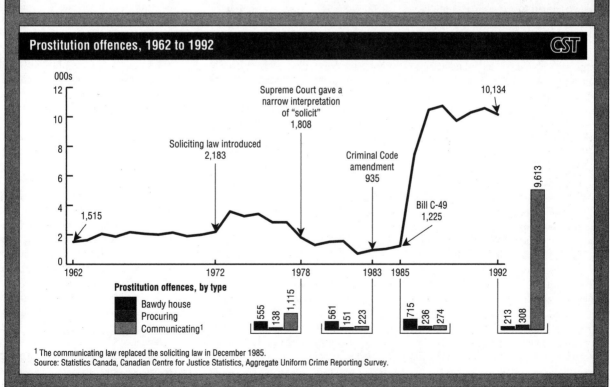

[1] The communicating law replaced the soliciting law in December 1985.
Source: Statistics Canada, Canadian Centre for Justice Statistics, Aggregate Uniform Crime Reporting Survey.

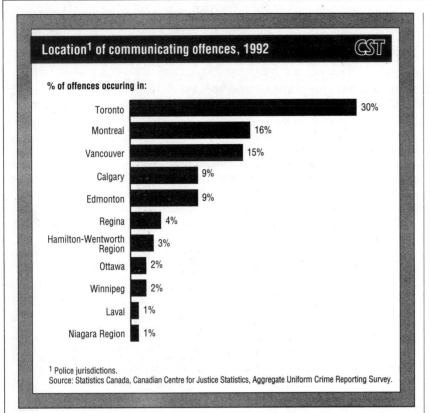

Location[1] of communicating offences, 1992   CST

% of offences occuring in:

Location	%
Toronto	30%
Montreal	16%
Vancouver	15%
Calgary	9%
Edmonton	9%
Regina	4%
Hamilton-Wentworth Region	3%
Ottawa	2%
Winnipeg	2%
Laval	1%
Niagara Region	1%

[1] Police jurisdictions.
Source: Statistics Canada, Canadian Centre for Justice Statistics, Aggregate Uniform Crime Reporting Survey.

soliciting section of the Code was also problematic because it did not define "public place," and it was not clear if it applied equally to female prostitutes, male prostitutes and customers.

In 1983, a Criminal Code amendment was introduced, specifying that the soliciting law applied to both female and male prostitutes. Later, in December 1985, the soliciting law was replaced with the communicating law (Bill C-49) which stands today. This law, applicable to both prostitutes (female and male) and customers, prohibits solicitation that impedes or otherwise interferes with the use of streets and public places.

Following the implementation of Bill C-49, those involved in the street trade became easy targets for police intervention, as is evidenced by the dramatic increase in the number of prostitution offences reported (7,426 in 1986, compared with 1,225 in 1985). However, since that time, the constitutionality of the communicating law has been challenged in many courts, resulting in variable enforcement practices across the country. It was not until May 1990 that the Supreme Court of Canada ruled in favour of the law's validity.

Most reported prostitution offences are for communicating Since many activities necessarily associated with prostitution are illegal, those involved are at constant risk of criminal prosecution. This is particularly true for those involved in the most visible aspect of the trade – street prostitution. Since 1986, when it became illegal to communicate publicly for the purposes of prostitution, most prostitution charges have been for communicating. In 1992, 10,134 prostitution incidents were reported by the police, 95% of which involved communicating offences. Bawdy house and procuring offences (recruiting a person to engage in prostitution) accounted for the remaining 5%.

The number of reported procuring offences is relatively small, at least in part, because traditional police methods are not always appropriate for enforcing sections of the Criminal Code involving procurement. Extensive police investigations are often required. In addition, offenders may be charged with related offences such as abduction, forcible confinement, weapons offences and sexual assault, which are not included in prostitution statistics.

Both prostitutes and customers can be charged under Canada's communicating

law. Prostitutes, however, may be at greater risk of being charged given their higher visibility. Although police and court information systems do not distinguish between customers and prostitutes, it is generally acknowledged that most prostitutes charged are female and most customers charged are male. Since 1986, the number of males charged has been relatively close to the number of females charged. In 1992, for example, 5,262 females and 4,695 males were charged with communicating for the purposes of prostitution. This suggests that the police are charging prostitutes and customers in close to equal numbers.

Highest proportions reported in Toronto, Montreal and Vancouver
Since 1990, the police have reported about 10,000 communicating offences annually. Among the 11 police jurisdictions where most of these offences are reported, the Toronto police report the largest proportion (30% in 1992), followed by the police in Montreal (16%) and Vancouver (15%). Together, 11 police jurisdictions reported 93% of all communicating offences in 1992. These same police jurisdictions reported 35% of all Criminal Code offences that year.

The number of offences reported among police agencies, however, is not necessarily indicative of the prevalence of street prostitutes and customers. Differences in police practices and resources have an impact on the volume of communicating offences reported among police agencies.

Who is entering the street trade?
While young women aged 12-17 comprise a very small proportion of women charged in communicating incidents (6% in 1992), research suggests that, for many prostitutes, the decision to enter the trade is made in youth. The Badgley Committee on Sexual Offences Against Children and Youth[3] found that one-half of prostitutes interviewed in 1984 entered the trade when they were under age 16, and almost all (96%) had become prostitutes before the age of 18. Prostitutes were, on average, aged 18 at the time of the Committee's interviews.

Considerable research has focused on those factors which may be important in guiding a young person's decision to prostitute. While findings are not conclusive, some researchers believe that this choice is often made within the context of abusive childhood experiences.[2,4] Others, however, argue that the decision to prostitute may be largely motivated by a rational expectation of financial gain.[5]

Research suggests many are runaways An overwhelming majority of prostitutes interviewed by the Badgley Committee had run away from home at least once – 93% of females and 97% of males. Further, 67% of females and 46% of males had run away several times.[4] Research also indicates that street prostitutes leave home at an earlier age than do other Canadians. Earls and David found that female prostitutes left home at an average age of 13.7 years, 3.6 years earlier than their counterparts who were not prostitutes.[6] Similar findings were reported for males.

The underlying problems associated with running away from home are often interrelated and highly complex. Fisher found that among young people who ran away more than once, family problems, such as parental drinking, parental conflict, family/child interaction problems, mental illness, spousal abuse and child physical or sexual abuse, were invariably present.[7] Also, a large proportion of those who ran away more than once (80%) were found to have been involved in delinquent activities, primarily as a means of support, and about one-fifth of these children reported having turned to prostitution.

Childhood sexual abuse may also be a factor Some studies indicate that childhood sexual abuse may be an important influence on young people's decisions to enter the street trade.[3,4,6,8,9] Although tentative, findings suggest that sizeable numbers of street prostitutes were sexually abused in childhood.

A comparison of data from two surveys commissioned for the Badgley Report indicates that prostitutes were at least twice as likely as other members of the population to have experienced a first unwanted sexual act involving force or threats of force.[4] More recently, Earls and David found that female and male prostitutes were more likely than non-prostitutes to have had some sort of sexual interaction with a family member.[6] Also, of young

people who had had a sexual encounter with a family member, this study found that among prostitutes it was more likely to have been a father or uncle, while among non-prostitutes it was more likely to have been a cousin of the same age.

While these findings support the view that prostitutes are more likely than non-prostitutes to have been sexually abused in childhood, other research suggests that the link to prostitution is not direct, but involves runaway behaviour as an intervening variable.[10] That is, adolescent prostitution can be viewed as a survival behaviour, suggesting that runaway prevention strategies aimed at providing supportive environments are needed, as are strategies to meet the everyday needs of runaway children.

A dangerous trade Street prostitutes face several health and safety risks. The 1984 Badgley Committee reported that about one-third of those interviewed were frequent or heavy users of alcohol or drugs and over one-half had contracted a sexually transmitted disease. About two-thirds had been physically assaulted while working as prostitutes, 44% of whom required medical attention. In addition, for many, prostitution led to broader ranges of deviance, including theft, assault and drug dealing.[3]

Homicide statistics highlight the dangers associated with the prostitution trade. During 1991 and 1992, 22 known prostitutes (all females) were murdered, representing 5% of female murder victims aged 16 and over. In 1991, 4 of the 14 prostitutes murdered were aged 16-17. In 1992, all prostitute victims were over age 17.

Murder cases involving prostitutes were less likely to be solved than those involving victims who were not prostitutes. For prostitute victims, an accused was identified in one-half of all cases (11 of the 22 cases) reported during 1991 and 1992. The comparable rate for all murders was 78%.

Customers were accused in 8 of the 11 cases of murdered prostitutes solved by the police in 1991 and 1992. Customers, however, were also victimized. During 1991 and 1992, 10 prostitutes were implicated in the murder of 8 victims, 4 of whom were believed to be customers.

Much remains unknown about street prostitution What is known about

prostitution pales in comparison to what is not known. Justice statistics tell us about those who come into conflict with the law, but we do not know how representative this group is of all prostitutes and customers. Research studies tell us about the experiences of prostitutes, but, while informative, findings are typically limited to small and often selective samples. What we do know is that, despite the introduction of a restrictive communicating law in 1985, the world's "oldest profession" persists in Canada. We also know that, sometimes, it persists at the expense of human life.

[3] Badgley Committee, **Sexual Offences Against Children**, Ottawa: Supply and Services Canada, 1984.

[4] J. Lowman, "Street Prostitutes in Canada: An Evaluation of the Brannigan-Fleishman Opportunity Model," **Canadian Journal of Law and Society**, 1991.

[5] A. Brannigan and J. Fleischman, "Juvenile Prostitution and Mental Health: Policing Delinquency or Treating Pathology," **Canadian Journal of Law and Society**, 1989.

[6] C.P. Earls and H. David, "Early Family Sexual Experiences of Male and Female Prostitutes," **Canada's Mental Health**, 1990.

[7] J. Fisher, **Missing Children Research Project: Volume 1, Findings of the Study**, Ottawa: Solicitor General of Canada, 1989.

[8] M. Silbert and A. Pines, "Sexual Child Abuse as an Antecedent to Prostitution," **Journal of Abuse and Neglect**, 1981.

[9] C. Bagley and L. Young, "Juvenile Prostitution and Childhood Sexual Abuse: A Controlled Study," **Canadian Journal of Community and Mental Health**, 1987.

[10] M. Seng, "Child Sexual Abuse and Adolescent Prostitution: A Comparative Analysis," **Adolescence**, 1989.

Lee Wolff and **Dorota Geissel** are senior analysts with the Canadian Centre for Justice Statistics, Statistics Canada.

• For additional information, see **Juristat**, Vol.13, No.4, Statistics Canada Catalogue 85-002 or contact Information and Client Services at (613)951-9023 or toll-free 1-800-387-2231, Canadian Centre for Justice Statistics, 19th Floor, R.H. Coats Building, Ottawa, Ontario, K1A 0T6.

Educational achievement of young Aboriginal adults

by Heather Tait

The Aboriginal population in Canada is young and growing quickly, and over the next few decades, a large number of young adults will be making the transition from school to work. Given that the labour market demands higher levels of schooling than ever before, obtaining a solid education is becoming increasingly important. A well-educated Aboriginal workforce is essential to meet the requirements of the labour market, and hence reduce high levels of youth unemployment and dependence on social assistance.

In general, the relationship between education and employment is clear: the unemployment rate for young Aboriginal adults without high school was 40% in 1996, compared to 9% for those with a university degree. Over the past decade, Aboriginal people in Canada have made some notable educational gains at both the secondary and postsecondary levels. Further improvements in young Aboriginal peoples' academic qualifications would continue to narrow this differential and so reduce the employment disadvantage faced by groups with lower educational levels. This article explores the educational attainment of young Aboriginal adults aged 20 to 29 in the 1980s and the 1990s, and compares their levels of schooling with those of other young Canadians.

Proportion of college and university grads doubles over past decade
Between 1986 and 1996, young Aboriginal adults improved their qualifications at every level of education. At one end, the proportion of young Aboriginal people (including current students) with less than a high school diploma fell from 60% in 1986 to 45% in 1996; at the other end, the share of those who completed their college education (refers to all postsecondary, non-university diplomas or certificates) increased from 15% to 20% during the same period. Progress was also evident at the university level: the percentage of those with a degree doubled, from 2% to 4%.

Despite these educational gains, in 1996 there were still large gaps in relative attainment between Aboriginal and non-Aboriginal people aged 20 to

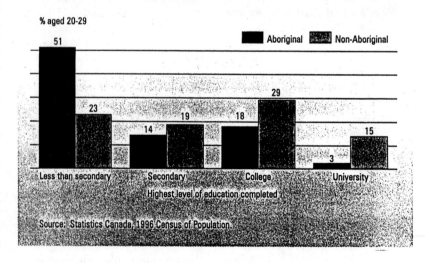

CST Nearly one in five young Aboriginal adults no longer attending school had completed college in 1996

% aged 20-29

Aboriginal ▮ Non-Aboriginal

	Less than secondary	Secondary	College	University
Aboriginal	51	14	18	3
Non-Aboriginal	23	19	29	15

Highest level of education completed

Source: Statistics Canada, 1996 Census of Population.

29. In fact, the gap widened during the decade for those with less than high school completion. While in 1986, Aboriginal people were 2.2 times more likely than their non-Aboriginal counterparts to have less than high school, by 1996 they were 2.6 times more likely to be without high school completion.

However, the opposite was true at the postsecondary level (including college, university and other post-secondary institutions), where the gap narrowed modestly, indicating a slight improvement in the relative position of Aboriginal people. For example, in 1986, Aboriginal people aged 20 to 29 were 60% less likely than non-Aboriginal people in this age group to have completed their postsecondary studies. By 1996, they were 50% less likely to do so.

The past decade's upward trend in Aboriginal education, however, may not be as significant as the figures suggest. During the 1986 to 1996 period, an increasing number of people, mostly those with North American Indian and Métis background, began to identify with an Aboriginal group, thus raising the total number of people who reported an Aboriginal identity on the Census. Many of these people were relatively well-educated and, as a result, may have helped push upward the average educational attainment of all young Aboriginal adults over the decade.[1]

Educational levels rise for both men and women

Although the educational attainment of both young Aboriginal men and women improved between 1986 and 1996, women had a somewhat higher

1. See also Guimond, E., A. Siggner, N. Robitaille and G. Goldmann. "Aboriginal Peoples in Canada: A Demographic Perspective." *Census Monograph Series*. Forthcoming.

CST What you should know about this study

Data in this article come from the 1986 and 1996 Censuses of Population and the 1991 Aboriginal Peoples Survey. In the 1986 and 1996 Censuses, two questions may be used to determine the size of the Aboriginal population: one on Aboriginal ethnic origin/ancestry and the other on Aboriginal identity. The 1996 total Aboriginal population estimate (799,010) used in this article is based on the identity question, which asked: "Is this person an Aboriginal person, that is, North American Indian, Métis or Inuit (Eskimo)?" The 1986 total Aboriginal population counts (455,130) were calculated by cross-tabulating data from both the ethnic origin and identity questions included in the questionnaire that year.

The large increase in the Aboriginal population between 1986 and 1996 cannot be completely explained by demographic factors, such as fertility and mortality. One must also consider that a significant number of people who did not report an Aboriginal identity in 1986 did so in 1996, most likely due to heightened awareness of Aboriginal issues. For the most part, the socio-economic characteristics of this new group were generally better than the characteristics of those who had previously identified. This contributed to some of the improvement observed in the socio-economic profile of the Aboriginal population as a whole during this period.

The Aboriginal Peoples Survey (APS) was a large-scale survey conducted as a follow-up to the 1991 Census. Persons who reported Aboriginal ancestry on the census questionnaires were asked in the APS about their identity. Slightly more than one million persons reported at least some Aboriginal ancestry, and just under two-thirds (625,710) self-identified as an Aboriginal person and/or a Registered Indian.

Incompletely enumerated reserves: In both 1986 and 1996, some Indian reserves and settlements were incompletely enumerated. In 1986, 136 reserves and settlements with an estimated population of 44,700 did not take part in the census. In 1996, 77 reserves, with an estimated population of 44,000, did not participate. These people are not included in this article.

School attendance: Because the 1986 Census did not ask about school attendance, 1986 and 1996 data compare highest-level-of-schooling figures for everyone (including students) in the specific age group. When only 1996 data are presented, figures cover only those who were not attending school at the time.

rate of success at most levels. For example, in 1996, the proportion of women, who had completed college was 21% compared with 19% of men. Similarly, a slightly higher share of women had completed their education at the university level.

Lone mothers, in particular, attended school more frequently than one would expect based on their often difficult circumstances. It is often stated that the responsibility of caring for children may make it more difficult for women to continue their studies, especially in lone-parent families where there is no spouse to help with childcare. However, according to the 1996 Census, Aboriginal lone mothers were more likely than mothers in two-parent families to be attending school. Indeed, some 30% of Aboriginal lone mothers were attending school, most on a full-time basis. This compared with 20% of Aboriginal women with children in two-parent families. Young Aboriginal mothers in both lone-parent and two-parent families most likely to be attending school had an incomplete postsecondary education.

Education cuts unemployment substantially

Without question, the higher the level of education, the lower the rate of unemployment for young adults who are no longer attending school. In 1996, young Aboriginal adults without a high school diploma reported an unemployment rate of 40%. In contrast, unemployment rates were only half as high for those with secondary (23%) or college (20%) completion. Young Aboriginal people with a university degree recorded the lowest rate, at 9%. The corresponding figures for the non-Aboriginal population aged 20 to 29 showed the same disparities between educational attainment and unemployment, although at considerably lower rates — 20%, 13%, 9% and 5%, respectively.

Métis lead the way in educational achievement

Canada's three broad Aboriginal groups — North American Indians (comprising Registered Indians and non-status Indians), Métis and the Inuit — have notably different levels of schooling, due mostly to their varying historical, economic, social and geographic circumstances. The opportunities available to them in the form of financial help also vary. For instance, Registered Indian and Inuit students are eligible to receive grants from the Postsecondary Student Support Program, which is funded through the Department of Indian Affairs and Northern Development. For the year 1997/98, a budget of $276 million assisted these students.[2]

Although most Métis people are not eligible for these grants, young

CST	Between 1986 and 1996, both Aboriginal men and women aged 20 to 29 increased their educational attainment				
		Men		Women	
Highest level of schooling completed	1986	1996	1986	1996
Less than secondary school	62%	48%	59%	42%
Secondary school	8%	13%	9%	11%
College	14%	19%	15%	21%
University	1%	3%	2%	5%
Incomplete postsecondary	14%	18%	16%	21%
Total number of people	42,110	65,385	46,800	71,595

Source: Statistics Canada, Censuses of Population.

CST — Between 1986 and 1996, the proportion of young Aboriginal adults with a university degree more than doubled

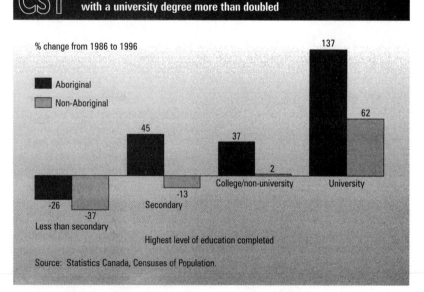

% change from 1986 to 1996

■ Aboriginal
▨ Non-Aboriginal

Highest level of education completed

Source: Statistics Canada, Censuses of Population.

Métis adults had the highest level of education in 1996. Several factors may have contributed to this. First, the Métis are less likely to live in remote communities or the far North than the other two groups, and thus have better access to postsecondary institutions. And second, the Métis have a longer history of formal education and a greater familiarity with other mainstream institutions than other Aboriginal people growing up in remote communities. Indeed, in 1996, some 21% of Métis aged 20 to 29 completed their college education compared with 17% of both North American Indian and Inuit people. Underscoring the same trend, 4% of Métis had university degrees compared with 2% of North American Indians and just under 2% of Inuit in their twenties.

In all three Aboriginal groups, however, those who did complete their postsecondary education tended to choose similar fields of study. The most popular field for all three was engineering and applied science technology, with 39% of Inuit and 27% of both North American Indians and Métis specializing in it. Within this field, the majority of people enrolled in the building technology trades (comprising construction, plumbing, welding and other similar trades). The next most common area of study was commerce, management and business administration, with nearly equal concentrations of North American Indians and Métis (22% and 24%, respectively) and a somewhat lower share of Inuit people (18%).

2. Department of Indian Affairs and Northern Development. 1998. Post-secondary Student Program Database. Inuit students account for roughly 1% (or 280) of the total number of students in this program.

 Family and money issues mostly responsible for young people not completing studies

In 1991, the Aboriginal Peoples Survey asked young adults who did not complete their postsecondary studies why they had decided not to continue. The reasons cited most frequently were family related and money issues, followed by a lack of interest or a dislike of school. Interestingly, women and men voiced different concerns. While the top reasons among women were family responsibilities (25%), the most important reasons among men related to money (18%).

However, it appears that with time some Aboriginal people may overcome these barriers. In general, Aboriginal people are more likely than other Canadians to return to school at older ages. The educational level of young Aboriginal adults may therefore improve as they get older.

Those in large cities most likely to hold degrees

Young Aboriginal people living in Canada's largest cities were the most likely to have completed a university degree, while those in rural First Nations communities (commonly referred to as reserves) were the least likely to have done so. And the differences were quite pronounced. For example, in cities with populations over 100,000, approximately 4% of Aboriginal youths had a university degree. This compared with just over 1% of those who lived on rural reserves.

Although pronounced, these disparities are not surprising because opportunities to pursue higher education and find employment tend to be limited in most rural reserves. While some isolated communities have access to satellite campuses, many people are still faced with the prospect of leaving their family, friends, community and way of life and traveling great distances to attend postsecondary institutions. Once enrolled, they are often confronted with unfamiliar surroundings and customs, resulting in feelings of isolation. Others are faced with "thought processes and ways of

knowing and learning that are a lot different than their own traditional ways."[3] Students may be discouraged when they find few or, in some cases, no other Aboriginal students and faculty on campus.[4]

Adding to these difficulties is the fact that many reserves are found in remote regions, where jobs are scarce and the land base inadequate. In these situations, people with high levels of formal education may feel obliged to leave their community in order to find employment.

Summary

From 1986 to 1996, there was much improvement in the educational achievement of Aboriginal people aged 20 to 29. While still falling below the levels of other Canadians, at the

3. Wilson, Darryl. 1998. "You Must Learn to Use Words Like Bullets." *Winds of Change*. Winter Issue. Boulder, Colorado, 24-30.

4. The Saskatchewan Indian Federated College. 1994. *Aboriginal Post-secondary Education: Indigenous Student Perceptions*. Report prepared for the Royal Commission on Aboriginal Peoples. Ottawa.

On April 1, 1999 Nunavut, Canada's third and newest territory, will become a legal and political reality. The existing Northwest Territories will be split, with Nunavut making up the eastern two-thirds of the area. The creation of the territory will result in various public-sector job opportunities for the Inuit people. One long-term goal is to create roughly 600 new jobs and to have a territorial government that is 85% Inuit (to match the proportion of Inuit persons who comprise the population of Nunavut). As a start, it is hoped that in 1999 the Inuit people will hold about 50% of all government jobs.[1]

These new positions require a well-educated workforce, but meeting the labour market demands of Nunavut will be challenging. Not only is there a small population base (24,665 people), but the educational attainment of Inuit in this territory is below that of other Aboriginal people. Nearly half (46%) of the Inuit population 15 years and over had less than grade nine education in 1996 and just over 1% had completed university.

Nunavut's younger adults appear similarly disadvantaged as their educational attainment fell substantially below that of other young Aboriginal people. Some 34% of young Inuit adults aged 20 to 29 had less than grade nine education compared with roughly 12% of other young Aboriginal adults.

At the other end of the scale, slightly more than 1% of Inuit youths had completed university compared with nearly 3% of all young Aboriginal people.

The new administrative structure will require a host of qualified individuals including those with training in human resources, senior government management, land and resource planning and computer technology. To meet the demand for a well-educated workforce, job-training, along with efforts to encourage Inuit children and young adults to stay in school, have become top priorities in recent years.[2] In 1996, the most common postsecondary qualification held by young Inuit people residing in Nunavut was engineering and applied science technology (32%), with the majority concentrated in fields such as welding, plumbing and construction. Commerce, management and business administration was the second most popular choice (19%), followed by education, recreation, and counseling (14%). In addition, 9% enrolled in science and technology, a field where, because of rapidly changing technology, experienced people are in great demand.

---

1. Laghi, Brian. July 4, 1998. "Inuit find no magic solution on the way." *Globe and Mail.* p. A6.

2. Ibid.

---

postsecondary level the educational gap between the two groups has narrowed somewhat over the past decade.

Higher education is one factor which may help Aboriginal people compete in a rapidly changing labour market. More advanced levels of schooling and a narrowing of the education gap between Aboriginal and non-Aboriginal people may improve young peoples' chances of finding suitable employment. As well, younger generations of Aboriginal children may also benefit, by having role models to follow.[5] These events, in turn, may reduce some of the socio-economic disparity that continues to exist between Aboriginal people and other Canadians. In addition, a well-educated group of young adults will be better able to contribute to the development of new government structures and institutions among all Aboriginal people.

Heather Tait is an analyst with Housing, Family and Social Statistics Division, Statistics Canada.

---

5. See Ponting, J. Rick. and Cora Voyageur. 1998. *An Hundred Points of Light: Grounds for Optimism in the Situation of First Nations in Canada.* Forthcoming.